MUSIC, EDUCATION, AND RELIGION

COUNTERPOINTS: MUSIC AND EDUCATION
Estelle R. Jorgensen, editor

MUSIC, EDUCATION, AND RELIGION

Intersections and Entanglements

EDITED BY
ALEXIS ANJA KALLIO,
PHILIP ALPERSON,
AND HEIDI WESTERLUND

INDIANA UNIVERSITY PRESS

This book is a publication of

Indiana University Press
Office of Scholarly Publishing
Herman B Wells Library 350
1320 East 10th Street
Bloomington, Indiana 47405 USA

iupress.indiana.edu

© 2019 by Indiana University Press

All rights reserved
No part of this book may be reproduced or utilized in any form or by any means, electronic or mechanical, including photocopying and recording, or by any information storage and retrieval system, without permission in writing from the publisher. The paper used in this publication meets the minimum requirements of the American National Standard for Information Sciences—Permanence of Paper for Printed Library Materials, ANSI Z39.48-1992.

Manufactured in the United States of America

Library of Congress Cataloging-in-Publication Data

Names: Kallio, Alexis Anja, editor. | Alperson, Philip, [date] editor. | Westerlund, Heidi, editor.
Title: Music, education, and religion : intersections and entanglements / edited by Alexis Anja Kallio, Philip Alperson, and Heidi Westerlund.
Description: Bloomington : Indiana University Press, 2019. | Series: Counterpoints: music and education | Includes bibliographical references and index.
Identifiers: LCCN 2018049691 (print) | LCCN 2018051365 (ebook) | ISBN 9780253043740 (e-book) | ISBN 9780253043719 (cl : alk. paper) | ISBN 9780253043726 (pb : alk. paper)
Subjects: LCSH: Music—Religious aspects. | Music—Instruction and study.
Classification: LCC ML3921 (ebook) | LCC ML3921 .M883 2019 (print) | DDC 780.71—dc23
LC record available at https://lccn.loc.gov/2018049691

1 2 3 4 5   24 23 22 21 20 19

This work was supported by the Center for Educational Research and Academic Development in the Arts (CERADA) at the University of the Arts Helsinki, the ArtsEqual project funded by the Academy of Finland's Strategic Research Council from its Equality in Society Programme (Project no. 293199), and the Global Visions through Mobilizing Networks project funded by the Academy of Finland (project no. 286162).

CONTENTS

Introduction / Alexis Anja Kallio, Heidi Westerlund, and Philip Alperson 1

Part 1. Tensions and Negotiations

1. On the Role of Religion in Music Education / Estelle R. Jorgensen 15

2. Selective Affinities: Concordance and Discordance at the Intersection of Musical, Educational, and Religious Practices / Philip Alperson 31

3. The Performativity of Performance: Agency at the Intersection of Music and Religion in School / Heidi Westerlund, Alexis Anja Kallio, and Heidi Partti 55

Part 2. Identity and Community

4. Shaping Identities through Religious Music Engagement: A Case Study of an Australian Catholic Girls' School / Janelle Colville Fletcher and Margaret S. Barrett 71

5. Religion and the Transmission of Thai Musical Heritage in Thailand and the United States / Pamela A. Moro 87

6. The Believing-Belonging Paradigm: Music, Education, and Religion in Contemporary Serbia / Ivana Perković and Biljana Mandić 99

7. Religious Repertoire in General Music Education: Spiritual Indoctrination or Cultural Dialogue? / Lauri Väkevä 111

Part 3. Navigating New Worlds

8. *Mysterium Tremendum et Fascinans*: Spiritual and Existential Experience and Music Education / Øivind Varkøy 129

9. The Sacred Sphere: Its Equipment, Beauty, Functions, and Transformations under Secular Conditions / Maria B. Spychiger 142

10. Music Education as Sacred Practice: A Philosophical Exploration / Frank Heuser 157

11. *Advocatus Diaboli*: Revisiting the Devil's Role in Music and
    Music Education / Alexandra Kertz-Welzel   171

Part 4. Emancipation, Regulation, and the Social Order

12. The Humanist Defense of Music Education in Civil and Religious
    Life: *The Praise of Musicke* (1586) and *Apologia Musices* (1588) /
    Hyun-Ah Kim   183

13. The Curious Case of *Good Morning Iran*: Music and Broadcast
    Regulation in the Islamic Republic / Erum Naqvi   196

14. When Hell Freezes Over: Black Metal—Emancipatory
    Cosmopolitanism or Egoistic Protectionism? / Ketil Thorgersen
    and Thomas von Wachenfeldt   208

Part 5. Agency and Social Change

15. Radical Musical Inclusion in Higher Education: The Creation of
    Foundation Music / June Boyce-Tillman   223

16. Religious Identities Intersecting Higher Music Education:
    An Israeli Music Teacher Educator as Boundary Worker /
    Laura Miettinen   238

17. Religion and Music in an Education for Social Change /
    Iris M. Yob   249

18. Dancing on the Limits: An Interreligious Dialogue /
    Belal Badarne and Amira Ehrlich   262

Music, Education, and Religion: An Invitation / Alexis Anja Kallio   273
Index   281

MUSIC, EDUCATION, AND RELIGION

Introduction

Alexis Anja Kallio, Heidi Westerlund, and Philip Alperson

Music, Education, and Religion: Intersections and Entanglements remedies a long-standing gap in music education scholarship by considering the ways in which music, education, and religion fuse together, overlap, connect, or conflict in theory and in practice. The rationale of this volume lies in the conviction that the various practical, social, cultural, ideological, and political constraints on music teaching and learning also engage with matters of religion, a thematic area that has been absent in scholarly work on music education, even when it comes to works attending to pluralism and diversity. In recognizing both enduring and new diversities in contemporary societies, the chapters in this book embrace a range of perspectives, including religious, contextual, geographic, historical, and theoretical standpoints and writings from the disciplines of music education, philosophy, cultural studies, sociology, anthropology, history, and ethnomusicology.

The timeliness of this inquiry arises from developments both within and outside the field of music education scholarship. Contemporary music education in the twentieth century focused by and large on the psychological, cognitive, aesthetic, and individual aspects of music making. The increasing prominence and prestige of instrumental music in the West, the influence of a recording industry that made musical works available in live and recorded media to a wide public, the development of formalist-oriented aesthetic theories, and a general secularization of formal education made it possible to articulate a demarcation between aesthetic musical experiences and the moral or cultural values of musical practices, with some proponents of music education even recommending that teachers consciously exclude "extramusical" understandings of musical material in their classes (e.g., Mark 1989; Reimer 1989, 1991). This separation of "purely" musical considerations from extramusical matters was urged even as some theories highlighted the conceptual and phenomenological similarities between some religious experiences and some aesthetic experiences (e.g., Reimer 1989).

Toward the turn of the millennium, however, scholarly discourses gradually shifted from a focus on purely musical aesthetic artifacts (e.g., Swanwick 1994) to music as a sociocultural practice (e.g., Alperson 1991; Elliott 1995). This shift occurred on a number of fronts. Instead of concentrating on individual listening experiences and a distanced appreciation of music, the emphasis of teaching and learning turned to the diversity of musical practices and music making. Music educators increasingly attended to the multitude of settings outside school music education, such as community music practices in Western and non-Western contexts (Higgins 2012; Veblen et al. 2013). With this renewed consciousness of cultural diversity in music education settings, some music educators urged that music be understood not only as something that people *do,* but as ways in which people *are* (Bowman 2004; Elliott 1990)—that is to say, the ways in which people understand, position, and present themselves in the world. This attention to diversity concurred with research in music psychology that focused on ways in which people construct and maintain their (multiple) identities through musical activities (Barrett 2009; MacDonald, Hargreaves, and Miell 2017; North and Hargreaves 2008). Accordingly, many music educators argued that the teaching and learning of music should incorporate students' own principles, values, and knowledge in musical praxis, as they reflect those in the surrounding society (see Regelski 2006).

This shift aligned with wider changes in learning theories in educational psychology, in which sociocultural views complemented narrower cognitive approaches (e.g., Sawyer 2002). Music learning was no longer theorized through individual cognitive representations of and skills in music of "the other" but through approaches that emphasized individuals' participation in, and contributions to, musical activities, processes of knowledge creation, and expressions of agency in communities of practice and networks. These developments affecting the field of music education suggest that music cannot be construed as a *thing* that stands distinct from one's religious or spiritual beliefs. Neither can music be considered to be an individual endeavor, isolated from social context. With this in mind, it is worth considering the religious dimensions of musical activities (Jorgensen 2003)—activities that also include those that take place in education contexts.

The notion that the religious or spiritual dimensions of music education warrant scholarly attention coincides with broader academic debates on the nature and extent of secularism in modern society. The philosophical heritage of the Enlightenment fueled an oft-made epistemological distinction between religious belief and secular reason (e.g., Taylor 2007), which led many philosophers and scholars to suppose that the rise of modernity, science, and rationality would lead ineluctably to an increasing disbelief in religion. In this way, Nietzsche could declare the death of God, Marx could describe religion as the opiate of the masses, Freud could speak of religion as an illusion, Durkheim could explain religion away in terms of its efficacy as a social institution, and Weber could see the tenets of Protestant religious ideology as fundamentally providing the core of the "spirit of capitalism" (Berger 2008). In line with such assumptions, the intersections of music, education, and religion have been positioned as increasingly irrelevant for contemporary societies—relics "of a bygone era when religion had cultural sway and political power but a factor that would continue to recede as secular forces took over" (Monsma and Soper 2009, viii).

However, predictions of the death of religion have proved to be greatly exaggerated. The notion of secularism itself and the binaries it presupposes (for example, religious thought vs. secular reason and public vs. private spheres) and the presumed univocality of religious belief have been subject to considerable scrutiny (Berger 2008; Habermas 2008; Taylor 2007). In addition, the new millennium has witnessed a resurgence of religious fervor and identity. This is most visibly expressed through expressions of religious fundamentalism, such as the rise of evangelical Protestantism in Western countries, expressions of Islamic fundamentalism in the Muslim world, new religious pluralisms in post-Soviet societies, the rise of fundamentalist Judaic sects in Israel, and the increasing influence of the Catholic Church in the global south. These developments have had far-reaching effects on the mechanisms of state, social institutions (not the least educational and legal institutions), international affairs, and personal, social, and political life. Such a resurgence of religiosity has led some to conclude that we live in a postsecular age. Postsecularism has not been discussed as "the end of the secular" (Lee 2017, 8), but rather an acknowledgment that demarcations between the religious, the spiritual, and the secular are entangled and unclear (Ratti 2013).

It is in this context that an investigation into the myriad connections between music, education, and religion is called for. *Music, Education, and Religion: Intersections and Entanglements* interrogates the ways in which the rituals and practices of music education are constructed and complicated by the forces of religion and belief. These are matters of great importance to the field of music education, affecting basic issues such as the legitimation of particular repertoires and practices of music in the curriculum; the kinds of perspectives, knowledge, values, and social relations that music education ought to foster; and even the matter of the inclusion and exclusion of students in the world of music education (Bowman 2007; Kallio 2015). If music is seen as a part and product of students' and teachers' lives, then the tensions, conflicts, and values that so often accompany matters of faith and religion must not be overlooked or dismissed.

Overview of the Book

Part 1: Tensions and Negotiations

Part 1 contains three chapters that describe and analyze the tensions that arise at the nexus of music, education, and religion, requiring negotiation by educators and students alike. It opens with Estelle R. Jorgensen's exploration of the benefits and challenges of teaching music as one of the humanities. She poses a justification for music educators and scholars to engage religions in realizing the intellectual, sensual, inspirational, imaginative, spiritual, and human experiences of music. She therefore emphasizes the importance of not only student, but also teacher, agency; a strong liberal arts component of teacher education; and a more distanced, critical approach to curriculum content. Engaging with music education policy and politics, Jorgensen outlines her hopes for a critical, creative, contextual, and constructivist approach to the teaching and learning of music in schools that can attend to the particularities, divergences, and nuances at the nexus of music, education, and religion.

Addressing the philosophical complexities of achieving what Jorgensen proposes, Philip Alperson's chapter explores some of the fundamental concepts and issues at the intersection of music, education, and religion. Beginning with a consideration of common understandings of the basic terms *music*, *education*, and *religion*, Alperson offers a survey of life-enhancing goods and life-diminishing harms that can attend to and complicate practices in religion, education, and music. Alperson argues that these goods and harms can carry different weights, can be thought of as primary and secondary to the practice in question, and can be achieved wittingly or unwittingly. He then applies this conceptual framework to the question of the place of religious material (and the notion of spirituality in particular) in the classroom, concluding that the recommendation to bring religious material into the music education classroom is fraught with a variety of conceptual and practical challenges.

In directing teachers to make space for multiple musical doings and beings in schools, as Jorgensen suggests, while also attending to the ethical and political complexity of doing so, as Alperson cautions, Westerlund, Kallio, and Partti's chapter focuses the discussion on the affordances made for and limitations placed on student agency and subjectivities in supposedly secular school music lessons. Particularly taking into consideration the increasing diversity of many student populations, they argue that a consensus of social values, moral frameworks, and worldviews—even if the consensus is one of neutrality—results in processes of (non)religious coercion or exclusion in the democratic school's music classroom. The chapter thus attends to the normative frames of religion or secularity in schools as an ethical and political matter.

Part 1 thus establishes that if, as Jorgensen implores, music education is to retain its artistic soul, it can never be a neutral undertaking. The intersection of music, education, and religion is not always harmonious, and while it gives rise to new possibilities for furthering social justice, it can also give rise to social tensions and potential harms. As a result, a paradox presents itself in which music educators in many contexts cannot afford to neglect matters of religion, but attending to the sacred is nevertheless a fraught and complex endeavor.

Part 2: Identity and Community

The chapters in part 2 engage in a discussion of the role of music in supporting multiple, and at times conflicting, religious identities in particular education contexts. Especially as many nations are contending with rapid cultural change, the chapters in part 2 consider the potential for music education to foster a sense of belonging or togetherness on the one hand, and on the other hand to fuel intercultural tensions or social and cultural exclusion. Opening this part, Janelle Colville Fletcher and Margaret S. Barrett extend the conversation on how student agency might be constituted or constrained in "secular" schools with a consideration of how adolescents' spiritual and religious identity work is shaped, within the context of music taught in an Australian Catholic school. Student narratives offer personal insights into their experiences and understandings of sacred, liturgical, and secular music at school. Fletcher and Barrett argue that music is a powerful expression of the sacred, contributing to individual identity formation and also a cohesive school community. The authors also raise important questions about how such a community identity contends with increasing diversity in students' religious affiliation—even in an explicitly Catholic school. Thus, they suggest that while religious music may serve as a catalyst for integration and inclusion, it may also serve as a point of differentiation and tension.

These tensions are brought to the fore in Lauri Väkevä's chapter, which examines both sides of a heated public debate on religious freedom and indoctrination in Finnish school music education. At the end of the school year, many Finnish schools celebrate with the singing of the Lutheran summer hymn *Suvivirsi*. Väkevä questions whether arguments for the omission of the hymn from school rituals reflect broader concerns for the inclusion of all students regardless of religious affiliation, or whether claims for its inclusion are warranted, either as a devotional practice of the religious majority or as a culturally significant tradition that has long ago been divorced from its religious origins. He concludes that if we are to engage in cultural dialogue rather than spiritual indoctrination, music educators need to be aware of the ideological justifications for the repertoires and practices that are employed in the cultivation of culturally reflective, ethical, and agential citizens.

While diversifying national populations heighten concerns over indoctrination through consensus or imposition, so too they present new possibilities for religious and nonreligious affiliation and identity. Ivana Perković and Biljana Mandić analyze the recent revival of religious music and Orthodox identity in contemporary Serbia, in both formal and informal education settings. The authors argue that the notable absence of music from the recently reintroduced primary school religious education curriculum reflects tensions in contemporary church-state politics, with religion serving as a vehicle for the protection and preservation of national identity. Neglecting the educational potentials of music here raises questions of whether students are learning religion, learning from religion, or learning about religion in Serbian schools. Conversely, with religious music being an everyday social and musical experience for participants in children's church choirs, Perković and Mandić argue that the process of learning is contextualized and integrated, shaping a sense of social cohesion through individual identity construction. These two contexts offer important insights into the distinction and overlap between private religiosity (believing) and public religiosity (belonging) in and through music education.

Whereas music and religious education may be seen to be reinstating a once-repressed religious and national identity in contemporary Serbia, belief and belonging appears somewhat different in Thai diasporic communities in the United States. While it might be assumed that Thai diaspora employ religion and music education as a means of retaining a sense of home in unfamiliar surroundings, Pamela A. Moro illustrates the ways in which the religious foundations of Thai music education also *produce* culture. Analyzing youth culture programs at Buddhist wats in the San Francisco area, Moro explains that such cultural transmission is simultaneously conservative and innovative. While religiously infused music education in these contexts emphasizes moral authority and preserves cultural heritage and tradition, it also allows for new forms of identity production among young participants and new forms of belonging and community as Asian Americans. Moro argues that this process of pursuing religion and music as a distinction of ethnic identity, while also "becoming American," has been necessary to establish recognition and legitimacy in multicultural America.

Part 2 emphasizes the role that context plays in the construction and articulation of religious and musical identities. Whether religious music recontextualized as cultural practice, the production of culture through religious music and the cultivation of communities in religious or secular schooling, or extracurricular choirs and community music activities, the functions of music in relation to individual and social identity are evidently complex—functions that are explored further in part 3 of this book.

Part 3: Navigating New Worlds

Music is often said to be able to capture something of human existence that goes beyond the intellectual, beyond the measurable. Similar discourses of transcendence surround religious experience, or spiritual belief. The chapters in this part of the book offer perspectives on the ways in which education might, or might not, attend to the existential, the ideological, or the spiritual in offering learners holistic critical engagements with music. Arguing against reductionist approaches to music education, Øivind Varkøy opens part 3 with a call for teachers to attend to the spiritual and existential layers of musical meaning by offering students powerful encounters with art. He suggests that much Nordic music education limits students' musical encounters by restricting education to the "outer side of the music"—that which is technically describable and easily graspable, rather that acknowledging the deeper layers of spirituality and existential experience. Varkøy characterizes this situation through Weber's notion of *disenchantment*, the fostering of a less poetic, less mysterious world and one that is overly reliant on modern Western rationality and empiricism. He also notes, however, that justification discourses in music education often rely on transformative potentials and "magical powers." Drawing on Kierkegaard's work *Either/Or*, Varkøy proposes that if teachers and students are to retain, or perhaps regain, some of the intensity and passion of musical experience, they need to move beyond the aesthetic and ethical stages of life to the religious.

Likewise appealing for music education to open up new worlds of meaning for students, Maria B. Spychiger considers the sacred sphere as a connecting zone between the factual world and *second worlds*, additional realities created by the human mind. In religious societies, she notes that these second worlds are divine, with churches and temples serving to connect these worlds of the gods with the human realm. She also notes, however, that music can play a key role in cultivating the sacred sphere and connect different worlds. Extending a psychological model of the person-environment relationship introduced by Lang (1993), Spychiger suggests that the sacred sphere retains its function even in a secular age. She argues that, as a specific ecology, music education ought to cultivate an awareness of other (spiritual) worlds if it is to make a wider range of cultures accessible. Spychiger concludes that education can engage and inspire learners through positioning the sacred as a searching area wherein they may enter new and old worlds of meaning, learning, and experiencing.

Frank Heuser begins his chapter in just such a sacred sphere. Noting the plurality with which individuals create their own sacred moments, distinct from religious doctrine or institutions, Heuser locates his discussion in what Charles Taylor (2007) refers to as the "imminent frame," a society in which individuals have an array of sacred-secular allegiances and options from which to choose. He draws parallels between the learning customs employed in music education and practices of spiritual traditions within the imminent frame. For example, he considers a conductor's pause before a performance as a small rite similar to that of a priest before a sermon, a signifier of reverence and of the sacred. In encouraging learners to explore their own identities without "treading on the forbidden territory of religious creeds" in secularized education contexts, Heuser finds hope in the themes of connectedness, community, and relationships with others. He argues that music is a powerful means of connection not only between individuals, but also for individuals to connect with their spiritual selves as well. Through exploring the guru/disciple relationship and adopting a multidimensional perspective of religion and spirituality, Heuser notes that spirituality—in sacred or secular forms—can play an important role in music teaching and learning.

Part 3 ends with an essay by Alexandra Kertz-Welzel that offers an important word of caution pertaining to the misuse of the powers of music education in matters of religion. Acknowledging some similarities between religious and intense musical experiences, but also acknowledging the potential for imposing religious value systems on students, Kertz-Welzel invites the reader on a metaphorical search for the devil in music education. Through Goethe's 1808 play, *Faust*, and Thomas Mann's 1947 novel, *Doctor Faustus*, she explores the likely, and perhaps unlikely, places where the devil can be found. Through the notion of Kitsch applied to music education, she locates the devil in overly simplistic, uncritical, sentimental characterizations of teaching and learning and also in music education that promises a renewed and healed world through the transformation of individuals and societies. Kertz-Welzel implores us to gain a more critical, dialectical awareness of how music is taught, why it is taught, and the goals toward which music education might aspire.

Thus, the chapters in part 3 focus on the potentials, but also the complexities, of navigating between the worlds of sacred and secular, and the worlds of music and education. In seeking deep, transformative, passionate, and transcendental experiences with music as part of teaching and learning, it is clear from these chapters that although these "other worlds" cannot be neglected, neither can they be welcomed unreflectively or uncritically.

Part 4: Emancipation, Regulation, and the Social Order

The potential misuse of religion or music in teaching and learning is continued in part 4, including three chapters that take the complex discussions of music, morality, and teaching to the foundational question of what music is in the first place, and what is considered *good* music, and by whom. Hyun-Ah Kim looks to the past in analyzing two Elizabethan apologetics that explore the value of music in civil and religious life. Defending music education against the common charge that music harbors symptoms of vanity and vice, the two treatises examined not only highlight the intrinsic value of music but also its value as a means to moral, spiritual, and religious ends. Although considerations of "the musician as an important agent of education and religious practice" is a perspective often overlooked in contemporary scholarship and music education practice, Kim reminds the reader that the discussions within this volume, and ideas conceiving of music and music education as ethical entities and political forces, are historically (in)formed, yet still insufficiently addressed.

Discussions of the value of music is a theme continued by Erum Naqvi as she undertakes a philosophical and musicological analysis of the regulation of music in Iran. As her point of departure, she describes a controversy arising from a television broadcast in 2014 that showed Iranian musicians performing. As Naqvi explains, the taboo that was broken here was not the broadcasting of the sounds of music, but the visual aspects of music making. The visual aspects of music making were at the time highly regulated by the authorities and labeled as problematic in line with particular religious concepts, political concerns, and questions of nationhood. Naqvi's chapter explores these understandings of music as they arise through interpretations based on the Qur'an and the hadith, but it also considers the regulation of music based on religious teachings as complicated by constructs of nationhood and the politics of postrevolutionary Iran. Arguing that "witnessing embodied acts of dexterity in performance" is a hallmark of Iranian classical music, Naqvi questions the educational ideologies underpinning understandings and valuations of musicality in Iranian classical music and how they are constructed and constrained in relation to religious doctrine.

Taking a closer look at one particular genre of music that often falls in the category of the improper, or even downright deleterious, Ketil Thorgersen and Thomas von Wachenfeldt consider the educational lessons that Black Metal music might have to offer school music education. Emphasizing the importance of musical and intellectual excellence and offering examples of many musicians displaying virtuosic ability and knowledge of diverse musical traditions, they explore Black Metal culture beyond the initial satanic, elitist, and misanthropic impressions one may have of the genre. Through the notion of cosmopolitanism, and interviews conducted with young musicians, Thorgersen and von Wachenfeldt approach Black Metal as a means and an analogy for music education to "explore, share, scrutinize, respect, and celebrate difference." Thus, although Black Metal might at first seem antithetical to the humane goals of democratic music education, Thorgersen and von Wachenfeldt suggest that if the school were to enter the dark realms, we might find new potentials for a critical, discomforting, open-minded music education.

Part 4 explores social norms and values as they are constructed by and reflected in musical performance and transmission. The chapters each contribute a different perspective on the values that guide teaching and learning and how understandings of morality, and of music, can be strengthened, confined, or unsettled by (anti)religious doctrine or belief.

Part 5: Agency and Social Change

If, as some previous chapters attest, both music and religion can foster a sense of community among diverse individuals and cultivate connections between different worlds and within oneself, the four chapters in part 5 turn their attention to the processes by which this can take place. The focus here is on how individuals or social groups might be afforded agency in enacting or navigating social change, acting as part of religious, musical, or educational communities. Considering the implications of fostering social cohesion in music education for music teacher education, June Boyce-Tillman seeks new ways to bring together multiple and dynamic religious identities in an inclusive postsecular music education community. In her chapter, she describes her own recent work at a university in the United Kingdom. Through queering the value systems embedded in traditional classical music curriculum models and subverting heteropatriarchal church structures, she advocates for a more collaborative approach that embraces diversity and different spiritualities. Radical musical inclusivity, in this context, is a tool for reconciliation, for social justice, and for peace.

The notion of an in-between space in which different spiritualities, religions, and music can meet is explored by Laura Micttinen. She examines religion as part of higher music education teachers' professional identity work in Israel, considering how teachers negotiate their own identifications when teaching students in a religiously oriented teaching context. Miettinen offers insights into the experiences of an Orthodox Jewish music teacher working within a segregated ultra-Orthodox Jewish educational context, in which religious values and norms define the boundaries of teaching content and method. Through the reflections of this teacher, Miettinen describes her work as a boundary worker, in that she acts as a bridge, but also a border, between different but related worlds. Such intercultural competence, she argues, can contribute to the formation of a liminal zone, a third space in which the ethical, cultural, and religious complexities of music education can engage in dialogue and produce new, culturally sensitive, ethically oriented understandings, learnings, and ways of interacting.

Exploring such an ethical commitment to promoting positive social change in and through music education, Iris M. Yob looks at three university outreach projects that aim to foster social unity among divided groups in the United Kingdom, address the needs of underprivileged youth in the United States, and offer music therapy and education to students with learning disabilities. The ways in which religion intersects work conducted in each of these three cases offers insights into the positive contributions and challenges that religion might bring to an education for social change. Yob suggests that if we are to work together in music, music educators need to take into account the complexities of lived experience, both religious and musical, in working toward mutual well-being and a common good. This entails the acknowledgment of sameness and difference and a commitment to the inclusion of all, even though inclusion may not always be comfortable.

Belal Badarne and Amira Ehrlich offer a dialogue between two sides of a society characterized by sociopolitical tensions and socioreligious segregation. As religiously observant music educators, Badarne and Ehrlich are each required to navigate numerous discrepancies between Jewish and Muslim religious doctrines and musical practices. Through an interreligious and intermusical conversation that dances "on the limits," Badarne and Ehrlich are positioned as cultural change agents, challenging the divisive, segregated socioreligious norms of Israeli society in searching for new opportunities for mutual understanding and identification. They conclude that their chapter serves as an illustration of "small and simple acts of hope," a model of collaboration in interreligious dialogue in music education. Yet it is also useful to engage in our own conversations with this chapter, hoping to fill the gaps that arise in our own research and teaching practices at the intersections of music, education, and religion.

Thus, having traversed considerable ground (indeed, venturing to "other worlds" and back), the chapters in this final part of the book illustrate what enacting social change at the nexus of music, education, and religion might look like in various contexts.

In the final contribution to the discussions in this book, Alexis Anja Kallio offers a response to the preceding chapters and a provocation for future theoretical and practical work. She firstly outlines the epistemological issues that arise from within and between the discussions presented in this volume, the first work attending to the intersection of music, education, and religion in decades. Accordingly, while the preceding chapters offer new insights, rich descriptions, and analyses, new ideas and questions are also raised, which Kallio suggests may provide the foundation for future conversations and inquiries. She invites readers to not only continue the rigorous work begun here in more depth, in different contexts, and by attending to new and different perspectives, but also to construct a critique of the emerging scholarship at the intersection of these three fields, so that we may challenge ourselves and each other in advancing our understandings and practices.

ALEXIS ANJA KALLIO is a music education researcher at the Sibelius Academy, University of the Arts–Helsinki, working as part of the Global Visions through Mobilizing Networks: Co-developing Intercultural Music Teacher Education in Finland, Israel, and Nepal project. She is coeditor of the *Nordic Yearbook of Music Education Research*.

HEIDI WESTERLUND is Professor of Music Education at the Sibelius Academy, University of the Arts–Helsinki, Finland. She currently leads two large-scale research projects: The Arts as Public Service: Strategic Steps towards Equality (ArtsEqual) and Global Visions through Mobilizing Networks: Co-developing Intercultural Music Teacher Education in Finland, Israel, and Nepal. She is co-editor of the book *Collaborative Learning in Higher Music Education* and editor-in-chief of the *Finnish Journal of Music Education*.

PHILIP ALPERSON is Professor Emeritus of Philosophy at Temple University in Philadelphia. He is editor of *What Is Music?*, *The Philosophy of the Visual Arts*, and *Diversity and Community* and former editor of the *Journal of Aesthetics and Art Criticism*.

References

Alperson, Philip. 1991. "What Should One Expect from a Philosophy of Music Education?" *Journal of Aesthetic Education* 25, no. 3: 215–42.
Barrett, Margaret S. 2009. "Sounding Lives in and through Music: A Narrative Inquiry of the Everyday Musical Engagement of a Young Child." *Journal of Early Childhood Research* 7, no. 2: 115–34.
Berger, Peter. 2008. "Secularization Falsified." *First Things* 180: 23–27.
Bowman, Wayne. 2004. "The Song Is You: Symposium on Musical Identity." *Action, Criticism and Theory for Music Education* 3, no. 1: 1–9.
———. 2007. "Who Is the 'We'? Rethinking Professionalism in Music Education." *Action, Criticism, and Theory for Music Education* 6, no. 4: 109–31.
Elliott, David J. 1990. "Music as Culture: Toward a Multicultural Concept of Music Education." *Journal of Aesthetic Education* 24, no. 1: 147–66.
———. 1995. *Music Matters: A New Philosophy of Music Education*. New York: Oxford University Press.
Habermas, Jürgen. 2008. "Secularism's Crisis of Faith: Notes on Post-secular Society." *New Perspectives Quarterly* 25: 17–29.
Higgins, Lee. 2012. *Community Music: In Theory and in Practice*. New York: Oxford University Press.
Jorgensen, Estelle. 2003. *Transforming Music Education*. Bloomington: Indiana University Press.
Kallio, Alexis A. 2015. *Navigating (Un)Popular Music in the Classroom: Censure and Censorship in an Inclusive, Democratic Music Education*. Studia Musica 65, Sibelius Academy of the University of the Arts Helsinki. http://urn.fi/URN:ISBN:978-952-329-014-3.
Lang, Alfred. 1993. "Zeichen nach innen, Zeichen nach außen – eine semiotisch-ökologische Psychologie als Kulturwissenschaft." In *Welt der Zeichen – Welt der Wirklichkeit*, edited by P. Rusterholz and M. Svilar, 55–84. Bern: Verlag Paul Haupt.
Lee, Raymond L. M. 2017. "Reconciling Religion, Spirituality and Secularity: On the Post-secular and the Question of Human Mortality." *International Journal of Philosophy and Theology*. https://doi.org/10.1080/21692327.2017.1285718.
MacDonald, Raymond, David Hargreaves, and Dorothy Miell, eds. 2017. *Handbook of Musical Identities*. Oxford: Oxford University Press.
Mark, Michael L. 1989. "A New Look at Historical Periods in American Music Education." *Bulletin of the Council of Research in Music Education* 99: 1–6.

Monsma, Stephen V., and J. Christopher Soper. 2009. *The Challenge of Pluralism: Church and State in Five Democracies*. Lanham, MD: Rowman and Littlefield.

North, Adrian, and David J. Hargreaves. 2008. *The Social and Applied Psychology of Music*. Oxford: Oxford University Press.

Ratti, Manav. 2013. *The Postsecular Imagination: Postcolonialism, Religion, and Literature*. New York: Routledge.

Regelski, Thomas A. 2006. "Reconnecting Music Education with Society." *Action, Criticism and Theory for Music Education* 5, no. 2: 2–20.

Reimer, Bennett. 1989. *A Philosophy of Music Education*. Upper Saddle River, NJ: Prentice Hall.

———. 1991. "Essential and Nonessential Characteristics of Aesthetic Education." *Journal of Aesthetic Education* 25: 193–214.

Sawyer, Keith. 2002. "Emergency in Psychology: Lessons from the History of Nonreductionist Science." *Human Development* 45: 2–28.

Swanwick, Keith. 1994. *Musical Knowledge: Intuition, Analysis, and Music Education*. London: Routledge.

Taylor, Charles. 2007. *A Secular Age*. Cambridge, MA: Harvard University Press.

Veblen, Kari K., Stephen J. Messenger, Marissa Silverman, and David J. Elliott. 2013. *Community Music Today*. Lanham, MD: Rowman and Littlefield.

Part 1
Tensions and Negotiations

1 | On the Role of Religion in Music Education

Estelle R. Jorgensen

Something is amiss in general education at all levels, where the study of the humanities and the world's musical traditions are diminished and marginalized. Much is lost when intellectual, inspirational, imaginative, spiritual, and humane experiences are devalued in education. Bypassing education in the sense of the search for wisdom—what philosopher Alfred North Whitehead (1929, 14) termed "religious" education—through literalist thinking devoid of artistic soul creates a myopic focus on the mastery of technical skills and prosaic vocational information. In the United States, notwithstanding calls during the past decades for a broader view of musical study within a wider societal and cultural context,[1] academic curricula in music education remain comparatively narrow, technical, and vocational. Elementary and secondary school music programs are pervasively populist and performative and place less emphasis on the study of esoteric musical traditions that require a musical education within the context of the humanities. Constitutional prohibitions against the establishment of religion have lately been read by the courts to require exclusion of religious music, or any course or program whose title smacks of religious music, from publicly supported music study and performance in schools (Perrine 2013, 2016, 2017). Although the earliest school music textbooks included sacred songs and hymns, the use of religious music and texts has declined to the point where today's textbooks are manifestly secular (Keene 2009; Mark and Gary 2007). The study of religious music in publicly supported universities and colleges is justified mainly on aesthetic, artistic, and vocational rather than religious grounds.

Rich possibilities exist for engaging religions, emphasizing the importance of music and the humanities in music curricula, and recognizing the power of intellectual, sensual, inspirational, imaginative, spiritual, and humane experiences in music among the other arts and humanities. As I explore some of the contributions and pitfalls of teaching music as a humanity and critically engaging religions in music education from an internationalist perspective, but situated in the United States, my focus in this chapter is on three questions that are central to an examination of the role of religion in music education. They are: Why should music education broadly construed critically engage religions? What conceptual challenges arise for music education when it engages religions? How can music educators navigate practically the intersections of music, education, and religion?[2] I approach these questions as a citizen of the world and resident in the United States, with an international perspective gleaned in my native Australia, during sojourns in Canada and England, and from travels in Europe and Asia.

Although the languages and means by which one expresses oneself musically, educationally, and religiously differ in important ways, and the questions they address are distinctive, these symbolic systems also share important commonalities. Human expressions of felt life—emotional, physical, and intellectual—are done and undergone, holistic and atomistic, literal and figurative, conscious and unconscious, enacted and ideational, theoretical and practical, sensual and spiritual, traditional and transformative. Straddling these disparate polarities, they encompass what philosophers of education Israel Scheffler (1991) and Iris Yob (1997) have termed cognitive emotions and emotional cognitions, respectively—that is, feeling in the service of thought, and thought in the service of feeling. Practically speaking, in navigating this territory, I find myself in what philosopher of education Deanne Bogdan (1998, 73) has characterized as "the eye of paradox." Music, education, and religions dwell in realms of imaginative, intuitive, and figurative thought and action.[3] As musician educator June Boyce-Tillman (2000) has observed, musical, educational, and religious ways of thinking and doing have been subjugated in the West (and in some other parts of the world), and they are fragile, vulnerable, and susceptible to being rendered lifeless. The animating, enriching, and ennobling qualities of their dynamic thought and practice can be literalized, systematized, strangled, desiccated, and destroyed. Because of these possibilities, music and religious educators, and protagonists of the other arts and humanities need to remain watchful and ensure that music, education, and religion thrive. With these considerations in mind, I turn to the questions at the heart of this chapter.

Why Should Music Education Critically Engage Religions?

Among the possible responses to this question, I focus on the following: the relationship between religion and spirituality, the interrelationship of music with other aspects of culture, the presence of explicit religious connections within music, the importance of critiquing the values that underlie religious beliefs and practices, the challenges to religious power structures and institutional resistance to critique, and the importance of resisting fundamentalism and dogmatism. Religion has often been associated particularly with spirituality, but this is not always the case.[4] Spirituality can also be experienced through the arts, myths, rituals, and the like. To borrow US philosopher Susanne Langer's (1957) approach, there is Spirituality with a capital S and spiritualities, some of which may be religious and others artistic or musical. A study of religion is not necessary for students to experience spirituality; they may also know spirituality through such subjects as music and the other arts, literature, science, and mathematics. Still, when music educators engage religions, students may access a broader array of spiritual experiences than they may know through a secularized music education. Teachers can prompt such experiences and evoke a sense of reverence, wonder, and awe in the face of beliefs and practices that may at once be musical and religious. As they critique and construct these experiences, teachers and their students can gain a deeper insight into themselves, the world around them, and whatever lies beyond. Yob (2011) argues for the importance of spiritual experience in education, which she sees as accessible through the arts as well as through religion. Her argument shares much with Langer's approach of distinguishing between Art with a capital A and the arts, of which music is one. Briefly put, although religions and the arts share elements, they also have their distinctive interests and features.

Coming to know music is a matter of grasping its interconnectedness with the other arts, the humanities, the institutions, and the sociocultural contexts within which it is experienced. During the past few decades, researchers such as Alperson (1987), Clayton, Herbert, and Middleton (2003), DeNora (2003), Scott (2002), and Shepherd (1991b) have compellingly made the case for the interconnectedness between music, society, and culture. Music is variously regarded as subject and object; structure and function; process; a distinctive art form with its own beliefs, practices, and norms; and a holistic enterprise that involves ritual, dance, the visual arts, storytelling, drama, song, speech, and instrumental music making. Often music is strictly codified and sometimes carries religious and mythical significance. Over time, music has become a specialized art form, and classical traditions have evolved independently from the vernacular traditions from which they draw inspiration and to which they contribute. The distinctiveness and esotericism of these classical traditions have set them apart from ordinary musical practices and other art forms. As they have become institutionalized, they have taken on a life of their own in a preoccupation with the mastery of their own beliefs, values, and practices that are intellectualized, specialized, reified, and objectified. This self-absorption is in tension with the cultural, societal, and institutional elements that make them possible and support, undermine, or otherwise affect them.

While the case for these tensions in classical traditions may be especially clear, other musical traditions also have devotees for whom musical practices remain separated from everyday life. I think, for example, of a young Hmong singer, instrumentalist, and dancer, the son of the village shaman in a Laotian village, whose exquisite performance of his traditional music, as I witnessed, could be thought about and intellectualized, specialized, and reified.[5] As I reflected on the singer's performance, it seemed important to dignify the artistry of his unforgettable musical performance. His performance evidenced the same devotion, intensity, fidelity, spirituality, power, and artistry as have some outstanding performances in the classical traditions that I have witnessed.[6]

Notwithstanding the clearly articulated links between music, the other arts and humanities, and the wider societal and cultural context, the process of coming to know music intimately and in practical terms often tends to become focused on the music itself, as if it were something apart from the rest of lived life. This need not be the case. Within the Western classical tradition, watching Anu Tali conducting the Sarasota Orchestra in a performance of Prokofiev's

Symphony no. 1 and Sibelius's Symphony no. 2 (Rife 2014; Williams 2014), I was struck by what this Estonian conductor brought to these performances that reflected her own grasp of Nordic culture and the traditional music of Finland, Russia, and the Baltic states. During rehearsals of this music, the musicians' attention was undoubtedly on their ability to collectively express the scores, and their rehearsals were no doubt driven by the urgency of preparing a performance within a limited time. Still, their performance expressed these cultures and constituted a window into them. Where performances are augmented with a wider systematic study of the cultures of which they are a part, music is better understood as part of a social and cultural experience.

The varieties of music of the world are also shot through with religious references and elements. Composer Arvo Pärt is quoted as describing the role of his faith as an Eastern Orthodox Christian on his composition as follows: "Religion guides all the processes in our lives, without us even knowing it.... It is true that religion has a very important role in my composition, but how it really works, I am not able to describe" (Robin 2014).[7] A vast part of the Western classical choral repertoire especially consists of music written explicitly for liturgical purposes. Much US country music is affected by Christian belief and interrelated with gospel music, and one better understands jazz as one grasps the power of blending traditional African and Christian beliefs and practices in jazz performances. In the East, as I witnessed the performance of a Chinese orchestra in Singapore with its interplay of Western and Eastern elements and tunings, I began to grasp the power of Chinese mythology and storytelling and the important theatrical role in music making. A brilliant water-puppet performance accompanied by traditional instrumentalists and singers who doubled as narrators, which I attended in Ho Chi Minh City, Vietnam, was likewise evocative of animistic and mythic thought. These examples illustrate the seeming impossibility of coming to a rich knowledge of music without also understanding the myths and religions that shape, contribute to, and are influenced by musical beliefs and practices.

Regarding music as an interrelated part of the wider culture also requires understanding the values that ground beliefs and practices and, as I have suggested in earlier writings, a systematic transformation (Jorgensen 2003, for example). The need for critical perspectives on music, education, and religion that are the premise of this book arises from the importance of interrogating the values that underlie them. One's practices express the beliefs, ideas, and ideals by which one lives and that one prizes and loves. When widely held, these beliefs become a common means of adjudicating music, educational practices, and religions. They may be so deeply and commonly held as to be unconscious. Tiryakian (1973, 199) uses the term "assumptive frames of reference" to connote these commonplaces. Gendered ways of musical, educational, and religious expressions are among such underlying, perhaps unquestioned, values. Throughout history, women and girls have been less able to receive educational opportunities or contribute to musical and religious formal practices.[8] The claims of contributive and distributive justice require that these practices be interrogated (Jorgensen 2015). If practices arise from belief systems as they also contribute to them, this interrogation requires a critique of the values that are expressed musically, educationally, and religiously. One may also speak musically of the alternative scale systems, tunings, and instruments that undergird sonic expectations and come to be cultural commonplaces. Challenging these systems and musical expectations likewise requires critiquing the values that give rise to them, often rooted in social and cultural beliefs and practices of which religion may be a part. It also means unsettling the taken-for-granted order of things in music as in wider society—a process that has ethical as well as musical repercussions.

This critique challenges the power structures underlying musical, educational, and religious institutions. Viewed organically, institutions form around shared beliefs, values, and practices that are manifested in social structures, functions, and processes. Self-interest in growth and survival propels institutions to resist and contest those beliefs, values, and practices that run counter to their own and to seek, where possible, to expand or maintain the sphere of their influence. Whether they be musical, educational, or religious, matters of power and influence are critical for the order they seek to maintain. Critiquing a musical tradition, educational system, or religion inevitably prompts institutional resistance to such criticism. Philosopher Michel Foucault's analysis of Western history in terms of the quest for power and the inevitable contest of ideas and practices that follow it suggests that this human predicament is inescapable, and that critique is not without risk.[9]

Institutions and the belief systems with which they are associated are also subject to fundamentalism. Where beliefs—be they musical, educational, or religious—are held narrowly, uncritically, literally, and rigidly, adherents may be unable or unwilling to see the value in alternative perspectives or to view the world more broadly in terms of "multiplicities and pluralities" (Greene 1988, especially chap. 4). As Scheffler (1991) notes, dogmatism, a sense of conviction, and the unwillingness to be surprised provide a sense of security. Although it can prompt a broader view of music and music education, too often fear of difference and of uncertainty fosters fundamentalist imaginations and contributes to narrow and rigid thought and practice. In the absence of a robust education in the humanities and public spaces in which ideas and practices can be debated, people do not develop the critical capacity to interrogate fundamentalisms wherever they appear or to think creatively, broadly, generously, and inclusively about different others. Even though critique carries a significant risk of the displeasure of those with vested interests in the status quo, ensuring a humane and civil society requires such interrogations. Critique is imperative as a means of contesting fundamentalist imaginations and opening public spaces for all human beings to participate fully in society and its cultural life, in what June Boyce-Tillman (ch. 15 in this volume) refers to as a radically inclusive stance.

What Conceptual Challenges Arise for Music Education When It Engages Religions?

Among the conceptual issues at the intersection of music education and religion, I essay brief responses to considerations of the limits of music education, what is meant by the notion of "religious engagement" in music education, and the role of the context in which music education is conducted in shaping religious engagement. Thinking about the limits of music education, of what it is and what it is not or cannot be, I am left with an ambiguous solution. Some conceptions of education are narrower than others. For example, education construed as training focuses necessarily on the skills needed in musicking in a musical tradition, whereas music education construed as enculturation is a much broader conception that encompasses music as a part of the culture of which it is a part. Other construals that I have examined, namely schooling, education, pedagogy, and socialization, fall somewhere between focused sonic and technical skill formation and broad social and cultural formation (see Jorgensen 1997). While each construal has value, when taken alone it is found to be wanting.

Although my own broad conception of education has much in common with John Dewey's (1916, 1929) ambivalence between the words *culture* and *experience*—an idea rooted in the ancient world—I am reluctant to relinquish narrower educational conceptions. As I've suggested in earlier work (1997), more restrictive notions of education have important insights to offer into discipline in schooling, growth in education, educational leadership and apprenticeship in pedagogy, social structures and processes in socialization, and anthropological perspectives and humane purposes in enculturation. I see these different insights on education dialectically, in tension, sometimes synergistically (as Reimer 2003 would prefer), and in dynamic intersection. The breadth of educational purposes might suggest that in the most specific of these definitions, education as training might exclude religious considerations in some settings, for example in secular school settings, and might include them in others, for example in the preparation of Church of England choristers in choir schools. Alternatively, conceived of broadly in terms of enculturation, or living a way of life culturally, religion is necessarily included because it constitutes a part of cultural life. My preference for a broad educational and cultural view leads me to suggest that music education in all settings include this array of types or facets of education, although possibly with different emphasis from time to time and place to place. Any music education that encompasses enculturation should necessarily engage religion because it is an aspect of human culture, and one would expect to find it included within music education broadly defined.

In terms of what counts as music, my response has been that music is what people say it is (Jorgensen 1997, ch. 2). In societies that do not have a word for music, what we think of as music in the West constitutes a part of an interrelated arts ritual in which instrumental and vocal sounds play an important part along with dance, theater, art, storytelling, and myth. This reality suggests thinking of music education as encompassing the polarities of a primarily sonic experience on the one hand and a holistic artistic ritual in which sound plays accompanying and even ancillary roles on the other. The degree to which music has been almost entirely focused on sound throughout history has varied. In our own time, I see a return to an emphasis on spectacle in musical performance, especially in popular culture. Likewise, music is importantly linked to the shared expectations evident in the various institutions in which it is experienced, including family, religion, commerce, government, and the music profession. In schools conducted under the aegis of the public or the state, values articulated by the state are preeminent in music education, whereas in religious schools, religious values predominate (Jorgensen 1997). Each institution has its own values that underlie the music education conducted under its aegis. Thus, a music school conducted by the Yamaha company is expected to serve as an agent for selling Yamaha pianos and other musical instruments, an instructional website is expected to provide information on various topics of interest to people who choose to visit it, a music school conducted within a Jewish tradition is required to instruct the young in liturgical music, and an elementary school music program conducted by French political authorities is expected to represent French educational values.

My problem with an institutional derivation of music education is that all institutions are flawed and limited in one respect or another. One of them, taken alone, does not suffice as a vehicle for music education. Nor are institutions mutually exclusive. Religious imperatives may saturate much familial life and governmental policy. Commercial imperatives can affect much religious, familial, and governmental belief and action. Each impinges on the others. These realities mean that although one might wish to include them all within music education, in the process of including them tensions, conflicts, and synergies abound. As in the case of education, this approach to music can include more than it excludes. These intersections make it more difficult to limit the reach of music education. It is both a musical enterprise concerned with what people say music is—that is, the plethora of beliefs, practices, values, and traditions that count as music and are practiced around the world—and an educational enterprise that encompasses a gamut of activities ranging from quite specific training in technical skills to broader objectives of enculturation.

This said, one may still sharpen the definition of music education by remembering that music and religion are distinctive. Yob (1992, 1995a, 1995b, 2003) observes that religions want answers to existential questions: Where did I come from? What is the meaning of my life? Where am I going? The arts, however, are interested in how these meanings are made in ways that are grasped through the various sensory modalities. Religious answers to these questions are enormously potent because the reality of mortality and the mystery of human existence leave one fearful of the unknown and of ceasing to exist in this world. Human fear of ceasing to be and a desire for satisfying existential explanations empower the religions with their various myths, rituals, and beliefs designed to answer these questions and alleviate these anxieties. While grasping these matters, musicians give voice to human experience through sound, sight, and touch within an array of private and public rituals. When musicians confront these existential questions, as they often do, their interest lies in how they express thought and feeling and represent it intelligibly in musical ways and constructions. When performing or listening to a performance of the Mahler Symphony no. 2 (Resurrection), for example, one understands Mahler's idealism and optimism in the face of death, while also attending to the host of stylistic, formal, and structural details in the composition combined within a sense of the whole. These musical ideas are represented in the musical score and its performance within a familiar concert ritual on a specific occasion. Problematic though it be in its sheer breadth, I cannot see how one can escape this reality. Despite one's interest in intrinsically "musical" questions, religious questions remain. Practically speaking, I cannot separate the reality of Mahler's theological worldview from this composition. For me, the composition and its composer are integral to grasping and illumining each other. Obviously, this may not be the case with every piece of music. Still, when it is, and religious issues are clearly implicated, religious questions also need to be addressed within music education.

Music education also transpires in different religious contexts. In some countries, such as the United Kingdom, religion is established; that is, it is the state religion. When such is the case, a music educator can freely engage religious music. Indeed, it is to be expected that a teacher would include music that would enable the young to fully participate in the established religion. Such a position privileges the established religion over other religions, and its music over that associated with other religions. In other countries that take an antiestablishment position on religion, such as the United States, in which general education is conducted in ways that avoid establishing a religion, including religious music in the music curriculum becomes more challenging, and a secular approach may result.

In today's multicultural world with its global impacts on societies, large minority populations who espouse different religions than the majority complicate the situation in countries in which a religion is established. Even where religions are not formally established, or where an antiestablishment view of religion is maintained by the state, the presence, for example, of large Muslim minority populations in historically Christian, Hindu, and Buddhist countries or of religiously diverse populations resulting from mass immigration can lead to heightened religious sensitivities in state-supported schools and colleges. Since democratic societies committed to humane and civil values seek to protect the rights of minorities as well as the majority, the religious values, beliefs, and practices of minorities are also accommodated to some degree in publicly supported schools. For example, the children of Jehovah's Witnesses may be excused from singing patriotic songs, just as Muslim boys and girls may be afforded instrumental music education in private settings that do not offend their religious values. Holiday concerts may be substituted for Christmas concerts to avoid offending atheists, agnostics, or the adherents of other faith traditions. Whether religion is established or not established, the necessity of these accommodations within a multicultural milieu suggests that it is easier for music teachers to avoid repertoires with specifically religious or liturgical associations and to secularize their music curricula than to directly engage religions and the music associated with them. Where music education dwells on the fringes of the core curriculum in general education and is offered primarily as an elective that relies on attracting students, teachers may reason that avoiding the possibility of religious conflicts and appealing to largely secular musical interests would be a safer course of action for them to pursue.

Rather than abandon engaging religions and religious music in music education, especially in publicly supported educational institutions, a better solution would be to interrogate religious values and their claims in public spaces. For example, social justice construed in terms of natural law would suggest that all have a right to a knowledge of their musical culture (Jorgensen 2015). This position is taken in the United Nations *Convention on the Rights of the Child* (United Nations General Assembly 1989). Yet, this view clashes with notions of social justice construed in theological terms, in which gendered differences are enshrined in religious beliefs, where some may have more rights to musical participation than others (Jorgensen 2015). For example, notwithstanding her wishes to learn to play a didgeridoo, an Australian Aboriginal girl does not have the right to do so within her traditional culture. The didgeridoo is a male preserve, undergirded by assumptions about masculinity, femininity, and musical and spiritual power. Where the claims of these different value sets are contested in the public spaces of publicly supported education, democracies rely on dialogue as a means to a practical solution in the interests of civility and humanity. The Aboriginal girl may learn to play the didgeridoo in a publicly supported school, even though she is denied it in her traditional culture. Once she knows how to play the instrument, her prowess may necessitate changes in her people's culture. This is exactly what happened in North America when women learned how to sing in the colonial singing schools: they then demanded to participate fully in the singing of their churches (Howe 2014).[10] Public education also brought about a liberalization of theology in the American Protestant churches as people sang their way into different theological conceptions of God and into different understandings of their direct access to God and their equal standing before God. The process of change in understanding is often messy, especially when religious interests are unwilling to compromise, authorities are intransigent, and adherents resort to violence. If democracies are to survive, music educators, as educators generally, need to cultivate critical thinking and the capacity to interrogate the interests and values of institutions and groups that are not necessarily aligned with humane thought and practice.

There are also important questions about what "religious engagement" by music educators means. In the context of publicly supported music education, I use the term to refer to approaching religions dispassionately and comparatively as a means of understanding the beliefs and practices of each one. Instead of proselytizing one's students or indoctrinating them into a religion, one seeks to help them understand the various faith traditions, their beliefs, practices, and values and critically interrogate them to grasp their contributions and detractions and their intersections with music.[11]

Musicians approaching these matters are likely to examine such questions within the context of repertoire. Studying musical pieces and performing them can open an understanding of how particular theological perspectives are expressed variously within the pieces studied. In earlier writing (Jorgensen 1993), I apply and extend theologian Paul Tillich's (1986) analysis of the interrelationship between the visual arts and ultimate reality and unpack several types of religious experience expressed in particular musical examples. It becomes clear in this analysis that various conceptions of God and of spirituality are expressed and reinforced in various types of religious and musical experience, be they mythical, mystical, prophetic-protesting, prophetic-critical, or ecstatic spiritual. Each of these experiences offers aspects that the others lack. While I am left with the prospect of a dilemma, in which it is important to rescue the best of each while avoiding the worst, the broad and comparative view I propose offers a problematic, inclusive, and critical approach to engaging religions in music education. The broader and richer the array of the repertoire, the more likely teachers and their students can grasp religious perspectives comparatively and experience the variety of approaches to spirituality associated with religious and musical traditions. Philosopher of religion Martin Marty (2005) conceives this broad and comparative approach to religions through the metaphor of hospitality, in which there is an openness to the insights of different faiths, their various expressions of spiritual life, and their different intersections with the broader societies and cultures in which they are embedded. In music education, Charlene Morton (2004) expresses a similar idea in her view of musical cosmopolitanism as a music educational value.

Within contexts in which religion is established, or in religiously supported schools, religious engagement may easily be restricted to indoctrination, as the young are inducted into the religion of which they are expected to become members. Although indoctrination has a place in all education that seeks to inculcate certain beliefs and values, if it results in closed-mindedness or dogmatism, it may stunt further growth and development by failing to value sufficiently those perspectives that diverge from the beliefs and practices being inculcated. There is wisdom in approaching the religions broadly, critically, and comparatively as a means of helping the young in a faith tradition to better understand the various beliefs and practices of others. Education construed as wisdom grasps both the breadth of multiplicities and the depth of particularities in knowledge of religion, music, and other things. One is better able to see, both literally and figuratively, the distinctions between religions and the threads that draw them together within human experience. In music education, one can experience them, to some degree, spiritually; one may know them not only intellectually but sensually and emotionally. The engagement I envisage is constructive and critical, theoretical and performative, thought and felt, spiritual and sensual, dispassionate and passionate.

Aside from these conceptual issues, the question of how to engage religion and music within music education remains. Music education straddles the realms of the theoretical on the one hand and the practical on the other. Equally pressing are matters concerning how music teachers can address religions in the work of music education. Such matters are somewhat vexed, and the approaches teachers might wish to enact are sometimes difficult to implement because of their relative powerlessness in the wider educational process. Finding solutions often means thinking systemically in matters of public policy.

How Can Music Educators Navigate Practically the Intersections of Religion and Music Education?

Music educators confront the practical problem of how to plan a course of action that values the study of musical and religious beliefs and practices within the broader context of the humanities and fine arts in general education. It is also imperative to think critically about the possibilities and pitfalls that may eventuate when one plunges into this middle ground of intersections, synergies, contradictions, and dissonances. I suggest four principles that may guide the ways in which music education engages religions constructively and critically. These concern issues of music teacher empowerment and situational thought and practice, an interactive, dynamic, and contextual approach to music curriculum, music teacher preparation and the liberal arts, and the role of political action.

First, music teachers need to be empowered to make decisions about their own instructional situations wherever possible. In doing this, they need to think reflexively about their beliefs, values, attitudes, and practices. This critical interrogation needs to be an important aspect of their decision making, as they consider and determine what they should do. Regarding teachers as agents responsible for enacting practices consistent with their beliefs may be more easily accomplished in the academy, where the tradition of academic freedom is more firmly rooted than in elementary and secondary education. Still, the stress on the normalization and standardization of education at all levels, requirements by professional accrediting bodies, and the imposition of politically motivated strings attached to government funding and programming make it more difficult for music teachers at all levels to craft music programs with their own students in mind. Because sensitivities arise within a global policy context of engaging religions in musical education, it is easier for teachers to approach religions within the frames of their instructional settings and with their own students in mind. A teacher's choice of repertoire for study by their students makes it possible to deal with religious questions that can appeal to them in ways that standardized approaches may not. Particularities, divergences, and nuances are often crucial in effectively meeting these students' aptitudes, backgrounds, interests, impulses, and needs. The teacher's knowledge of her or his students is crucial in planning ways in which to deal with the religious questions that invariably arise in music making and taking.

This approach requires that teachers think critically and constructively about the most appropriate approaches in their situations and possess the courage and skill to determine and implement approaches that the circumstances merit. A situational approach to music teacher decision making is often at odds with public policy in the broader educational environment, which results inevitably in a patchwork of approaches rather than a uniform and focused approach. Accordingly, music teacher professional organizations needed to create public spaces that foster dialogue among music teachers and create opportunities for them to work together to develop common ground and shared approaches. Instead of treating teachers as technicians who follow prescribed approaches, educational leaders and policymakers need to trust teachers more than is too often the case. They need to empower teachers individually and collectively as professionals to craft the ways in which their students engage the subject matter to effectively meet their needs and interests and guide them toward wisdom.

Second, implementing a program of music educational engagement with religions and the humanities necessitates a broad and liberal teacher preparation. Since music needs to be studied humanely and artistically, teachers require a background in the humanities to make the connections, which in turn requires a strong liberal arts component. If teachers are to engage religions critically while also meeting the needs and interests of their students, teachers need the courage and ability to critically examine the ideas and practices that they have been bequeathed and the skills to shape their own curricula in ways that help their students. This means rethinking much music teacher education that has traditionally focused on transmitting instructional methods developed by others and has not dealt extensively and critically with religions within the context of the humanities. Thinking creatively and critically this sort of curriculum development requires intellectual engagement, breadth of perspective, and diverse and specialized skill sets. Humanistic and intellectually engaged teaching requires, most important, imagination and intellectual verve. These expectations need to be built into continuing education for music educators. Without these qualities, attempts to engage religions within music education must surely flounder.

Third, the principal means whereby music teachers can engage religions is through their curricula—the points where their beliefs manifested themselves in the subject matter and their students' engagement with it. In thinking of engagement in this sense, I consider the ways in which students interrelate with the subject matter, view it, internalize it, reject it, transform it, or otherwise make it their own. Regarding curriculum as the intersection between subject matter and students recognizes the importance of the structures and processes of religious thought and practice as viewed by its experts and exponents on the one hand and the students' perceptions, interests, desires, and impulses on the other. Dewey recognizes that the young first approach subject matter intuitively or, as Whitehead would say, romantically, from the perspective of their own idiosyncratic understandings (Dewey 1902; Whitehead 1929). Gradually, however, throughout the educational process, students come to an understanding of the subject matter as experts and exponents would see it—a stage that Whitehead characterizes as generalization. Generalization need not mean that students necessarily internalize the values underlying that subject matter. Rather, they can distinguish between the ways in which the subject is articulated and their own preferences. These considerations provide useful ways of looking at the practical predicament of music educators who seek to engage religions in their curricula.

Fourth, in those situations in which the music curriculum is dictated by state and accrediting bodies, it is important to find the political means to insist on change as a matter of public policy.[12] In the past, music educators have relied on three principal sources of support in this process: the public at large, educators, and musicians (Jorgensen 1983). Politicians and educational policymakers have been susceptible to pressure by those with a specific agenda in the educational process, especially when such actors muster collective action. In today's world, the mass media and the internet are other possible sources of empowerment, especially when confronted with corporate influence in political and educational life. Musicians share interests with artists in other fields who can be allies. Demonstration also has undeniable power, as do example and musical composition and performance as ways of creating model approaches that others may want for themselves. One cannot think practically about music education change without also thinking and acting politically, economically, and in community with individuals and groups, organizations, and institutions that share one's interests. To this end, models of music programs that contextualize musical study within the wider culture and constructively and critically engage the religions in a broad approach to music education, would be a potent means of garnering the support of musicians, educators, and the public at large for systemic change in music education (see Jorgensen 2003).

Conclusion

In sum, I have unpacked responses to questions about the reasons why music education broadly construed needs to critically engage religions, conceptual problems that arise in the process, and practical ways in which music educators can engage religions. Clearly, although the responses to these questions are problematic, it is possible to deal constructively and critically with the conceptual challenges raised by the intersection of religions and music education and to develop practices consistent with these objectives.

ESTELLE R. JORGENSEN is Professor Emerita of Music Education at Indiana University and is on the doctoral faculty of Walden University. She is author of *Transforming Music Education* (Indiana University Press, 2003), *The Art of Teaching Music* (Indiana University Press, 2008), and *Pictures of Music Education* (Indiana University Press, 2011). She is editor of the journal *Philosophy of Music Education Review* and the book series *Counterpoints: Music and Education*.

Notes

1. Shepherd (1991a) prods music educators toward a more critical and humane approach to musical study and notes music's contribution to intellectual development. In a similar vein, Hanson (2014) laments the decline of the humanities in the academy that has resulted in what he sees as a loss of an important source of intellectual development and wisdom as academic study has become pervasively prosaic, vocational, and technical. I am indebted to Forest Hansen for bringing this reference to my attention. Concerns about a possible decline in the importance of the humanities in education are also echoed in observations about the fate of classical music. See Vanhoenacker (2014).

2. For a perspective on defending music education as a humanity in general, see Kim, "Humanist Defense," chapter 12 in this volume.

3. Some of these complexities are unpacked by Alperson in chapter 2 in this volume.

4. On the interrelationship between the spiritual and the sacred, see Varkøy, chapter 8 in this volume; Spychiger, chapter 9 in this volume; Heuser, chapter 10 in this volume; and Kertz-Welzel, chapter 11 in this volume.

5. Feld (2012) makes a compelling case for a growing understanding of the rich meaning underlying the traditional music of the Kaluli people of Papua New Guinea. Contrary to the notion that classical musical compositions have an exclusive claim to objectifying and reifying these traditions, Feld demonstrates that while the Kaluli people think of their music differently than classical musicians in the West might do, they nevertheless think about music aesthetically. Likewise, it was clear in the case of the Hmong musician that he thought deeply about his music making quite apart from his musical performance. For him, his music is spiritually powerful, and what he thinks and does is crucial in evoking a desired result.

6. This approach values the common humanity evident in distinctive musical practices. See Gaita (2000).

7. Pärt attended a series of performances in New York City and Washington, DC, in May and June 2014 as part of the Arvo Pärt Project.

8. For an early groundbreaking study of women and music, especially in relation to religion, see Drinker ([1948] 1995). Also see Jorgensen (1995). For a study of the restrictions on women's participation in congregational singing in the Massachusetts Bay Colony and the impact of the singing schools on changing women's roles in church music from the latter part of the eighteenth into the nineteenth centuries, see Keene (2009), chapters 1 and 2.

9. See, for example, Foucault (1977, 1982). For a short introduction to Foucault's ideas on power, see Felluga (2011).

10. On the connection between singing schools as part of wider social movements and women's participation in Protestant church singing, see Jorgensen (1995).

11. Väkevä examines aspects of the role of indoctrination in music education in chapter 7 of this volume.

12. See, for example, Yob, chapter 17 in this volume.

References

Alperson, Philip, ed. 1987. *What Is Music? An Introduction to the Philosophy of Music.* University Park: Pennsylvania State University Press.

Bogdan, Deanne. 1998. Review of "In Search of Music Education" by Estelle R. Jorgensen. *Philosophy of Music Education Review* 6, no. 1 (Spring): 71–73. http://www.jstor.org/stable/40327115.

Boyce-Tillman, June. 2000. *Constructing Musical Healing: Wounds That Heal.* London: Jessica Kingsley.

Clayton, Martin, Trevor Herbert, and Richard Middleton, eds. 2003. *The Cultural Study of Music: A Critical Introduction.* New York: Routledge.

DeNora, Tia. 2003. *After Adorno: Rethinking Music Sociology.* Cambridge: Cambridge University Press.

Dewey, John. 1916. *Democracy and Education: An Introduction to the Philosophy of Education.* New York: Macmillan.

———. 1902. *The Child and the Curriculum*. Chicago: University of Chicago Press.
———. 1929. *Experience and Nature*. London: Allen and Unwin.
Drinker, Sophie. (1948) 1995. *Women and Music: The Story of Women in Their Relation to Music*. New York: Feminist.
Feld, Steven. 2012. *Sound and Sentiment: Birds, Weeping, Poetics and Song in Kaluli Expression*. 3rd ed. Durham, NC: Duke University Press.
Felluga, Dino Franco. 2011. "Modules on Foucault: On Power." *Introductory Guide to Critical Theory*. Last modified January 31. West Lafayette, IN: Purdue University. http://www.purdue.edu/guidetotheory/newhistoricism/modules/foucaultpower.html.
Foucault, Michel. 1977. *Discipline and Punish: The Birth of the Prison*. Translated by Alan Sheridan. New York: Pantheon.
———. 1982. "The Subject and Power." In *Michel Foucault: Beyond Structuralism and Hermeneutics*, 2nd ed., edited by Hubert L. Dreyfus and Paul Rabinow, 208–26. Chicago: University of Chicago Press.
Gaita, Raimond. 2000. *A Common Humanity: Thinking about Love and Truth and Justice*. 2nd ed. London: Routledge.
Greene, Maxine. 1988. *The Dialectic of Freedom*. New York: Teachers College Press.
Hanson, Victor Davis. 2014. "The Death of the Humanities." *Defining Ideas*, January 28. https://www.hoover.org/research/death-humanities.
Howe, Sondra Wieland. 2014. *Women Music Educators in the United States: A History*. Plymouth, UK: Scarecrow.
Jorgensen, Estelle R. 1983. "Engineering Change in Music Education: A Model of the Political Process Underlying the Boston School Music Movement (1829–1838)." *Journal of Research in Music Education* 31, no. 1 (Spring): 67–75.
———. 1993. "Religious Music in Education." *Philosophy of Music Education Review* 1, no. 2 (Fall): 103–14.
———. 1995. "Women, Music, and the Church: An Historical Approach." In *Women and the Church: The Feminine Perspective*, edited by Lourdes E. Morales-Gudmundsson, 35–55. Berrien Springs, MI: Andrews University Press.
———. 1997. *In Search of Music Education*. Urbana: University of Illinois Press.
———. 2003. *Transforming Music Education*. Bloomington: Indiana University Press.
———. 2015. "Intersecting Social Justices and Music Education." In *Oxford Handbook on Social Justice and Music Education*, edited by Cathy Benedict, Patrick Schmidt, Gary Spruce, and Paul Woodford, 7–28. New York: Oxford University Press.
Keene, James A. 2009. *A History of Music Education in the United States*. 2nd ed. Centennial, CO: Glenridge.
Langer, Susanne K. 1957. *Problems of Art: Ten Philosophical Lectures*. New York: Scribner's.
Mark, Michael, and Charles L. Gary. 2007. *A History of American Music Education*. 3rd ed. Lanham, MD: Rowman and Littlefield.
Marty, Martin E. 2005. *When Faiths Collide*. Malden, MA: Blackwell.
Morton, Charlene. 2004. "Response to Bennett Reimer: 'Once More with Feeling: Reconciling Discrepant Accounts of Musical Feeling.'" *Philosophy of Music Education Review* 12, no. 1 (Spring): 55–59.
Perrine, William M. 2013. "Religious Music and Free Speech: Philosophical Issues in *Nurre v. Whitehead*." *Philosophy of Music Education Review* 21, no. 2 (Fall): 178–96.
———. 2016. "The Rehearsal and Performance of Holiday Music: Philosophical Issues in *Stratechuk v. Board of Education*." *Philosophy of Music Education Review* 24, no. 2 (Fall): 131–50.

———. 2017. "*Bauchman v. West High School* Revisited: Religious Text and Context in Music Education." *Philosophy of Music Education Review* 25, no. 2 (Fall): 192–213.

Reimer, Bennett. 2003. *A Philosophy of Music Education: Advancing the Vision.* Upper Saddle River, NJ: Prentice Hall.

Rife, Susan L. 2014. "Sarasota Orchestra Director Takes Charge." *Sarasota Herald Tribune*, February 22, 1A, 7A.

Robin, William. 2014. "His Music, Entwined with His Faith: Arvo Pärt's Pieces Are Not Only Spiritual, but Church-Specific." *New York Times*, May 18, AR 14.

Scheffler, Israel. 1991. *In Praise of the Cognitive Emotions and Other Essays in the Philosophy of Education.* New York: Routledge.

Scott, Derek B. 2002. *Music, Culture, and Society: A Reader.* Oxford: Oxford University Press.

Shepherd, John. 1991a. "Music and the Last Intellectuals." *Journal of Aesthetic Education* 25, no. 3 (Fall): 95–114.

———. 1991b. *Music as Social Text.* Cambridge, UK: Polity.

Tillich, Paul. 1986. "Art and Ultimate Reality." In *Art, Creativity, and the Sacred*, edited by Diane Apostolos-Cappadona, 219–35. New York: Crossroad.

Tiryakian, Edward A. 1973. "Sociology and Existential Phenomenology." In *Phenomenology and the Social Sciences*, vol. 1, edited by Maurice Natanson, 187–222. Evanston, IL: Northwestern University Press.

United Nations General Assembly. 1989. *Convention on the Rights of the Child*, December 12. Document A/RES/44/25. http://www.cirp.org/library/ethics/UN-convention.

Vanhoenacker, Mark. 2014. "Requiem: Classical Music in America Is Dead." *Slate*, January 21. http://www.slate.com/articles/arts/culturebox/2014/01/classical_music_sales_decline_is_classical_on_death_s_door.html.

Whitehead, Alfred North. 1929. *The Aims of Education and Other Essays.* New York: New American Library.

Williams, Gayle. 2014. "Tali Brings Orchestra's Energy Out." *Sarasota Herald Tribune*, February 22, 7B.

Yob, Iris M. 1992. "Religious Metaphor and Scientific Model: Grounds for Comparison." *Religious Studies* 28, no. 4: 475–85.

———. 1995a. "Religious Emotion in the Arts." *Journal of Aesthetic Education* 29, no. 4 (Winter): 23–38.

———. 1995b. "Spiritual Education: A Public School Dialogue with Religious Interpretations." *Religious Education* 90, no. 1 (Winter): 104–17.

———. 1997. "Cognitive Emotions and Emotional Cognitions." In *Reason and Education: Essays in Honor of Israel Scheffler*, edited by Harvey Siegel, 43–57. Dordrecht, Neth.: Kluwer Academic.

———. 2003. "Thinking Constructively with Metaphors," *Studies in Philosophy and Education* 22, no. 2 (March): 127–38.

———. 2011. "If We Knew What Spirituality Was, We Would Teach for It," *Music Educators Journal* 98, no. 2 (December): 41–47, http://mej.sagepub.com/content/98/2/41, doi: 10.1177/0027432111425959.

2 | Selective Affinities: Concordance and Discordance at the Intersection of Musical, Educational, and Religious Practices

Philip Alperson

Introduction: From Elective to Selective Affinities

In 1809, the German writer, artist, and scientist Johann Wolfgang von Goethe completed a novella, *Die Wahlverwandtschaften*, in English *Elective Affinities* (Goethe 1971). The novel's plot centers on the decision of a wealthy couple, Baron Eduard and his wife Baroness Charlotte, to invite two friends to live with them at their country estate. The book tells the story of the fateful consequences of that invitation.

Goethe's book has been the object of critical attention from its time of publication to the present day, a span of more than two hundred years (Adler 1990; Goehr 2008; Tantillo 2001). Part of the book's interest is suggested by its title. The phrase "elective affinities" is a technical term derived from eighteenth-century scientific attempts to identify and order dispositions of chemical elements to form combinations with one another. These chemical affinities were said to be "elective" (*Wahl* in German), not in the sense that the connections were somehow a matter of choice but rather in the technical sense that certain affinities or coherences tend to occur in the natural order of things. The attractions seem to be elective, that is, "preferred," by nature. Scientists of the time, including the French chemists Étienne-François Geoffroy and Pierre-Joseph Macquer and the Swedish chemist Torbern Bergman, constructed charts or "tables of affinities" representing the degrees of attractive and dissociative forces of the then known elements.

It is part of the fascination of the novella that Goethe moved the idea of elective affinity from chemical table to human fable, suggesting by way of an elaborate chemical/literary metaphor that in matters of the heart and other human affairs are also deeply embedded natural attractions or affinities that affect human relations. In Goethe's story, various kinds of affinities are exemplified not only in the developing relationships among the characters and the exchange of human partners that is the key to the plot, but also in the dialogue of the characters, as they discuss human relations using the technical terminology of chemical elective affinity theory. One of the characters (Charlotte) suggests that the relationships between groups of people such as classes, social circles, and occupations, might also be affected by the forces of elective affinity.[1]

Goethe was not the first to propose the idea that human relations were essentially motivated, if not driven, by deeply embedded relations of affinity. In the early fifth century BC, the Greek philosopher Empedocles had theorized that four fundamental elements—earth, air, fire, and water—mingle and separate through the powers of love and strife to compose the nature of all living things. Nor was Goethe the last. After Goethe's work, the pioneering sociologist Max Weber used the idea of elective affinities as a conceptual tool to examine the relationship between the Protestant work ethic and the notion of a "calling" or secular vocation, on the one hand, and the "spirit of capitalism" and the rational pursuit of economic gain, on the other, thereby demonstrating a connection between the rational pursuit of economic gain and moral and religious significance (Weber 1905; see also Howe 1978).

What strikes me about the trope of elective affinities, especially in Weber's hands, is the suggestion that not only chemical elements—or even human relations—but, indeed, entire realms of human endeavor and practices might have affinities or dispositions to combine with one another. In this chapter, I take my cue from the general idea of elective affinities to explore some basic conceptual issues on the possible affinities among three areas of human practice: music, education, and religion.

My plan is to begin with some rather abstract conceptual considerations, moving increasingly toward concrete, practical issues. I shall start by indicating why it might reasonably be thought that the areas of music, education, and religion do have deep affinities, especially in some of their shared goals. I shall then move on to the stronger claim that the collaboration of practices in the fields of music, religion, and education might enhance the achievement of some of these goals, thereby serving to sustain their practices or otherwise favor each other's continuance. I shall identify a particular version of this enhancement thesis, which I shall call "the additive hypothesis." I shall then argue that while the additive hypothesis might at first seem attractive, especially insofar as it comports with the high regard in which we generally hold music, education, and religion, the hypothesis fails to take into account some of the complications and practical problems that arise in actual practices in these fields. I shall then turn to one set of practical issues that arise when music, education, and religion come into contact with one another in the music education classroom. I shall argue, finally, that one should approach the intersection of musical, educational, and religious practices, *not* as a site of natural elective affinities, but rather as an arena of potential "selective" affinities. And I shall urge that one needs to approach connections among these domains with considerable caution.

Extensional Adequacy

Is it even possible to arrive at useful generalizations about the realms of music, education, and religion, in consideration of their enormous diversity of practices?

Put in more technical terms, is it reasonable to think that we could arrive at strict definitions of these three pursuits that would provide us with extensional adequacy, that is to say, definitions that would correctly apply to exactly the same things, including all things we intuitively think belong in the category and excluding all things we think do not?

Consider the case of religion. There is no single belief or doctrine espoused by all religions. Take the matter of the postulation of supernatural or transcendental deities. Judaism, Christianity, Islam, Sikhism, and Bahá'í are monotheistic religions, asserting the existence of a single supernatural being. Ancient Greek religion was polytheistic. Some religions seem to be a blend: Hinduism postulates the existence of a supreme being, Brahman, who can be worshipped in many forms. Arguably, the same might be said about the Christian triune conception of God. Beliefs in personal deities do not play a role in Zen Buddhism, which might better be described as a religion of immanence, where transcendence, if the word is to be used at all, refers not to a transcendental metaphysical realm but rather to an elevated state of consciousness or being brought about through meditative discipline. Some religions worship animal or ancestral spirits (zoolatry) or nature itself. There is no agreement about what sorts of physical objects might enable or become proper objects of religious responses. In some traditions, inanimate objects such as relics, statues and crosses, or food and drink such as bread and wine are venerated. In others, livings things such as cows and trees, or natural phenomena such as the River Ganges, are considered sacred. In some religions, certain edifices or places are denominated as centers of religious practice; in others prayer or meditation can take place anywhere. Some religions are associated with large complex institutions, but it is also possible to be religious in the sense of having a personal relationship with something—a transcendental god, perhaps. Nor can we identify any single ritual, practice, worldview, mode of experience, or feeling common and peculiar to all religions. Some religions favor rational argumentation as a mode of religious understanding; others assert the authority of sacred text or the pronouncement of religious leaders; still others look to mystical experience. The variety of religious doctrines, beliefs, and practices seems deep indeed (Alston 1967). One wonders, then, what exactly counts as a religion.

Education, too, comes in many forms. Of course we often think of education in terms of formal institutions such as schools, colleges, and universities. But much education occurs informally outside the walls of institutions—in homes, among friends, traveling, on the streets, at leisure, at work, from novels and comic books, from the internet, from mass media, and the movies. The aims of education can be construed very broadly, as in the case of a liberal arts education that strives not only to introduce students to history and culture, but also to develop critical habits of thought and receptivity toward life in general. Other sorts of education are more narrowly focused: to train students to be computer programmers, fashion designers, priests, or violinists. Some educational programs have a relatively fixed term of study defined by a number of credits hours or semesters. Alternatively, education may be understood as a lifelong project. Some educational programs clearly delineate between the role of teacher or master on the one hand and the student or apprentice on the other. Other educational contexts are more collaborative, as when less experienced musicians sit in with more experienced ones. Educational programs may be directed toward particular age groups, as in the cases of preschool, kindergarten, and adult education, but they need not be: community chess lessons in the park are age-blind.

Music also seems to resist easy definition. Of course, we may think of music in terms of what goes on in the concert hall, especially in terms of the performance of instrumental chamber and orchestral music in the Western diatonic tradition. But instrumental music is only a part of what we enjoy as music. Music may—and frequently does—involve the admixture of words, drama, costume, and dance, not to mention the effects of sophisticated lighting, celebrity, fashion, and bling. Music may be polytonal, microtonal, atonal, or nontonal. It may involve or even consist primarily of ambient or environmental sound. It may be composed and performed in accordance with strict and familiar guidelines. It may be improvised. Or relatively random. Music may involve an audience hearing a performance in real time in a single physical location such as a concert hall, or its audience might be dispersed worldwide and asynchronously by means of recordings or the Web. Some music, such as singing in the shower, has no audience, unless one is thought to be singing to the walls or to oneself. Music may be more or less or captured and passed on to new generations by means of notation and instructional manuals. But some musical traditions rely on oral transmission for its preservation. In the face of all this variety, one might reasonably ask: Are the complexities, fluidities, and differences among the various practices of music, education, and religion simply too unruly and diverse to capture conceptually?

Many—perhaps most—human practices are not amenable to strict definitions indicating necessary and sufficient conditions that enable us to state decisively whether something does or does not belong as a member of the class in question. This is true not only for music, education, and religion but also for art, games, and other human practices, affairs, groupings, and relations. And yet, as Wittgenstein (1953) points out, despite the fluidities of practices we nevertheless make sense of these categories, not by means of sets of necessary and sufficient conditions, but rather because we understand that in each of these practices there is a range of overlapping similarities among the instances of a class, where no one feature is common to all, but where some group of characteristic or typical features is commonly present. There are, as we say, family resemblances. In the same way, we can talk meaningfully about our understanding of such things as religion, education, and music. Among the characteristics commonly associated with religion are beliefs in supernatural beings, a distinction between sacred and profane objects, certain sorts of experiences, prayer, and so on, even though no one of these features is present in all instances of religion. Characteristics common to education might include the notion of discipline or interdisciplinary study, the distinction between teacher and student, the existence of formal and informal structures, concepts of critical thinking, practical reason, vocational training, and so on. In the case of music, we might think of the notion of a listenable auditory field whether tonal or not, the idea of performance, the concept of art, the possibility of a notational system, the existence of musical instruments, an emphasis on skill, expression, or musicality, and so on. Which of these characteristics should be the proper focus of attention? Context will be our guide.

The Enhancement Thesis: Integral Goods

In the specific context of the intersection of practices of music, education, and religion, I would like to focus on one characteristic in particular that I think is not, strictly speaking, a defining feature of these fields but that, I suggest, is commonly a part of our thinking about them. I propose that we think of these endeavors functionally, as enterprises, that—at their best—promote various kinds of social and personal enhancements. Education, religion, and music can be seen as three dimensions of human flourishing, aspiration, and happiness. That is to say, at their best, each of these domains aims at securing various kinds of goods. We cannot hope to come up with an exhaustive list of what these life-enhancing goods are, but let me indicate what I take to be some of the more prominent ones.

The goals of education, the forms of good to which they aspire, might be said to include the transmission of knowledge and culture; the training of skills; the development of cognitive, emotive, and social capacities; and the education of people as citizens. Education can promote the inculcation of correct habits and virtue, the attainment of social justice, and the emancipation and freedom from oppression and discrimination based on race, gender, class, ethnicity, nationality, or other factors.

What goods might be associated with religion? Religion is often said to be a source of meaning and value or an overall sense of the purpose of things; a guide to a worthy and satisfying life; a foundation for ethical principles; and a provider of material, psychological, and spiritual support for the poor, the underprivileged, and the wealthy. Religion can help us to cope: it can be a place of peace, harmony, or solace, a home where one can feel a part of a community and have a sense of personal identity and self-worth by virtue of shared belief, vocation, or ritual. It can serve as an anodyne for a sense of isolation or existential estrangement. Religion may be thought to be a link to a transcendent realm, a means of salvation in a fallen world, a reminder or exemplification of the mystery of things, or an answer to troubling questions about the meaning of human finitude and what happens to us after our deaths. Religion can be both a source of consolation and, as Maimonides ([1190] 1904) famously put it, a guide for the perplexed.

Music, too, can be a site of human enhancement. Creating and listening to music typically involve the development and refinement of particular human skills and capacities and seems to most people a source of enrichment, fulfillment, and happiness. Music can be appreciated for its manifold and profound aesthetic qualities as well as for its wealth of expressive and symbolic meanings. It is often seen as a paradigm of human creativity and culture. All the arts, Walter Pater famously says, aspire to the condition of music. Music can be regarded as a system of communication, or part of larger systems of communication, and it can be a marker of personal and social identity. As such, it can serve as a means of expression and activism, promoting social understanding, order, and change. Music can help people get through difficult periods, when they're down and troubled and they need a helping hand. Music can aid in the recovery from depression, pain, and suffering, in the music therapist's lab, in one's living room, even while jogging. These then are some of the goods traditionally attributed to the enterprises of religion, music, and education.

In looking over even this provisional list, one can see that the range is varied, profound, and of obvious relevance to human flourishing. One can also see areas of overlap in the various ways that music, education, and religion can be thought to contribute to personal and social enhancement. Each area identifies the development of relevant skills or cognitive capabilities. Each might be thought to engage particular ranges of emotion. Each recognizes certain provinces of knowledge. Each area identifies ranges of pleasure, enjoyment, or satisfaction. There are communal aspects to activities in each of the three areas. Each provides an avenue of self-expression and a site for the articulation of deeply held values. We might summarize these affinities at a very general level by saying that music, education, and religion are activities that help to make life enjoyable and meaningful, and in so doing contribute to human dignity, worth, and happiness.

The Additive Hypothesis

Now, it is tempting at this point to suppose that since music, education, and religion are singly capable of contributing to human enhancement and since, as we have just seen, there is a considerable overlap or complementarity in the goods that might be enabled through these practices, then the beneficial effects of these endeavors might be strengthened in their combination. Let us call this the additive hypothesis. The enhancement might be of goods characteristic of the individual fields or of some emergent good or set of goods arising from the combination or blending of the practices. In calling such a view a "hypothesis" I do not mean that people who hold such a view are putting forward a hypothesis in the strong scientific sense, that is, a predictive proposal advanced as a solution to a problem whose truth requires some degree of empirical substantiation by observation or experimentation. I intend rather a weaker sense of *hypothesis*, along the lines of a conjecture or even a tacit assumption, that the additive salutary effects of the combination of musical, educational, and religious methods, doctrines, or practices will be equal to or greater than the salutary effects of musical, educational, or religious methods, doctrines, and practices considered separately. Such a view might be semiconsciously held, something vaguely felt rather than something held in the mind in clear propositional terms. There may be a psychological appeal to the additive hypothesis; it is only natural to think that since we value the goods proclaimed by each of these fields singly, that we would do well by joining forces, as it were, thus securing new or greater goods in their combination.

I now want to suggest that the additive hypothesis stands in need of careful and critical elaboration. I say this partly on the basis of some very general technical considerations I can mention here only in passing. Following philosopher Peter Geach, I take goods to be attributive, not predicative terms, by which I mean that when we call something a good we are not saying that something possesses some absolute property, goodness, in the way that an apple might possess the property of redness or have a spheroid shape. Rather, when we say a thing is good we mean that it is good relative to some standard: it is good for someone or for something or in some respect (Geach 1956).

This means that if we were to compare things with respect to their goods, as we do in the case of the additive hypothesis, we would have to ascertain what it is these things are good for before we could determine whether or in what way their combination might somehow enhance each other's goodness. Suppose we were to argue, for example, that some combination of religious doctrines, beliefs, or methods would be beneficial in the music education classroom. To make good on such a claim we would at a minimum have to be able to specify what the combination would be good for: some desired effect, use, or function, perhaps, which would arise in the combination of practices.

But notice that there is no *a priori* reason to suppose that because one thing is a good in respect to a particular use and another thing is good even with respect to the same use, the two things taken together will result in an enhanced collaborative good with respect to that use. The fact that both chocolate mousse and marinated herring taste good does not guarantee that marinated herring on top of chocolate mousse will taste good, even though we are considering them each and jointly as good with respect to the same thing: how good they taste. The proof of the pudding is in the eating. It just turns out that the idea of combining chocolate mousse with marinated herring is a bad idea.[2] Similarly, we might say that being independent-minded is taken to be a virtue and that getting along well with others is taken to be a virtue. But, as it turns out, being independent-minded can interfere with getting along well with others, just as getting along with others may dull the spirit of independent thinking. In the matter of the assessment of goods we must, as Wittgenstein says, look and see.

So, it looks as if the additive hypothesis, taken as a general inclination to look for amiable connections among the domains of music, education, and religion, however tempting or psychologically satisfying it may seem, cannot take us very far until we have a better grasp of what specific sorts of goods are at stake and what the actual prospects for goodness are in the case of particular practices and combinations. Which is to say we must consider not only the goods that can arise as a result of religious, educational, and musical practices, but also the harms they may cause.

Associated Harms

Let us return to the case of religion. While it is true that religion—at its best—can be seen as promoting human flourishing and aspirations and securing some of the goods we mentioned earlier, it is also true that religion has been a source of grievous harms. Chief among these are the related evils of religious intolerance and religious hatred that have fueled some of the worst horrors the world has known. Religion has been a factor, in some cases the driving factor,[3] in some of the worst massacres, wars, and atrocities in human history: the Roman persecutions of Christians under Nero, the military expeditions by western Christians in the Crusades to check the spread of Islam in the eleventh through thirteenth centuries, the Thirty Years' War between Protestants and Catholics in the seventeenth century that reduced the population of present-day Germany by somewhere between 25 percent and 40 percent, the extermination of 6 million Jews in Nazi Germany and German-occupied territories in the World War II; conflicts among Sunni Muslims, Shiite Muslims, Druze, and Christian Lebanese in the Lebanese Civil War (1975–91), ongoing strife between Jews and Arabs in Israel and Palestine, between Muslims and Hindus in Pakistan and India, between Buddhists and Muslims in Myanmar and Sri Lanka, between Catholics and Buddhists in South Vietnam, and between Hui and Uyghur Muslims in China. Boko Haram, whose aim is to establish a fully Islamic state in Nigeria, was responsible for a suicide attack on a United Nations building in Abuja in 2011, repeated burnings of schools and villages, brutal attacks that have killed thousands of people, and, in 2014, the mass abduction of more than two hundred schoolgirls (Felter 2018; Williams and Guttschuss 2012). Osama bin Laden cited the Western hatred of Islam as a prime reason why he masterminded the 9/11/2001 terrorist attacks that killed nearly three thousand people (bin Laden 2002). The Islamic State in Iraq and the Levant (ISIS/ISAL) issued a contract ultimatum (*dhimma*) to Christians living in Mosul in 2014: leave Mosul, convert to Islam, pay a protection fee (*jizya*), or die by the sword. Mosul, which had a Christian population of about 60,000 as recently as 2003, had by 2014 been virtually emptied of Christians (BBC 2014a). The terrorist mechanisms of ISIS include the separation of families, forced religious conversions, forced marriages, beheadings of civilians, sexual assault, and sexual slavery, carried out in the name of Wahhabist Islam. In 2014, the Pakistani Taliban attacked a school in Peshawar, massacring 145 people, 132 of them children (BBC 2014b). One is simply at a loss to understand the scope and horror of the sad, tragic history of religious violence and depredation.[4]

These are examples of large-scale atrocities arising from interreligious and interdenominational intolerance and hatred. There are also the indignities, social and cultural exclusions, and invidious consequences that are evident in the everyday life and work of individuals who become the victims of theocratic fascism. Galileo was famously brought before the Roman Inquisition in 1632, condemned, and placed under house arrest for his scientific work, in particular for his defense of the Copernican heliocentric theory of astronomical movement. Spinoza was excommunicated in 1656 by the Portuguese Jewish community in Amsterdam for his philosophical work. Salman Rushdie was the victim of a fatwā issued by the spiritual leader of Iran, the Ayatollah Khomeini, who declared that Rushdie's novel, *Satanic Verses*, was a blasphemy against Islam. The Dutch film director Theo van Gogh was murdered by Mohammed Boyeri, a Dutch-Moroccan Muslim, who objected to van Gogh's film, *Submission*, which criticized the treatment of women in Islam. The government of Afghanistan investigated the *Afghanistan Express* newspaper for blasphemy when the paper published an article raising the question whether Muslims should embrace even the possibility that more than one God exists (Craig 2014).

Nor does one have to be influential or have a high public profile to be affected by social exclusion in everyday life. Children may be pressured into participating in classroom holiday rituals celebrating religious traditions they may not share, and they may be ostracized if they do not comply. They may be asked to join in group prayer before sporting events, whether they share the prevailing creed or not. Or whether they are believers at all.

Indeed, religious harms extend not only to believers but also to nonbelievers. In the United States, where there is a strong conviction in the minds of many that religious faith and morality are inextricably linked, one might think twice before publicly mentioning one is an atheist. Polls consistently show that atheists are the least trusted, most hated identifiable group in the United States. When asked in a 2006 University of Minnesota poll which group "does not at all agree with my vision of American society," atheists topped the list at 46 percent, followed in order by Muslims (26%)—and this was after the terrorist attacks of 9/11—homosexuals (23%), Hispanics (20%), conservative Christians (14%), recent immigrants (13%), and Jews (8%). When asked which group "I would disapprove [of] if my child wanted to marry a member of this group," atheists again were the winners, coming in at 48 percent, easily defeating their closest rivals Muslims and African Americans (Edgell, Gerteis, and Hartmann 2006). And if asked whom people would be least likely to vote for in a presidential election, atheists again lead the list, beating out Muslims, gays and lesbians, and Mormons (Jones 2012). Trial lawyers in the United States are advised by trial consultants to remind jurors, if they know they are judging an atheist, that atheists are human (Keene and Handrich 2010). It is no wonder that US political candidates and, indeed, US presidents, find it obligatory to end public speeches with the phrase, "God bless America." This in a country where the first amendment to the United States Constitution, the so-called "Establishment Clause," was designed to build "a wall of separation between Church & State," as its author, Thomas Jefferson, put it (Jefferson [1802] 1978).

Religious intolerance may be tied to or exacerbated by other forms of discrimination such as nationalist, ethnic, and racial prejudices, as in the case of the racist threats and atrocities perpetuated by the US white supremacist hate group, the Ku Klux Klan, who look to the authority of Christian scripture to support their allegations of the inferiority of blacks, Catholics, Jews, and immigrants. Hence, the symbolic significance of cross burnings (Wade 1987, 185). Similarly, as Simone de Beauvoir, Kate Millett, Mary Daly, and others have argued, there is embedded in the founding myths of the Abrahamic religions of Judaism, Christianity, and Islam—the male godhead, the idea of Eve as a secondary, imperfect, and morally defective man—a deep vein of androcentrism, if not misogyny, an "othering" of women that has enabled the legitimation of women's confinement and subservience (Mikaelsson, forthcoming). And so, women are discouraged or forbidden from admittance to the clergy or participating in other forms of religious ritual. Orthodox Judaism forbids women from constituting a *minyan* (prayer quorum). In Israel, Orthodox Jews prohibit women from praying in public at the Wailing Wall. In 2012, the Afghani Taliban, on the authority of their interpretation of Islamic law, stoned a woman to death for being seen in public with a man. In 2014 in Sudan, Mariam Yehya Ibrahim, an eight-month-pregnant wife and mother raised as a Christian by her mother, was pronounced guilty of apostasy and sentenced to be hanged after first being lashed one hundred times when she refused to renounce Christianity and embrace the Muslim religion of her father (Associated Press 2014). And in the United States, where 55 percent of the population depends on employer-based programs for health coverage, the Supreme Court has ruled that so-called "closely held" corporations such as family-owned companies, were "persons" entitled to assert their "sincerely held" religious beliefs and to exempt themselves from covering certain sorts of women's birth control as preventive health care, even when the health or the life of the woman would be in jeopardy because of conditions such as congenital heart disease or Marfan syndrome. In this way, the religious beliefs of even a few corporate owners directly affect the ability of thousands of women to control their reproductive lives and overall health. Within days of the Supreme Court ruling, Gordon College, a Christian college in Massachusetts, sought exemption from a federal ban on antigay discrimination (Allen 2014), while a second Christian institution, George Fox University in Oregon, denied a transgender student on-campus housing on religious grounds (Borgen 2014). It is an open question how many other forms of discrimination will be enabled on the grounds of protecting "sincerely held" religious beliefs in the United States.

To this point we have been speaking of harms primarily insofar as they may be said to be born out of religious doctrine and belief. But harms can also arise from the action or inaction of religious institutions. One thinks of the Catholic Church's complicity in and attempts to conceal cases of child sexual abuse. In the United States alone, in a fifty-year period ending in 2002, more than ten thousand cases of clergy sexual abuse were reported to diocese officials. Of 4,392 priests accused of sexual misconduct, only 6 percent were convicted and only 2 percent received prison sentences (John Jay College of Criminal Justice 2004). In 2013, the Office of the United Nations High Commissioner for Human Rights criticized the Holy See (Center for Constitutional Right 2015) for its violence against children worldwide, citing cases of sexual abuse of children by members of the church and the "code of silence" imposed by the church, as well as the torture and cruel treatment of children, referring to slavelike conditions and physical and sexual abuse committed against girls working in the church-run Magdalene Laundries in Ireland through 1966.[5] The 2009 Ryan Report of the Irish Commission to Inquire into Child Abuse documented child abuse cases in sixty residential reform schools run by the Catholic Church in Ireland from 1936 to 1970 (Office of the Minister for Children and Youth Affairs 2009).

Let us leave this account of some of the harms wrought by religion and turn our attention to education. As we have seen, critical thought and analysis cultivated through education can help to identify, transmit, and thereby secure those bodies of knowledge, values, and traditions that a society holds as ideals, to enable individuals to lead full and fruitful lives. It would be a mistake, however, to see the effects of education as goods *simpliciter*.

Notwithstanding the manifold pleasures of education pursued for its own sake, education can also bring its share of frustration, anxieties, and disappointments. To a certain extent learning to cope with such difficulties is simply a part of life and, indeed, overcoming obstacles, learning to manage failure, and learning from one's mistakes can themselves yield a sense of accomplishment, if not enjoyment. Nevertheless, if educators and educational programs are not sensitive to matters of access and bias and to the cognitive, emotional, social, and developmental differences among students—if, for example, curricula and testing apparatuses are too rigid—students may experience needless anxiety and fears and may even be set up to fail.

In thinking about the potential and actual harms of education, consider also the matter of the political economy of education. Educational institutions, from primary schools through universities, have in recent years and in certain countries been under pressure to operate under principles imported from the corporate world. The basic idea is that educational institutions are conceived as "service institutions" in which educators are regarded as workers who have to be "managed" effectively in order to provide the best service—the provision of "products" for their "customers." Efficient management is seen as a matter of increasing worker "accountability" and "productivity," which in turn depend on identifying "measurable outcomes." As one management guru has put it, what can be measured can be seen; what cannot be measured cannot be seen.[6]

The emphasis on productivity measurements has had serious and harmful effects up and down the educational system in countries where this set of values has taken hold. In Britain, for example, the 1986 national Research Assessment Exercise and its successor program, the Research Excellence Framework have assessed the quality of university research on a point system favoring programs with "economic impact," resulting in the closure of university departments, narrowing the curriculum, and encouraging university lecturers to game the system by orienting their research to amass countable publications by, for example, cutting up large manuscripts into smaller chunks in order to increase the number of publications. The turn to managerialism in higher education has hit arts and humanities researchers especially hard (Shepherd 2009; Warner 2014). Secondary schools in Britain are ranked in "league tables" according to their aggregate performance on grades achieved by students taking the General Certificate of Secondary Education tests (United Kingdom Department of Education 2014). In the United States, where the market-based approach to education has made major inroads, the governor of Texas has recommended ranking university faculty according to cost per student. US colleges and universities also rely on the exploitation of cheap labor, in the interest of "efficiency," engaging legions of part-time adjunct teachers who receive low wages and no health or retirement benefits, to teach their courses. Currently more than 50 percent of US university faculty are part-time adjunct teachers.

The insistence on measurable productivity has also led to an increasing emphasis on standardized tests, according to which not only students but also teachers and schools are judged. In some states in the United States, high school teachers whose students do not score well on the tests are threatened with dismissal, a possibility underwritten by two major pieces of federal regulations, the "No Child Left Behind" act of 2001 (PL 107-110), which required all public schools receiving federal funding to administer statewide standardized tests annually to all students, and the "Race to the Top" Fund of 2009 (American Recovery and Reinvestment Act of 2009, PL 111-5), which offered $4.35 billion in competitive funding to states that agreed to evaluate teachers by student test scores. It is not surprising that students study for the tests and teachers teach for the tests. Indeed, the structure of the school system itself is changing to accommodate the demand for corporate efficiency and the adoption of market-based restructuring of schools. The privatization of schools has taken funds and resources from underperforming schools, shifting them toward private charter schools or voucher-based institutions, to allow parents increasing "consumer choice" among service providers. This has hit socioeconomically disadvantaged groups hard, especially urban schools with diverse and immigrant populations and children whose first language is not English, since this population does not do as well on standardized tests written in English. Overlaid on this is an emphasis on those subjects of direct benefit to the corporate world, the so-called STEM fields: science, technology, engineering, and mathematics.

I mention these developments not simply because the nostrums of "efficiency" and "accountability" displace the idea of teachers as professionals with standards of autonomy and responsibility and accordingly diminish what talented and dedicated teachers do in the classroom. These trends also cause specific harms to students and to society generally. As Randall Allsup and Heidi Westerlund have argued in the case of the music classroom, the damage being done in the name of what John Dewey calls the quest for certainty can be seen in the deemphasis on teacher agency, in particular the capability of teachers to guide students in the development of ethical or moral imagination in the face of the uncertainties and ambiguities that life presents (Allsup and Westerlund 2012). Defunding arts and humanities education, reducing funding to underserved populations, recasting general education as a worker supply system, constricting the notion of knowledge production to science, technology, vocational training, and corporate "entrepreneurialism"—these are all harms that affect students, teachers, and society as a whole.

The dangers go even more deeply. We have said that one of the goods that can come from education is the transmission of deeply held beliefs to new generations of students. But consider the roles education can play with respect to beliefs. Bertrand Russell makes a helpful distinction, differentiating between liberal education, on the one hand, whose goal is free and unbiased discussion and the freedom to question any belief if one can support the questioning by solid argument, and, on the other hand, what Russell calls "edification"—the bolstering of beliefs that favor the authorities and whose appeal rests on the desire to preserve a stable society and perpetuate the institutions of State (Russell 1951).

There are two realms of harm this distinction reveals. First, the emphasis on education as the transmission of received opinion that promotes stability runs the risk of stifling creativity and rewarding conformity over spontaneity, original thinking, and eccentricity. I am not thinking so much about the brand of eccentricity of, say, Oscar Wilde, who is reputed to have taken his pet lobster out for a walk on a leash, but rather the free spirit of the individuality of human beings that, as John Stuart Mill notes, is one of the elements of human well-being, happiness, and social progress, and one of the main means by which people discover new truths and resist the tyranny of opinion. Individuality is one of the first casualties of an education that puts too much stress on what Mill calls "the despotism of custom" (Mill 1859, chapter 3).

In short, education always carries with it the dangers of indoctrination—the inculcation of preconceived values—and this enables a second set of potential harms, namely, as educators and social critics including Paolo Freire (1970, 1994), Ivan Illich (1971), Michel Foucault (1975), Henry Giroux (1983), bell hooks (1994), and others have argued, that educational systems have their own political characters and they can function as a means of social control perpetuating social inequality. As Freire (1994) points out, educational systems do not operate in value-free ways. Put in Foucauldian terms, schooling may be understood as a form of "disciplinary technology," like the prison or the Panopticon itself, a mechanism of surveillance and social regulation connecting knowledge and power devised to police behavior and neutralize disorder through confinement, time management, and a system of punishments and rewards (Deacon 2005). When we think of indoctrination, it is tempting to think of the overt examples such as the reeducation camps of China, Vietnam, and Korea. But the threat of indoctrination and surveillance can exist anywhere.

Let us turn finally to music. Does it make sense to speak of musical harms? It may seem odd even to ask the question. Music is one of those activities that seems so positive to so many people. We virtually equate being musical with being human. Music is interesting in this regard in part because of a widespread historically established tradition of regarding music autotelically—as having an end or purpose in itself—and in listening to music autonomously for its own sake (Hanslick [1854] 1986; Kivy 1991). For this reason, it is helpful to distinguish two categories of musical harms: (1) those harms internal to the practice of creating, listening to, and appreciating music autonomously, which we shall call intrinsic harms, and (2) those harms external to the practice of creating, listening to, and appreciating music autonomously, which we shall call extrinsic harms, bearing in mind that this distinction may not be so easily made in practice.

Let us start with intrinsic musical harms. We know that there are such things as musical jokes such as the false endings in Haydn's String Quartet in E-flat, op. 33, no. 2 ("The Joke"). Are there any purely musical harms? There are. Playing out of tune, playing wrong notes, playing too fast, playing too slowly, missing a repeat sign, playing with too heavy a vibrato—the list is very long. These are examples of failing to observe prevailing technical and stylistic standards of performance practice within specific musical traditions. Violation of these norms can cause pain to those performers and audience members who hold to certain standards of performance practice and who can detect these failings. There are also internal musical harms that arise within the social protocols of musical performance. One can behave badly in the case of improvised jazz, for example, by violating protocols of soloing in ensemble situations: playing a chorus that is stylistically incongruous with the tune, for example, or soloing for twelve choruses when the three players before you have taken two choruses each. These are harms that are violations of musical practice although, to be sure, they have a social dimension (Alperson 2010). Audiences can inflict parallel harms by crackling candy wrappers, by failing to stifle coughs during a musical performance, by clapping too soon or—worse—by leaving a cell phone on during a performance.

Music may also inflict extrinsic harms, harms that extend beyond the world of music autonomously conceived. Music can be a marker for and can reinforce social stratification. It is not at all uncommon for people to judge other people on the basis of the kinds of music they listen to. What would it say to you about me if I told you that my favorite kind of music was rap? Or chamber music? Or Tuvan throat singing? The phenomenon is caught memorably in Nick Hornby's novel, *High Fidelity*, in which a character judges people not according to the content of their character, but according to the content of their record collections. A customer asks a clerk in Robert Fleming's second-hand vinyl store whether he can have a copy of Stevie Wonder's pop tune, "I Just Called to Say I Love You." No, you cannot, the clerk says, "because it's sentimental, tacky crap, that's why not. Do we look like the sort of shop that sells fucking 'I Just Called to Say I Love You'?" Rob asks the clerk how he could drive a potential customer away like that. The clerk replies, "He offended me with his terrible taste" (Hornby 1995, 53–54). Through this fictional episode, Hornby joins forces with the social theorist Pierre Bourdieu, who argues that judgments of taste are acts of social positioning, markers of upbringing, education, and social origin, bound up with systems of disposition ("habitus") characteristic of differences between classes and class fractions (Bourdieu 1984). Music is not alone among human practices in its ability to foster discrimination and cause harms by means of this sort of stratification; but music is a familiar mode of legitimating social difference. You are what you hear.

Music can also be employed instrumentally in a variety of moral contexts, for both good and ill. Music can be used to undermine autonomy, regulate behavior, and enforce compliance with social norms and mores in strictly managed societies such as the military. Reveille can be used to wake up the troops in the morning and songs may be used to bolster comradery, courage, and bravado in preparation for battle, and in this way can be an accomplice to nefarious military conflict. National anthems may evoke pride in country at political rallies and football games, but they may also stoke the fires of war and hatred (Alperson 2014). Historical memory and associations can also play a part. Programming

Wagner in Israel is always a risk because of the painful associations in the minds of many between Wagner and anti-Semitism and the appropriation of Wagner's musical works by the Nazis.[7] Styles and genres of music can also be the bearers of social damage: the lyrics and videos of much hip-hop music are hypermasculinist, homophobic, and misogynist, exaggerating stereotypically male behavior, presenting objectifying and hypersexualized representations of women, and normalizing the abuse, exploitation, and victimization of women in general and women of color in particular (Durham, Cooper, and Morris 2013). Music has been weaponized as a component of "harsh interrogation" torture techniques to inflict emotional, psychological, and physical pain and suffering in detention camps at Bagram Air Force Base in Afghanistan, Mosul Air Force Base in Iraq, and the Guantánamo Bay detention facility in Cuba (Cusick 2008).

Music, by virtue of its powerful aesthetic and emotive force, also can deaden critical reflection and foster social and political quietism. Aristotle long ago noted that music can be used as means of relaxing, and for this reason he classed music with other relaxation agents such as sleep, dancing, and deep drinking (Aristotle 1993). But the charge here goes further than the pursuit of the pleasant. Precisely because music can create an alternate musical universe, it is possible to steep oneself in musical phenomena themselves, and in so doing remove oneself from the realities of the world. There is a particularly touching performance of the song "I Wish I Was in Dixie" by the vocal group the Hi-Lo's (1960). "Dixie," recognizable to many by its first line, "O, I wish I was in the land of cotton," is a remembrance of plantation life in the nineteenth-century US South. Performance of the song, which originated in US blackface minstrel shows, is often a flashpoint in the United States, as the song is fraught with political meanings that continue to excite high passion. For some, the song conjures up pride in Southern culture and heritage. For others, the song stands as an expression of racism, expressing sympathy for a world of racial discrimination, segregation, and slavery. And yet, much of this meaning falls away when the Hi-Lo's sing the song, such is the power of Gene Puerling's meticulous, closely harmonized arrangement and the group's haunting, pitch-perfect performance, all of which transcends or, some would say, masks the concrete cultural and historical conditions alluded to by the lyrics. Music in this way is a retreat from life. Put your headphones on and you can insulate yourself from other people as well.

Taking Stock: The Question of Spirituality

Let us take stock. We have before us a short survey of some of the principle goods and harms that can attend to and that complicate practices in religion, education, and music. These goods and harms carry weights that depend on context and perspective. To someone deeply enrapt in a piece of music or under the ecstatic sway of a particular religious experience, other goods, such as the sense of belonging to a larger musical or religious community, may seem remote or absent from consciousness completely. The widespread harm being done to inner-city schools by the increasing privatization of public school may seem a long way off from the lonely child feeling frustrated by his multiplication tables. Moreover, goods may be primary or they may be secondary or tertiary (etc.). A primary good resulting from introducing sacred music into a music education classroom might be an enhanced understanding of a culture. A secondary or associated harm might be the creation of an atmosphere of exclusion. Finally, goods and harms can be achieved wittingly or unwittingly. They are goods and harms nonetheless. All this is part of the big picture. With these points in mind, let us now see how they might play out in practice. I would like to concentrate on one sample issue. Let us consider the question of the place of religious material in the music education classroom.

What do we mean by religious "material"? If by material we mean the sacred texts and sacred music of a particular religion, and if by religion we mean a religion identifiable in part in virtue of a distinctive set of doctrines and beliefs, and if by music education classroom we mean a classroom in a religious institution, of course the materials may be a means of furthering understanding and appreciation of the tenets of the religion in question or providing aids to worship, which would be goods in relation to sustaining and promoting the religion favored by the institution. Martin Luther, for example, argued that hymns should be promoted in the service of the church as a means of grace and salvation. Luther suggested three reasons why music might be advantageously combined with religion in an educational context: (1) singing spiritual songs is good and pleasing to God, (2) hymns are a way to further the word of God and Christian doctrine, and (3) the young "might rid themselves of amorous and carnal songs, and in their stead learn something wholesome" (Luther [1525] 1983). Since, however, as we have seen, religions have been a source of both goods and harms, the promotion of the religion itself is something subject to further evaluation, even in the case of religiously affiliated institutions.

In the case of secular educational institutions, the case becomes more complicated, since the place of religious education in a public institution is itself a matter that needs to be addressed. This is not a fatal consideration. The common way to address the issue is to distinguish between the promotion or proselytizing of religion on the one hand and the study of religion, considered as one component of culture or civilization, on the other. In this regard, certainly in the West, the contribution of religious music has been unmistakably profound, not only in terms of its importance to religious culture but also in terms of the sheer magnificence of so much religious music and its role in Western culture generally. On these grounds, one can make a plausible argument for the inclusion of religious music in the secular music education classroom, assuming that one of the goals of music education is to expose students to music as a dimension of history and culture, in one's own culture and in the culture of others (Jorgensen 1993; Yob 1995).[8]

That said, there is nevertheless a certain principled reluctance in some quarters to feature religious music, or to bring religious materials into the classroom. This reluctance may stem from several considerations. First, there is a concern for the sensitivities of students and the worry that students will experience a sense of social exclusion, even when the material is handled by the teacher in a sensitive and respectful way. Some people also are fundamentally wary of religion per se. Some people disbelieve in certain religious tenets, and who, as a matter of moral and intellectual integrity, do not wish to materially support an enterprise they find intellectually unsustainable, if not psychologically suspect. Some people refuse to live under the sway of what they see as an illusion motivated by fear (Russell [1927] 1957), or by the longing for a father figure who might protect one against the forces of nature (Freud [1928] 1962). There are people who are chary of some or all of the other religious harms we have documented and who do not wish to be complicit in the furtherance of moral harm. Even if religion is a consolation, it is not, some argue, a consolation worth having.

These are some of the reasons why the move in recent years to discussions of spirituality in the music education classroom is so fascinating. Now, of course, it is possible to think of the introduction of spirituality into the classroom in terms of exposing students to sacred or religious music. And it is possible to talk about spirituality insofar as it tied closely to the doctrines and beliefs of established religions. In these regards, talk about spirituality in the classroom would be subject to some of the same cautions and reservations we have discussed. Some recent proponents of spirituality in the classroom, however, have explicitly tried to put distance between the concept of spirituality and the concept of religion. It has been said that spirituality refers to a certain kind of consciousness or experience that, while it may be facilitated by religious rituals and practices, may equally be occasioned by music or other things, and that spirituality is not bound to any particular doctrinal, ritualistic religion, bound by dogma in belief and practice, or indeed bound to religion in general (Palmer 2010). Thinking of spirituality as a characteristically human capacity "frees spirituality from the domain of religion," it is argued (Yob 2010). Spirituality, it is said, is not tied to "institutionalized religions or their work in education as a means of indoctrination" (Jorgensen 2011).

But if the consciousness of spirituality is not essentially tied to religion, how are we to understand it? One way to understand spirituality is to see it as closely related to aesthetic experience. That would help us to understand not only what kind of experience is being picked out by the term but also why the experience has relevance to the music education classroom. Music might be thought of, for example, as providing a "path" or a "bridge" to this sort of spiritual experience, either because music leads to the characteristic experience of spirituality itself or because the aesthetic experience of music and the experience of spirituality are fundamentally similar, in which case we might speak of the experience of "musical spirituality" (Bogdan 2003), or even that musical spirituality is a *kind* of aesthetic experience (Bogdan 2010; Palmer 2010). Speaking in this vein would also help us understand one other thing. Both religion and music can afford experiences of great power and richness, experiences that often seem different from, if in fact they do not rise above, the prosaic experiences of daily life. The idea of spirituality might help to explain why this is so.[9]

The comparison between spiritual experience and the aesthetic experience of music is part of a larger debate: Is there a similarity between aesthetic experience and religious experience generally speaking? It has seemed so to some. It has been said that religious and aesthetic experience are both rapturous or peak experiences, experiences of awe, wonder, or the sublime, somehow richer than run-of-the-mill experiences. Artistic and religious activity alike are often characterized as taking us into new territory or giving us new perspectives by making clear something we have not previously seen or going beyond the mere givenness of experience. The theologian Rudolf Otto famously speaks of religious experience as numinous, a form of consciousness that has the qualities of a "mysterium tremendum": awe-fulness, overpoweringness, energy, and the wholly other, "that which is quite beyond the sphere of the usual, the intelligible, and the familiar." The numinous is directly present in religious experience, Otto tells us, but it may be expressed indirectly in the appreciation of natural objects, as when we stare in wonder at a rose, as well as in sublime and magical impressions in art, as in the intimations of the mystical effects of the sounds and silences of Bach's Mass in B minor (Otto, [1923] 1958, 26, 60–74). Others have spoken of aesthetic experience and religious experience alike as being characterized fundamentally by a kind transcendence (Bogdan 2003; Martland 1996; Reimer 1995) or "transfiguration" (Shusterman 2008).

There are no doubt some similarities between some religious experiences and some experiences of music, and both musical and religious experiences can be powerfully moving. The problem is in understanding just how far we can push the analogy between religious and aesthetic experiences of music. For a start, the concept of aesthetic experience is itself suspect. It is not clear that there is such a thing as aesthetic experience, if by this one means that there is a special state of mind that one can adopt at will and that must exist prior to any aesthetic experience. It is true that we may sometimes listen to music vigilantly, paying special attention to such musical features as melody, rhythm, harmonic movement, intonation, and so on, "for their own sake." But what we are doing in such cases is simply paying attention. There is nothing further to be gained by calling the action or state of mind aesthetic. Moreover, even with respect to this kind of attention, it is arguable that paying close attention to purely musical qualities is the only proper way to respond to music (Dickie 1964; Sparshott 1982, 472–74).[10] To be sure, we may listen to music carefully, we may read novels carefully, and we may watch films carefully. But the distinctive aesthetic qualities and characteristics we perceive are conditioned by the particular works in front of us, by the histories, institutions, and predispositions that enable and surround them, and especially by the culturally embedded habits and dispositions we bring to the works as we bring these works into our lives. So there is no general "aesthetic" experience on which all our engagements with the arts are based; and it is a mistake to think that the aesthetic is the only road to art.[11]

Can we strengthen the analogy between aesthetic experience and religious experience then simply by eliminating the pesky term *aesthetic* and get on with the business of describing the experiences appropriate to musical works of art and to religion? Not really. The more specific our descriptions of musical experience get, the more diffuse the analogy with religious experience gets. One might speak, for example, of the rapture or ecstasy one can feel in the presence of the beautiful in music, and perhaps some religious experiences have a rapturous or ecstatic character. But some readings of so-called aesthetic experience emphasize, not active participation and ecstasy, but rather (as in the hands of Schopenhauer) an attitude of retreat or withdrawal from the world. Detachment might comport well with certain descriptions of mystical experience or Buddhist meditation, but it seems at odds with the idea of rapturous or ecstatic experience. Moreover, as Francis Sparshott (1976) has pointed out, the emphasis on detached or serene contemplation of the sensory appearances of things seems at odds with at least certain religious tenets: rather than turning from the world to something higher or seeing the world in the light of something higher, the attitude makes "the world the plaything of one's subjectivity. One could take this to be a religious experience only by deifying one's subjectivity" (Sparshott 1976, 110, 112).

Indeed, there is a more general parallelism here: in religion, as in the arts, we confront a complex web of systems of belief, attitudes, and related practices. To make religious experience primary in religion runs the risk of segregating religion from the serious concerns of life and thereby transform it into something that is not religious at all, just as emphasizing aesthetic experience in the arts separates them from the actual histories and institutions of art (Sparshott 1976, 112). Music can elicit a great variety of experiences, especially when we think of music in the context of the everyday situations in which we find music created and enjoyed. The diversity of religious experiences may also be considerable, including the experiences of awe, mystery, guilt, shame, regret, and adoration.

So, it looks as though in considering the analogy between aesthetic and religious experience, we are on the horns of a dilemma: if we leave the concepts of aesthetic and religious experience open we run the risk of undermining the analogy because we do not have the specificity we need to evaluate the analogy; if we further specify the terms *aesthetic* and *religious* the dysanalogy increases. And if one were to try to further specify the notion of spirituality by reintroducing more specific doctrinal metaphysical concepts, such as the way in which music "talks for the soul"—something that is neither matter nor mind (Yob 2010)—then one of the key strategic advantages of the spirituality position—that it maintains a distance from religion by maintaining religious practice while rejecting religious doctrine—is lost. We can see, then, that the proposal that one can and one ought to bring spirituality into the music education classroom is indeed fascinating, but it is a recommendation that brings with it its own set of conceptual and practical challenges.[12]

Let me end by returning to Goethe and Weber. Throughout this chapter, I have tried to show that there are, to be sure, many affinities at the intersection of music, education, and religion. Some of the practices that arise at this intersection can, to employ a musical metaphor, be concordant or harmonious with one another. But when we take into account the wide of range of goods and harms that surround musical, educational, and religious practices, we realize that the affinities we think we see are not simply enshrined in the natural order of things. There are discordances, incongruities, and, frankly, disturbing consequences to consider. In light of this complicated state of affairs, we would do best to proceed with caution and be selective in our employment of them.

PHILIP ALPERSON is Professor Emeritus of Philosophy at Temple University in Philadelphia. He is editor of *What Is Music?*, *The Philosophy of the Visual Arts*, and *Diversity and Community* and former editor of the *Journal of Aesthetics and Art Criticism*.

Notes

I wish to thank Alexis Kallio, Mary Hawkesworth, Elizabeth Wood, and Martin Donougho for their helpful comments on an earlier version of this chapter. I also thank my colleagues at the Sibelius Academy of Music at the University of the Arts–Helsinki and the University of Music and the Performing Arts–Graz, where some of the thoughts in this essay were developed. The faults that remain are entirely mine.

1. It is an open question whether Goethe himself intended his application of principles of chemical attraction to human relationships to be literal or metaphorical. The ambiguity can be seen in Charlotte's comment:

> It needs little imagination to *see in* these elementary forms people one has known; what they especially suggest is the social circles in which they live. But most similar of all to these inanimate things are the masses which stand over against one another in the world: the classes, the professions, the nobility and the third estate, the soldier and the civilian.... It is in just this way that truly meaningful friendships can arise among human beings (Goethe 1971, 52, my italics).

The captain's language is similarly equivocal: "It really does look *as if* one relationship was preferred to another and chosen instead of it" (Goethe 1971, 54, my italics).

2. I set aside the possibility that there exists a culture in which such a concoction is found delicious. I am an attributive relativist with respect to goods but I am an absolutist about the taste of chocolate marinated herring mousse.

3. I am explicitly not proposing a mono-causal explanation of the examples of violence I here adduce. I take it as a given that religion may be one of multiple causes, including socioeconomic, economic, military, personal, familial, and other factors, contributing to personal, social, ethnic, and religious hatred and violence.

4. It is sometimes claimed that such violence is a perversion of authentic religious creed: these actions are "not *really* Muslim," "not in accord with the *true* tenets of Christianity," a result of "extremist," "radical," "militant" *interpretations* of Buddhist beliefs, and so forth. I find such claims disingenuous, setting aside as they do the evident extent to which religious violence has in fact been motivated by religious sentiment. My purpose in this section is in any case to identify actual harms done in the name of religion, not to adjudicate doctrinal debate.

5. The Magdalene Laundries were asylums set up in the nineteenth and twentieth centuries in Europe and North American to house "fallen women." The laundries in Ireland have been the subject of three well-known films: Steve Humphries's 1998 documentary, *Sex in a Cold Climate*, Peter Mullan's *The Magdalene Sisters* (2002), and Stephen Frears's *Philomena* (2013).

6. "Unless we determine what shall be measured and what the yardstick of measurement in an area will be, the area itself will not be seen" (Drucker 1993, 74).

7. Without wanting to get too far afield, one can distinguish between negative emotions that occur fictionally and negative emotions experienced or understood by the listener or viewer. In the case of the film version of the musical *Cabaret*, an elderly man in a beer garden fictionally expresses a feeling of unease as he watches a youth in a brown shirt emblazoned with a swastika who starts a hymn to the Fatherland, "Tomorrow Belongs to Me," and who is then joined by other patrons in the garden. Audience members may understand or experience their own sense of dread as they watch the film.

8. Note the emphasis on instruction. One might accept the instructional value of introducing spirituality into the classroom but object on pedagogical grounds to the use of such material for therapeutic purposes. David Carr (2008) mounts such an objection, favorably citing R. S. Peters's precept that the main function of the teacher is to train and instruct, not to help and cure. I am not sure one can clearly maintain so strict a distinction.

9. I concentrate on the aesthetic sense of spirituality here because of its centrality in the music educational literature. David Carr (2008) helpfully enumerates several senses of musical spirituality—music of ecstasy and transport, music of consolation, motivating music, healing music, devotional music, and music without purpose—some of which I discuss here in passing.

10. This is not to say that the idea of aesthetic *qualities* is superfluous. Time prevents me from going further into this matter.

11. This helps to explain why when studio artists, musicians, poets, actors, and filmmakers are put in the same room, they do not necessarily have a lot to say to each other.

12. There are many other issues that arise when we think about the confluence of musical, educational, and religious practices that, in the interest of space, we cannot consider here. I have not addressed, for example, the question whether the embrace of spirituality in the classroom might have a role to play in inculcating habits of virtue or of otherwise developing moral sensibility. I have not discussed the connection between spirituality and mysticism or the practical pedagogical question of how a teacher actually goes about guiding a student in the development of inner states of consciousness. Nor have I addressed some of the fundamental philosophical questions about religious belief, in particular the arguments for and against the existence of God, the matter of the divine attributes, the problems that evil and suffering pose for theism, the varieties of disbelief and skepticism about religion, or the status of miracles.

References

Adler, Jeremy. 1990. "Goethe's Use of Chemical Theory in His Elective Affinities." In *Romanticism and the Sciences*, edited by Andrew Cunningham and Nicholas Jardine, 263–79. New York: Cambridge University Press.

Allen, Evan. 2014. "Religious Exemption to Hiring Rule Urged: Bias on Sexual Orientation at Issue; Gordon College Leader Joins Request." *Boston Globe*, July 4, A.1.

Allsup, Randall, and Heidi Westerlund. 2012. "Methods and Situational Ethics in Music Education." *Action, Criticism, and Theory for Music Education* 11, no. 1: 124–48. http://act.maydaygroup.org/articles/AllsupWesterlund11_1.pdf.

Alperson, Philip. 2010. "A Topography of Musical Improvisation." *Journal of Aesthetics and Art Criticism* 68, no. 3: 273–80.

———. 2014. "Music and Morality." In *Ethics and the Arts*, edited by Paul Macneill, 21–31. Dordrecht: Springer.

Alston, William. 1967. "Religion." In *The Encyclopedia of Philosophy*, edited by Paul Edwards, 7: 140–45. New York: Macmillan.

Aristotle. 1993. *Politics*. 1339a, Translated by William David Ross. Chicago: Encyclopaedia Britannica.
Associated Press. 2014. "Sudan: Woman Sentenced to Death after Refusing to Renounce Her Faith." *New York Times*, May 16, A14.
BBC. 2014a. "Iraqi Christians Flee after Isis Issue Mosul Ultimatum." *BBC News*, July 18. http://www.bbc.com/news/world-middle-east-28381455.
———. 2014b. "Pakistan Taliban: Peshawar School Attack Leaves 141 Dead." *BBC News*, December 16. http://www.bbc.com/news/world-asia-30491435.
bin Laden, Osama. 2002. "Letter to America." *The Guardian*, November 24. http://www.theguardian.com/world/2002/nov/24/theobserver.
Bogdan, Deanne. 2003. "Musical Spirituality: Reflections on Identity and the Ethics of Embodied Aesthetic Experience in/and the Academy." *Journal of Aesthetic Education* 37, no. 2: 80–98.
———. 2010. "The Shiver-Shimmer Factor: Musical Spirituality, Emotion, and Education." *Philosophy of Music Education Review* 18, no. 2: 111–29.
Borgen, Daniel. 2014. "Department of Education Grants George Fox Religious Exemption; Says College Can Refuse Trans Students On-Campus Housing." *PQ Monthly*, July 11.
Bourdieu, Pierre. 1984. *Distinction: A Social Critique of the Judgement of Taste*. Cambridge, MA: Harvard University Press.
Carr, David. 2008. "Music, Spirituality, and Education." *Journal of Aesthetic Education* 42, no. 1: 16–29.
Center for Constitutional Rights. 2015. *United Nations Recommendations for Vatican Accountability for Sexual Violence in the Church*. https://ccrjustice.org/UnitedNationsRecommendsVaticanAccountability.
Craig, Tim. 2014. "New Afghan Government Investigates Newspaper for 'Blasphemous Article.'" *Washington Post*, October 22. http://www.washingtonpost.com/world/asia_pacific/new-afghan-government-investigates-newspaper-for-blasphemous-article/2014/10/22/d8ffc136-59ea-11e4-b812-38518ae74c67_story.html.
Cusick, Suzanne. 2008. "'You Are in a Place That Is Out of the World . . .': Music in the Detention Camps of the 'Global War on Terror.'" *Journal of the Society for American Music* 2, no. 1: 1–26.
Deacon, Roger. 2005. "Moral Orthopedics: A Foucauldian Account of Schooling as a Discipline." *Telos*, no. 130 (Spring): 84–102.
Dickie, George. 1964. "The Myth of the Aesthetic Attitude." *American Philosophical Quarterly* 1: 56–65.
Drucker, Peter F. 1993. *Management: Tasks, Responsibilities, Practices*. New York: HarperBusiness.
Durham, Aisha, Brittney C. Cooper, and Susana M. Morris. 2013. "The Stage Hip-Hop Feminism Built: A New Directions Essay." *Signs* 38, no. 3: 721–37.
Edgell, Penny, Joseph Gerteis, and Douglass Hartmann. 2006. "Atheists as 'Other': Moral Boundaries and Cultural Membership in American Society." *American Sociological Review* 71: 211–34.
Felter, Claire. 2018. "Nigeria's Battle with Boko Haram." Council on Foreign Relations. August 2018. https://www.cfr.org/backgrounder/nigerias-battle-boko-haram.
Foucault, Michel. 1975. *Discipline and Punish: The Birth of the Prison*. New York: Random House.
Freire, Paulo. 1970. *Pedagogy of the Oppressed*. New York: Continuum.

———. 1994. *Pedagogy of Hope: Reliving the Pedagogy of the Oppressed*. New York: Continuum.
Freud, Sigmund. (1928) 1962. *The Future of an Illusion*. Translated by W. D. Robson-Scott. London: Hogarth.
Geach, Peter. 1956. "Good and Evil." *Analysis* 17, no. 2: 32–42.
Giroux, Henry. 1983. *Theory and Resistance in Education: A Pedagogy for the Opposition*. South Hadley, MA: Bergin and Garvey.
Goehr, Lydia. 2008. *Elective Affinities: Musical Essays on the History of Aesthetic Theory*. New York: Columbia University Press.
Goethe, Johann Wolfgang von. 1971. *Elective Affinities*. Translated by R. J. Hollingdale. London: Penguin.
Hanslick, Eduard. (1854) 1986. *On the Musically Beautiful*. Translated by Geoffrey Payzant. Indianapolis: Hackett.
The Hi-Lo's. 1960. "I Wish I Was in Dixie." Columbia Records CS8300, Track 11.
hooks, bell. 1994. *Teaching to Transgress*. New York: Routledge.
Hornby, Nick. 1995. *High Fidelity*. New York: Riverhead.
Howe, Richard Herbert. 1978. "Max Weber's Elective Affinities: Sociology within the Bounds of Pure Reason." *American Journal of Sociology* 84, no. 2 (September): 366–85.
Illich, Ivan. 1971. *Deschooling Society*. New York: Harper and Row.
Jefferson, Thomas. (1802) 1978. "Letter to the Danbury Baptists." *Library of Congress Information Bulletin* 57, no. 6. Washington, DC: Library of Congress. https://www.loc.gov/loc/lcib/9806/danpre.html.
John Jay College of Criminal Justice. 2004. *The Nature and Scope of the Problem of Sexual Abuse of Minors by Catholic Priests and Deacons in the United States, 1950-2002*. Washington, DC: United States Conference of Catholic Bishops.
Jones, Jeffrey M. 2012. "Atheists, Muslims See Most Bias as Presidential Candidates." Princeton, NJ: Gallup.
Jorgensen, Estelle. 1993. "Religious Music in Education." *Philosophy of Music Education Review* 1, no. 2: 103–14.
———. 2011. "How Can Music Education Be Religious?" *Philosophy of Music Education Review* 19, no. 2: 155–63.
Keene, Douglas, and Rita Handrich. 2010. "Panic over the Unknown: America Hates Atheists." *The Jury Expert* 22, no. 2: 50–60.
Kivy, Peter. 1991. *Music Alone*. Ithaca, NY: Cornell University Press.
Luther, Martin. (1525) 1983. Preface to Johann Walther's *Wittenbergisch Geistlich Gesangbuch*. In *The Hymns of Martin Luther Set to Their Original Melodies*, edited by Leonard Woolsey Bacon. New York: Charles Scribner's Sons, xxi. Cited in Leslie Spelman. 1951. "Luther and the Arts," *Journal of Aesthetics and Art Criticism* 10, no. 2 (December): 166–75. Quotation appears on 168–69.
Maimonides. (1190) 1904. *Guide for the Perplexed*. 2nd ed. Translated by M. Friedländer. London: Routledge and Kegan Paul.
Martland, T. R. 1966. "An Analogy between Art and Religion." *Journal of Philosophy* 43, no. 18: 509–17.
Mikaelsson, Lisbeth. Forthcoming. "Religion." In *Oxford Handbook of Feminist Theory*, edited by Mary Hawkesworth and Lisa J. Disch.
Mill, John Stuart. 1859. *On Liberty*. London: Longman, Roberts and Green.
Office of the Minister for Children and Youth Affairs: Department of Health and Children. *Report of the Commission to Inquire into Child Abuse*. 2009. Dublin, Ire.: Stationery

Office. https://www.dcya.gov.ie/documents/publications/Implementation_Plan_from_Ryan_Commission_Report.pdf.

Otto, Rudolf. (1923) 1958. *The Idea of the Holy*. Translated by John W. Harvey. London: Oxford University Press.

Palmer, Anthony. 2010. "Spirituality in Music Education: Transcending Culture, Exploration III." *Philosophy of Music Education Review* 18, no. 2: 152–70.

Public Law PL 107-110, the No Child Left Behind Act of 2001.

PL 111-5, the American Recovery and Reinvestment Act of 2009.

Reimer, Bennett. 1995. "The Experience of Profundity in Music." *Journal of Aesthetic Education* 29, no. 4: 1–21.

Russell, Bertrand. (1927) 1957. *Why I Am Not a Christian and Other Essays on Religion and Related Subjects*. New York: Simon and Schuster.

———. 1951. "The Best Answer to Fanaticism—Liberalism." *New York Times*, December 16.

Shepherd, Jessica. 2009. "Humanities Research Threatened by Demands for 'Economic Impact.'" *The Guardian*, October 12.

Shusterman, Richard. 2008. "Art and Religion." *Journal of Aesthetic Education* 42, no. 3: 1–18.

Sparshott, F. E. 1976. "Religious Experience and Aesthetic Experience." In *The Challenge of Religion Today*, edited by John King-Farlow. New York: Science History Publications.

———. 1982. *The Theory of the Arts*. Princeton, NJ: Princeton University Press.

Tantillo, Astrida Orle. 2001. *Goethe's Elective Affinities and the Critics*. New York: Camden House.

United Kingdom Department of Education. 2014. *School Performance Tables*. http://www.education.gov.uk/schools/performance.

Wade, Wyn Craig. 1987. *The Fiery Cross: The Ku Klux Klan in America*. New York: Simon and Schuster.

Warner, Marina. 2014. "Diary: Why I Quit." *London Review of Books* 36, no. 17 (September 11): 42–43.

Weber, Max. 1905. "Die Protestantische Ethik und der 'Geist' des Kapitalismus." *Archiv fur Sozialwissenschaft und Sozialpolitik* 20, pt. 1: 1–54.

Williams, Daniel, and Eric Guttschuss. 2012. *Spiraling Violence: Boko Haram Attacks and Security Force*. New York: Human Rights Watch.

Wittgenstein, Ludwig. 1953. *Philosophical Investigations*. Translated by G. E. M. Anscombe. Oxford, UK: Basil Blackwell.

Yob, Iris M. 1995. "Religious Music and Multicultural Education." *Philosophy of Music Education Review* 3, no. 2: 69–82.

———. 2010. "Why Is Music a Language of Spirituality?" *Philosophy of Music Education Review* 18, no. 2: 145–51.

3 | The Performativity of Performance: Agency at the Intersection of Music and Religion in School

Heidi Westerlund, Alexis Anja Kallio, and Heidi Partti

Although media and technology are offering teachers and students richer and more diverse musical opportunities than ever before, hands-on music making and performance are still often promoted as the ideal for meaningful learning in schools. Whereas performance in schools once equated to the choral singing of national and religious repertoires (Keene 1982; Pajamo 1976), such narrow definitions of what was seen as musically good have largely been replaced by multicultural repertoires and ideals. For example, in Finland, the recently introduced National Core Curriculum for Basic Education (Finnish National Board of Education 2014) emphasizes the role of music instruction in guiding pupils to attain an appreciative and inquisitive attitude towards cultural diversity and the multiplicity of musical meanings (Finnish National Board of Education 2014, 141). In learning about cultures and difference through performance, music has increasingly been considered not as an artifact to learn about, in terms of its history or in terms of cultivating an aesthetic appreciation among students, but as social action. As such, the performance of different musics has been seen as one way to bring together students of different musical, ethnic, cultural, and religious identities and backgrounds. However, taking into account the inherent diversity of school populations, the social character of musical performance means that there is a heightened, or at least more explicit, potential for tensions and conflicts to arise between the values and beliefs embedded in students' identifications and those legitimized through the selection of school repertoires.

In this chapter, we explore the potentials for conflict that exist at the intersection of music, education, and religion, as performances in schools elicit enactments of the religious or nonreligious beliefs of students and those of the school.[1] This is often a meeting between multiple, incongruent, and often noncomplementary worlds. Drawing on the concept of performativity, through illustrations from the Finnish context, we argue that when music, education, and religion intersect in musical performance, complex questions arise about identity, subjectivity, and agency—requiring ethical and political negotiation from both teachers and students. This chapter has three main sections: First, we examine how feminist philosopher Judith Butler's concept of performativity might extend and complicate our understanding of musical performance in formal music education contexts.[2] When applied to the intersections between music, education, and religion, the lens of performativity allows us to reconsider the prevalent views on identity in contemporary multicultural music education, to consider identities not as singular, stable categorizations, but as multiple, situational, and under constant negotiation. These dynamic ideas of who students are and who they are becoming, are here seen to be constituted through performativities in, and through, musical performance. Second, we locate this discussion in the rituals and musical performances of the diverse, comprehensive school context, which we argue is a distinct type of public space. The boundaries established in separating this—often assumed to be secular—public space from the ideologies and doctrines associated with religious institutions may be seen to have resulted in a "collective amnesia" (Clarke 2009, 3). We question whether such amnesia, through the exclusion of religious histories, beliefs, values, and identities of students, and indeed teachers, can succeed in constructing a nonpartisan, *inclusive*, and *neutral* community. Finally, we consider the place of agency within these processes of school community building. We argue that through reconsidering the prevalent notion of recognition in multicultural music education scholarship, we might better attend to the power dynamics of inclusion and exclusion as they manifest in and through music education in the secular school. Although drawing on examples from the Finnish music education settings and curriculum documents, the chapter is by no means restricted to the Finnish context only. As a whole, the chapter aims to contribute to the theorization of social justice in music education.

Complicating Musical Performance

In recent decades, music education scholarship has emphasized multiculturalism not only as a means of recognizing the diversity of musical material and performance practices in the world, but also as a "social ideal; a policy of support for exchange among different groups of people to enrich all while respecting and preserving the integrity of each" (Elliott 1990, 151). The praxial turn toward the "apprenticeship tradition" (Schrag 1992) has offered an important contribution to *how* multiculturalism is navigated in schools. Through its various iterations (e.g., Alperson 1991; Elliott 1995; Bowman 2002) praxialism has shifted the focus of music education from a more distanced, normative, aesthetic appreciation of master works to musical action, through a hands-on, contextualized approach. In short, music has been conceptualized not as a thing, but as a verb, as seen in the concept of musicing (Elliott 1995).

This shift of perspective to regard music as something we do, has meant that music(s) ought not to be seen as something external to our identities but as collective doings involving the "exploring, affirming, and celebrating" (Small 1998) of musical, and other, values, beliefs, and relationships. By resisting idioms peculiar to schools and turning instead to the values and goods of music already found within communities and societies, scholars have extended the conceptualization of music from something we *do*, to something that we *are* (Elliott and Silverman 2015). This may be seen as particularly relevant for young people taught in schools as they negotiate their own conceptualizations of the self in relation to others, context, and situation within and beyond the peer group. Importantly, through this understanding, the school not only needs to take into account who students *are,* but also attend to ethical questions of who they are *becoming* (Bowman 2002; Kallio 2015; Karlsen and Westerlund 2015).

In making space available for multiple musical doings and beings in schools, careful repertoire selection has been thought to support and contribute to each student's identity construction (Elliott 1995, 212). Accordingly, cultural recognition has guided teacher's selections of musical repertoire for classes and school performances (Drummond 2005; Elliott 1995), and lessons have paid close attention to the ethnocultural characteristics of music (Volk 1998, 4). This focus on ethnic diversity and cultural representation has seen school music take considerable strides toward making lessons more accessible for more students. In the process, however, it has neglected other diversities, such as the religious identities of students and religiously defined musical practices. Although perhaps not explicated in curricula or music education scholarship, religious values and beliefs may be intricately bound with musical expression and musical performance—as musical doings.

There has been considerable criticism of multicultural approaches that direct teachers to select repertoire and activities solely on the basis of their perceptions of students' ethnic backgrounds. For instance, Karlsen (2013) and Sæther (2008) have argued against teachers relying on their own assumptions about *who* their students are, noting that in the Nordic countries immigrant students often wished to conceal their ethnic-geographical musical identities, as they seek to fit in with what they perceived to be mainstream school culture. Students did not wish to be categorized as Other, even if it were a *musical* Other. In many cases, if the teacher were to include music that was representative of these students' assumed backgrounds, "what may have been intended as an act of cultural inclusion and recognition from the teacher's side would instead have functioned as an act of social alienation" (Karlsen 2013, 172). In Sæther's (2008) study in Sweden, immigrant students defined the quality of their music lessons not in terms of whether their *own* music was recognizable in school repertoires, but rather according to their own level of engagement, the cooperation between students, and the cohesion that was achieved through playing popular music—which they saw as a broader "youth culture." However, this desire to fit in through performing youth culture together is not unproblematic. As Karlsen and Sæther both note, conflicts may arise between students' engagements with popular music at school and the values and religious convictions of their families. Understanding musical meaning as something that arises through social action, diversity as it relates to the social constructions of race, history, culture, and religion—among others — can intersect with music making. Therefore, music making with others may not *always* result in social cohesion. Moreover, if music is understood as action, as something we *do,* as music making intersects with religion, it also intersects with other social constructs that accompany religious beliefs and practices, such as gender. For instance, in the United Kingdom, Harris (2003) found that "Muslims are almost unanimously unhappy about the idea of boys and girls being taught together at secondary age," particularly in the "secular" performing arts.

In considering the complexity of student identifications in, and through, music, the feminist lens put forward by Judith Butler (2007) allows for identity to be understood not as something you already are (a "being"), but as something that is performed again and again (a "doing") in one's becoming. If, then, to participate in music is also such a doing (as something we *are*), we are also doing identity *through* music making, as praxialist philosophers have long pointed out. This means that there need not be a "doer behind the deed," but the doer "is variably constructed in and through the deed" (Butler 2007, 195). There is no subject prior to the cultural field that it negotiates. In this sense, musical performance is *performative*, as an impersonation of ethnic, cultural, linguistic, geographical, or religious identities and norms that, through repetition, constitute the self. Extending Butler's focus on linguistic constructions of identity to music, we might understand the work of the *performative* in the school music context as "draw[ing] upon and recit[ing] a set of linguistic/[musical] conventions which have traditionally worked to bind or engage certain kinds of effects. . . . This power of recitation is not a function of an individual *intention*, but is an effect of historically sedimented linguistic/[musical] conventions" (Butler 1995, 134). Nevertheless, it is important to note that this process is not so simple as to say that by performing a Japanese Hichiriki flute piece the student is constituted as Shinto. Or that by singing the "Hallelujah Chorus" from Handel's *Messiah*, the student is constituted as Christian. Rather, in this account, the subject of the student is constituted not just through negotiating and reproducing, but also contesting identities in any given musical performance. This in turn (re)enforces the boundaries of which identities are made possible, thinkable, sayable, or musicable. The imposition of normative categories is "thus not a repressive act by one subject against another," but it is rather this categorization that "makes possible the formation of the subject . . . a reiterated effect of a structure" rather than any singular action (Butler 1998, 255). Religiosity, irreligiosity, or any identification between may thus be in conflict with a musical practice or music educational practice. For instance, as mentioned earlier, the common school practice of girls and boys playing and singing together is one that may clash with religious doctrine or identifications.

Hence, musical performativity is not simply a matter of trying on roles and identities, to discard at the end of music making in class. Rather, if musicing is a social process of becoming oneself, performances in schools (and the possible repetitions of negotiations or nonnegotiations) may be seen as constituting the subjectivities of students. In other words, as the negotiations involved in musical performativity are not necessarily easy and may be emotionally charged, they are not to be seen as simply intellectual tasks, creative exercises or fictive identifications to be conducted for musical learning to take place, but rather as normative frames within which students become who they are. We can then further ask by means of an oversimplified dichotomy of religious/nonreligious, how does assumed secularization constitute the subjectivities of religious students in schools? Or vice versa, how might (explicitly or implicitly) religious music repertoires constitute the subjectivities of students who identify themselves as irreligious or antireligious? While individual instances are complicated by various identifications, categorizations, and performativities of (non)religiosity (among any number of other performativities), how normative frames of religiosity or nonreligiosity afford or limit student agency is, ultimately, an ethical and political question.

The School as Public Space

Butler's analysis of the performative conceptualizes the world as something not necessarily chosen by the individual. Therefore, some crucial conditions are set for teaching and learning when viewing school music education through the lens of the performative of performance, particularly when it comes to assumptions of shared identifications. First, whereas many other school subjects may be approached more or less through individual work, performance in the music classroom and group situations requires at least some semblance of cohesion, typically achieved through a collective approach to music making. The musical ensemble—be it a peer group, a class, a choir, an orchestra, or rock band—is then required to participate in a common process of identification, through sharing values, beliefs, and ideals as part of the musical performance. Moreover, school performances are often at least partially public, meaning they are framed in ways by which individuals present an image of themselves for acceptance by, or at least the appreciation of, audiences beyond their peers or immediate colearners. Therefore, processes of identification do not take place backstage in private but are required to be performed in front of others—emerging through a negotiated relationship between self-image and public image (Jenkins 2008, 93).

Second, ignoring religious identities in secularized public schooling does not necessarily afford each student an equal opportunity to exercise agency and may negate the inherent heterogeneity of school populations. Indeed, some researchers argue that a secularist order is itself based on discriminatory universalism, "since it does not recognise the particularities of religious bodies in the public space" (Poulter, Riitaoja, and Kuusisto 2016, 70). Grounded in the philosophies of the French revolution and eighteenth-century Enlightenment thinking, secularism as a *neutralizing* concept separated religion from concerns of the public domain, rather seeing faith as an individual, private, personal matter. This widespread, and in many places widening, rift between the private-religious and secularized public sphere is manifest even in research fields such as the sociology of religion (e.g., Clarke 2009, 14). Consequently, religion is often thought to have nothing to do, or *ought* to have nothing to do, with comprehensive, state-run schooling, seen through the legislative divides between church and state in the curricula of the United States, Australia, and the United Kingdom, for example. Yet researchers have stressed that even in secularized contexts, there is no "such a thing as a neutral public space or neutral education.... They are always social, political and historical constructions" (Poulter, Riitaoja, and Kuusisto 2016, 78). The religious diversity of school populations is therefore not erased simply through secular mandates.

This assumption that secular schooling is somehow neutral can suppress, marginalize, or erase students' own (non)religious identities. This possibility raises questions about how inclusive a secular music education can be, if in restricting the religious content or identifications of school repertoires we also impose a neutralizing framework on students' expressions. This is particularly relevant if we take into account that only about 15 percent of the world's population identifies as nonreligious or atheist (Castells 2010, xviii). The cohesive aims of school music making and the inherent diversity of the worldviews of student populations may thus come into conflict when processes of community building collide with individual (non)religious identities and values. This importance of recognizing, rather than restraining, multiple beliefs, religions, and value systems is now understood to be an integral part of Finnish comprehensive education, and schools are encouraged to direct pupils in both acknowledging and critically reflecting on the values they encounter, as well as in building their own worldviews (Finnish National Board of Education 2014, 15).

Through the Butlerian perspective, secular music education practices can be understood to be just as much social rituals as religious music education practices. Through these rituals, secular communities are necessarily normative, regulating students (and indeed teachers) through processes of interpellation. Jackson and Mazzei (2012) describe this interpellation as acts of hailing: "This hailing (or, "Hey, you!") is an act of forming the subject to comply with and obey the laws of its domain" (74). Hailing, we argue, can take place not only through religious musical repertoire, but also when conformity to secularization, or at least the suppression of one's own religious identity, is the anticipated outcome. According to Butlerian logic, discursive (or musical) interpellations are attempts to pull or put someone "in their place," forcing individuals into subjection according to social norms. This interpellation is not descriptive, but inaugurative, in the sense that it "seeks to introduce a reality rather than report on an existing one" (Jackson and Mazzei 2012, 79). For instance, in our own institution, some student music teachers have refused to perform ancient Finnish pagan music as part of a compulsory folk music course. These student teachers explained that performing this musical tradition would be a violation of their Christian faith and understandings of what music is for. Through their justifications for not participating in this particular performance, the Sibelius Academy's student music teachers *contested* and also *produced* understandings and meanings of their own Christianity, of the paganness of the ancient folk music, and of the secular normative educational framework that interpreted the religious and the pagan not as issues of identity but rather as historical, cultural knowledge.

Hence, it is not necessarily clear which musical repertoires are experienced as religious, so to speak, as it is (re)inscribed through performativities of performance. For instance, as Lauri Väkevä suggests in this volume, it is possible that most Finnish school students do not experience the singing of the summer hymn

Suvivirsi as particularly religious, as the song has long been considered a part of Finnish cultural heritage, heralding the end of the school year and the beginning of summer holidays. The relations between music and religious experiences are thus contingent and under constant negotiation, and this complexity extends from the role(s) that music plays in religious institutions and activities to considerations of which genres, styles, and instruments are considered appropriate for believers, or communal services, rituals, festivals, devotions, and prayer (Brown 2014). Indeed, the distinction between religious music and nonreligious music "is a variable and fluid one" (Brown 2014, 124), and which musics are considered to be religious, by whom, and in what circumstance vary from one individual to another, and from one situation to another. What is important, however, is whether this music is interpellative; whether the musical performance hails and forms the subject to obey the laws of its domain. It can be argued that, for some, Suvivirsi certainly works as a citational practice through which available identities are regularly (re)constituted.

Although any social act constitutes subjectivity through the ritualized repetition of norms, it might be argued that school rituals represent perhaps the most canonized forms of such acts where music and religion intersect, and where musical acts of interpellation can take place. It has been noted that school rituals and musical performances in rituals reveal the "deep grammar of school culture" (Nikkanen and Westerlund 2017, 117), and "function as stagings of the body, as symbolic actions, as aesthetic spectacles and ethical events" (Wulf 2008, 45). In this way, school music can also shape the social relations of the school, oscillating between conflict and processes of integration. Ritualization thus legitimizes values and ideals that are desirable as "fundamentally a way of doing things to trigger the perception that these practices are special" (Hollywood 2002, 112). With this in mind, a distinction often made is between teaching *about* religious holidays in the classroom and *celebrating* them (as has been stated in the State of Washington's Office of Superintendent of Public Instruction [2018] Equity and Civil Rights guidelines, as just one example of many). In music rituals, however, the boundaries between teaching about and celebrating are blurred, since music making is a social performance of who we are and who we aspire to become. It is important to note that participating in school celebrations through collective music making, such as through performing the Finnish summer hymn *Suvivirsi*, is often presented as nonnegotiable, and the only way to resist the citational practice is to merely listen or to leave.

If, as we have suggested, our engagements with music in school always carry the potential to be religiously loaded, schools are never wholly secular or neutral. Rather, schools are a particular kind of public spaces where conflict and tensions are unavoidable products of collaborative work, community, and constant negotiation. Uncritical assumptions of secularity thus negate the dynamic political and ethical negotiations that constitute (non)religious musical meanings and student identities through the performativity of performances. Moreover, as secularization projects conflict with situational performativities, these political and ethical negotiations can be seen as not taking place in a way that is natural or free. Yet this consideration does not exclude the importance of the creation of community in a school context. The invocation and making of the "us" through concerted action in school rituals is not, however, related just to past communities and their ethnicities but could be "bound up with a future that is yet to be lived out" (Butler 2015, 169) and in this way be seen as forms of political performativity in which the conditions of coming together are constantly under negotiation (Westerlund, Partti, and Karlsen 2017).

As already mentioned, a multicultural ethos informing the selection of musical repertoires within a secularized school environment has been intended to "extend the reference of 'us' as far as we can" (Woodford 2005, 89), including more students as part of a cohesive school community. However, if school performances take into account the performativity of the performance, such a neutralizing, assimilatory approach may negate students' complex and dynamic (non)religious identities, resulting in processes of exclusion more than inclusion (Kallio 2015). Prioritizing consensus in terms of secularization, or assuming an automatic consensus to take place through school performances, limits which religious identifications are legitimized in the school context through insisting that "certain kinds of . . . events be narrated [or performed] only one way" (Butler 1997, 134).

Agency and Recognition

The challenges of performance, particularly as they relate to matters of religion, thus arise when engaged in as a collective. As the focus in recent scholarly work has been on cultivating a school community through music making together, individual agency, and its place in relation to the collective, has been somewhat neglected (Schmidt 2012). Hence, with musical performance and the performativity of identities both seen as doings, a central concern for music teachers is how difference can be performed within the public spaces of the school community—in which agency is key. Instead of seeing agency as an ability to act on and within the world to make choices that are willed rather than determined, Butler suggests that agency is rather derived from within the constitution of subject, when a subject's performative acts both reproduce and contest the foundations and origins of stable identity categories (Butler 2007, 195). The subject is generated through "*a regulated process of repetition* that both conceals itself and enforces its rules," and agency "is to be located within the possibility of a variation on that repetition" (Butler 2007, 198; emphasis orig.). From this perspective, the Finnish student music teachers who refused to perform ancient Finnish pagan music because of their Christian faith, contesting the nonreligious identity of an otherwise pluralist musician, multicultural music teacher, and curriculum worker, *performed* agency. For them, this music was not neutral. Through this example, it may be seen that there is a difference between learning about Finnish pagan music and performing this music, with the performative act of performing seen to reproduce the identity category associated with any given repertoire. The irony here is that the same student music teachers may, in their future careers, accompany the hymn *Suvivirsi*, which arguably is a ritual that interpellates the student subjects in schools in exactly this same way.

Agency, here, is thus not simply referring to the ability to do or think outside interpellative categorizations. Butler (2004) notes an important paradox: that agency is both constrained and dependent on normative categories imposed on individuals, in a social world they never chose—in this way, the paradox of agency is the *"condition of its possibility"* (Butler 2004, 3, emphasis added). The Christian student teachers' performative contestations against the assumption of secularized schooling would not be possible if they had not been asked to perform pagan music that conflicted with their own religious subjectivities. Imposed identity categorizations are thus sites of "necessary trouble" (Jackson and Mazzei 2012), allowing for relational conflicts that produce nuanced and contextualized understandings of one's own identifications and those of others in any given situation.

Hence, the canonized rituals and musical repertoires of the school music context not only foreclose (Butler 1998) the agential options made available to students but provide the necessary conditions for the recognition of the student as a viable subject. In her work on immigrant students' musical agency in Finland, Norway, and Sweden, Karlsen (2013) demonstrates how some students were happy to be identified musically according to their or their parents' homeland and others found it was a limiting categorization, particularly in the school context. Karlsen argued that such identity negotiation "not only draws on but also *produced complexity*" (172, emphasis added) in music lessons and school life as a whole. Therefore, although the experience of recognition is necessary for us to become socially viable beings, this recognition needs to be recognized as a matter of power "with the problem of who qualifies as the recognizably human and who does not" (Butler 2004, 2). As part and parcel of cultivating a school community, teachers should allow for recognition also referring to the possibility of *not* being labeled according to normative identity categories. Moreover, expressions of subjectivity can be silent, erased, or hidden. Performativity can emerge as provisional, an error, or a mistake. As Butler writes, "If a subject were constituted once and for all, there would be no possibility of a reiteration of those constituting conventions or norms. That the subject is that which must be constituted again and again implies that it is open to formations that are not fully constrained in advance. Hence, the insistence of finding agency as resignification" (Butler 1995, 135). The performative is therefore a social ritual where the modalities of practice are powerful, precisely because they are so insistent and insinuating.

In this way, Butler's understanding of recognition reaches beyond the voluntarist notion of self and recognition that liberal multiculturalism has suggested. In contemporary multicultural liberalism, "Indigenous subjects are called on to perform an authentic self-identity of prenational, 'traditional' cultural difference" (Butler and Athanasiou 2013, 76), and students are expected to strengthen this identity, which is reserved and defined for them by the dominant understanding of cultural diversity and identity. The public space of the school thus serves as a site where contests for recognition are waged between different, and at times opposing, (non)religious doctrines, practices, values, and musical expressions

(Kallio 2015). This recognition, as a site of power, is one means "by which the human is differently produced" (Butler 2004, 2).

Beyond Neutrality

In this chapter, we have extended earlier theorizations of musical performance in education to consider the potential conflicts and tensions that arise at the intersection of music and religion in school. We have aimed to demonstrate how music education is not only simply a matter of transmitting neutral knowledge, even in secular schooling, and that there is a need to consider how various (non)religious identifications are produced in the school context, particularly in musical performances as expressions of assumed collectives. The development of secularism as "epistemic ethnocentrism" (Poulter, Riitaoja, and Kuusisto 2016, 69) has created a false assumption that students arrive at the music classroom having left their (non)religious backgrounds or beliefs at the door. In reality, students' identities, values, and beliefs may foreclose certain musical practices if they are to identify with particular religious doctrines. Through highlighting the performativity of musical performance, we have argued that students are constituted (but not determined) through the practices of music making and how the making and remaking of subjectivities through the performative processes means that students may be continually resignified. Identity categories such as Muslim student, Catholic student, or secular school are therefore signifiers laden with different, and situated, social, historical, political, and ethical meanings.

If citizenship and a democratic approach to education takes equity and social justice as a central premise, questions may be raised whether equity is achieved through the dismissal of difference through adopting what is believed to be a religiously neutral, secular stance. With the diversity within school populations, it may be questioned whether we can assume a consensus of social values, moral frameworks, and worldviews, even if that consensus is one of educational neutrality. Instead, the assumption of neutrality isolates the student to navigate between religion-based home cultures and secular school culture alone. Paradoxically, secularization also prevents us from recognizing that, despite the presumed neutrality, schools still include historically established religious musical repertoires, particularly in festivities and ceremonies. Assuming secularization thus obfuscates the political modalities of the most fundamental ethical questions.

We therefore suggest that in attending to the intersection of music, education, and religion, we need to recognize the messiness, the contradictions, the complexity, and the politics of practices previously seen as perhaps simply cognitively challenging but ultimately socially harmonious musical performance. The teacher in today's diverse schools is required to make conscious attempts to understand which musics and musical practices interpellate religious identities, and which school rituals may result in processes of (non)religious coercion or exclusion. In navigating this complexity, difference is not an obstacle to overcome. Rather, there is a need to understand diversity in music education beyond the idea of an expansion of knowledge in and through musical practices of the world and to see curricular content itself as a potentially conflicting and contested arena for constituting agency. When conceptualizing musical performance as an inclusive practice in school, we therefore need to constantly search for, and respond to, the ethical and political dimensions of musical performance—the performativity of performance.

HEIDI WESTERLUND is Professor of Music Education at the Sibelius Academy, University of the Arts–Helsinki, Finland. She currently leads two large-scale research projects: The Arts as Public Service: Strategic Steps towards Equality (ArtsEqual) and Global Visions through Mobilizing Networks: Co-developing Intercultural Music Teacher Education in Finland, Israel, and Nepal. She is coeditor of the book *Collaborative Learning in Higher Music Education* and editor-in-chief of the *Finnish Journal of Music Education*.

ALEXIS ANJA KALLIO is a music education researcher at the Sibelius Academy, University of the Arts–Helsinki, working as part of the Global Visions through Mobilizing Networks: Co-developing Intercultural Music Teacher Education in Finland, Israel, and Nepal project. She is coeditor of the *Nordic Yearbook of Music Education Research*.

HEIDI PARTTI is Acting Professor of Music Education at the Sibelius Academy, University of the Arts–Helsinki, Finland. She is coeditor of the book *Visions for Intercultural Music Teacher Education* and coauthor of *Säveltäjyyden Jäljillä*, a book on composing pedagogy.

Notes

This study has been conducted as part of the ArtsEqual research project, funded by the Strategic Research Council of the Academy of Finland and its Equality in Society strategic research program (project number 293199) and the Global Visions through Mobilizing Networks project funded by the Academy of Finland (project number 286162).

1. The authors acknowledge that terms such as *religious* and *nonreligious* are an oversimplification of the wide variety of worldviews held by individuals, even those who explicitly align themselves with particular religious organizations or doctrine, or those who distance themselves from organized religion altogether. As various scholars have pointed out (see, e.g., Woodhead 2013), religiosity and spirituality is becoming increasingly dispersed, taking various forms of multireligiosity. For the purposes of this chapter, we use the terms in their broadest sense, pertaining to beliefs about extraordinary realities.

2. The concept of performativity has been applied in a number of different fields. With origins in the work of John L. Austin on the philosophy of language, in this chapter we apply the concept beyond speech acts to refer to other means of communication.

References

Alperson, Philip. 1991. "What Should One Expect from a Philosophy of Music Education?" *Journal of Aesthetic Education* 25, no. 3: 215–42.

Bowman, Wayne. 2002. "Music's Significance in Everyday Life." *Action, Criticism, and Theory for Music Education* 1, no. 2: 1–4.

Brown, Frank Burch. 2014. "Musical Ways of Being Religious." In *Oxford Handbook of Religion and the Arts*, edited by Frank B. Brown, 109–29. Oxford: Oxford University Press.

Butler, Judith. 1995. "For a Careful Reading." In *Feminist Contentions: A Philosophical Exchange*, edited by Seyla Benhabib, Judith Butler, Drucilla Cornell, and Nancy Fraser, 127–44. New York: Routledge.

———. 1997. *Excitable Speech: A Politics of the Performative*. New York: Routledge.

———. 1998. "Ruled Out: The Vocabularies of the Censor." In *Censorship and Silencing: Practices of Cultural Regulation*, edited by Robert C. Post, 247–60. Los Angeles: Getty Research Institute for the History of Art and the Humanities.

———. 2004. *Undoing Gender*. London: Routledge.

———. 2007. *Gender Trouble: Feminism and the Subversion of Identity*. 2nd ed. New York: Routledge.

———. 2015. *Notes toward a Performative Theory of Assembly*. Cambridge, MA: Harvard University Press.

Butler, Judith, and Athena Athanasiou. 2013. *Dispossession: The Performative in the Political*. Cambridge, UK: Polity.

Castells, Manuel. 2010. *The Power of Identity*, 2nd ed. Chichester, UK: Wiley-Blackwell.

Clarke, Peter B. 2009. Introduction to *The Oxford Handbook of the Sociology of Religion*, edited by Peter B. Clarke, 1–27. Oxford: Oxford University Press.

Drummond, John. 2005. "Cultural Diversity in Music Education: Why Bother?" In *Cultural Diversity in Music Education: Directions and Challenges for the 21st Century*, edited by Patricia Shehan Campbell, John Drummond, Peter Dunbar-Hall, Keith Howard, Huib Schippers, and Trevor Wiggins, 1–11. Brisbane: Australian Academic.

Elliott, David.1990. "Music as Culture: Toward a Multicultural Concept of Music Education." *Journal of Aesthetic Education* 24, no. 1: 147–66.

———. 1995. *Music Matters: A New Philosophy of Music Education*. Oxford: Oxford University Press.

Elliott, David, and Marissa Silverman. 2015. *Music Matters: A Philosophy of Music Education*, 2nd ed. Oxford: Oxford University Press.

Finnish National Board of Education. 2014. *Perusopetuksen opetussuunnitelman perusteet* [Finnish National Agency for Education]. Helsinki: Opetushallitus.

Harris, Diana. 2003. "A Practical Guide on How to Teach Music to Muslims." Paper presented at the UNESCO Regional Meeting on Arts Education in the European Countries, Canada, and the United States of America, Helsinki, Finland. Accessed March 1, 2016. https://wayback.archive-it.org/10611/20160107120723/http://portal.unesco.org/culture/en/files/40530/12669214963musicmuslims.pdf/musicmuslims.pdf.

Hollywood, Amy. 2002. "Performativity, Citationality, Ritualization." *History of Religions* 42, no. 2: 93–115.

Jackson, Alecia Y., and Lisa A. Mazzei. 2012. *Thinking with Theory in Qualitative Research: Viewing Data across Multiple Perspectives*. New York: Routledge.

Jenkins, Richard. 2008. *Social Identity*, 3rd ed. New York: Routledge.

Kallio, Alexis A. 2015. "Navigating (Un)Popular Music in the Classroom: Censure and Censorship in an Inclusive, Democratic Music Education." Studia Musica 65, Sibelius Academy of the University of the Arts Helsinki. http://urn.fi/URN:ISBN:978-952-329-014-3.

Karlsen, Sidsel. 2013. "Immigrant Students and the 'Homeland Music': Meanings, Negotiations and Implications." *Research Studies in Music Education* 35, no. 2: 161–77.

Karlsen, Sidsel, and Heidi Westerlund. 2015. "Music Teachers' Repertoire Choices and the Quest for Solidarity: Opening Public Arenas for the Art of Living with Difference." In *The Oxford Handbook of Social Justice in Music Education*, edited by Cathy Benedict, Patrick Schmidt, Gary Spruce, and Paul Woodford, 373–87. Oxford: Oxford University Press.

Keene, James A. 1982. *A History of Music Education in the United States*. Hannover, NH: University Press of New England.

Nikkanen, Hanna, and Heidi Westerlund. 2017. "More Than Just Music: Reconsidering the Educational Value of Music in School Rituals." *Philosophy of Music Education Review* 25, no. 2: 112–27.

Pajamo, Reijo. 1976. *Suomen koulujen laulunopetus vuosina 1843–1881* [Singing lessons in Finnish schools from 1843–1881]. Helsinki: Suomen musiikkitieteellinen seura. Acta musicologica fennica 7.

Poulter, Saila, Anna-Leena Riitaoja, and Arniika Kuusisto. 2016. "Thinking Multicultural Education 'Otherwise'—from a Secularist Construction towards a Plurality of Epistemologies and World." *Globalisation, Societies and Education* 14, no. 1: 68–86.

Sæther, Eva. 2008. "When Minorities Are the Majority: Voices from a Teacher/Researcher Project in a Multicultural School in Sweden." *Research Studies in Music Education* 30, no. 1: 25–42.

Schmidt, Patrick. 2012. "Ethics or Choosing Complexity in Music Relations." *Action, Criticism and Theory for Music Education* 11, no. 1: 149–69.

Schrag, Francis. 1992. "Conceptions of Knowledge." In *Handbook of Research on Curriculum: A Project of the American Educational Research Association*, edited by Philip W. Jackson, 268–301. New York: Macmillan

Small, Christopher. 1998. *Musicking: The Meanings of Performing and Listening*. Middletown, CT: Wesleyan University Press.

State of Washington's Office of Superintendent of Public Instruction. 2018. *Equity and Civil Rights—Religion in Schools*, April 17. http://www.k12.wa.us/Equity/Religion InSchools/default.aspx.

Volk, Terese M. 1998. *Music, Education, and Multiculturalism: Foundations and Principles*. New York: Oxford University Press.

Westerlund, Heidi, Heidi Partti, and Sidsel Karlsen. 2017. "Identity Formation and Agency in the Diverse Music Classroom." In *Handbook of Musical Identities*, edited by Raymond MacDonald, David Hargreaves, and Dorothy Miell, 493–509. Oxford: Oxford University Press.

Woodford, Paul. 2005. *Democracy and Music Education: Liberalism, Ethics, and the Politics of Practice*. Bloomington: Indiana University Press.

Woodhead, Linda. 2013. "Neither Religious or Secular: The British Situation and Its Implications for Religious-State Relations." In *Contesting Secularism: Comparative Perspectives*, edited by Anders Berg-Sorensen, 137–62. Farnham, UK: Ashgate.

Wulf, Christoph. 2008. "Anthropological Research in Education: Towards a Historical-Cultural Anthropology of Education." In *Kasvatustieteen tila ja tutkimuskäytännöt: Paradigmat katosivat, mitä jäljellä?* [The status and research practices of education: paradigms were lost, now what's left?], edited by Pauli Siljander and Ari Kivelä, 33–49. Helsinki: Finnish Educational Research Association.

Part 2
Identity and Community

4 | Shaping Identities through Religious Music Engagement: A Case Study of an Australian Catholic Girls' School

Janelle Colville Fletcher and Margaret S. Barrett

Introduction

The philosopher Durkheim and theologians Schleiermacher and Otto (in Mariña 2009) draw parallels between music and religion, arguing that expressions of the sacred, such as those made through music, are more important than the institutions of the church in establishing religious identity. For adolescents, music is a powerful tool for making meaning and functions as a mode of symbolic transformations (Langer 2009), thus contributing to their identity work. The theologian Otto (in Strenski 2015) also draws a parallel between music and religion, both of which provide avenues to greater understanding of the worlds in which we live. Given these parallels and relationships between music and religion, it may be speculated that music is a shaping force in adolescents' religious identity work. This chapter explores the ways in which music functions in a Catholic girls' school and focuses specifically on students' perceptions of the ways in which music shapes their religious observance and spiritual experience.

Music and Identity Work

Many theorists have identified the ways in which music supports adolescents' identity work. DeNora (2000, 2003) describes how music is used as a resource to make sense of lifeworlds and serves as a tool for world building. Music can be used as a social dialogue and to express personal meanings and has the ability to influence behavior. D. H. Hargreaves (1967) and D. J. Hargreaves and North (1997) argue that social interaction, social institutions, and our social environment shape musical identities.

Bennett (2000) provides a sociological view of youth culture and music, examining how music subcultures influence adolescent lifestyles and identity work. Bennett's view clearly acknowledges music as a symbolic activity whereby youth use music as a cultural resource in order to develop a sense of belonging among their peers, to develop a collective identity, and to gain a further understanding of how they identify themselves and others in their social worlds. Bennett recognizes the importance of examining music in the lives of adolescents through a sociological theoretical framework and emphasizes the reflexive nature of musical identity work whereby adolescents reflect on others who "occupy their lifeworlds" (2001, 141).

MacDonald, Hargreaves, and Miell (2002) describe the "importance of musical communication" to young people (462). Such communication plays a strong role in their identity work. MacDonald et al. emphasize the fundamental role that music plays in a variety of aspects of young people's identity work, such as "the negotiation, construction and maintenance of identities" (463).

Music for adolescents is more than entertainment or distraction. Instead, it produces a "life philosophy" that encompasses a complete lifestyle, a set of values, and a common language (Barna 2001). Music provides a "distinctive identity" and a way of creating a shared identity. Barna argues that music is an important "self-defining resource" for adolescents, which shapes their values and ideals.

Catholic Education in Australia

Compulsory education within the Australian school system is offered through three school systems: Government, Independent, and Catholic.[1] Catholic schools comprise the larger proportion of nongovernment schools in Australia. Enrollments in Catholic schools continue to increase (ABS 2011), despite the decrease of Catholic-affiliated students attending the schools (NCEC 2013). Catholic schools provide an education that is imbued with Christian values, Catholic philosophies and traditions including the study of religion as a subject, school liturgies, Masses, and spiritual retreats.

The Catholic school system is one of the oldest educational institutions (Bryke, Lee, and Holland 1995), yet there is limited research in this sector. The research that has been undertaken has focused largely on the religious curriculum (such as Rossiter 2010, 2011) or aspects of the schools' operation and organization (Bryke, Lee, and Holland 1995), with less attention to other facets of Catholic education, particularly adolescents' identity work and the role of music in this work.

An emerging issue in Catholic schools is a significant change in the demographic profile, with fewer Catholics and more non-Catholics enrolling in these schools each year (Chambers 2012). Chambers argues that Catholic schools need "to find the best way to express their Catholicity in a changing educational environment" (186). Similarly, other authors (Grace and O'Keefe 2007; Pascoe 2007) state that Catholic schools are continuing to search for the best way to cater to their schools' changing religious needs with this greater religious diversity in the student body.

The pressures of living in an increasingly secularized society has made sustaining a Catholic identity increasingly difficult for adolescents (Barbot and Heuser 2017; Rymarz and Graham 2006). "Religious individualism" and "moral relativism" are significantly escalating in Australia, replacing more traditional religious observance, particularly among young people (Buchanan and Rymarz 2008), which may be attributed to increasing secularization. Because of these factors, Catholic education must reflect a "worldview that integrates faith, life and culture. [It needs to] reflect the multi-faith context and reality of contemporary schools" (Archdiocese of Brisbane n.d.).

The link between religion and identity has often been overlooked in literature across a range of disciplines, including religion, sociology, and education (McAdams 1993). Rossiter (1999) suggests that many youth studies reflect a need for young people to make meaning and develop a sense of self. Few studies explore adolescents' experience of Catholic education and the role of music in that experience. This research aims to address this gap.

Religious Music

Scally (1994) argues that educators must first learn to understand adolescents and their lived experience before trying to educate them. She suggests that music provides one avenue for exploring this phenomenon. For Scally, "their music is the most effective source, because it is the most common imaging system for them today. Music always mirrors culture's images, issues and values, and provides valuable tools for education and ministry" (245). She suggests using music as a tool to communicate with teenagers and that music can become a powerful medium within religion. Joncas (1997) articulates how scripture can find new life through music as it connects and engages the emotions. Therefore, religious music experience in all its forms may play an integral part in helping teenagers to form their religious identities. For the purposes of this chapter, we define religious music as music employed in a sacred context, which may include liturgical music (sacred music that is written specifically for and connected with liturgical action [Sacrosanctum Concilium 1963]) or secular music that is adapted for sacred purposes.

While extensive literature exists on liturgical music within the church, limited literature interrogates the nature of religious music as defined within a Catholic school setting. As mentioned, the literature acknowledges the way in which music, religion, and schooling are all powerful influences on adolescents' personal, social, and religious identity work. The existing limited research, however, applies a macro or micro lens to the ways in which Catholic schools utilize religious music and the purposes it serves. By drawing on the significant impact music, religion, and schooling have on adolescents' identity work, this research aims to link the three concepts together in order to investigate religious music in Catholic schools and the impact it has on adolescent identity work (see fig. 4.1).

Methodology

As a project that seeks to understand adolescents' lived experiences, we have adopted a qualitative interpretive case-study research approach (Stake 1995). Qualitative inquiry "locates the observer in the world" and provides a naturalistic and interpretive approach to research, making the "world visible" (Denzin

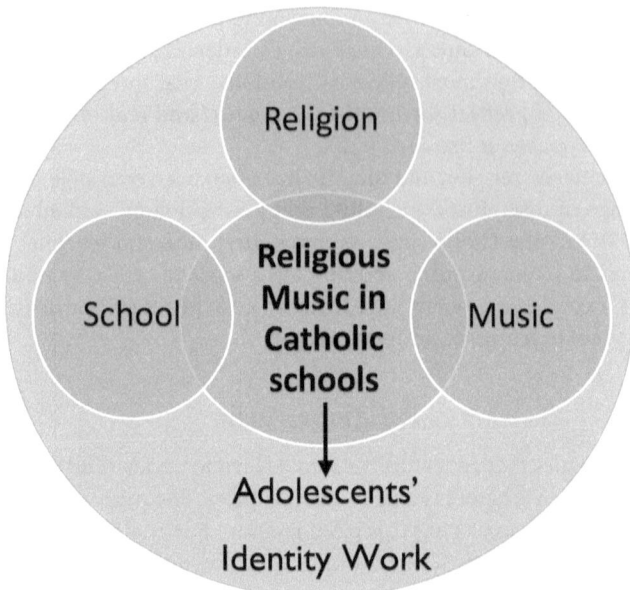

Figure 4.1. Influences on adolescents' identity work; religion, school, and music. This research focuses on the center circle, the overlap between these three influences.

and Lincoln 2002, 3). The research was undertaken at an all-girls Catholic secondary school in metropolitan Australia. Data were generated through observation and individual and group interviews with fourteen year-12 students.

The interview data were analyzed through narrative analysis and analysis of narrative methods (Polkinghorne 1995). The observation data were analyzed to identify the places in which students engaged with religious music and the nature of their participation. The findings have been reported as narratives, providing rich accounts of the participants' experiences and understandings of the phenomenon. Figure 4.2 depicts a general outline of the research methods, revealing five stages of inquiry.

1. **Selection of participants:** Identify schools; contact gatekeeper; Catholic Education Office, and school principal.
2. **Participant identification and recruitment:** Gain further information about the school context, music, and religious programs. Work with key staff member to recruit participants.
3. **Data generation:** Unobtrusive observations in a range of contexts. Group interviews. Individual interviews.
4. **Data interpretation:** Narrative analysis. Interviews transcribed and checked. Analysis of the narratives to draw conclusions and themes.
5. **Ethical considerations:** Evaluation, trustworthiness, credibility, transferability, dependability, confirmability, limitations.

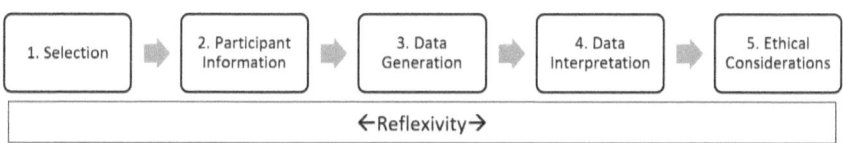

Figure 4.2. The process of conducting the case study.

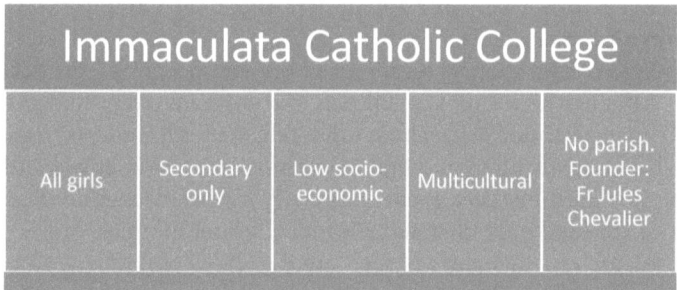

Figure 4.3. The social context and general information about the culture of the case school.

The Context: Immaculata Catholic College

Immaculata Catholic College, an all-girls Catholic secondary school in Australia, was chosen for the case study (see fig. 4.3). This school is unusual in that it enrolls students from multicultural and multifaith backgrounds, with a high proportion of Muslim students.

Immaculata Catholic College offers education through affordable fees and substantial scholarship opportunities and thrives on a wide range of cultures. The school's ethos emphasizes inclusivity and a sense of community. The school has approximately six hundred students, 2 percent of whom are indigenous students, and 50 percent of the students have a language background other than English.[2]

The school places great value on multiculturalism; the student body represents more than fifty cultures and thirty languages, and 122 students are enrolled in the English as a Second Language (ESL) program at the school. The school also has approximately one hundred students who are from an Afghan, Iranian, Iraqi, or Middle Eastern background, many of whom are Hazara refugees from Afghanistan.[3]

The school provides many support programs to assist students who are new to Australia. School celebrations and public recognition of various cultural or religious events are commonplace, one of which is the school's annual multicultural night. This night features music, dance, costumes, and food from the families and communities of various backgrounds at the school and celebrates their various cultural traditions. The school has a strong ESL program, with many support staff to assist refugees and other students who lack English language skills. During Ramadan, a sacred month in the Islamic calendar, the school provides classrooms at recess and lunchtimes during which Muslim students can fast without the temptation of the food other students are eating. The school permits the Muslim students to wear headscarves and long sleeves as part of their observance of Islamic tradition. In the corner of the grassed area not far from the entrance to the chapel is an Islamic prayer space, made of mosaics created by a group of Muslim students at the school. Other than the Islamic prayer space, the school is clearly identifiable as a Catholic college, with statues of the Virgin Mary in the school yard and a crucifix and posters displaying Catholic saints or Bible verses in every room.

The religious education program is a core component of the school curriculum. Although based on Catholicism, the program offers students the opportunity to explore and learn about other religions. All students, regardless of religious belief, are required to attend the religious education lessons and to complete tasks assigned by their teacher. Similarly, Catholic school retreats (which are days of spiritual and religious reflection), school liturgies, prayer services, and Masses, are essential parts of the Catholic school philosophy, and students are expected to attend. The Catholic events are inclusive of students of all faiths, many of whom volunteer to do Bible readings, say prayers, or sing in the liturgical choir, despite their religious differences. The school's ethos is based on Father Jules Chevalier's values, including compassion, social justice, and nurturing faith (Arthur 2014).[4] While the music department is relatively small for a school of its size, many musical opportunities are available for students, including both curricular and cocurricular activities. Music is offered to every year group, and students may elect to participate in a range of ensembles, including an African drumming ensemble and a ukulele ensemble.

The Participants

As the focus of the study is the role of religious music experience in adolescents' lived experiences and identity work, participants were recruited from year 12 (17–18 years old). Participants were in their final year of schooling and had a history of experience in religious music participation over four years of secondary schooling, and they were therefore able to reflect on their secondary school journey as it approached completion. Accordingly, they were identified as key informants on the experience. To access a range of perspectives, eighteen students were recruited, initially assigned to three categories of participation in music: students who classified themselves as musicians (five students); students who classified themselves as nonmusicians (five students); and, a mixed group of these two categories (four students). These students participated in group interviews on the experience. Two students from each group were invited to participate in follow-up individual interviews, but this varied with the participants' availability and willingness. A total of fourteen students completed the planned data-generation processes (see table 4.1).

Table 4.1. Participants in the study.

Groups Interviews	Student Names	Individual Interviewees
Group A: Music students (those who classify themselves as musicians)	5 girls (Grace, Nina, Kate, Jasmine, Carina)	Kate Jasmine
Group B: Nonmusic (those who classify themselves as nonmusicians)	5 girls (Anh, Tasmyn, Chang, Hanh, Diu)	Chang Anh
Group C: Mixed (mixed group of musicians and non-musicians)	4 girls (Chi, Lisa, Nhi, Jennifer)	Chi

The students declared a range of faiths, including Catholic, nonpracticing Catholic, Buddhist, spiritual (nonreligious), Lutheran Christian, and agnostic. The case study aims to create a snapshot of how students in this Catholic school participate in everyday religious music experiences, the meanings they derive from this experience, and its role in their identity work.

Using an interpretivist paradigm suggests that adolescents' lifeworlds are central to the research process and acknowledges the subjective character of adolescents' experiences. The data were generated through observation and individual and group interviews with fourteen girls enrolled in year 12 over the course of one school term (ten weeks). The participants shared stories and accounts of their experiences of religious music at school and the meanings they attributed to them. The data were interpreted through a process of narrative analysis in order to "systematic(ally) search for meaning" (Hatch 2002, 148). Through thematic analysis and analysis of narrative approaches, key findings revealed the importance of religious music in shaping various aspects of adolescents' identity work, including social identity, personal identity, and spiritual identity work.

Key Findings

Religious music is an integral part of these adolescents' religious experience, schooling, and identity work. The key findings of this study emphasize the multifaceted influence of religious music on adolescents' identity work, including their religious identity, social identity, and personal identity. In the following sections findings are presented and supported by narrative accounts.

Religious Music Supports Religious Identity Work

Religious music supports adolescents' religious identity work by providing a time when adolescents can engage with music and lyrics individually and independently. Religious music was reported as being more flexible in meeting adolescents' identity needs than other aspects of religious practice, such as spoken prayer. Religious music was identified as the most influential religious practice for adolescents' religious identity, fostering a deeper spiritual and religious connection. When music is chosen inappropriately, however, it can disrupt spiritual and religious focus. Traditional Catholic music, such as hymns, was generally the preferred music choice over popular Christian music, because it was tied to liturgical action and reinforced the message of the service. In contrast, secular music, used in spiritual and religious ways, allowed adolescents of all faiths to connect and draw their own personal meanings from the music. This use of music is illustrated in the following narrative account, which draws on group and individual interviews undertaken by the first author, Janelle Fletcher.

RELIGIOUS CONNECTION IN AND THROUGH MUSIC

I asked the participants in a group setting whether music can influence their beliefs or values in life, and the girls automatically reflected on their experiences of music in Mass, particularly with a song they like called "Shine, Jesus Shine," technically a Protestant rather than Catholic hymn. They discussed how all the girls in the school enjoy and sing that song, complete with the hand actions, and how they enjoy it regardless of whether they are religious or to which tradition they belong.

> KATE: I think music kind of gives the way of connecting with things, so even in church, like, everyone at school would just be so bored if it was talk, talk, talk, talk and the fact that we've got music in between kind of gives them a break and it makes it more relatable.

Participants identified the way that music was often more engaging than speaking at Masses. Jasmine commented that the music itself does not make individuals change their beliefs, rather it may widen their perspective on life, values, and religion.

> JASMINE: It can give you other views on your religion but, yeah, I doubt it could actually make you go "Oh, that's a good song Adele, I'm going to become a Hindu" [all laughing]. You wouldn't completely alter your life, you might just look at things slightly differently.

Kate insistently states that the school has not helped her religious identity, despite her initial comment at the start of the interview that she is now more open to religion than she was prior to high school.

> KATE: I don't think it helped—I wasn't very religious before I came to this school, but then I came here and they started talking about all these amazing things, like God walking on water, and I was like "What the hell, no one can do that" or Jesus or whoever [girls laughing].
> INTERVIEWER: Can you relate to it?
> KATE: Yeah, I just, I just listen to the stories and think that's crap—no one does that.

Kate went on to say how learning more about her peers and their religious beliefs has encouraged her to be more open-minded to religion, more so than the religious teachings themselves.

SUPPORTING RELIGIOUS IDENTITY

For Grace, the school has helped her religious identity through imparting Christian values and helping her to recognize what is important in life.

> GRACE: We're very Dominican-minded and we always go out and we volunteer for things. We do things as a school community and we help out our community's old. I guess that really shows—I think the school's values as well.

It is interesting, though, that when I asked participants what should be changed, particularly in the liturgical music at their school now, they said, "nothing."

> HANH: I like it, I like the way they set it up and stuff.
> JENNIFER: I want more songs.

I ask what sacred music means to them.

> LISA: A time of peace in sacred music, a time of peace.
> CHANG: I think its music . . . like kind of reflects what your religion is altogether.

Anh talks to me about her confusion with her own religious identity. It is surprising that she says that she relies on music to support her faith, and she states that being open-minded is the best way to be.

> ANH: Yeah I'm still confused, I just depend on music like that is—I've got my faith in that.

On describing having faith in her music, she states,

> ANH: It's just there like it's a constant thing that's always gonna be there . . . [It's] helped me through my hard times, so I'm just gonna keep depending on them [the songs] to get me through and hope that, you know, that I'll always have faith in music.

LITURGICAL MUSIC AS A SPACE FOR REFLECTION

Liturgical music helped Lisa to become more reflective about the message of the Mass and her relationship with God.

> LISA: It's, like, reflective. . . . Like it gives you a chance to sort of like think back, like, especially if it's after the priest has been talking. . . . It gives you a chance to, like, think about what he said and how it kind of relates to you? Like, that's personally how it is for me, but I guess it's not for everyone.

Shaping Identities and Religious Music Engagement 79

PERCEPTIONS OF SECULAR MUSIC

The group identifies situations in which secular music has been used inappropriately at Catholic events.

> NHI: At retreat this year, we went into prayer and two girls started singing "Marry You" by Bruno Mars [a secular song] and I was so confused. [girls laughing]
> CHI: [strongly agreeing] Yeah, totally unrelated.
> NHI: [continuing] And when they finished and then I was like, "What just happened?" like how is that relatable to religion at all?

Jennifer explains that she prefers traditional Catholic music at religious events:

> JENNIFER: I would rather stick with what we have . . . 'coz it seems more, mmm, spiritual.

It appeared that the girls value the importance of tradition in a religious setting and have expectations about the sacred nature of liturgies, possibly influenced by their Catholic and Christian upbringings.

Religious Music Fosters Positive Social Identity Work

Religious music supports adolescents' sense of group identity in the way it fosters a unique school identity. Participants identified the way in which certain songs are identified as distinctive to their school community, defining them as independent from other Catholic schools. Participation in religious music practices also fostered an institutionalized Catholic identity, as participants shared a common understanding of Catholic expectations and rituals. What is most significant, religious music provided a space within which adolescents could unite to sing in a special and common identity, allowing them to feel a sense of community and belonging. Religious music brought feelings of empowerment, acceptance, togetherness, and belonging.

BUILDING COMMUNITY THROUGH RELIGIOUS MUSIC

The participants describe the importance of traditional music in any type of religious community, as it brings a sense of connectedness.

> TASMYN: I think the school is pretty important 'coz when we have Masses we sing, like, the "Shine, Jesus Shine," the one that we always (sing).

Diu explains how the song "Shine, Jesus Shine" signifies Immaculata and reminds them that all the girls have something in common:

> DIU: It signifies Immaculata Catholic College as a community 'coz we learnt that, like, at year 8 and it's carried around with us to year 12, and it makes us more, like, together and just more united.

INTERVIEWER: So that particular hymn, you identify yourself as being an Immaculata girl?
DIU: Yeah 'coz everyone engages in the song and the action of the song.

Diu's comment indicates the way the girls associate their collective identity with their school's favorite religious song. Anh provides a personal example:

ANH: It wasn't until year 9 that it kind of hit me that this was an Immaculata song and it actually felt like I belonged somewhere. . . . Yeah, it just made me feel like I belonged. Every time that song comes on it just feels nice, 'coz not everyone talks to each other, well we're all friends, but you don't always get to catch up with someone and sometimes it feels a bit, like you're isolated from some people and when you sing that song it just feels like everyone's just come together, as, like, a whole community, and you feel like you belong somewhere . . . in, like, one particular clique.

The liturgical music gave the girls a sense of community, acceptance, and belonging. When I asked them whether they would like to hear other modern hymns or contemporary songs in the Masses, the participants disagreed and said that they like the traditional songs. The participants seemed to have a special connection to the songs and the tradition of the school.

CHANG: It's not, like, just music to us . . . it sort of brings us together. . . . It doesn't have a religious meaning to us [per se]."

Chang acknowledges, though, if it wasn't for the religious tradition in her school, that particular experience may not exist. Diu agreed that the song brought "everyone together."

CARINA: Yeah, like even the other girls, who don't have, like, religious beliefs, they still sing the song because you feel that you're a community when you're all singing it.

The participants clearly saw the song "Shine, Jesus Shine" as a way of coming together as a community.

MUSIC AS A MEANS OF ESTABLISHING POSITIVE EMOTIONS

The participants identified that singing and participating in liturgical songs does not necessarily make the students Catholic, but rather creates a sense of community.

GRACE: We only know the chorus [all laughing] and mumble through the rest of it. But half the people who sing it, like, I can guarantee the majority of them wouldn't believe in Jesus, but, um, because of the—it's very upbeat and it's happy, people want to sing along to it.

Shaping Identities and Religious Music Engagement 81

LISA: I think it does, you know, even like when we have that Mass where everyone goes to even the non-Catholic girls can join in with the songs you know they're still doing something in Mass.

Music was identified as a way for all students, regardless of religious affiliation, to participate and share in singing the songs together.

Religious Music Shapes Personal Identity Work

The adolescents' personal identity work is shaped by religious music as they engage with the routines and rituals of Catholic practices. Many participants identified the importance of consistency and structure in creating stability and familiarity within their personal worlds. Religious music also enabled a time of quiet reflection, when adolescents could be at peace with themselves and each other. For some, religious music provided an opportunity for personal expression, through singing, worshipping, reflecting, and engaging with others. Through these religious music experiences, the students felt a stronger sense of self-worth (Ebie 2005).

IDENTITY WORK IN AND THROUGH COMMUNITY AND FAITH

I asked Anh in an individual interview what it means for the girls when they are all singing that song together:

ANH: I think it's a bit of everything, you know, you get to praise God and Jesus but you get to do it in a really fun way, you get to join in with the whole community and everyone can be as one . . . you know?

The song is a way for students to fulfil their identity needs through both a sense of belonging and faith.

MUSIC'S ROLE IN SPIRITUAL CONNECTION AND IDENTITY

In an individual interview, Anh tells me that attending Mass makes her feel more connected spiritually, and she tries hard to stay focused and learn from the Mass:

ANH: I try to understand what the message of the Mass is rather than just sitting there and complaining "it's too boring." . . . I try to piece things together to try and see what they're trying to say and what the songs are and why the songs are put there and everything and just reflect on that.

She says that her feelings during Mass are fairly neutral, but she is moved when the choir sings:

ANH: It feels kind of powerful and you feel like you belong, well, I feel like I belong. It sort of feels weird, but you sort of feel blessed for this opportunity to connect the whole entire school . . . even though it's not my religion, but I get the opportunity to do that, and, like, when I receive my blessing that's kind of nice as well. It feels kind of like they are accepting you even though you're not part of the religion, so you feel like you do belong.

She says that after Mass she also feels more reflective and keeps in mind the message of the Mass. It affects her throughout that day and, sometimes, even days later. Anh also says that it is important for students to learn about other religions:

> ANH: I think it's just, well, you can expose other students to other, you know, new worlds that they probably never even heard of. . . . I didn't even know about the Muslim religion until I got here, I didn't know anything about it, so, you know, you open students' eyes and if they like it, they do, and if they don't, they don't, but I think it's good to have variety.

Anh even states that this could be a tactic for strengthening one's Catholic identity:

> ANH: I think it could . . . for example, I have a belief but I don't agree with you . . . I think it would just make you more passionate about what you believe in? Or if you could have the same agreement you'd be, like, oh yeah, I think.

The participants described teenagers' religiosity and spiritualty today. Nhi responds bluntly: "nonexistent." She elaborates further, however, stating that she is more spiritual than Catholic, despite having grown up around the Catholic faith. She states, however, that the Catholic faith has helped her with important moral and ethical considerations and in being a good person, and she thus considers it important to continue teaching teenagers about Catholicism.

> NHI: Well, I'm Catholic and grew up in a Catholic family, went to a Catholic primary school and a Catholic high school and I don't know, it's just—I wouldn't say that I'm overly religious where everything I do is, like, for God, but—I am a very spiritual person and I think because I've, you know, like the Catholic faith has been part of my life, that's the reason. It's hard to explain. It's, like, taught you morals and ethics, which nowadays comes more in a spirituality than it does religion. And in my sense, you've got a big part of if I do something wrong I always think "oh no, God's going to punish me" and stuff like that so it does have a big effect on my life.

Conclusion

Catholic schools provide an important place in which adolescents' spiritual and religious identity work is shaped (Chambers 2012; Grace and O'Keefe 2007; Pascoe 2007). Including music in the schools' religious traditions and rituals provides a medium through which adolescents can explore their identity work, but there appears to be little significant research in this area. This chapter has sought to present an understanding of the ways in which Catholic schools use, produce, and shape music in Catholic traditions and rituals and provides further insights for educators into the impact that music has on adolescents' identity work. Crucial work of the chapter was to outline the ways in which students in this Catholic setting engage with religious music (liturgical and secular) and its function in their identity work. It is clear that music is a key to engaging youth culture (Scally 1994), because music plays a vital role in adolescents' identity work (Bennett 2001; MacDonald et al. 2002). Therefore, the utilization of religious music to support adolescents' identity work was apparent and multifaceted, not only in supporting their religious identity, but also through fostering positive social identity work among their peers and personal identity work (Barbot and Heuser 2017).

The research reported in this chapter also reveals some significant gaps: while the case study's school promotes a multiculturalist policy in its acceptance of a range of religious affiliations, it should be noted that none of the research participants were recruited from the school's Muslim population. The absence of these students' voices may be attributed to a range of factors, including the role of music in the Islamic faith, the degree to which these students felt able to engage in discussions of music, or indeed the relative importance of music in their lives. Catholic school populations have become increasingly diverse in their students' religious affiliations. Religious music may act as a catalyst to integrate and engage students of different religious backgrounds, but the belief that music can become a common ground may not hold true. This situation challenges educators to consider adolescents' point of view—their narratives—to further support various aspects of their identity work in Catholic schools and to consider the ways in which music can build community and a collective identity among the students.

JANELLE COLVILLE FLETCHER is Head of Music and Senior Lecturer at Tabor College of Higher Education in South Australia and a research fellow with the University of Queensland. Her research interests include musical identity, adolescents' engagement in music, music education at secondary and tertiary levels, and religious music.

MARGARET S. BARRETT is Professor and Founding Director of the Creative Collaboratorium at the University of Queensland in Australia. Her research focuses on pedagogies of creativity and expertise, identity work in music, early musical development, engagement in music and arts activity, and music program evaluation.

Notes

1. Catholic schools are fee-paying schools partially funded by government; the enrollment fee depends on the affiliated order, gender, boarding facilities, year levels of schooling, the location, and the social precedence.

2. Data gathered from the school in 2011.
3. Data gathered from the school in 2011.
4. Data gathered from the school mission statement in 2011.

References

ABS (Australian Bureau of Statistics). 2011. Profile ID Census. *Community Profiles.* http://www.censusdata.ABS.gov.au/census_services/getproduct/census/2011/communityprofile/0.
Archdiocese of Brisbane. n.d. "Contemporary Contexts of School Religious Education." In *The Shape of Religious Education.* Accessed January 22, 2019. http://www.rec.bne.catholic.edu.au/The%20Shape%20of%20Religious%20Education/Pages/Contemporary-Contexts-of-School-Religious-Education.aspx.
Arthur, Tony. 2014. "Jules Chevalier and the Transformation of Society." *Compass Review* 48, no. 2 (Winter): 15–17. http://compassreview.org/autumn14/7.pdf.
Barbot, Baptiste, and Brianna Heuser. 2017. "Creativity and Identity Formation in Adolescence: A Developmental Perspective." In *The Creative Self: Effect of Beliefs, Self-Efficacy, Mindset, and Identity,* edited by M. Karwowski and J. Kaufman, 88–98. London: Elsevier Academic.
Barna, George. 2001. *Real Teens: A Contemporary Snapshot of Youth Culture.* Ventura, CA: Gospel Light.
Bennett, Andy. 2000. *Popular Music and Youth Culture: Music, Identity and Place.* Basingstoke, UK: Palgrave Macmillan.
———. 2001. *Cultures of Popular Music.* Buckingham, UK: Open University Press.
Bryk, Anthony. S., Valerie. E. Lee, and Peter. B. Holland. 1995. *Catholic Schools and the Common Good.* Cambridge, MA: Harvard University Press.
Buchanan, Michael. T., and Richard Rymarz. 2008. *An Introduction to Catholic Education: Current Perspectives.* Terrigal, Australia: David Barlow.
Chambers, Michael. 2012. "Students Who Are Not Catholics in Catholic Schools: Lessons from the Second Vatican Council about the Catholicity of Schools." *International Studies in Catholic Education* 4, no. 2: 186–99.
DeNora, Tia. 2000. *Music in Everyday Life.* Cambridge: Cambridge University Press.
———. 2003. *After Adorno: Rethinking Music Sociology.* Cambridge: Cambridge University Press.
Denzin, Norman K., and Yvonne S. Lincoln. 2002. "Introduction: The Discipline and Practice of Qualitative Research" In *The SAGE Handbook of Qualitative Research,* 3rd ed., edited by Norman K. Denzin and Yvonna S. Lincoln, 1–32. Thousand Oaks, CA: Sage.
Ebie, Brian D. 2005. "An Investigation of Secondary School Students' Self-Reported Reasons for Participation in Extracurricular Musical and Athletic Activities." *Research and Issues in Music Education* 3, no. 1: article 5. http://ir.stthomas.edu/rime/vol3/iss1/5.
Grace, Gerald. R., and Joseph. O'Keefe, eds. 2007. *International Handbook of Catholic Education: Challenges for School Systems in the 21st Century,* Vol. 2, *Catholic Education.* Dordrecht: Springer.
Hargreaves, David. H. 1967. *Social Interactions in Secondary School.* London: Routledge.
Hargreaves, Douglas. J., and A. C. North. 1997. *The Social Psychology of Music.* Oxford: Oxford University Press.

Hatch, J. Amos. 2002. *Doing Qualitative Research in Education Settings.* Albany: State University of New York Press.

Joncas, Jan Michael. 1997. *From Sacred Song to Ritual Music: Twentieth-Century Understandings of Roman Catholic Worship Music.* Collegeville, MN: Liturgical Press.

Langer, Susanne. K. 2009. *Philosophy in a New Key: A Study in the Symbolism of Reason, Rite, and Art.* Cambridge, MA: Harvard University Press.

MacDonald, Raymond. A. R., Douglas. J. Hargreaves, and Dorothy. E. Miell. 2002. "Musical Identities." In *Musical Identities* [e-book], edited by R. A. R. MacDonald, D. J. Hargreaves, and D. E. Miell, 462–70. Oxford: Oxford University Press.

Mariña, Jacqueline. 2009. "Friedrich Schleiermacher and Rudolf Otto." In *Oxford Handbook of Religion and Emotion,* edited by John Corrigan. https://dx.doi.org/10.1093/oxfordhb/9780195170214.003.0026.

McAdams, Dan. P. 1993. *The Stories We Live By: Personal Myths and the Making of the Self.* New York: W. Morrow.

NCEC (National Catholic Education Commission). 2013. *Catholic Education in Australia: Insight Document.* https://www.ncec.catholic.edu.au/resources/research/400-australian-catholic-schools-2013/file

Pascoe, Susan. 2007. "Challenges for Catholic Education in Australia." In *International Handbook of Catholic Education* (787–810). Dordrecht Springer.

Polkinghorne, D. E. 2005. "Language and Meaning: Data Collection in Qualitative Research." *Journal of Counseling Psychology* 52, no. 2: 137–45.

Rossiter, Graham. 1999. "Historical Perspective on the Development of Catholic Religious Education in Australia: Some Implications for the Future." *Journal of Religious Education* 47, no. 1: 5–18.

———. 2010. "A Case for a 'Big Picture' Re-orientation of K–12 Australian Catholic School Religious Education in the Light of Contemporary Spirituality." *Journal of Religious Education* 58, no. 3: 5–18.

———. 2011. "Reorienting the Religion Curriculum in Catholic Schools to Address the Needs of Contemporary Youth Spirituality." *International Studies in Catholic Education* 3, no. 1: 57–72.

Rymarz, Richard M., and John Graham. 2006. "Drifting from the Mainstream: The Religious Identity of Australian Core Catholic Youth." *International Journal of Children's Spirituality* 11, no. 3: 371–83.

Sacrosanctum Concilium. 1963. *Constitution on the Sacred Liturgy.* December 4, 1963. Vatican: Sacrosanctum Concilium. http://www.vatican.va/archive/hist_councils/ii_vatican_council/documents/vat-ii_const_19631204_sacrosanctum-concilium_en.html.

Scally, Anna. 1994. "Music: The Key to Youth Culture." *Catholic World* 237, no. 1421: 244–46.

Stake, Robert. E. 1995. *The Art of Case Study Research.* Thousand Oaks, CA: Sage.

Strenski, Ivan. 2015. *Understanding Theories of Religion: An Introduction.* 2nd ed. West Sussex, UK: Blackwell.

Vatican. 2013. Vatican II—The Holy See. http://w2.vatican.va/content/Vatican/en.html.

5 | Religion and the Transmission of Thai Musical Heritage in Thailand and the United States

Pamela A. Moro

The performance of music in the Thai classical tradition, both in Thailand and among Thai living in the United States of America, is shaped by Buddhism and by a sacred worldview shared by performing artists of South and Southeast Asia. In Thailand, religion has long provided opportunities for performance but also frames specific understandings of knowledge and teacher-student relationships. In recent decades, religion has invigorated and reinforced the transmission of musical heritage that, in the mid-twentieth century, was perceived as vulnerable or endangered. In somewhat different ways, Thai people in North America rely on music and dance instruction at Buddhist temples to navigate the development of identity and values among youth.

Thai classical music is an elite tradition, cultivated historically in royal and noble courts but with roots in village life and temple rituals. The music emphasizes heterophonic ensembles, especially of melodic percussion instruments. Solo performance, both vocal and instrumental, is also important, as is music as accompaniment to classical dance and theater. Thai musical structures and performance practices share much with other traditions across Southeast Asia, while the music's theoretical foundations and sacred context bespeak distant roots in India. Though once relying on master-disciple relationships and oral/aural transmission, in the late twentieth century, much music instruction became institutionalized within schools, university music departments, and a national system of performing arts conservatories.

While at first glance Thai music education in the context of religion may appear to be a conservative force, the two extended cases I explore here point to how religion and education *produce* culture in inventive ways. I begin by introducing several concepts developed in contemporary anthropology, to identify links between culturally based understandings of heritage and pedagogies rooted in religion. I then move to an overview of Thai religion as relevant to music and music education before exploring the two cases.

My experiences as a researcher on Thai music and as a friend to performers, teachers, and students of the music, started in the 1980s. I was a graduate student in anthropology, with a strong background in European musical performance but also some familiarity with the gamelan music of Java. I studied the

Thai language and, in the mid-1980s, pursued research in Bangkok that became my doctoral dissertation. My aim was to update some earlier studies of Thai classical music by Western writers in light of a resurgence of Thai (especially urban and middle-class) interest in traditional arts. While relying on qualitative research methods such as interviews and observation, I also participated by practicing several musical instruments and following teachers as they went about their work. My career unfolded in the United States as a professor at small private universities, with occasional opportunities to return to Thailand for more research. In 2007, I spent several months in residence at Chiang Mai Rajabhat University as a guest of the Thai music program. In 2011, I began getting to know Thai people in the San Francisco Bay Area of California, where arts and culture programs, especially for youth, are supported by Buddhist temples.

Heritage, Religious Pedagogy, and the Framing of Cultural Objects

For the past several decades, much theoretical work in anthropology and related fields has been concerned with questions about cultural reproduction, seeking to identify where and how individuals maneuver within broad social forms or how they invent new patterns of power, discipline, and resistance. Such questions are crucial in two areas of my study: *cultural heritage* (including music, ritual, and other expressive forms closely tied to claims of group identity) and *pedagogy associated with religion*. Both rely on culturally constructed understandings of the past. I use the term *heritage* not to refer to artifacts, sites, or unchanging customs associated with past times or personalities, but as a process that transmits ideas about the past, as (re)contextualized in the present. "Heritage is a product of the present that draws on an assumed imaginary past, and justifies itself by reference to an equally assumed imaginary future" (Ashworth 2011, 21). Paradoxically, heritage may be delineated and defined by human actors who claim it as enduring tradition. Groups embracing classical Thai music today inevitably position themselves through images of a prestigious past (Myers-Moro 1989; compare Herzfeld 2003). Similarly, education—including music education—rooted in or supported by religious systems may gain legitimacy through a perceived stability, from a moral authority rooted in the past. As Adely and Seale-Collazo (2013) note, "Religious education is often understood as reproductive, as primarily concerned with maintaining moral authority and orthodoxy, or preserving knowledge. However, religious pedagogical projects are inevitably constrained and shaped by relations of power, patterns of human practice, and the reality that all forms of authority or hegemony must respond to . . . ongoing cultural transformations" (344). While we might expect music education rooted in religion to be traditional and unchanging, in fact—like other cultural forms—it is constantly and creatively inventive in the face of social, political, and economic changes.

It is the researcher's task to pay attention to the meaning imputed, or assigned, by participants. Richard Handler (2011), drawing on the influential work of Goffman (1974), advocates an emphasis on *frames* for such analyses. Frames transform human interaction to demarcate play, fantasy, sport, homage, and parody. Handler notes that a focus on framing can help us understand cultural objectification—the treatment of ritual or other aspects of culture as objects or things "at once possessed by a social group and representative of it" (41). Following Handler, I treat the musical heritage of Thailand, and the religiously associated education system that transmits and (re)invents it, as such a cultural object, made meaningful in new ways through framing by participants as heritage. In this light, we may see religion as a force that can invigorate—not fossilize—Thai music making today.

Overview of Religion in Thailand, as Relevant to Musical Performance

Music, religion, and education are entwined in Thailand—and throughout South and Southeast Asia—in numerous ways, from historic patterns of daily community life to politically resonant constructions of national identity, and including symbolic correspondences between musical structures, worldview, and other cultural content.

Theravada Buddhism in History and Social Life

The societies of mainland Southeast Asia, including Thailand, have been strongly shaped by the Theravada branch of Buddhism, with ancient sources in India and Sri Lanka. Buddhism as a whole, dating back to four or five centuries BCE, has always been an international faith, but numerous divisions developed over time, and local patterns integrated with regional cultures. The integration of spirit cults, magical beliefs, and Hindu- and Chinese-derived content led some to use terms like *syncretism* and *hybridization* to characterize Thai religion (Guelden 2007; Kitiarsa 2005, 2012).

Ethnographic descriptions of twentieth-century Thai life emphasize the key role of Theravada monastic communities in both village and city life. Groups of monks live together at the temple compound or *wat*, but whole communities or neighborhoods interact in and around the wat. The wat is a focus for coordinated community activities, including daily offerings of food (important in the spiritual lives of women, in particular, who prepare and donate the food), the organization of calendrical rites and festivities, and temporary ordinations that serve as rites of passage for male youth. They are often sites of considerable pride.

Historically, Theravada Buddhism has been deeply tied to conceptions of kingship, rule, and power. The faith remains the state religion and is one of three key institutions promoted after the World War II era: king, nation, and religion (Keyes 1987). Today, 94.6 percent of the Thai population is Buddhist, and most Thai seamlessly equate Thai culture (including folk religious practices, spirit cults, and Hinduism) with Thai Buddhism, leaving a somewhat awkward space for those in the nation who profess Islam and Christianity (CIA World Factbook 2019).

Conceptions of Thai National Culture

In the last decades of the twentieth century and up to the present, class- and region-based constituencies began to vie for power in Thailand, ultimately leading to the post-2005 political turmoil and an army coup in 2014. During these decades, a middle-class movement to promote an urban-based national identity, indebted to elite and monarchical culture, became significant, driven in part by a sense of pride in the Thai civilization, promoted as a contribution to humanity. Such a movement is not new, and earlier efforts to create a national culture date back to the mid-nineteenth-century kings. Thai classical music and Thai Buddhism are important components of this heritage, displayed for tourists, affirmed by the royal family, and supported by public educational institutions. For the Thai musicians I know, the political context is of little relevance. For Thai in the San Francisco Bay Area of California, notions of Thai heritage function as a source of prestige, and a sense of legitimacy is very important.

Temple Rituals and Holidays as Occasions for Music

Thai Buddhists participate in religion to a great extent through rituals and holidays, which, whether tied to the calendar or to the human life cycle, provide occasions for musical performance, often with the temple as a site. In all, music demarcates sacred time and space. For example, seasonal temple festivals in northern Thailand emphasize processions of drum-and-gong ensembles; cremations and other life-cycle rites may draw on distinct repertoires and ensembles, as do *tham khwan* rituals for calling spirits back to the body, and merit-making rituals, related to the doctrine of karma. Another example is *Thet Mahachat*, an October holiday featuring recitations elaborating the last human life of the Buddha, performed by a monk with high oratorical skills. The narrative is presented in thirteen chapters, with instrumental music performed between chapters. This is just one of several forms of skilled oratory and chant that Buddhist monks in Thailand may perform. Monks do not perform as musicians per se, and these expressive forms are considered not music but preaching, even though they have value as entertainment as well as religious ritual (compare Miller 1992, 186). Even if the recommended instrumentation and repertory is not possible, *some kind* of traditional music will demarcate portions of lengthy ritual events, such as those mentioned above. Wats in Thailand can also be sites for music and dance for more purely entertainment purposes, especially with children as performers.

Musical Structures and Worldview

Some authors suggest a correspondence between South and Southeast Asian musical structures and religious worldview (for example, Becker 1981 and 1988; Bohlman 2005). These musical forms emphasize the repetition of cyclical patterns, especially lengthy metric structures, and do not develop in a teleological movement toward a conclusion. There is no forward movement, no development in the Western classical sense, though the music certainly can escalate, through speed and volume, toward rapid and exciting endings. Pieces can be extended through improvisation and embellishment of basic units of melody. Patterns may parallel views of the afterlife, reincarnation, and a sense of historical time moving in giant cycles, as opposed to a Western, Christian-based sense of developing toward an end-result conclusion or salvation (Asad 1993).

Hindu-Buddhist Understandings of Knowledge and Musical Power

Thai musicians and dancers have their own religious practices, emphasizing lines of transmission between deities, teachers, and disciples. They include maintenance of altars in instructional settings and periodic rituals (*way khruu* ceremonies) that honor teachers and initiate students into stages of learning associated with tiers of repertory, which I will address later in this chapter. These observances recognize a pantheon of deities associated with the origins and transmission of the performing arts. Hindu deities, represented materially by dancers' papier-mâché masks, manifest in performance and are associated with musical sound. They necessitate etiquette on how musical instruments and the human body are engaged in performance. Musical knowledge itself is shaped by this context, and the teaching and learning of music and dance are regulated through ritual elaboration. This musical knowledge is powerful. It has the power to bless and affirm and to protect the most advanced musicians when they perform sacred repertory that is seen as supernaturally risky. (The most detailed study of *way khruu* is Wong 2001; also Myers-Moro 1993, chapter 6; more recent studies include Binson 2009a and 2009b.)

The most skilled and knowledgeable musicians I have met in Thailand, without exception, take the spiritual side of music very seriously. This is something they value and want to pass along to their students. For some master musicians, their devotion extends to encouraging religious faith among their students even beyond the specific realm of musical performance, for example, by exposing students to Buddhist teaching from respected elders, or by taking students to visit sacred sites. Guiding a student's moral development is part of the job of being a teacher of Thai music.

Now that we have seen how music, religion, and the transmission of musical knowledge intersect in Thailand, two examples will help us consider further how conceptions of heritage and religiously informed music education can yield inventive processes.

Religious Ritual in Thai Music Education Today

Thai educational institutions—except for those specifically serving Muslims and Christians—integrate Buddhism, as well as related Hindu, folk, and animist content, into campus life. School children start the day with Buddhist prayers, and Buddhist holidays are observed through days off. On school and university grounds, Buddha images receive honored space, as do shrines for Phra Phikanet or Phra Phikanesuan (Ganesha), the elephant-headed Hindu deity associated with learning, and shrines for spirits associated with the geographic place or land. Around the music department, however, students and instructors engage in religious observances in addition to those of the general school or university population. Instructional spaces for Thai music require that people remove their footwear, because they contain sacred images and objects and are sites for frequent ritual action among educators and students.

Such objects and ritual actions are visible constituents of the sacred worldview crucial to education in Thai classical music. Various forms of *way khruu* rituals, touched on earlier, literally "honor teachers." Musicians distinguish small observances, such as maintenance of altars with daily or weekly offerings, from annual events that require significant planning and include a large number of participants. Large *way khruu* are officiated by a senior teacher who has received ritual permission from elder, respected musicians to perform the sacred text of the event, which typically lasts more than three hours. The event invokes deities, blesses musical instruments, and ends with rites that initiate students, giving them sacred permission—and significant social affirmation—to study progressively more difficult repertory. As part of the ritual, each music student in attendance will make an offering and receive a blessing. Like many rituals around the world, the events are multisensory, with a visual emphasis on an elaborate, creatively designed altar, with its offerings of food and flowers, photographs and statuary, and the striking presence of musical instruments. These elaborate altars are set up by advanced music students, often working days in advance to complete the work required. (For shorter *way khruu* rituals, such as before a concert, teachers may assemble a portable altar, perhaps including only a few deity images and incense.) At some points during the long event, respectful silence or soft recitation is required of participants; toward the end, the focus breaks up a bit and people may perform musical instruments for each other in small groups and mingle informally. This is during the long phase when students are initiated; one by one, each must sit inside the *khong wong yai*, a circular bronze metallophone, and play a short melodic passage while their wrists are held by a teacher.

Way khruu rituals, in various forms, are associated with many kinds of specialized knowledge and its transmission, in Thailand, including martial arts and traditional medicine. From the mid-twentieth century, a version has been celebrated annually in the public schools for general educators. They were described to me by one Thai woman as "teacher appreciation day," a term that does not fully capture the spirit or function of the occasion. To my knowledge, it is among musicians that *way khruu* has been most lavishly elaborated, especially when staged by large public universities and conservatories. In the 1980s, only a small number of senior teachers held ritual permission to officiate the events. Their number was intentionally expanded, however, in the 1990s in an effort to widen participation in the ritual and music in general, undoubtedly recognizing the potential for the ritual to motivate students. Visiting Chiang Mai Rajabhat University, part of a public university system, in 2007, I observed that organizing, officiating, and providing music for *way khruu* were significant and fairly frequent opportunities for student-musicians and faculty to perform music. Because a qualified officiant is required, senior musicians with the skill to lead the ceremony—with their advanced students assisting—may be invited to lead *way khruu* at numerous sites in the community.

The elaborate, inclusive *way khruu* event was popularized during the decades when the Thai schools successfully developed programs in Thai music education, roughly starting in the 1970s and 1980s. During the World War II era, Thailand's government controlled traditional arts to the point of prohibition for some genres, if deemed backward (often because of their connections to working-class or rural populations), and forced modernization for others. Even in the 1970s, few Thai schools offered Thai music instruction in depth, and even high-quality universities had extracurricular Thai music clubs but not Thai music departments or study programs. The growth of educational programs in Thai music, even at the undergraduate and graduate degree levels, is a success story and source of pride for today's musicians. Private studios associated with master teachers, which is not unlike the old days, have also resurged. From a functionalist perspective in anthropology, we can see how *way khruu* rituals contribute by serving sociocultural needs. They motivate and commend youth participation in music learning. Students need only have studied music for a short while before they will be initiated into the lowest level. (Progressively smaller numbers of students will advance to the higher of five levels of initiation, at subsequent *way khruu*.) The rituals encode and reinforce a set of values: they teach the sacred worldview of musicians, respect for senior teachers and for learning in general, and humility before those with more experience (see Binson 2009a).

If young students show dedication to serious musical practice, his or her teacher will conduct a small private version of *way khruu* with them, to initiate them into formal study. Short *way khruu* are also required before public performances. Such performances are often experiences of joy and pride for young students, their teachers, and their parents. At their briefest, the rites involve a small offering of incense and flowers and prayers guided by the teacher. There has been some growth in preperformance *way khruu* in recent years, now using the same material culture and iconography as the larger events. Among Thai in the United States, some public performances now move what was once a backstage altar out to the side of a publicly visible stage, foregrounding ritual that in the past would have been private. This suggests a reframing of the event as cultural objectification or consciously claimed heritage (Brosius and Polit 2011).

Musical Heritage at Thai Buddhist Temples in California

Since the 1970s, Thai living in North America and Europe have organized diaspora community life around wats that serve, just as in Thailand, as both religious and social centers (Bao 2005, 2009; Cadge 2005; Numrich 1996). Many non-Thai visit Thai weekend food courts to eat noodles, soups, and other foods just as at marketplaces in Thailand, sold in part as fundraising to support the wat. In 2011, I carried out several months of fieldwork with two Thai Buddhist temples in California, in the San Francisco Bay Area cities of Fremont and Berkeley. Both wats host what they call "culture programs" for youth, which include training in Thai language, Buddhism, dance, and music—daily during the summer, and weekly during the school year. Initially, senior women, who had migrated to the United States as adults, were the performing arts instructors. In the 1990s, however, both wats developed arrangements with Thai universities that annually send over groups of young resident teachers who take primary responsibility for daily or weekly instruction. (Resident monks take care of religious instruction; see Kitiarsa 2010 for a full study.) In an institutional sense, the programs are highly developed transnational ones that provide a religious context that promotes the learning of music and dance by framing heritage for new needs.

In today's world, terms like *religion*, *politics*, *culture*, and *ritual* are both lay concepts and social science concepts. Handler writes, "Such terms are compromised because . . . they are at once native terms and analytic terms. We try to use a term like 'ritual' to make sense of what people are doing but one of the things people are doing is borrowing terms like 'ritual' from social scientists to make sense of their own world" (2011, 42). Quite explicitly, the culture of Thailand, as they understand it, is what the parental and grandparental generations in the California wats hope to teach to youth. Such culture is a version of Thai heritage (domestically in Thailand as well as in diaspora) shaped in part by the Thai state and thus related to state-supported educational curricula, tourism, and class-based prestige. Perhaps the fundamental goal is the teaching of Thai language, and what parents described to me as values, especially in etiquette, gender, the body, and aesthetics. Pursuing these goals through Thai dance and music is seen as a wise choice, because of the embodied nature of these activities. They inscribe culture on individuals (Farnell 1999; Wulff 2011) by emphasizing sensory bodily experiences: habits, routines, and all the semiconscious and unconscious encounters that form the stuff of identity, memory, and familial love. Young students learn the sacred worldview of the performing arts through homage to deities at every lesson, initiation rites, and—if a qualified officiant visits from Thailand—at larger *way khruu* events.

We must be careful, in the context of this volume, not to overemphasize or overdetermine the role of religion here. The pedagogy of Thai music, whether at institutions in Thailand or in the diaspora, is not uniquely "religious" but is pedagogy associated with, and entwined with, religion. Yet to young people of Thai ancestry in the United States, music, dance, and language are indeed taught alongside Buddhism—in (or very near) the same space. Wats in California are all-at-once social, physical, and sacred spaces, demarcated by geography, architecture, language, smells and tastes, sounds, and bodily experiences of gesture, posture, clothing, adornment. But the purpose of the culture programs is not to propagate Buddhism per se. True enough, Thai temples outside Thailand receive financial and institutional support from the Thai government, evidence of what one scholar calls a missionary intent on the part of the state (Kitiarsa 2010). Yet we must stretch our understanding of religion—Thai Buddhism as religion, and the wat as a sacred site—by recognizing the seamless connections between religion and culture, their isomorphism from the Thai and Thai diaspora perspective. Many young adults and youth with whom I have spoken describe their participation at the wat as "about" culture and identity, not about religion in an ideological sense. They understand Thai Buddhism as a bundle of experiences that is part of a greater bundle of multigenerational, Thai-identified experiences that traverse continents and time periods. If anything, the version of Buddhism that they may articulate owes as much to white middle-class American understandings of Buddhism (with its emphasis on meditation and household decor) as to the sermons and rituals of the wat.

To some degree, the culture programs at wats in California indeed fit a conservative model of religious education, emphasizing moral authority and aiming to preserve tradition. This is perhaps how the older-generation participants see it. But from the vantage of younger participants, other forms of identity emerge, of which they themselves are in charge. At the Thai temple in Berkeley, California, among prominent leaders in the program are women now in their thirties, born in Thailand, largely raised in the United States, highly educated, and experienced as dancers and performers. They have become guides to younger Thai Americans, for example, by taking teenagers on visits to Thailand specifically to explore aspects of their heritage. These and other young Thai Americans bring their own understandings of identity to the community, connected in some ways to emerging, broader forms of identity as Asian Americans. Some find a degree of subcultural capital or ethnic cool in their Thainess or adopt the distant sense of nostalgia that their parents and grandparents feel toward Thailand. (See Maira 2012 for an insightful study of similar patterns among Indian American youth.) When speaking English, some Anglicize the pronunciation of their names. They take part in, or supervise children who take part in, public folk festivals and multiethnic diversity celebrations—new frames for performance, identity, and heritage. Virada Chatikul (2006) made a short film, *Boonkhun*, about the culture program at the Berkeley wat, emphasizing participants' perceptions of identity and belonging. Participants use Thai religion as one tool for framing identity and their own maturing positions within the diaspora community.

The wat as a locus for Thai community building in the United States conforms to patterns long unfolding among other immigrant populations, pursuing religion—and its associated performing arts—as a way to hold onto a distinctive identity while also becoming American. A major vein in the scholarly literature on immigration and ethnicity in the United States concerns the role of religion, observing that religion in immigrant communities generally contributes to an ethnic identity in a way that is acceptable, nonthreatening, or even celebrated by dominant groups (Min 2002). In the United States, religion has been the most legitimate form of ethnic expression and always a source for group formation. For example, Hindu Indian religious groups in southern California have sought to "become Hindu" with a dedication and level of participation exceeding that in India, positioning themselves as Americans yet retaining at least a symbolic level of ethnicity (Kurien 1998, 2002). Kurien proposes that such a movement involves "staking out a place at the multicultural table" (1998, 61). Like Hindus from South

Asia, Thai Americans have had to build their own religious/community institutions, based in part on the congregational model of US Christian and Jewish organizations, because umbrella organizations associated with their faith did not exist. If staking out a place at the multicultural table involves, to some degree, pursuing forms of difference that are safe or affirmed by the majority, it is possible that the educational system in the United States, as well as religion, is an important factor. Schools and universities in the United States attempt to celebrate ethnicity at holidays or community festivals, in clubs associated with particular identity groups, and through inclusive curricula and pedagogy. Thus, public educational institutions provide metamessages about the kinds of difference, and the forms difference might take, in multicultural America, in inevitable but perhaps unacknowledged dialogue with community groups as self-authoring agents.

To conclude, I must note that I have not yet encountered any explicit questioning of the appropriateness of religion in Thai music education, in Thailand or among Thai in California. For the musicians I know best, it is unthinkable that Thai music would not be entwined with its sacred worldview and rituals. Why should we expect otherwise? North Americans and Europeans, cherishing the separation of public and private spheres where religion is concerned, might be surprised by the religiosity of Thai music education. Yet anthropological theory emphasizes that the secular is historically produced, every bit as much as the religious, not universally the same and not inevitable (Cannell 2010). For participants in Thai music, controversy about religiously based education may never arise. Resistance may arise among disenfranchised people excluded from elite sources of prestige and power, including religious minorities—perhaps not directed so much at music education but at the whole package of state-supported heritage. There are real consequences and material effects associated with the public role of religion in the Thai nation, which we cannot ignore for the sake of easygoing cultural relativism and tolerance. Yet, if we focus on the perspectives of participants at this time, we see that religion is not a tool for exclusion but a force for energizing what had been dwindling performing arts.

PAMELA A. MORO is Professor of Anthropology at Willamette University in Salem, Oregon. Her research includes work on music and musicians in Thailand, religion and ritual, LGBT/feminist choral singing, and anthropological perspectives on the violin from a global perspective.

References

Adely, Fida, and James Seale-Collazo. 2013. "Introduction to Special Issue: Ethnographies of Religious Education," *Anthropology and Education Quarterly* 44, no. 4: 340–44.

Asad, Talal. 1993. *Genealogies of Religion: Discipline and Reasons of Power in Christianity and Islam*. Baltimore, MD: Johns Hopkins University Press.

Ashworth, Gregory J. 2011. "Heritage in Ritual and Identity" In *Ritual, Heritage, and Identity: The Politics of Culture and Performance in a Globalised World*, edited by Christiane Brosius and Karin M. Polit, 19–38. London: Routledge.

Bao, Jiemin. 2005. "Merit-Making Capitalism: Re-territorializing Thai Buddhism in Silicon Valley." *Journal of Asian-American Studies* 8, no. 2: 115–42.

———. 2009. "Thai-American Middle-Classness: Forging Alliances with Whites and Cultivating Patronage from Thailand's Elite." *Journal of Asian-American Studies* 12, no. 2: 163–90.

Becker, Judith. 1981. "Hindu-Buddhist Time in Javanese Gamelan Music." *Study of Time* IV: 161–72.

———. 1988. "Earth, Fire, Sakti, and Javanese Gamelan," *Ethnomusicology* 32, no. 3: 385–91.

Binson, Bussakorn. 2009a. "Rites and Beliefs of Music in Thailand's Lanna Region." *Fontes Artis Musicae* 56: 299–313.

———. 2009b. "The Role of Food in the Musical Rites of the Lanna People of Northern Thailand." *Rian Thai International Journal of Thai Studies* 2: 45–69.

Bohlman, Philip V. 2005. "Music: Music and Religion in India." In *Encyclopedia of Religion*, 2nd ed., edited by Lindsay Jones, 9: 6278–87. Detroit: Thomson Gale.

Brosius, Christiane, and Karin M. Polit, eds. 2011. *Ritual, Heritage, and Identity: The Politics of Culture and Performance in a Globalised World*. London: Routledge.

Cadge, Wendy Heartwood. 2005. *The First Generation of Theravada Buddhism in America*. Chicago: University of Chicago Press.

Cannell, Fenella. 2010. "The Anthropology of Secularism." *Annual Review of Anthropology* 39: 85–100.

Chatikul, Virada, producer and director. 2010. "Boonkhun." DVD, 22 min. San Francisco: Thai Cultural Center.

CIA World Factbook. 2019. "People and Society: Thailand." April 19. https://www.cia.gov/library/publications/the-world-factbook/geos/th.html.

Farnell, Brenda. 1999. "Moving Bodies, Acting Selves." *Annual Review of Anthropology* 28: 341–73.

Goffman, Erving. 1974. *Frame Analysis: An Essay on the Organization of Experience*. New York: Harper & Row.

Guelden, Marlane. 2007. *Thailand: Spirits among Us*. Singapore: Marshall Cavendish.

Handler, Richard. 2011. "The 'Ritualisation of Ritual' in the Construction of Heritage." In *Ritual, Heritage, and Identity: The Politics of Culture and Performance in a Globalised World*, edited by Christiane Brosius and Karin M. Polit, 39–54. London: Routledge.

Herzfeld, Michael. 2003. *The Body Impolitic: Artisans and Artifice in the Global Hierarchy of Value*. Chicago: University of Chicago Press.

Keyes, Charles F. 1987. *Thailand: Buddhist Kingdom as Modern Nation-State*. Boulder, CO: Westview Press.

Kitiarsa, Pattana. 2005. "Beyond Syncretism: Hybridization of Popular Religion in Contemporary Thailand." *Journal of Southeast Asian Studies* 36, no. 3: 461–87.

———. 2010. "Missionary Intent and Monastic Networks: Thai Buddhism as a Transnational Religion." *Journal of Social Issues in Southeast Asia* 25, no. 1: 109–32.

———. 2012. *Mediums, Monks, and Amulets: Thai Popular Buddhism Today*. Seattle: University of Washington Press.

Kurien, Prema. 1998. "Becoming American by Becoming Hindu: Indian Americans Take Their Place at the Multicultural Table." In *Gatherings in Diaspora: Religious Communities and the New Immigration*, edited by R. Stephen Warner and Judith G. Wittner, 37–70. Philadelphia: Temple University Press.

———. 2002. "'We Are Better Hindus Here': Religion and Ethnicity among Indian Americans." In *Asian America: Building Faith Communities*, edited by Pyong Gap Min and Jung Ha Him, 99–120. Walnut Creek, CA: AltaMira.

Maira, Sunaina. 2012. *Desis in the House: Indian American Youth Culture in NYC*. Philadelphia: Temple University Press.

Miller, Terry. 1992. "A Melody Not Sung: The Performance of Lao Buddhist Texts in Northeast Thailand." In *Selected Reports in Ethnomusicology: Text, Context, and Performance in Cambodia, Laos, and Vietnam*, edited by Amy Catlin, 161–88. University of California–Los Angeles.

Min, Pyong Gap. 2002. "A Literature Review with a Focus on Major Themes." In *Religions in Asian America: Building Faith Communities*, edited by Pyong Gap Min and Jung Ha Him, 15–36. Walnut Creek, CA: AltaMira.

Myers-Moro, Pamela. 1989. "Thai Music and Attitudes towards the Past," *Journal of American Folklore* 102: 190–94.

———. 1993. *Thai Music and Musicians in Contemporary Bangkok*. Center for Southeast Asia Studies Monograph No. 34. University of California–Berkeley.

Numrich, Paul. 1996. *Old World Wisdom in the New World: Two Immigrant Theravada Buddhist Temples*. Knoxville: University of Tennessee Press.

Wong, Deborah. 2001. *Sounding the Center: History and Aesthetics in Thai Buddhist Performance*. Chicago: University of Chicago Press.

Wulff, Christoph. 2011. "Performativity and Dynamics of Intangible Cultural Heritage." In *Ritual, Heritage, and Identity: The Politics of Culture and Performance in a Globalised World*, edited by Christiane Brosius and Karin M. Polit, 76–94. London: Routledge.

6 | The Believing-Belonging Paradigm: Music, Education, and Religion in Contemporary Serbia

Ivana Perković and Biljana Mandić

During the last decade of the twentieth century, the revival of Orthodoxy in Serbia has been driven by fundamental historical, political, economic, social, and other changes.[1] After a period of marginalization during the socialist regime, the Serbian Orthodox Church (re)gained its integrated role during the 1990s, a difficult decade of deep moral, cultural, and spiritual crisis. Orthodoxy became the essential factor in the revived Serbian identity, and sociologists of religion describe its role "as a continuous and the only reliable guardian of tradition and historical memory" (Blagojević 2008, 41). Later, when the wars in the former Yugoslavia ended, the restored religiosity did not recede; rather, at least in Serbia, the situation was stabilized in the sense of a high confessional and religious, mostly Orthodox, self-identification on the part of the people. This reaffirmation of religious values affected interest in religious music. The music of worship had an important role in the process of the creation and construction of the new social and Orthodox identity, which led to the creation of church choirs in almost all the cities and many of the villages inhabited by Serbs. The generally positive attitude toward religious music caused professional music ensembles and associations (choirs) to turn to public and liturgical performances and recording the music of worship, and composers began to write new sacred pieces and to harmonize or arrange traditional Serbian chants.

Faced with the increase in public expectations and demands, the Serbian educational system reacted in 2001 with the (re)introduction of religious education in primary and secondary schools (after a nearly fifty-year hiatus). It was a compulsory elective subject (the other option being civic education), with the general goals to "acquaint students with the faith and spiritual experiences of their own Church and religious community, to enable them to acquire an integrated religious view of the world and life, and to . . . preserve and cultivate their own religious and cultural identity respectively" (Joksimović 2003, 213).

Such a state of affairs raises various questions. What is the general role of Orthodox music in the context of current religious education? Is the increase in religiousness/spirituality in Serbia accompanied by suitable musical activities in the educational context? How does practicing Orthodox music affect the identity of the school-age children and their teachers? What kind of knowledge is gained, or could be gained, when music and religion "meet" in the educational program?

To address these questions we have carried out a critical exploration of the modes of presence of religious music, in both formal and informal educational contexts for children of school age. Two main educational settings have been analyzed: compulsory, governmentally administered, and regulated education in primary schools (religious education—the Orthodox catechism); and the less formal educational setting of children's church choirs, organized outside school hours.

Music's Role in Spiritual Connection and Identity

Our theoretical perspective relies on the work of the sociologist Grace Davie and her typology of religious beliefs and belonging. Her influential concept, although questioned by some sociologists, has found its application in several areas, including in writing about churches, in the statements of religious leaders, in religious journalism, and so on (Davie 2012). Although Davie does not operationalize the concepts of believing and belonging fully, the first term refers to subjective religion (regular prayer, belief in God, belief in life after death, and the like), and the other features more objective aspects (church attendance, Baptism, etc.; Davie 1994). We find the way Isabella Kasselstrand elaborates Davie's idea of belonging very useful: she sees belonging as about more than attending church or participating in church activities. In her opinion, religious belonging includes membership (belonging to), identification (feeling that one belongs), and participation in religious rituals (Kasselstrand 2015).

To the best of our knowledge, the possibilities of the believing-belonging typology of religiosity have not been utilized much (if at all) in research on music and education. But the introduction of the sociological distinction between personal, subjective, or private religiosity (believing) and public, institutional, objective religiosity (belonging) is useful because of the light it may cast on our understanding of the dynamic relationship between music, education, and religion. Music may be a powerful catalyst in both believing and belonging. It may dynamically affect the way believing is developed and practiced, and it certainly has a direct influence on modes of belonging. From the theoretical perspective, the introduction of the believing-belonging model into our discussion on music, education, and religion has two important implications: one involving issues of epistemology and another involving issues of identity.

Religious knowledge is not necessarily verbal, and religious matters often exist beyond language. The gap between knowing and saying is particularly important for worship, since one of the most essential features of worship is "a sense of being in the presence of that which is beyond capture by human concepts" (Sloboda 2005, 351). As far as Orthodoxy is concerned, apophatic theology is based on the understanding that language is inadequate for the expression of God's nature. According to the twentieth century Orthodox theologian Vladimir

Lossky, "the human mind and human language are incommensurate with the divine reality" (Nichols 1999, 34). Music communicates certain things that cannot be communicated in any other way; the nature of musical knowledge may also be beyond language, as is the case with religion. In the educational context, the knowledge gained through religious music has a strong self-reflexive dimension (Radford 2001). Given the opportunity to musically express themselves, students can imagine and assert a reality that is truly their own.

Religious identity has an integrative nature; a sense of belonging is an important human need, and shared religious identities and beliefs build strong ties between members of a community. According to the philosopher Alain de Botton, the sense of community is central (De Botton 2012), even in contemporary atheist spirituality (Comte-Sponville 2007). It is interesting to compare June Boyce-Tillman's insightful comments in this volume, on fostering community at the university level in Britain, with the integrative role of religious identity for school-age children in Serbia.

Congregational identity is dynamic, mobile, and continuously formed and reformed through interactions between members of the religious community. Similarly, the processual nature of music makes it important in articulating personal and collective identity. As Simon Frith puts it, "music seems to be a key to identity because it offers, so intensely, a sense of both self and others, of the subjective in the collective" (1996, 110). From an educational point of view, engagement in music is a communal event that connects students and gives them "larger truths about what it means to be alive and human" (Palmer 2010, 164).

One Serbian sociologist of religion argues that, at the beginning of the twenty-first century, Orthodox Serbs "are religious in a manner of traditional belonging without believing" (Đorđević 2009, 64). Although it is statistically accurate, we find his image too generalized for the diverse Serbian society and want to evaluate whether his notion can be accepted or rejected within our framework. More precisely, we are interested in what can be learned when the two particular categories of Davie's typology ("believing and belonging" and "belonging without believing") are applied to the renewed connections between music, religion, and the education of school-age children in Serbia. Categories of "believing without belonging" and "not believing and not belonging" will not be elaborated on further here, as this research did not provide sufficient data to reach definite conclusions on those phenomena.

Since these topics have not been addressed in current (or previous) studies on music pedagogy in Serbia, or in research on musicology more generally, we cannot rely on published data or previous analysis. Therefore, our methodological approach combines the analysis of administrative documents, interviews with a small number of informants—four religious education teachers (Nena, Vlada, Bilja, and Anđelko) and three (plus one) conductors of children's choirs (Jelena, Maja, Ana; Nena is both a teacher and conductor), conducted especially for this publication during June and October of 2015—and relevant internet resources and personal experience and insights. Much work remains to be done, and this study is the first attempt to define this area of research at many different levels.

Religious Education in Serbia

Religious education in Serbia "was introduced under chaotic circumstances, shortly after the democratic changes following 5 October 2000, to which it was directly linked" (Aleksov 2004, 341). As a result, many problems occurred, including the issue of shared, but not clearly defined, responsibilities between the church and the state. The lack of integration of religious education into the official educational system governed by the Ministry of Education[2] has caused many problems, including a discrepancy between the content of textbooks and the practice of teaching, where religious teachers had to—and still have to—rely on their own resources.

The brochure "Religious Instruction in Schools in Serbia," prepared by the Ministries of Education and of Religious Affairs in 2001, stressed the importance of religious and cultural identity for the subject of religious education. Among the reasons for the selection of the Orthodox catechism was that parents often mentioned their expectations for "exploring the culture, religion, history" and "better understanding of national and European culture and art" (Joksimović 2003, 152). As Davie suggests, cultural memory associated with religion in modern Europe relies on artistic objects (including musical artifacts) and involves the "overlapping between the religious and the aesthetic spheres" (Davie 2000, 174). Aesthetic involvement in music is "both personal and at the same time a part of a unified common experience, and the sense of unity between the subjective self and the objective universe" (Radford 2001, 158). In that sense, it is close to spiritual and religious experience.

But the official curricula for Orthodox catechism in primary school (prescribed by the Serbian Ministry of Education) makes no mention of music or chant. It is interesting that Orthodox iconography, architecture, literature (the lives of the saints) and Serbian epic poetry are among the teaching content recommended for the second grade of primary school, but there is no reference to Serbian chant or congregational or choral singing. We can only make assumptions about why music has been omitted when other arts have been included. Perhaps the authors of the curriculum thought that music—as nonverbal, nonrepresentational, and nonvisual—is less accessible than painting, architecture, or literature. Or they may have considered that the introduction of music would require certain special skills that are not necessary when dealing with other arts. Whatever the reason, the unique educational potential of "music, where cognition and emotion meet" (Sloboda 2005, 333), the union so close to Orthodox believers, or the opportunities that making music as a source of knowledge can offer, have been missed. For example, in the curricula for the first and second grade of primary school available on the website of the Institute for the improvement of education, we read "The teaching of the Orthodox catechism in the first and second grade . . . should prepare students to accept that existence is a matter of participation, that is, that person is unity with other person" (ZUOV, n.d.). It goes without saying that the simple pleasure of communal singing would facilitate the acceptance of this—for children of this age—complex content. On the other hand, curricula continuously stress the importance of "membership": "What is most important, and that is the main objective of the catechism, is that students become members of the liturgical community. . . . Pupils should, whenever possible, attend—or refer to—the liturgical assembly" (ZUOV, n.d.).

Throughout the Orthodox church, music is regarded as a "form of Orthodox worship in its essence"—the same attitude is held by the Serbian Orthodox Church, evident through the words of the first Serbian patriarch St. Sava (1174 or 1175 to 1236): the soul of the monastery is "service in singing," the analyzed curricula have ignored this point. The contradiction becomes even greater when one thinks about the potential of music to bring together the religious and aesthetic, the goal almost explicitly stated by Serbian governmental institutions, but omitted from the official educational strategy. This phenomenon provokes a simple question: who actually controls religious education in Serbia?

A strong national concern has been the most important link between the church and secular politics in Serbia (Drezgić 2010). For the political authorities, the role of the national Orthodox Church is more important for its integrative function—in the sense of belonging—than for the promotion of religious beliefs. At this point, it becomes clear that the omission of music from the official curricula for religious education reflects a political, not religious, motivation. "Belonging without believing" here is a matter of national identification, a road to a "distant shared memory, which does not necessarily entail shared belief, but which still governs collective reflexes in terms of identity" (Hervieu-Léger 2006). In other words, it is not about religion at all, but about national belonging and identification through the perception of religion as the key vehicle for the protection and preservation of the nation.

On the other hand, the answers provided by religious education teachers imply different things. All the interviewed teachers agree on two points: the curriculum and textbooks are not appropriate for the age of the children, and their experience from teaching shows that songs make learning easier and knowledge more permanent. In some cases, music can be used to overcome issues arising from the first point, for example, when teaching the creation story from the book of Genesis in the first grade. Our informants emphasize that pupils at the age of six or seven grasp the long and complex content easily thanks to the simple strophic song "Stvorio je Bog" ("God created"). What is more important, they do not forget the song.

One informant provided similar observations and further elaborated on issues of the contextualization of the content, noting that the introduction of already familiar tunes in teaching gives the children the opportunity to build on existing (musical) knowledge: "The concepts discussed in the songs remain permanently adopted and it's easier for children to understand their meaning. . . . They are directly and personally involved in singing the song, they are direct participants and try to work it out better" (Vlada).

As Orthodox believers, teachers of religious education do not have doubts about whether their pupils are learning religion, learning *from* religion, or learning *about* religion. The first option is predominant, since their teaching is faith-based, and the object of their instruction is to "enable pupils to come to believe in the religion or to strengthen their commitment to it" (Schreiner 2002, 5). Some teachers emphasize the strong link between singing and believing and belonging:

> The ultimate goal of catechism is to bring the child to God and the Church.... So, while educating the children in the Church... we are trying to prepare them to be "citizens of the Kingdom of Heaven." To achieve this goal, the most important thing is their participation in the Divine Liturgy.... In that sense, singing is very important: when they learn to sing the Divine Liturgy, the children (as well as adults...) have that feeling of being a part of the one "Body of the Church." (Nena)

On the one hand, participation in the singing and chanting of the prescribed liturgical hymns is considered an important spiritual tool for drawing us closer to God—the "sung prayer"—and as an expression of believing. On the other hand, participation in the one "Body of the Church," which implies the simultaneity of self and others, the subjective and the collective, is significant for religious belonging. For some of our informants the Serbian chant, the authentic musical expression of the Serbian Orthodox Church since the eighteenth century, is an important tool in achieving course objectives: "The melodies of the traditional Church chant develop godliness among children" (Vlada). The singing of consecrated melodies, hymns used daily in regular church practice in Serbian churches and monasteries, also develops a sense of belonging.

There is one more important point. When asked about the sense of belonging within religious education, all our informants commented on Serbian national history, the motherland, the Serbian language, and folk music, and none of their comments dealt with religious belonging: membership, identification, and participation in religious rituals. Complex relationships between the state, educational institutions, and the Orthodox Church affect religious education. As the subject of "double jurisdiction," it cannot avoid a certain overlapping between the religious and political domains, where issues of belonging and identification are constantly revisited.

Children's Choirs

Revitalized Orthodoxy in contemporary Serbia has stimulated the foundation of numerous children's church choirs, and the incorporation of liturgical music into repertories of existing (secular) choirs. In 1999, the famous children's choir *Kolibri* (Hummingbird), working under the National Broadcasting Company, RTS, introduced sacred music into its repertory, on the initiative of their conductor for many years, Milica Manojlović. The first work performed by them was the best-known cycle of sacred choral music in Serbian history, the Divine Liturgy of St. John Chrysostom, composed by Stevan Stojanović Mokranjac in an arrangement specially produced by Vojislav Ilić, the celebrated Serbian conductor and composer. The CD featuring the Divine Liturgy was the best-selling CD of "art music" of PGP-RTS, the music production branch of the Serbian Broadcasting Company.

Three years later, in 2002, St. Simeon's Academy Day was celebrated with a performance of *The Serbian Divine Calendar*, written by contemporary Serbian composer Vera Milanković. Certain movements from the cycle were also performed by the *Kolibri* choir. "What civic society needs is to find an emotional and aesthetic pleasure in spiritual music"—was the composer's comment in the preface of the work (Milanković 2006, 5). The fact that "innocent children" accept the religious doctrines contained in the text, even if they are too complex for their age, provoked serious criticism in the mass media (Milanković 2003, 22). It is interesting that supporters of the religious repertory stressed that spiritual music has an important role in the shaping of civic identity. If religious education is something different from, or at least separated from, civic education in the Serbian educational system, what then is the role of religious music in civic identity? Through the complicated and intertwined process of national, class, and religious identity (re)construction in Serbia during the 2000s, the power of music with religious references was recognized by the media. Intensive support from the media—from the most powerful media entity, the National Broadcasting Company as well—has influenced the articulation of the discourse of "belonging without believing," where belonging is expressed more at the level of nationality than of Orthodox Christianity.

An insight into the activities of children's church choirs may offer some answers. As their work has not been researched previously, this part of the study will put a stronger emphasis on the informative angle, and the considerable number of quoted informants' replies will serve as a basis for further arguments. In contrast to the primarily secular choruses, for church choirs religious music is an everyday, actual, social, and musical experience. But even if their shared musical actions, deeply rooted in the church, reflect integrative aspects of their religious environment, they also provide a stable informal learning environment, where extensive knowledge is gained and multiple identities are built. In August 2014, goals and objectives of the choir of the Ascension Church in Belgrade were published on the website of the church: "The aim of the existence of this choir is not only the musical enrichment of children, but also the introduction of the rich tradition of the liturgical chant to our children. Of particular importance is the children learning and getting used to the liturgy for their active participation, as believers in worship" (Ascension Church 2014).

Some children's choirs have emerged from catechism schools held at churches, founded during the 1990s, prior to the official introduction of religious education in Serbian schools. Common expressions of praise through the singing of religious verses, set to simple tunes, seemed like a natural extension of Sunday school activities. Other choirs were founded during the 2000s, after some new churches were built. The choir singers are children between the ages of 3 and 15 years, usually members of the parish community. Not all the children come from families of believers, although such cases are prevalent. Children from religious families are encouraged and supported by their parents to participate in all aspects of church life, including singing at the worship services, musical socializing after the Divine Liturgy, choral rehearsals, and so on. In this sense, participation in the choir encourages religious enthusiasm and offers further support to believing and belonging. Our informants stated, however, that it sometimes happens that an (unbaptized) child who sings in the choir brings her or his parents to church, and some even to baptism (Jelena). In such cases, music is an agent of change, not only of personal attitude toward religion, but also of an entire family's point of view.

Choir membership is free, which is an additional motivation for gifted children from families of a lower economic status. Some conductors recruit even nonmusical children: "I can see that some children are lagging behind in musical development, that others are disturbed. . . . Then something happens, and they start singing beautifully. There are two such girls who even opted for music later" (Maja). The dominant ethos is based on the principle of belonging, while making music is the glue that holds everything together.

The engagement of the choirs varies, mostly according to the conductor's selections. Some choirs participate regularly in the Divine Liturgy, and others sing several liturgical hymns each Sunday or for every feast. There are choirs that sing only on certain occasions, for example, during the festive procession around the church and for vespers on "Vrbica" ("Little Willows"—a Serbian Orthodox custom on Lazarus Saturday),[3] and others gather in the singing of spiritual, nonliturgical songs in the churchyard after the Divine Liturgy. One informant noted that "singing after liturgies on major holidays is the most joyous and magnificent, everyone wants to participate. When adults hear children singing, they are amazed, sometimes even ashamed when they see how much the children know, and they do not know" (Nena).

Conductors select the pieces to be sung, in consultation with the rector of the church, from among the compositions that they find most suitable for the level and preferences of the children. Some decisions are deeply personal and based on individual religious, educational, aesthetic, artistic, and other views. Some informants expressed preference for chanting in unison over singing in harmony: "When the monophonic liturgical singing of our children is accompanied by ison [drone], their facial expressions are different; the entire atmosphere is changed, calm" (Maja).

In certain ensembles, the selection depends on what the children like. If they recognize some music as beautiful, spiritual, sublime, and so on, they will sing it for several years: "Once I was amazed when I brought "Svjati Bože" [Holy God] by Kornelije Stanković to younger grades in school. Their energy of singing was unforgettable—not the beauty of the singing, they still have not learned the piece, but they recognized the spiritual beauty of music in the traditional Serbian Church melody that excited them" (Ana).

In the Orthodox liturgical setting, music serves the text, and so choral conductors pay close attention to the text. Children should have a basic understanding of the text and its content, even if it is in Church Slavonic, the official language of worship of the Serbian Orthodox Church. This language is practically foreign to the children, and rehearsals often begin with translating and commenting on the most important messages conveyed through the text. Conductors have developed a personal sensitivity to the texts and individual methods in introducing children to religious texts: "Children have to understand that these are not 'little songs,' but prayers to God! I explain the meaning of the text and translate it into Serbian simultaneously, so that they can understand it in the same way as we adults do" (Jelena).

In some other children's choirs, Church Slavonic words are learned by repetition: "They are just rhythmically 'rapping' the text, phrase by phrase, till they learn it" (Ana). All conductors pay careful attention that children learn to enunciate and articulate the text in a clear and natural manner.

Participation in a church choir offers a range of knowledge to children. From the perspective of the believing-belonging model, the fact that the process of learning is contextualized and integrated is more important than the individual areas in which children acquire knowledge or the amount of factual knowledge or skills they take on. The internal and external church ambience is a special and unique learning environment, where architecture, images, sounds, fragrances, and so on are united with Orthodox spirituality and perpetual loyalty to the tradition. Such an environment, characterized by aesthetic and artistic stability, reduces the impact of daily unpredictability, rapid changes in socioeconomic conditions, disturbed systems of values, and so on. In such a milieu, traditional learning focused on topics is replaced by a sophisticated intersection of believing-belonging, living and learning, collaboration and engagement. Children are motivated by the emotional, evocative, transformative, and other powers of music. It is not rare that children "from atheist families who know nothing about Orthodoxy ask to sing in our Church over and over again" (Ana). Indeed, one conductor's strong experiences with religious music ("the most intense experience of music," Gabrielsson 2010, 551) within a liturgical context, had a ripple effect on her own religiosity.[4]

The knowledge gained through participation in the children's choir is an umbrella concept: on one hand, it includes theoretical and practical action and factual knowledge of music, religion, ethics, art, history, culture, and other areas; on the other hand, it is a knowledge that helps "the person to maintain the cognitive structure of the self.... What a person defines as his or her being" (Csikszentmihalyi and Schiefele 1992, 172).

As previously mentioned, different types of knowledge are combined to enable children to participate musically in worship: "Things are carried simultaneously on several levels: a practical knowledge of music, the church, general education, religious education, music theory.... All aspects are taught at the same time.... It's a mix, a drop of this, a drop of that, essences, to make them able to accept something" (Jelena).

Apart from being realistic, this approach puts learning in the practical and current context of a national and Orthodox Church.

In addition, conductors emphasize that musical participation in church choirs affects children's behavior and social cohesion through the process of identity construction. Social cohesion is particularly important in overcoming difficulties and conflicts: "We all feel like a family. Everyone's acting like brothers and sisters; this is especially true for the church choir. I never felt this in the school choir. Conflicts occur in the church choir, but rarely, and they are easily overcome" (Maja). Different aspects of belonging to a group that shares religious values and musical preferences are important for personal, as well as for collective, identity. Thus, singing in the choir helps children navigate the process of development and transformation.

Conclusion

This chapter has analyzed the role of music in the relationship between believing and belonging in the Serbian formal and informal educational context, in a historical moment marked by an greater interest in and influence of religion. In particular, this chapter has argued that two types of relationships are relevant for the subject: "belonging without believing" and "believing and belonging," where belonging may have a national or religious dimension. The first one is practiced more openly, with the support of governmental institutions and with more prominent media coverage. Sociological claims that Serbian Orthodox society could be described in terms of "traditional belonging without believing" are confirmed by our analysis of the official discourse and the role of music in religious education (within a formal educational context) and public performances. The other model, "believing and belonging," is less visible in the public sphere, but no less vital, and uses music as the mediator for religious understanding, beliefs, and identification. At the intersection between believing and belonging, music reinforces these effects in an informal educational context and strongly affects the process of contextualized learning.

IVANA PERKOVIĆ is Professor in the Department of Musicology, Faculty of Music, University of Arts, in Belgrade, Serbia. She is the author of books on the Serbian Oktoechos modal system, Serbian choral church music, and the history of the Faculty of Music in Belgrade.

BILJANA MANDIĆ is Assistant Professor at the Faculty of Philology and Arts, University of Kragujevac, in Serbia, where she is Head of the Music Theory and Pedagogy Program. She is the author of six textbooks and two manuals in the field of music education.

Notes

Research for this article was done partly in the context of the project "Identiteti srpske muzike u svetskom kulturnom kontekstu"/Identities of Serbian Music in the World Cultural Context/ ref. no. 177019, supported by the Ministry of Education, Science and Technological Development of the Republic of Serbia.

    1. Eastern Orthodoxy is the main religion in Serbia: almost 85 percent citizens are adherents of the Serbian Orthodox Church. For this reason, this study deals only with Orthodoxy.

2. Currently the Ministry of Education, Science, and Technological Development.
3. Lazarus Saturday: the Saturday before Palm Sunday.
4. "The most beautiful liturgy I experienced was in Bliškovo Monastery in Montenegro. I do not know how we sang, it was a vortex of energy, even now it gives me chills. I don't know what we sang, we just sang and felt abnormal energy. It came from the altar, through us, I didn't isolate it—God, thank you" (Ana).

References

Ascension Church in Belgrade. 2014. "Choir." Accessed August 1, 2015. http://њњњ .вазнесењскацрква.српe/en/2014-08-01-17-40-10/2014-08-05-15-48-48.html
Aleksov, Bojan. 2004. "Religious Education in Serbia. Religion." *State and Society* 32, no. 4: 341–63.
Blagojević, Mirko. 2008. "Desecularization of Contemporary Serbian Society." *Religion in Eastern Europe* 27, no. 1: 37–50.
Comte-Sponville, André. 2007. *The Little Book of Atheist Spirituality.* Translated by Nancy Huston. New York: Viking Press.
Csikszentmihalyi, Mihaly, and Schiefele Ulrich. 1992. "Arts Education, Human Development, and the Quality of Experience." In *Arts in Education: Ninety-First Yearbook of the National Society for the Study of Education,* edited by Bennett Reimer and Ralph A. Smith, 169–91. Chicago: University of Chicago Press.
Davie, Grace. 1994. *Religion in Britain since 1945: Believing without Belonging.* Oxford, UK: Blackwell.
———. 2000. *Religion in Modern Europe: A Memory Mutates.* New York: Oxford University Press.
———. 2012. "From Believing without Belonging to Vicarious Religion: Understanding the Patterns of Religion in Modern Europe." In *The Role of Religion in Modern Societies,* edited by Detlef Pollack and Daniel Olson, 165–76. Abingdon, UK: Routledge.
De Botton, Alain. 2012. *Religion for Atheists: A Non believer's Guide to the Uses of Religion.* London: Hamish Hamilton.
Đorđević, Dragoljub. 2009. "Religiousness of Serbs at the Beginning of the 21st Century: What Is It About?" In *Revitalization of Religion: Theoretical and Comparative Approaches,* edited by Danijela Gavrilović, 57–64. Niš, Serbia: YSSSR.
Drezgić, Rada. 2010. "Religion, Politics and Gender in the Context of Nation-State Formation: The Case of Serbia." *Third World Quarterly* 31, no. 6: 955–70.
Frith, Simon. 1996. "Music and Identity." In *Questions of Cultural Identity,* edited by Stuart Hall and Paul du Gay, 108–27. London: Sage.
Gabrielsson, Alf. 2010. "Strong Experiences with Music." In *Handbook of Music and Emotion: Theory, Research, Applications,* edited by Patrik N. Juslin and John Sloboda, 547–74. New York: Oxford University Press.
Hervieu-Léger, Danièle. 2006. "The Role of Religion in Establishing Social Cohesion." *Eurozine,* August 17. http://www.eurozine. com/articles/2006-08-17-hervieuleger -en.html.
Joksimović, Snežana, ed. 2003. *Verska nastava i građansko vaspitanje u školama u Srbiji* [Religious and civic education at schools in Serbia]. Belgrade: Institut za pedagoška istraživanja.
Kasselstrand, Isabella. 2015. "Nonbelievers in the Church: A Study of Cultural Religion in Sweden." *Sociology of Religion* 76, no. 2: 1–20.

Milanković, Vera. 2003. *Kolibri* [Hummingbird]. Belgrade: RTS.
———. 2006. *Serbian Divine Calendar*. Belgrade: Clio.
Nichols, Aidan. 1999. *Light from the East: Authors and Themes in Orthodox Theology*. London: Sheed and Ward.
Palmer, Anthony. 2010. "Spirituality in Music Education: Transcending Culture, Exploration III." *Philosophy of Music Education Review* 18, no. 2: 152–70.
Radford, Mike. 2001. "Aesthetic and Religious Awareness among Pupils: Similarities and Differences." *British Journal of Music Education* 18, no. 2: 151–59.
Schreiner, Peter. 2002. "Models of Religious Education in Schools in Europe." Paper presented at the Strategy Development Seminar of the Oslo Coalition on Freedom of Religion or Belief, Oslo, December 7–9, 2002. folk.uio.no/leirvik/OsloCoalition/Schreiner1202.doc.
Sloboda, John. 2005. *Exploring the Musical Mind: Cognition, Emotion, Ability, Function*. Oxford: Oxford University Press.
ZUOV (Institute for Improvement in Education). n.d. Nastavni planovi i programi. Accessed July 15, 2015. https://zuov.gov.rs/nastavni-planovi-i-programi/.

7 | Religious Repertoire in General Music Education: Spiritual Indoctrination or Cultural Dialogue?

Lauri Väkevä

The Case of *Suvivirsi*

There is a recurring leitmotif in Finnish discourse that intimately concerns the subject of this book. Every spring, the common practice of singing a particular hymn in public schools is questioned, leading to a more-or-less heated discussion of the relationship between education, religion, and music. The hymn is called *Suvivirsi* (lit., "Summer hymn"), number 571 in the Finnish Evangelical Lutheran hymnal (*Virskirja* 1986). *Suvivirsi* is commonly sung in public ceremonies of Finnish schools to herald the beginning of the summer holiday, making it one of the best-known Lutheran songs in Finnish culture.[1]

Those who question the presence of *Suvivirsi* in public-school ceremonies usually refer to the regulation restricting devotional practices in Finnish public schools. This regulation is based on the Finnish Constitution, which acknowledges every citizen's positive and negative freedom of religion, stating that "no one is under the obligation, against his or her conscience, to participate in the practice of a religion" (Constitution of Finland 1999, 3). *Suvivirsi* is a Lutheran hymn, and because Lutheran hymns are composed in order to be sung as part of religious rituals, incorporating them into a public-school ceremony implies that the latter is a religious ritual (see, e.g., Heinimäki and Niemelä 2011).[2] There have been various responses to this argument. Because the premise that denominational religious material should not be imposed on every student is widely accepted, justifications for maintaining the practice have been mainly sought by denying the validity of the other premise, namely, that singing *Suvivirsi* makes a school ceremony devotional.

Many of those who defend the singing of the hymn at school refer to its central place in Finnish cultural tradition, which, according to the argument, distances a religious song (or at least this one) from its original religious meaning when sung in a school ceremony intended for all Finns. Hence, singing the song in a church would be an entirely different thing from singing it as part of a school gathering. Some also argue that *Suvivirsi* has significance as a national symbol, making it worthy for all Finns to sing, regardless of their faith, as a token of their patriotic sentiment—which is perhaps somewhat surprising, since the hymn is of Swedish origin![3]

The debate over *Suvivirsi* in schools has, for the most part, remained informal, waged in the pages of newspapers by various public interest groups and politicians.[4] But senior bureaucrats have also intervened in such disputes. Such thread of discussion arose in March 2014 when, in response to an anonymous complaint filed to the Finnish Chancellor of Justice, Deputy Chancellor Mikko Puumalainen issued the following statement (excerpt):

> I see it as problematic from the standpoint of religious freedom and equality that ... events ... are organized in schools that have religious content and that can be even taken as confessional by content.... Ceremonial traditions may include confessional elements, even if the ceremonies would not otherwise be religious or confessional.... While one particular hymn would not ... change the ceremony to religious practice, such particular hymn can still have significance from the standpoint of freedom of religion (Uskonnon harjoittaminen kouluissa 2013, 8).[5]

Puumalainen justified this as follows:

> Even if following the traditions can be valuable in itself, in legal surveillance one has to take as one's point of departure the content of the tradition from the standpoint of, among other things, fundamental rights. To maintain that the school ceremonies are part of Finnish culture and tradition is likely to create an oppressing element.... Because the teachers are in an authority position in relation to the underage students, in [ceremonial] situations the oppressive element may become emphasized and can amount to the child's fear of being left out. It is also necessary to ask why the common festivals or end-of-the-season ceremonies in school should ... be integrated into the practicing of religion, and in this way, why their communal nature should be broken.... Both from the standpoint of negative freedom of religion and European Court of Human Rights juridical practice, it would be better justified ... that, no events led by the teachers, other school personnel, or personnel of a congregation that include content of certain conviction would be organized in schools (Uskonnon harjoittaminen kouluissa 2013, 9–10).

Referring to earlier decisions by the European Court of Human Rights (ECHR), Puumalainen argued that it might be seen as unethical to subject someone to certain religious practice in public school against his or her will, even when the context would not be predominantly religious. Puumalainen also stated that "references to the traditions do not ... liberate the state from its duty to obey the rights secured in the European Convention on Human Rights" (Uskonnon harjoittaminen kouluissa 2013, 4).

Even if the practice of singing *Suvivirsi* was not really the main point of Puumalainen's statement, he implied that even one hymn could be interpreted as a religious practice when sung as part school ceremonies intended for the participation of all students. Indeed, when asked by the media about how *Suvivirsi* should be dealt with in schools from then on, the chancellor's representative specified that "*Suvivirsi* is also religious," thus implying it would not be an exception to the rule (Reinboth 2014a).

Thus, the hymn again became the focus of public debate, also made timely by the impending end-of-school ceremonies. On the basis of Puumalainen's statement, the National Board of Education began checking the instructions to be issued to schools, despite considerable dissent from some educational administrators and teachers (Yleisradio 2014a). Fueled by immense media coverage, a wave of public protest erupted, led by several politicians and opinion leaders, who used the case of *Suvivirsi* as an opportunity to indicate their public stances on matters of religion, culture, and society. The Office of the Deputy Chancellor received more than one hundred complaints in response to Puumalainen's statement (Yleisradio 2014e), some of which assumed that Puumalainen had specifically targeted *Suvivirsi* in making his statement. The public debate also became fertile ground for the expressing of extreme social and political views: "Now these hymnbook clowns, counselors and deputy counselors of justice etc. collect sympathies to their decisions from immigrants, gays, and all sorts of atheists" (Reinboth 2014b).

In the ensuing public discussion, several politicians testified about the validity of the Constitutional Law Committee's earlier decision that singing a hymn in a public-school ceremony should be seen as a cultural tradition rather than as devotional practice. Some also argued that to oppose singing *Suvivirsi* in such ceremonies is to oppose the ways of the Finnish cultural majority, and thus impinged on their positive freedom of religion. The debate culminated in one representative of the nationalist party "the Finns," Vesa-Matti Saarakkala, proposing a new law for the Finnish Parliament that would secure the place of Christian devotional practices in public schools (Saarakkala 2014). Around the country, there were also public demonstrations where people sang *Suvivirsi* together, voicing their support for its inclusion as part of school celebrations.

So efficient was the public counterstrike, that considerable pressure arose for the Constitutional Law Committee to reevaluate the matter.[6] A new statement was issued after the committee had consulted legal experts (Yleisradio 2014b), making it clear that Finnish schools can continue the practice of singing *Suvivirsi* and other hymns in public-school ceremonies, and that such singing does not impinge on anyone's negative freedom of religion, as the hymns are not considered religious within such a context. This decision apparently satisfied the majority, but for some it may still raise two questions: What makes a song religious in the first place? And on what premises can it be decided that a religious song becomes secular in another context? (Yleisradio 2014d).

It seems that a line was crossed in the 2014 *Suvivirsi* disputes, politicizing the entire discussion. While politicians of every stripe defended the singing of *Suvivirsi*, representatives of the nationalist party were exceptionally vocal, perhaps empowered by their recent success at the polls. All this may be taken as a sign of an emerging need to renegotiate the role of the majority denomination in Finnish public educational institutions, as the society is rapidly gaining awareness of its multiculturality and multireligiosity. Majority rights were certainly brought to the fore. Whether religious minorities were, or continue to be, heard in this discussion, largely depends on how well they are able to present their case in future debates.

The Changing Role of Religious Music in Finnish Public Schools

If there is a notion that unifies contemporary observations on the state of Finnish society, it is that, today, the society faces an increasing multitude of views on politics, society, and culture. This is also true of religious views (Kallioniemi 2005). Nevertheless, Finnish society has remained relatively monoreligious. Despite the steady decrease in membership in the Evangelical Lutheran Church, as of December 2013, 75.3 percent of the population still officially associated themselves with this denomination (Statistics Finland 2013); indeed, it has been said that Finland is the most Lutheran country in the world. Whatever the reality, it can hardly be doubted that the Evangelical Lutheran church has played a decisive role in shaping Finnish cultural sensibility and identity and that music has been one of the fields where this shaping has taken place.

As in other European countries with a Protestant majority, the singing of a religious repertoire in Finnish schools has a long history (Pajamo 1976; Vapaavuori 1997), and Lutheran hymns have played an important role in Finnish public education from the Reformation to the twenty-first century. In addition to teaching children applicable skills and knowledge, Finnish schools were for a long time expected to prepare students for congregational life. Consequently, when the Finnish common school (*kansakoulu*, lit., "folk school") was established in the latter half of the nineteenth century, it was largely seen as a preparatory school for confirmation. While the operation of public schools was transferred from the church to the state in 1866, religious songs were still assumed to constitute the most important repertoire for singing in schools. That said, it is worth noting that in the state-regulated common school, the role of singing religious material was not understood to be merely congregational. Rather, hymns and other religious songs were seen to contribute to the holistic education of the child. This thinking was in line with the Lutheran view that a religious upbringing and an education for secular life should blend seamlessly.[7] It was also in line with Luther's personal conviction that congregational singing has an important role in ensuring an individual's wellbeing.[8]

In sociological terms, the fact that hymn singing was accepted to have various roles in the school already in the nineteenth century can perhaps be understood as a first sign of ideological differentiation, which eventually disconnected religious education from music education. The process took a considerable amount of time. In the 1985 National Core Curriculum, "music of the religions" was still seen as one of the six mandatory content areas of music education (*Peruskoulun opetussuunnitelman perusteet* 1985; *Peruskoulun opetuksen opas: musiikki* 1987, 1).[9] The late 1980s also witnessed the issuing of a national plan for teaching Lutheran hymns in comprehensive schools (*Peruskoulun virsisuunnitelma* 1987; see also Pajamo 1988, 1991). In the 1994 National Core Curriculum, religious repertoire was no longer mandatory, no doubt reflecting a change from subject-oriented lesson planning to a more open curriculum. It may also be seen as a manifestation of increasing differentiation between religious and secular education. In the 2004 National Core

Curriculum, hymns were mentioned only as part of the Lutheran religious education curriculum (*Perusopetuksen opetussuunnitelman perusteet* 2004, 204–5), which meant that students from other denominations were no longer obligated to learn or perform them. In this light, it is perhaps understandable that some people oppose singing Lutheran hymns as part of public-school ceremonies intended for all students. After all, even the national curriculum states that hymns belong *exclusively* to Lutheran religious education. Then again, the long history of congregational songs in public education may explain why many Finns are also reluctant to relinquish hymn singing altogether.[10]

Religious School Music as a Practice of Civil Religion

I have thus far discussed the reluctance of many Finns to accept the claim that such hymns as *Suvivirsi* should be omitted from public-school ceremonies because of their religious connotations. Does such reluctance suggest a need to recognize the rights of the religious majority, as I have suggested? Or, does it reflect a wider concern for the education of all students? In this section, I will examine this question from the standpoint of civil religion.

Stemming from Rousseau's theory of the social contract (Rousseau 2019 [1762], bk. 4, ch. 8), civil religion refers to a public mentality that unites a state by providing its operations with an aura of the sacrosanct, defining the identity of its inhabitants as citizens. In Rousseau, such a mentality consists of "social sentiments without which a man cannot be a good citizen or a faithful subject" (bk. 4, ch. 8). Rousseau took civil religion, not such as is practiced in church but in state-owned institutions, to be necessary for the social cohesion of a state. Émile Durkheim (1961) later argued that schools were one such institution where civil religion was to be implemented. In turn, Robert Bellah (1967, 1) has argued that civil religion manifests as "a set of beliefs, symbols, and rituals" that marks "certain common elements of religious orientation that the great majority of [citizens] share." Noticing the semisecular character of such beliefs, perhaps civil religion can also be understood as a secularized, nontheistic version of a theistic religion. As such, the concept may offer an opportunity to understand why those who are not attracted to ecclesiastical religions might nevertheless partake in seemingly devotional practices and rituals in the public sphere. This would mean that the state would assume the institutional role that was previously assigned to the church or other religious bodies.

To return to our theme of religious music in Finnish public schools, it is worth noting the ways in which music education was advocated when the first common-school curriculum was introduced (Pajamo 1976; Väkevä 2015). The very first public arguments over what music should be taught in common schools focused almost exclusively on three kinds of songs: religious, national, and folk songs.[11] While the demand for singing a religious repertoire in Finnish schools was based on the vital role that such singing had in Lutheran congregational life, ideals noting the importance of national and folk songs drew on the values of national romanticism, which implied that education in the arts should serve the realization of the spiritual *telos* of the budding nation. This was also the function that many Finnish intellectuals granted to the arts: they saw artworks as expressions of national spirit, devoted to the political cause of the national state, manifest in the culture of an ethical community that is comparable to the other civilized societies in Europe.[12] It can be argued that music thus served a dual role in the formation of the Finnish nation: on one hand, providing a means for growing the people into political maturity; on the other, providing symbols that signified that Finns were capable of producing their own culture, thus justifying the nation's position among the ranks of civilized nations.

Against this backdrop, it is easy to understand why the functions of the state and religion have coalesced in Finnish history. As Mikkola (2004) has argued, it is possible to interpret Finnish nationalism as a social phenomenon motivated by religion and at the same time as a religion in itself (see also Alasuutari 1996). In sociological terms, Finnish nationalism may be understood as an ideologically guided system of belief that has gradually differentiated itself from the belief system of the Evangelical Lutheran Church, with this process already taking seed in the mid-nineteenth century. Even if such a differentiation can be understood as a process of secularization, from another perspective it offers the basis for seeing religious sentiments as the responsibility of the state, as part of a larger cultural political project. Even today, as the commonly heard tripartite motto *Koti, Uskonto, Isänmaa* ("Home, religion, fatherland") suggests in Finnish public discourse, there appears to be a longing for a "comprehensive, self-contained, and integrated system of representation" that could relieve the anxiety of social differentiation and cultural fragmentation of late modern society and its fragmenting institutions (Anttila 1993, 122; see also Sevänen 1998).

Such "unifying systems of representation" may be theoretically understood from the standpoint of interpenetration. As developed from Parson's ideas by Münch (2001), *interpenetration* refers to cultural processes, in which two or more differentiated social "spheres of action" overlap with the aid of a "voluntaristic order" that provides the basis for their reintegration. Through such reintegration, the effects of social differentiation may be augmented, with common interests binding differentiated social systems together. According to Münch (1987, 21, 27), such common interests frame their own "zones of interpenetration" that help social actors apply shared ideological resources in coordinating and justifying their actions in diverse social systems.

On the basis of Münch's theory, Sevänen (1998) has argued that, because of interpenetration, modernist differentiation took place in Finnish society within a framework of a tightly knit infrastructure that united the interests of people operating in different spheres of action. The first indication of this unification was the potential of nationalism to appeal to people across social boundaries. Another unifying factor may have been the symbolic order of the Lutheran church, which, despite the secularization of Finnish society during the twentieth century, has proved to be a powerful ingredient in the cultural identification of the civic mentality.

The arts, music included, can also be taken as zones of interpenetration, because they also provide unifying ideological symbolic orders that help people to coordinate their lives between social systems. When symbolizing national aspirations, the arts offer "safe" places for people's interests to convene, for they support the political project of recognizing a unified nation, in spite of differing religious or other personal beliefs. From this standpoint, the current widespread acceptance of religious singing in Finnish public schools can perhaps be seen as a manifestation of a civil mentality that resists modern differentiation. In this sense, hymn singing in schools might also serve to transcend the lines demarcated by differentiated social institutions, by becoming an institution in itself. Whether people outside the Lutheran majority are to accept such institutions as guiding their lives depends on whether they agree that the symbolic order of the majority serves the common cause of the entire nation. Be that as it may, it is surely more convenient to argue for inclusion of a religious repertoire in Finnish school ceremonies on cultural or national terms than in terms of religious upbringing.

Singing *Suvivirsi* in a Public-School Ceremony: Critical *Bildung* or Spiritual Indoctrination?

This takes us to my final theme, which I will approach armed with the German concept of *Bildung* (*sivistys* in Finnish).[13] *Bildung* has had different interpretations in educational literature, but the reading that has mostly influenced Finnish discourse originated in the eighteenth- and early-nineteenth-century writings of Herder, Hegel, and the so-called New Humanists active in the German language area. For Hegel, *Bildung* marked a process through which an individual subject grows into full spiritual maturity in terms of the ethical order (*Sittlichkeit*) of a society.[14] If *Bildung* is interpreted in this way as an endogenous process of self-cultivation, a question emerges: what is the relationship of this process to publicly maintained and regulated education? This problem has largely defined continental educational philosophy in the modern era. One possible response to the problem is to make a distinction between socialization and *Bildung* and to argue that *both* influence the way education is organized (Siljander 1997). Such a position reminds us that, whenever social institutions are intervening with processes of *Bildung*, issues of power necessarily arise (Siljander, Kivelä, and Sutinen 2012; Väkevä 2012).

Critical notions of *Bildung* can be understood as perspectives that focus on this relation between self-cultivation and the coercive effect of society. From the standpoint of critical theory, this relation is mediated by social institutions that justify their operations in ideological terms. While school is undoubtedly the most important pedagogical institution in modern societies—and thus is an important framing condition for *Bildung*—family, religious organizations, and other social formations also influence the process of self-cultivation. In a highly differentiated late modern society, with a variety of interest groups that negotiate how education should intervene with the growth of the individual, the cultural interpenetration of social systems may offer a common symbolic ground on which to build consensus. From the critical standpoint, however, interpenetration may also conceal underlying ideological tensions that need to be brought to light, analyzed, and—when found to be problematic—contested (Kincheloe 2007; Nielsen 2007; Sünker 2006).

Often, when the negative consequences of education on an individual's growth are considered, the concept of *indoctrination* pops up. Many educational theorists have held this term to mark an educative process gone wrong, even if, before the mid-twentieth century, the word was not commonly applied pejoratively (Thiessen 1993). According to contemporary definitions, *indoctrination* refers to a process in which students are inculcated into certain doctrines, or bodies of principles (MOT 2013, s.v. *indoktrinaatio*). Severely restricting the students' freedom of self-determination, indoctrination presents itself as antithetical to *Bildung* and, thus, is a critical point on which to anchor a discussion of the relationship between school and society.

In recent years, some educational theorists have argued that the concept of indoctrination is not precise enough to be used as a means of educational criticism (Puolimatka 1997; Tan 2004; Thiessen 1993).[15] According to these critics, philosophical attempts to define indoctrination fail—not because indoctrination does not occur, but because it is not easy to see how certain subject matter, certain ways of teaching, or even certain intentions and purposes fulfill its conditions. Whether teaching is to be understood as indoctrination is thus a very contextual matter.

Attempts to define indoctrination are often criticized as support for religious, moral, or political education (Puolimatka 1997). But charges of indoctrination have also been raised against secular education. For instance, according to Wahlström (2009, 158), the European Convention of Human Rights was originally conceived to "secure an education that was not indoctrinating," as after World War II, Western Europe sought a way to articulate educational ideals that were antagonistic to those that guided education behind the Iron Curtain, especially ideals that opposed religious education. For many representatives, an important goal of the European human rights project was to secure Western European parents' right to decide the religious education of their children. Such rights were generally understood to be necessary conditions for *Bildung*. In this light, it is easy to see why accusations that equate religious education with indoctrination are frequently met critically in European pedagogical discussion.

If we return to the Finnish *Suvivirsi* debate, it is also interesting to note that in 2014 the original complaint addressed to the Finnish chancellor of justice asked him "to investigate, whether public and publicly funded . . . schools and upper high schools *(lukiot)* . . . operate against the provisions of equity and freedom of religion and conscience, as articulated in European Convention of Human Rights, when organizing religious practices during the school hours" (Uskonnon harjoittaminen kouluissa 2013, 1). The complainant observed that "the habit of including the practicing of religion in [school] activities . . . leads to dividing the students into two groups according to their conviction" (1). Such segregation, according to the complainant, takes place frequently in "school services, religious day's opening ceremonies (*aamunavauksissa*), and other religious events organized in schools."

Two observations are in order here. First, both the original complaint and the ensuing statement of the deputy chancellor interpreted the human rights convention primarily from the standpoint of negative freedom of religion, even if the convention was originally established with positive freedom of religion in mind. Whether this is the best way to address the case of religious music in schools today may be problematized on the basis of this historical fact, without entering into discussion about the educational benefits of such music. The crucial issue would then be, whether hurting the negative freedom of a minority is sometimes necessary in order to secure the positive freedoms of the majority, or vice versa.[16] This is surely a contextual and political issue, which means that the tables are easily turned with societal change. Second, the original complaint was not targeted exclusively at the Finnish tradition of singing *Suvivirsi*, or any other song, but more generally against imposing devotional practices of certain denominations on all students. While *Suvivirsi* may be seen as a positive symbol for national-cultural consensus, and its incorporation into a public-school ceremony may be taken as a polite egalitarian nod to the authority of the religious majority, its acceptance as educative content that is necessary for the general *Bildung* process of every student may be disputed on the basis of its being a Lutheran hymn. Then again, the song can also be defended on the same grounds.

The complaint that ignited the 2014 *Suvivirsi* debate seems to have been motivated by the observation that Finnish schools frequently work in cooperation with major congregations (mainly the Evangelical Lutheran), organizing public events and ceremonies together. According to the complaint, when addressed to all students, such ceremonies may be problematic, not only in theoretical terms of endangering the negative freedom of religion, but also because they lead to treating minority students in a potentially indoctrinating manner or at least insensitively—for instance, when non-Lutheran Evangelical students have to be led outside the ceremonial hall during a ceremony that should accommodate all students, which seems to be the case in some schools. At the most intense phase of this discussion, a public report addressed to the Ministry of Education and the Board of Education, signed by two representatives of the "www.et-opetus.fi" community (dated May 11, 2014),[17] also testified that many non-Lutheran parents, teachers, and students have experienced problems in cases in which Lutheran religious performances and public prayers have been organized in public schools.[18] While such practices may be taken as examples of how education supports *Bildung* by addressing a subject matter that holds deep significance to many Finns, they may also be taken as antithetical to the ideal of *Bildung*, perhaps even as indoctrinatory, to the degree that they do not involve the critical selection of educational content in relation to the students' emerging life contexts. In critical theories of *Bildung*, such informed selection would be a key determinant of education done right.

Conclusion

To summarize this discussion, at present, a number of Finns, perhaps even an increasing number, seem not to be satisfied with the Constitutional Law Committee's decision to include Lutheran hymns in public-school ceremonies on the grounds that they contribute to the cultural or civic *Bildung* of all students. For these Finns, it is a living option to consider all hymn singing as religious practice, and cases where such singing is expected from all as forms of religious, or perhaps spiritual, indoctrination. This view does not have to depend in any way on the changing roles and multiple functions of the religious repertoire in Finnish culture. A hymn is a hymn, and as such, cannot (and perhaps should not) sever its association with Lutheran devotional life.

From the standpoint of this opinion group, it would be probably be the safest bet to organize public-school ceremonies in ways that could not be associated with religious rituals, at least in any direct way. Then again, even if *Suvivirsi* has obviously won a place in the hearts of the Finnish majority, to oppose its singing in public-school ceremonies does not deny its cultural or national significance. While it is a hymn, it is a historical landmark in the Finnish school singing repertoire and can be appreciated (or depreciated) accordingly. What the opposition to it can remind us of is that, today, Finnish public schools increasingly cater to a variety of students from different cultural backgrounds within or outside the nation's borders, expressing a variety of different attitudes toward devotional practices, together with an increasing awareness of their rights to both positive and negative freedom of religion. As time goes by, such attitudes may also inspire criticism against secular forms of religion, perhaps even leading to changing the symbolic orders of interpenetration targeted at unifying the Finnish people as a nation. If this takes place, other symbolic orders might be needed, and to the degree that they may be incorporated into education, they must be chosen with an eye both on the global, continental, and national legalization and on the critical need to educate individuals as culturally reflective ethical agents. Music educators should be aware of such factors and, when needed, show tolerance toward differing views, including when they contest traditional ways of music making.

Acknowledgments

This study has been conducted as part of the ArtsEqual research project, funded by the Strategic Research Council of the Academy of Finland and its Equality in Society strategic research program (project number 293199).

LAURI VÄKEVÄ is Professor of Music Education at the Sibelius Academy, University of the Arts–Helsinki, Finland. He is the editor of *Future Prospects for Music Education: Corroborating Informal Learning Pedagogy* (together with Sidsel Karlsen) and of *De-Canonizing Music History* (together with Vesa Kurkela).

Notes

This chapter is based on my keynote presentation at the Critical Perspectives on Music Education and Religion conference at Sibelius Academy of the University of the Arts, Helsinki, August 21, 2014.

1. The history of *Suvivirsi* goes back to late seventeenth century, when it was added to the Swedish hymnal. The song soon also found its way into the Finnish hymnal and today it is one of the most commonly sung Lutheran hymns in Finland. The hymn was probably composed in 1697 by an anonymous author. The lyrics are usually supposed to have been written by the bishop of Gotland, Israel Kolmodin. According to the tradition, the good bishop was inspired by the natural beauty of the Hånger spring near Visby (Virsikirja 571 Jo Joutui Armas Aika).

2. Finnish Evangelical Lutheran Church defines a hymn as "a song, religious in content, fit to be sung together" and further characterizes the practice of singing hymns as "declaration, teaching, pastoral care, prayer, and experiencing community" (Virret ja muu musiikki 2014; see also Virsikirja 1986)

3. Some say that *Suvivirsi* is based on German melody; others say it is based on a Swedish folk tune.

4. For instance, Finnish Union of Freethinkers and church-related opinion groups.

5. All translations are mine.

6. The vice chair of the committee, Outi Mäkelä, had earlier commented (for Yleisradio 2014c) that it is strange that the deputy chancellor wants to "raise confusion with such a matter" and doubted the authority of the chancellor to issue statements of such a nature. Also, the president of Finland made a short comment on the matter, wondering whether the deputy chancellor does not have more important duties.

7. As discussed, for example, in Luther ([1524] 1987).

8. See, for example, Eggert (1983). Also the chief architect the first Finnish common-school curriculum, Lutheran clergyman Uno Cygnaeus stated that school singing is imperative, as it "unites and uplifts hearts" (1910, 198). Singing should be studied "not only for later life, but to refresh and refine time together in the school itself" (Cygnaeus 1910, 199).

9. In the form of congregational service music, music of different denominations and appreciation of great works of church music.

10. Taira (2012) argues that there is a historical connection between Lutheranism and Finnishness in Finnish discourse and that atheism has traditionally been associated with anti-Finnishness. From this standpoint, the reluctance to give up hymn singing in schools may reflect the institutionalization of the Lutheran faith in Finnish society and how it has been reflected in the collective psyche of the majority.

11. But many teachers and educational administrators continued to oppose singing secular songs in school at the end of the nineteenth century, and there is reason to believe that a religious repertoire continued to be the most important subject matter in common-school singing classes until the mid-twentieth century.

12. The need for constructing a cultural profile for the Finnish nation was driven by the colonial status of Finland over the centuries. There is no space here to discuss Finnish nationalism in any extensive way. It should be noted, however, that cultural and religious institutions have played an important part in the process of creating and maintaining the country's independence, in concert with educational institutions.

13. It is often stated that *Bildung* does not translate easily into English. The Finnish dictionary defines *"sivistys"* as "knowledge and spiritual maturity" that is acquired "by way of education" or through a "process of self-cultivation" (MOT 2013, s.v. *sivistys*).

14. Hegel describes this process thoroughly in *The Phenomenology of Spirit* (Hegel 1976). For a discussion of the relation between *Sittlichkeit* and *Bildung*, see *Elements of the Philosophy of Right* (Hegel 1991, §145–57).

15. One way to develop this critique is to scrutinize attempts to define indoctrination and to show that all of them fail (Puolimatka 1997). For instance, to criticize teaching that does not base its content on scientific inquiry as indoctrination can fail when the content includes notions that cannot be scientifically justified (such as moral principles and, perhaps, religious beliefs). Moreover, it is not clear how to define a doctrine as the content of indoctrination: for instance, it is not always easy to draw a line between scientific theories and doctrines. Another attempt to define *indoctrination* is to pay attention to how the teacher teaches. For instance, if the students are not provided opportunities to critically consider all relevant options for the notion to be learned, or the grounds for believing it as true, they may be said to be indoctrinated. Critics have argued in opposition to this that there are beliefs that have no alternatives or that are axiomatic in the sense that they need no further reasons. Besides, it may be maintained that it is impossible to consider all living options for all educational content, especially at the lower grades. It has been further suggested that one way to define *indoctrination* is by identifying the intention or objective of the teacher as indoctrinatory. Such attempts have also raised criticism, for it is not clear how such intentions are identified unless the teacher is vocal about his or her attempt.

16. This may also be true in the more specific case of music education: according to Bowman (2007), music education is always both inclusive and exclusive.

17. The purpose of the online community is to provide information about a nondenominational school subject that is named "Ethics" in the English translation of the Finnish national curriculum (*elämänkatsomustieto*, lit., "life stance knowledge"). This subject is mandatory for students who do not participate in religion classes.

18. One of these communications was issued by a teacher who reported having had to participate in a church- and state-funded *Virsivisa* (lit., "Hymn quiz") project despite being non-Lutheran. Funded by the Finnish Evangelical Lutheran Church and the Finnish Board of Education, the project aims to teach Lutheran hymns to students of the third and fourth grades as part of their everyday schoolwork (http://www.virsivisa.fi; see also "Tällainen on Virsivisa" 2014). Some juridical experts have seen the quiz as problematic because it also was meant to be played outside the Lutheran religion classes. As the constitutional law professor Veli-Pekka Viljanen argued for *Helsingin Sanomat*, *Virsivisa* can perhaps also be taken as a different case than the practice of singing *Suvivirsi* in school ceremonies, for such practices can be seen as "religious traditions practiced in Christmas festivities or other distinct events" rather than as cases of the teachers incorporating "religious materials systematically in other teaching" ("Tällainen on Virsivisa" 2014).

References

Alasuutari, Pertti. 1996. *Toinen tasavalta: Suomi 1946–1994* [The second republic: Finland 1946–1994]. Tampere, Fin.: Vastapaino.

Anttila, Jorma. 1993. "Käsitykset suomalaisuudesta—traditionaalisuus ja modernisuus." In *Mitä on suomalaisuus?*, edited by Teppo Korhonen, 108–34. Helsinki, Fin.: Suomen antropologinen seura.

Bellah, Robert. 1967. "Civil Religion in America." *Dædalus* 96, no. 1: 1–21.

Bowman, Wayne. 2007. "Who Is the 'We'? Rethinking Professionalism in Music Education." *Action, Criticism, and Theory for Music Education* 6, no. 4: 109–31. http://act.maydaygroup.org/articles/Bowman6_4.pdf.

Constitution of Finland. 1999. https://www.finlex.fi/fi/laki/kaannokset/1999/en19990731.pdf.

Cygnaeus, Uno. 1910. *Uno Cygnaeuksen Kirjoituksen Suomen kansakoulun perustamisesta ja järjestämisestä* [Uno Cygnaeus's writings for establishing and organizing Finnish common school]. Edited by Gustaf F. Lönnbeck. Helsinki, Fin.: Kansanvalistus.

Durkheim, Emile. 1961. *Moral Education.* New York: The Free Press.

Eggert, Kurt J. 1983. *Martin Luther, God's Music Man.* http://www.wlsessays.net/files/EggertLuther.pdf.

Hegel, Georg W. F. 1976. *Phenomenology of Spirit.* Oxford: Oxford University Press.

———. 1991. *Elements of the Philosophy of Right.* Cambridge: Cambridge University Press.

Heinimäki, Jaakko, and Jussi K. Niemelä. 2011. *Kamppailu Jumalasta: 12 erää uskosta* [The struggle over God: 12 rounds of faith]. Helsinki, Fin.: Helsinki-kirjat.

Kallioniemi, Arto. 2005. *Uskonnonopetuksen haasteet kulttuurisessa murroksessa.* Helsinki, Fin.: Didacta Varia.

Kincheloe, Joe L. 2007. "Critical Pedagogy in the Twenty-First Century: Evolution for Survival." In *Critical Pedagogy: Where Are We Now?*, edited by Peter McLaren and Joe L. Kincheloe, 9–42. New York: Peter Lang.

Luther, Martin. (1524) 1987. "To the Councilmen of All Cities in Germany That They Establish and Maintain Christian Schools." Translated by Albert T. W. Steinhaeuser. In *Works of Martin Luther*, 4: 74–97. Albany: AGES Software. http://media.sabda.org/alkitab-8/LIBRARY/LUT_WRK4.PDF.

Mikkola, Kati. 2004. "Uskonto, isänmaa, isänmaausko: Uskonnollisen argumentaation ulottuvuudet Topeliuksen Maamme kirjassa" [Religion, fatherland, fatherland-religion: the dimensions of religious argumentation in Topelius's *Maamme* book]. In *Uskonnon paikka: Kirjoituksia uskontojen ja uskontoteorioiden rajoista* [The place of religion: writings on the borders of religions and theories of religion], edited by Outi Fingeroos, Minna Opas, and Teemu Taira, 209–44. Helsinki, Fin.: Suomalaisen kirjallisuuden seura.

MOT. 2013. *MOT Kielitoimiston sanakirja* [MOT dictionary of the Institute of the Languages, Finland]. http://ezproxy.uniarts.fi/login?url=http://mot.kielikone.fi/mot/taideyliopisto/netmot.

Münch, Richard. 1987. *Theory of Action: Towards a New Synthesis Going beyond Parsons.* London: Routledge and Kegan Paul.

———. 2001. *The Ethics of Modernity: Formation and Transformation in Britain, France, Germany and the United States.* Lanham: Rowman and Littlefield.

Nielsen, Frede V. 2007. "Music (and Arts) Education from the Point of View of Didaktik and Bildung." In *International Handbook of Research in Art Education*, edited by Liora Bresler, 265–85. New York: Springer.

Pajamo, Reijo. 1976. *Suomen koulujen laulunopetus vuosina 1843–1881* [Singing teaching in Finnish schools 1843–1881]. Helsinki, Fin.: Suomen Musiikkitieteellinen.

———. 1988. *Peruskoulun virsitieto* [Hymn knowledge for comprehensive school]. Helsinki, Fin.: Kirjapaja.

———. 1991. *Hymnologian peruskurssi* [The basic course of hymnology]. Helsinki, Fin.: Sibelius-Akatemia. Kirkkomusiikin osaston julkaisuja 2.

Peruskoulun opetuksen opas: musiikki [The guide for teaching in basic education: music]. 1987. Helsinki, Fin.: Valtion painatuskeskus.

Peruskoulun opetussuunnitelman perusteet [Core curriculum for the comprehensive school]. 1985. Helsinki, Fin.: Valtion painatuskeskus.

Peruskoulun virsisuunnitelma [Hymn plan for the comprehensive school]. 1987. Helsinki, Fin.: Suomen ev.lut. kirkon keskushallinto.

Perusopetuksen opetussuunnitelman perusteet [Core curriculum for the comprehensive school]. 2004. Opetushallitus. Määräys 1-3/011/2004. Vammala, Fin.: Vammalan kirjapaino.

Puolimatka, Tapio. 1997. *Opetusta vai indoktrinaatiota: Valta ja manipulaatio opetuksessa [Teaching or indoctrination: power and manipulation in teaching]*. Helsinki, Fin.: Kirjayhtymä.

Reinboth, Susanna. 2014a. "Apulaisoikeuskansleri: Uskonnolliset tilaisuudet pois kouluista" [Deputy chancellor: religious events away from school]. Helsinki *Sanomat*, March 24. http://www.hs.fi/kotimaa/a1395629878403.

———. 2014b. "Suvivirsi aiheutti palautetulvan" [An overflow of feedback caused by *Suvivirsi*]. Helsinki *Sanomat*, April 25. http://www.hs.fi/kotimaa/a1398346003347.

Rousseau, Jean Jacques. (1762) 2019. *The Social Contract, or the Principles of Political Right*. http://www.constitution.org/jjr/socon.htm.

Saarakkala, Vesa-Matti. 2014. Lakialoite koulujen kulttuurikristillisten traditioden vaalimisesta [A bill upholding the cultural-Christian traditions of the schools], blog, March 26. http://www.saarakkala.fi/blogi/2014/03/26/330.

Sevänen, Erkki. 1998. *Taide instituutiona ja järjestelmänä: Modernin taide-elämän historiallis-sosiologiset mallit* [Art as institution and as system: the historical-sociological models of modern art life]. Helsinki, Fin.: Suomalaisen kirjallisuuden seura.

Siljander, Pauli, ed. 1997. *Kasvatus ja sosialisaatio* [Education and socialization]. Helsinki, Fin.: Gaudeamus.

Siljander, Pauli, Ari Kivelä, and Ari Sutinen, eds. 2012. *Theories of Bildung and Growth— Connections and Controversies between Continental Educational Thinking and American Pragmatism*. Rotterdam, Neth.: Sense.

Statistics Finland. 2013. *Väestö uskontokunnan mukaan ja osuus väestöstä 1950–2013* [Population by religious denomination and the share of the population 1950–2013]. http://tilastokeskus.fi/til/vaerak/2013/vaerak_2013_2014-03-21_tau_002_fi.html.

Sünker, Heinz. 2006. *Politics, Bildung and Social Justice: Perspectives for a Democratic Society*. Rotterdam, Neth.: Sense.

Suomen Evankelis-Luterilainen Kirkko. *Virsikirja* [Hymn book]. 1986. http://evl.fi/virsikirja.

Taira, Teemu. 2012. "More Visible but Limited in Its Popularity: Atheism (and Atheists) in Finland." *Approaching Religion* 2, no. 1 (June 8): 21–35. https://doi.org/10.30664/ar.67489.

"Tällainen on Virsivisa" [This is *Virsivisa*]. 2014. *Helsingin Sanomat*, May 26. http://www.hs.fi/kotimaa/a1401079533944.

Tan, Charlene. 2004. "Michael Hand, Indoctrination and the Inculcation of Belief." *Journal of the Philosophy of Education* 38, no. 2 (May 24): 257–67. https://doi.org/10.1111/j.0309-8249.2004.00380.x.

Thiessen, Elmer John. 1993. *Teaching for Commitment: Liberal Education, Indoctrination, and Christian Nurture*. Montreal: McQueen-Gills University Press.

"Uskonnon harjoittaminen kouluissa" [The practicing of religion in schools]. 2013. Apulaisoikeuskanslerin päätös [Decision by deputy chancellor] OKV/230/1/2013. http://www.okv.fi/media/uploads/ratkaisut/ratkaisut_2014/okv_230_1_2013.pdf.

Väkevä, Lauri. 2012. "Experiencing Growth as a Natural Phenomenon: John Dewey's Philosophy and the Bildung Tradition." In *Theories of Bildung and Growth*:

Connections and Controversies between Continental Educational Thinking and American Pragmatism, edited by Pauli Siljader, Ari Kivelä, and Ari Sutinen, 261–80. Rotterdam, Neth.: Sense.

Väkevä, Lauri. 2015. "Music for All? Justifying the Two-Track Ideology of Finnish Music Education." In *Critical Music Historiography: Probing Canons, Ideologies and Institutions*, edited by Vesa Kurkela and Markus Mantere, 45–56. Aldershot, UK: Ashgate.

Vapaavuori, Hannu. 1997. *Virsilaulu ja heräävä kansallinen kulttuuri-identiteetti: Jumalanpalveluksen virsilaulua ja-sävelmistöä koskeva keskustelu Suomessa 1800-luvun puolivälistä vuoteen 1886* [Hymn singing and the awakening national culture identity: the discussion about hymn-singing and melodies in service in Finland from mid-nineteenth century to 1886]. Saarijärvi, Fin.: Suomen kirkkohistoriallinen 173.

Virret ja muu musiikki [Hymns and other music]. 2014. Suomen evankelis-luterilainen kirkko [Evangelical Lutheran Church of Finland]. Accessed September 23, 2015. http://evl.fi/evlfi.nsf/Documents/8ED81ADA2486F346C225728B003F3787?openDocument&lang=FI.

Virsikirja 571. Jo Joutui Armas Aika. Virsikirja.fi. Accessed August 1, 2019. https://virsikirja.fi/virsi-571-jo-joutui-armas-aika/.

Wahlström, Ninni. 2009. "The Struggle for the Right to Education in the European Convention on Human Rights." *Journal of Human Rights* 8, no. 2: 150–61.

Yleisradio. 2014a. "Suvivirren laulaminen kouluissa uuteen harkintaan" [Singing *Suvivirsi* in schools to be reconsidered]. *Yleisradion uutiset*, March 24. http://yle.fi/uutiset/suvivirren_laulaminen_kouluissa_uuteen_harkintaan/7152153.

———. 2014b. "Suvivirren laulaminen voi jatkua kouluissa" [Singing *Suvivirsi* can continue in schools]. *Yleisradion Uutiset*, April 4. http://yle.fi/uutiset/suvivirren_laulaminen_voi_jatkua_kouluissa/7173951.

———. 2014c. "Suvivirsi-ratkaisun tehnyt apulaisoikeuskansleri vastaa arvosteluun: 'Emme kiellä mitään—toimme esiin ongelman'" ["The deputy chancellor that made the decision over *Suvivirsi* replies, 'We do not forbid anything—we have brought out a problem'"] *Yleisradion uutiset*, March 26. http://yle.fi/uutiset/suvivirsi-ratkaisun_tehnyt_apulaisoikeuskansleri_vastaa_arvosteluun_emme_kiella_mitaantoimme_esiin_ongelman/7157209.

———. 2014d. "Vapaa-ajattelijat: Missä vaiheessa virrestä on tullut muuta kuin uskonnon harjoittamista?" [Freethinkers: when did singing a hymn become something other than practicing religion?] *Yleisradion uutiset*, May 27. http://yle.fi/uutiset/vapaa-ajattelijat_missa_vaiheessa_virresta_on_tullut_muuta_kuin_uskonnon_harjoittamista/7265341.

———. 2014e. "Oikeuskansleri sai yli 100 kantelua Suvivirsi-linjauksesta—kanteluista ei enää selvityspyyntöjä" [Chancellor received over 100 complaints about Suvivirsi alignment—no more statement requests of the complaint]. *Yleisradion uutiset*, July 9. https://yle.fi/uutiset/3-7346720

Part 3
Navigating New Worlds

8 | *Mysterium Tremendum et Fascinans*: Spiritual and Existential Experience and Music Education

Øivind Varkøy

Music constitutes entire universes of meaning, large spectrums of potential experiences. Music (of any genre) contains acoustic layers, structural layers, physical layers, layers of tension, emotional layers, and spiritual and existential layers. According to the Danish music educator Frede V. Nielsen (1942–2013) all layers in music correspond to similar layers of awareness in people. Something in the one resonates with something in the other. This means that the layers of meaning in music only exist as possibilities, as potential, and that they must be actualized and perceived in the encounter with the experiencing subject. All types of layers of meaning have such a character: physical or structural as well as spiritual and existential (Nielsen 1994). Knowledge and reflection about the encounter is a prerequisite for the teacher to be capable of providing access to all the layers of meaning in music, including music's spiritual and existential layer, in his or her teaching.

In line with Nielsen, I argue that communication between music's spiritual and existential layer and the corresponding layers of human awareness often fails. Music education has a tendency to disregard the deeper perspectives in music, and a great deal of pedagogical work seems to concentrate on bringing the students into contact with the outer side of the music, that which is technically describable and easily graspable. This chapter offers a critical discussion of the situation—from a Nordic perspective.

The expression "spiritual and existential" refers to a special type of experience. We experience something that affects us on a spiritual and existential level. The question about meaning is innate; meaning in life—and the meaning of life. Reflections about choice, suffering, hope, joy, time, passion, death, happiness, intensity, and belonging are also natural. In previous works, I argue that the tendency to focus mainly on the outer side of the music, and the lack of focus on the layer of spiritual and existential meaning in music, takes away an important space for students to wonder and reflect about their own experiences in encounters with music (Pio and Varkøy 2012; Varkøy and Westby 2014).

Can the lack of music-educational focus on the spiritual and existential layer of musical experience then simply be because teachers do not know what art is? In the novel *Old Masters*, by Austrian author Thomas Bernhard (1989), a main character reproaches teachers for destroying their pupils' interest in art. He argues that, to begin with, all young people[1] are receptive to everything, including art: "The teachers . . . are through and through *petit-bourgeois* and instinctively act against their pupil's fascination by art and enthusiasm for art by reducing art and generally anything artistic to their own depressing stupid dilettantism and by turning art and generally anything artistic at school into their repulsive record playing and an equally repulsive and incompetent choral singing, which is bound to repel the pupils" (23). The character argues that teachers cannot explain to their pupils what art is, simply because they themselves do not know what it is. The teachers do not lead their pupils *toward* art, but push them *away from* art "into their revolting, sentimental vocal and instrumental *applied art*, which is bound to repel their pupils . . . instead of elucidating art, and especially music, to them and making it a lifelong joy (24).

If we look beyond this art of exaggeration, the story may hold important lessons. How can teachers destroy children's fascination with art? Although the reasons can be numerous, one may well be that these teachers "do not know what art is," as Bernhard suggests. What does it mean, then, not *knowing what art is*? I contend that a teacher who, because of a lack of qualifications, experiences, and reflection has a limited or reduced understanding of what music *can* mean in people's lives, and who, consequently, is not able to be open to *all* of the different kinds of meanings and experiences that can be found in the encounters between the music and the individual, "does not know what art is," and he/she is in danger of guiding the students "away from art." Then it is easy for the teacher not to understand the difference between "making music into a lifelong joy" (Bernhard 1989, 24) and organizing enjoyable music activities.

The teacher's perspective on music has a great deal of influence on what takes place in the lessons and what does not. The music teacher's perspective is among those things that enables and denies possibilities for the pupil's musical experience, and the teacher can therefore obstruct certain musical experiences. This challenging music-pedagogical situation—about which I argue that *different kinds of musical experience* in the classroom may be discussed in relation to choices made by the teacher—can be illuminated with assistance from the Danish philosopher Søren Kierkegaard's (1988) theory of stages on life's way, as well as Aristotle's (1999) concepts about music and music education.

Before turning to Kierkegaard and Aristotle, however, let us first focus on the striking parallels between musical experiences of a spiritual and existential character and mystical religious experiences. I think knowledge about such striking parallels can contribute to a better understanding of the music-educational fear of engaging in spiritual and existential musical experiences. To illuminate the Nordic culture's distance from (or even fear of) terms like *spiritual* and *religious* (a central term in Kierkegaard's philosophy), I will, before I turn to Kierkegaard and Aristotle, even relate my discussion to cultural processes of disenchantment and ritual rationality.

I am very aware that I do not speak from a neutral place. We all speak from one position or another, with some interest. The best we as authors can hope for, especially in a book like this, is that we do not hide this fact behind some sort of academic objectivity. Thus, the question all readers should ask of any text is, From what kind of philosophical position is this text written? My interest in the layer of spiritual and existential meaning in music as such, and the striking parallels between musical experiences of a spiritual and existential character and mystical religious experiences, is related to my own history of musical experiences—and my reflections related to these experiences, connected to a certain worldview—as described by Charles Taylor (2007): "the modern identity and outlook flattens the world, leaves no place for the spiritual, the higher, for mystery" (356). To me, music opens to what the ancients referred to as the *mysterium tremendum et fascinans*, an expression that suggests the chill and delight of facing the unnamable. This is my place, in the late-modern garden of experiences and reflections existing side by side.[2]

Striking Parallels

As stated, I have in previous works discussed the lack of music-educational focus on the spiritual and existential layer of musical experience. I have also discussed whether one possible explanation for the remoteness with which both music education and the music education research field approach spiritual and existential musical experience is that such experiences cannot be described technically, nor are they manageable (Guldbrandsen and Varkøy 2004, introduction). I have even discussed this problem in connection to the originally German term *Bildung*, as well as in connection to the fact that the field of spiritual and existential experiences is a quagmire of discussion about values and ideological contradictions, a battlefield full of philosophical, social, and personal identity constructions (Varkøy 2015a, 2015b).

In this chapter, I would like to develop this last point: the field of spiritual and existential experiences as a quagmire of discussion about values and ideological contradictions, a battlefield full of philosophical, social, and personal identity constructions. I will do so by emphasizing the striking parallels between musical experiences of a spiritual and existential character and mystical religious experiences. The pedagogical challenges and problems related to a kind of experience that is not technically describable or easily graspable and that can very easily become an ideological battlefield, should become even more pronounced when we focus on these striking parallels. The point is particularly relevant in secularized Nordic societies, in which people may find concepts like *spiritual* and *religious* to be very problematic in an educational discourse.[3] Secularization as a phenomenon in modern Western societies and its consequences for music education is discussed in a number of other chapters in this book. In chapter 9 of this volume, Maria Spychiger "deals with the question of what the sacred sphere is when a society is secular, or if an individual's second, fictional worlds are not religious, but may be found in literature, philosophy, film, music, science, and so forth." Frank Heuser in chapter 10 discusses "the emerge of secularity in the West." Westerlund, Kallio, and Partti in chapter 3 discuss how the "assumption that secular schooling is somehow neutral can suppress, marginalize, or erase students' own (non)religious identities, and moreover "as secularization projects conflict with situational performativities, these political and ethical negotiations can be seen as not taking place in a way that is natural or free."

Spiritual and existential experiences connected to powerful encounters between music and the individual are usually both shocking and jolting, and they can seldom be fully expressed in words. Moreover, these experiences are unpredictable. They can provide a form of insight or understanding. This understanding is transitory, however, and is not something one has permanent access to. The spiritual and existential experience is therefore a discontinuous occurrence, in itself a break with pedagogical continuity in which everything is planned in advance, as stated by the German philosopher of education Otto Friedrich Bollnow (1959), Since we never can predict or plan such encounters and experiences, the teacher's task is to make the pupils familiar with the entire universes of meaning and large spectrums of potential experiences that exist in music.

The characteristics of spiritual and existential musical experiences are almost identical to what is characteristic of religious, mystical experiences. In *The Varieties of Religious Experience*, the US philosopher and psychologist William James (1842–1910) distinguishes four characteristics of the religious mystical experience: (1) it is untranslatable and ineffable, (2) it provides a form of insight or understanding, (3) it is not something one has permanent access to, and (4) it is something one is exposed to, although the exposure may be a result of a long preparatory process (James 1902). These characteristics are also familiar in the context of the spiritual and existential musical experience.

The divine moment in a powerful musical experience is unpredictable and rare and cannot be manipulated through controlled didactical procedures. It is something one is exposed to. Powerful musical experiences certainly have their own specific features, but they are related to experiences and phenomena we find in religious mysticism.

German theologian and scholar of comparative religion Otto (2004) summarizes the mystical experience under the term *tremendum et fascinans*: something nameless that is perceived as both frightening and alluring. Otto turned to the experience of the sacred or numinous; the experience of the holy, the ineffable, the mysterious, the alien, and the frightening; "*das Ganz Andere*" (Otto 1917, 26).

Otto's is almost confusingly similar to a number of philosophers' descriptions of powerful aesthetic experiences. Immanuel Kant's (2005) notion of the sublime contains a similar duality of fear and fascination. Kant was contemplating the beautiful during an age in which music was typified by the classical Viennese ideals of harmony and symmetry; the age of Haydn, Mozart, and early Beethoven. To borrow from Friedrich Nietzsche (2008), we might say that it was primarily an Apollonian musical age. Nietzsche uses *Apollonian* and *Dionysian* to describe two central principles in Greek culture. All types of form or structure are Apollonian, as is rational thought. Drunkenness and madness are Dionysian, as are all forms of enthusiasm and ecstasy. Music, according to Nietzsche, is the most

Dionysian of the arts, since it appeals directly to humanity's instinctive, chaotic emotions and not to our rational minds.

But since the time of Haydn, Mozart, and early Beethoven, a fair amount of music of a more Dionysian character has flowed through history, beginning with Beethoven's later works and developing into a flood during the late Romantic and expressionist periods, while today we encounter it in a variety of rock music. Following the Norwegian musicologist and music therapist Even Ruud (1997), I argue that we today live in a (Western) music culture that, in many ways, is characterized by an existential dynamic pressure. Both contemporary popular music and the role of music in people's lives have this character, for example, in the context of identity construction.[4]

On the other hand, educational and cultural policy's reductionist approach toward musical experience, which is fixated on harmony, is also apparent. Much educational and cultural political thinking focuses on music as a means of developing harmonious personalities, of contributing to social understanding, respect, and harmony, and in general of healing individual and social wounds in the modern society (Røyseng and Varkøy 2014).

The problem here is certainly *not* that not all music is sublime, nor that music educators are not engaged in sublime music and the sorts of musical experience sublime music might evoke in their students. My point is, however, to focus on the marginalization of spiritual and existential experiences in music education. The paradox is that these deeper experiences seem to be very central in most people's engagement in music outside school. I argue that this pedagogical and political reductionism of musical experience, which focuses on the beautiful and marginalizes the sublime, is connected to the fact that Western societies since the Reformation have been characterized by a tendency toward disenchantment.

Disenchantment and Ritual Rationality

In *The Protestant Ethic and the Spirit of Capitalism*, the German sociologist Max Weber (1864–1920) argues that disenchantment causes the world to become more and more prosaic and less poetic, more predictable and less mysterious (Weber 2011). Connected to this process of disenchantment is the general hegemony of technical rationality. Rationality from the areas of technology and economy—which represents *the* character of modern Western rationality—has undoubtedly become an important component of modern bourgeois society's ideals of life (Varkøy 2013).[5] Weber emphasizes how the predilection for mathematically founded, rationalized empiricism in Protestant asceticism is an important aspect of the Puritan spirit of capitalism. This implies, for instance, that sports are valued only if they serve a rational purpose, and it also implies a general distrust of cultural products that cannot be directly connected to religious values. Weber even connects these ideas to concepts of upbringing.

But at the same time as disenchantment certainly occurs, music education and cultural politics tend to justify music from a belief in its transformative, magical powers; a ritual logic based on music' assumed magical powers to transform and heal. The problems of both society and individuals seem to be placed before the altar of art, and one prays, hoping and wishing for the best, as one must do when dealing with the logic of magic. Sometimes the magic works, and sometimes it doesn't. When art is included in regional policy, integration policy, health policy, and innovation policy, it is not primarily because of art's utility. It is the belief in the transformative power of art experiences. This ritual rationality concerns some sort of reenchantment. While technical or instrumental rationality (Weber 2011) is related to the disenchantment of the world, ritual rationality concerns re-enchanting a disenchanted world (Røyseng and Varkøy 2014).

Sometimes the ritual arguments about good music remind me of what, in theological circles, is labeled prosperity theology or glorification theology. In this understanding of the Christian faith—not least as we know it from evangelical and charismatic churches—the attitude toward the holy can be summarized in Janis Joplin's famous verse: "Oh Lord, won't you buy me a Mercedes Benz?" In prosperity or glorification theology, God seems to be valued primarily as some sort of butler, or a mega-handyman and a party-fixer of existence (Eagleton 2009).[6] In the ritual logic of the positive and healing qualities of art, art is God the party-fixer. Today's tsunami of instrumental reason necessitates a consumerist ideology even when it comes to ritual logic, yet this very ideology undermines the Protestant ethical attitude that made our modern Western societies possible (Žižek 2011).

Musical Experience and Kierkegaard's Theory of Stages on Life's Way

The dilemmas related to ritual rationality can be examined in light of Kierkegaard's attack on the bourgeoisie's educated Christianity, in which, in his view, the religious is reduced to a bourgeois piety. In a music-educational context, it will be interesting to discuss how the idea of music, as a party-fixer of existence, relates to a phenomenon such as spiritual and existential musical experience—linked as this kind of experience is to intensity and passion. Intensity and passion are concepts connected to Kierkegaard's theory of stages on life's way, a theory related to the classical antiquity theory of the three forms of life: the life of pleasure, the life of duty, and the life of reflection—as will be shown later in this chapter.[7]

In my view, in the case of spiritual and existential musical experience, we move toward a form of being that can be viewed in light of what Kierkegaard (1988) refers to as the religious stage—as distinct from the aesthetic and ethical stages on life's way. It is necessary to emphasize that the expression "religious stage" in my context is primarily a term for a way of being characterized by intensity and passion, independent of Kierkegaard's nineteenth-century philosophical-theological context. There is, however, one common denominator between religious faith and art, as formulated by the Polish author Witold Gombrowicz (2013): "Like faith, art fears only one thing: lukewarmness" (8–9; my translation from Norwegian).

Kierkegaard is considered to be the father of existentialism. Overall, Kierkegaard's existential philosophy centers on possible stages on life's way. The individual must intentionally determine which stage he or she aims to achieve. Such choices have the quality of leaps. The aesthetic sphere is the domain of immediacy, the ethical is the field of demand and duty, and the religious is the stage of fulfillment. Kierkegaard's presentation of the forms, or stages, of life, shows us the consequences of the various forms of life, and challenges us to choose. The guideline and objective of the stages of life is intensification. With each step, an increase in intensity and sincerity occurs.

Prior to each chosen stage lies the life of the philistine. The philistine is not the name of a stage, but of a form of life in which one does not connect with oneself but lives in a formulaic, habit-based life—a form of life preceding each existential choice. It is by making a choice that one renounces the philistine life and is thrown into the stages. In the book with the striking title *Either/Or*, the first two forms of life, or stages, are presented: the aesthetic and the ethical (Kierkegaard 1987, 1992). In the aesthetic form of life, one does not completely commit oneself to people or pursuits. One is a spectator, one constantly wishes to be able to tear oneself away. The aesthete is on a continual search for new impulses, he/she is eternally and desperately searching for new pleasures. The aesthete is full of contempt for trivial everyday life, the life of the philistine. When the aesthete wants to distance himself or herself from everyday life, he or she does so by building a life based on pleasure. Each obligation, every lasting commitment is threatening.

As a result of such a hedonistic way of life, one is never satisfied. As soon as one need is met, another need emerges—which demands immediate satisfaction. The perceptual sweetness in the aesthetic and the aesthete's continual hunt for new pleasures produces nothing more than despair. The way out of this despair is, according to Kierkegaard, connected to the ethical choice. The ethical stage is characterized by the assumption of responsibilities and obligations in a larger social and societal context. Seen from the outside, the ethical person is somewhat like the philistine, with a fixed income and a domestic life. But—while the philistine has allowed himself or herself to drift unconsciously with the current into a conventional life, the ethicist has consciously chosen this form of life. From his or her former lifestyle as a hedonistic aesthete, the ethical person chooses to turn to society and its demands and expectations. The ethicist is not, however, always able to live up to his or her ideals. *Either/Or* concludes, suggestively, with a sermon that advances the tenet that, in relation to God, we are always in the wrong.

This argumentation points toward the third stage; the *religious*, which is discussed in depth in Kierkegaard (1988). Kierkegaard's theory of stages—and particularly his religious stage—is linked to a discussion of what it means to be Christian. The entire discussion takes place within a theological-philosophical framework. According to Kierkegaard, faith suspends the ethical. Passionate and spiritually-demanding faith is the ultimate stage, in which the individual recognizes the paradoxical and absurd in the Christian concept of God: God is born as a human, dies on a cross, and rises again so that humankind may be delivered from its sins. According to Kierkegaard, one does not believe in such a story because it is rational, but because it is absurd. The Christian faith is, according to Kierkegaard, not a doctrine full of rules to live by—as it is for the ethical person.

Faith is a form of life that embraces the absurd, a break with every rationality. The believer casts himself or herself into the seventy thousand fathoms of water without a life vest or safety line. The intellect is swept aside, and it becomes possible to make a qualitative leap into the Christian faith. The object of faith is namely the paradox, which is the complete opposite of the rational. Faith is the irrational principle itself: "credo quia absurdum." We are confronted with the intellect's subordination to faith. To Kierkegaard, this is the highest point of individual freedom.

As noted earlier, the religious stage is characterized by intensity and passion. Kierkegaard employs an image from the field of art: "To take passion out of the lines of a play and in compensation have the orchestra fiddle a little is to prostitute poetry and is comic, just as it would be in actual life if the lover, instead of pathos in his breast, had a music box in his pocket for the crucial moment" (1988, 405).

Kierkegaard describes the aesthetic and ethical stages as being related to choices we make as human beings. Such choices are conscious, intentional, often both thoughtful and justified—and they have a purpose of pleasure or duty. To make the leap to the religious stage is also a matter of choice, although the choice does not usually entail accomplishing a goal.

I contend that spiritual and existential musical experience does not concern the aesthetic or the ethical but is about the religious; about passionately abandoning oneself, about the intense and unconditional surrender—not to a superficial hedonistic pleasure, but to a deeper kind of experience that will have existential meaning in life. It is about a break with the philistine's trivialities, as well as the aesthete's manifold pleasures, and the ethical person's eternal question, "What is it good for?" It is about casting oneself into seventy thousand fathoms of water, about venturing into risk zones where everything is different from what we are used to. As formulated by the French philosopher Jacques Maritain (1961), the artist's task is not to give the bourgeoisie a light intoxication after the meal, but to supply us with spiritual nourishment. The spiritual and existential musical experience can transport one to border areas, borderline experiences, and boundary crossings. I think that this way of thinking may challenge music-educational work that is limited to the music's outer side—in a productive way.

Aristotle and the Functions of Music

In Kierkegaard's philosophy and writings about art, morality, and faith, Aristotle (384–22 BCE) is offered considerable attention. The classical antiquity theory about the three forms of life (*bios apolaustikos*, *bios politicos*, and *bios theoretikos*) can be said to acquire flesh and blood in Kierkegaard's stages. The three forms of life in classical antiquity theory are even expressed in Aristotle's concept of music, which focuses on music as pleasure and recreation, as a means of character development, and as a virtuous activity.

While Plato seems to be more concerned with determining which type of music would be appropriate for achieving specific sets of educational aims and objectives, Aristotle (1995) focuses on the actual and practical use of music in a descriptive way—even if he is also clearly normative. Aristotle's concept of music and music education is clearly expressed in his work *Politics*. In Aristotle's (1999) view, each species has a particular nature, and the ideal life for that species is one that fulfills its nature. Human beings are the only species that have a rational soul (*logos*). To achieve happiness (*eudaimonia*), which represents the highest realization of human nature, the human being has to fulfill its nature as a rational being, as well as live in accordance with virtue or excellence (*areté*). The highest form of life consists of virtuous and valuable activity guided by the rational part of the soul. This form of life is exercised as a leisure activity (*scholé*), as opposed to work undertaken to earn a livelihood, which is characterized by the absence of leisure (*ascholia*). Virtuous activity (*diagogé*) does not come to us by chance, we are responsible for acquiring and exercising it (Sundberg 2000). The individual *chooses* to move into the virtuous condition or dimension through his own condition and attitude (Fossum, Varkøy, and Westby 2015).

Aristotle's concept of music centers on four main aspects, three of which should be viewed in connection to one another. The fourth aspect, *katharsis*, will not be discussed here, since it is Aristotle's discussion of the other three aspects, as they relate to each other, that is important in relation to Kierkegaard's stages. *Katharsis* is more a therapeutic than a philosophical or pedagogical concept.

These three aspects, which concern the function of music and its place in education, constitute three levels in ascending order. They correspond to Aristotle's concept of human development and his ranking of human activity. Each level is continued in and incorporated into the next level:

    3. Virtuous activity (*diagogé*)

   2. Character development (*ethos*)

  1. Pleasure/recreation (*paidiá, anapausis*)

Aristotle's empirical-psychological point of departure is the human being's natural affection for music. Music is a natural source of pleasure and joy. Aristotle recognizes music's quality as a central and profound source of experience and poses the question, Why should we appreciate and cultivate music? Should it be cultivated because of its potential for immediate pleasure and recreation? Or could it be that music contributes to an individual's personal development? Could it even be that music inspires virtuous activity (*diagogé*) and contributes to the development of wisdom and practical thought (*phronesis*)?

Aristotle determines that music could be significant to all three aspects. He is skeptical, however, about the growing acceptance of the aspect of pure pleasure (*hedoné*) in the society of his time. He observes that people are sometimes thrown off track in the pursuit of pleasure. The highest goal and purpose (*diagogé*) may well involve pleasure, but not of the lower kind (*hedoné*). Since there is a certain similarity between the different types of pleasure, the human being may confuse the higher type with the lower. Aristotle then evaluates music's possible functions in human development as one progresses through the stages toward the highest purpose or goal. During this process, the function of character development (*ethos*) is brought into play.

Like Plato, Aristotle is not a relativist. There is no doubt that he views some aspects as better than others. Music may, in Aristotle's view, further one's development toward a life of virtue and excellence (*areté*). This view corresponds with Plato's philosophy. According to Aristotle, it is an empirical fact that music affects us in both positive and negative ways. Because of its educational power, he grants music a privileged position in the development of character. Tonalities, melodies, and rhythms are considered to build character (*ethos*). One should therefore engage with music that is associated with and promotes moral character. Aristotle distinguishes between ethical and enthusiastic melodies, as well as those that promote the ability to act, and he groups tonalities in a similar manner. In contrast to Plato's stricter evaluation of tonalities, Aristotle maintains that it is possible to use any tonality, but in different ways and for different purposes (Sundberg 2000; Varkøy 2015c, ch. 1).

Music's function in character development thus opens the way for music's highest purpose and meaning—virtuous activity (*diagogé*). Music does not, however, thereby cease to act as a source of pleasure and recreation. Through music-assisted character development and the training of one's musical judgment, one reaches a level where it is possible to have a higher, spiritual, more virtuous, and reflective experience of music. This experience unifies the experience of pleasure and recreation with the experience of the good, the true, and the beautiful. One is satisfied in the right way about the right things. This function of music is the one that brings happiness (*eudaimonia*) and a life that corresponds to the highest realization of human nature. This way of thinking is clearly related to Aristotle's (1999) discussion of happiness and the good life, which links happiness in the long run (*eudaimonia*) to the realization of the *logos* aspect of human nature.

So What?

As stated earlier: The teacher's perspective on music is an important element in what enables and denies possibilities of musical experience for the student. Teachers need to engage in a level of reflection that ensures that they are capable of grasping the differences between the various layers of meaning that music offers. In the context of this kind of reflection, I argue that one would be better off if one related one's thinking to discussions like those presented by Kierkegaard and Aristotle, focusing on spiritual and existential musical experience as intense and unconditional surrender, not as superficial hedonistic pleasures, but deeper kind of experiences that will have existential meaning in one's life (*eudaimonia*).

The recognition of differences is a foundational for the act of *choosing*. For instance, the teacher may choose between guiding the pupils toward an aesthetic, ethical, or religious stage of musical experience (Kierkegaard 1988); focus on pleasure and recreation, character development, or virtuous activity (Aristotle 1995, 1999); or focus on the layers of musical meaning (Nielsen 1994), respectively.

My point is *not* that every music-educational situation should focus on a religious stage, virtuous activity, or spiritual and existential experience. I simply argue in favor of the teacher's professional knowledge of the different kinds of musical meanings and experiences and the importance of the educational act of choosing.

Kierkegaard's primary focus is on the *choice* and an either/or, attacking all attempts to allow opposing points of view to combine into a higher unity. He insists on regarding the aesthetic, the ethical, and the religious as distinct, fundamental categories. Aristotle is somewhat more inclusive, allowing for both/and, including both pleasure/recreation, character development, and virtuous activity, even though he evaluates music's possible functions in human development as one progresses through the stages toward the highest goal.

When Nielsen (1994) discusses how music-pedagogical work should involve communication between *all* the layers of meaning in the music on the one side and the individual on the other, he argues that the musical experience as spiritual and existential experience seems to be marginalized. But Nielsen is surely speaking more of a both/and than his countryman Kierkegaard.

In line with Nielsen, I argue that the music teacher ought to give students access to *all* kinds of musical experiences; spiritual and existential experiences as well as experiences of acoustics, structures, tensions, and emotions. This is surely an argument of both/and. Nevertheless, the teacher ought to also recognize the difference between the various kinds of layers of meaning in music. He or she has to understand the difference between organizing enjoyable music activities and making music into a lifelong joy (as Thomas Bernhard [1989] puts it)—of spiritual and existential experiences. This is an argument of either/or. Sometimes a choice is required. When spiritual and existential experiences seem to be marginalized in (Nordic) music education, the music pedagogical challenges seem to involve arguments of both/and, as well as arguments of either/or. There is a time for both/and—another time for either/or.

ØIVIND VARKØY is Professor of Music Education and head of the doctoral program at the Norwegian Academy of Music in Oslo, Norway, Visiting Professor in Music at Oslo Metropolitan University, and has previously been Professor and Visiting Professor in Musicology at Örebro University, Sweden. His research in the philosophy of music education has been published in Norwegian, Swedish, English, and German.

Notes

1. Except for those with certain sensory differences . . .
2. See Foucault (1986).
3. This may to some extent even be said about terms like *transcendence* and *uplifting*.
4. See also DeNora (2000).
5. See also Frank Heuser's chapter in this volume on the process of disenchantment.
6. See also Jenkins (2011).
7. See also Varkøy and Westby (2014).

References

Aristotle. 1995. *Politics*. Translated by Ernest Barker. Oxford: Oxford University Press.

———. 1999. *Den nikomakiske etikk* [*Nicomachean Ethics*]. Translated by Øyvind Rabbås and Anfinn Stigen. Oslo: Dagens Bøker Book Club.

Bernhard, Thomas. 1989. *Old Masters: A Comedy*. Translated by Evald Osers. London: Quartet.

Bollnow, Otto Friedrich. 1959. *Existenzphilosophie und Pädagogik*. Stuttgart, Kohlhammer.

DeNora, Tia. 2000. *Music in Everyday Life*. Cambridge: Cambridge University Press.

Eagleton, Terry. 2009. *Reason, Faith, and Revolution: Reflections on the God Debate*. New Haven, CT: Yale University Press.

Fossum, Hanne, Øivind Varkøy, and Inger Anne Westby. 2015. "The Act of Choosing in Music Education." Paper presented at the International Society of Philosophy of Music Education Conference, Frankfurt am Main, June 6.

Foucault, Michel. 1986. "Of Other Spaces." *Diacritics* 16 (Spring): 22–27.

Gombrowicz, Witold. 2013. *Dagboken 1959–1969* [*Diaries 1959–1969*]. Translated by Agnes Banak. Oslo: Flamme.

Guldbrandsen, Erling E., and Øivind Varkøy. 2004. *Musikk og mysterium* [Music and mystery]. Oslo: Cappelen Akademisk.

James, William. 1902. *The Varieties of Religious Experience*. London: Longmans, Green & Co.

Jenkins, Philip. 2011. *The Next Christendom: The Coming of Global Christianity*. Oxford: Oxford University Press.

Kant, Immanuel. 2005. *Critique of Judgement*. Mineola, NY: Dover.

Kierkegaard, Søren. 1987. *Either/Or*, part 2. Translated by Howard V. Hong and Edna H. Hong. Princeton, NJ: Princeton University Press.

———. 1988. *Stages on Life's Way*. Translated by Howard V. Hong and Edna H. Hong. Princeton, NJ: Princeton University Press.

———. 1992. *Either/Or*, part 1. Translated by Alastair Hannay. London: Penguin.

Maritain, Jacques. 1961. *Kunstnerens ansvar* [The responsibility of the artist]. Translated by Howard V. Hong and Edna H. Hong. Oslo: Cappelen.

Nielsen, Frede V. 1994. *Almen musikdidaktik* [General music didactics]. Copenhagen: Christian Ejler's.

Nietzsche, Friedrich. 2008. *The Birth of Tragedy*. Translated by Douglas Smith. Oxford: Oxford University Press.

Otto, Rudolf. 1917. *Das Heilige* [The holy]. Breslau: Trewendt & Granier.

———. *Das Heilige* [The holy]. 2004. Munich: C. H. Beck.

Pio, Frederik, and Øivind Varkøy. 2012. "A Reflection on Musical Experience as Existential Experience: An Ontological Turn." *Philosophy of Music Education Review* 20, no. 2 (Fall): 99–116.

Røyseng, Sigrid, and Øivind Varkøy. 2014. "What Is Music Good For? A Dialogue on Technical and Ritual Rationality." *ACT: Action, Criticism and Theory for Music Education*, 13, no. 1: 101–25. www.act.maydaygroup.org.

Ruud, Even. 1997. *Musikk og identitet* [Music and identity]. Oslo: Universitetsforlaget.

Sundberg, Ove Kristian. 2000. *Musikktenkningens historie: Antikken* [The history of music philosophy: antiquity]. Oslo: Solum.

Taylor, Charles. 2007. *A Secular Age*. Cambridge, MA: Belknap.

Varkøy, Øivind. 2013. "Technical Rationality, Techne and Music Education." In *Professional Knowledge in Music Teacher Education*, edited by Eva Georgii-Hemming, Pamela Burnard, and Sven-Erik Holgersen, 39–50. Aldershot, UK: Ashgate.

———. 2015a. "Bildung: Between Cultural Heritage and the Unknown, Instrumentalism and Existence." In *The Routledge International Handbook of the Arts and Education*, edited by Mike Fleming, Liora Bresler and John O'Toole, 19–29. London: Routledge.

———. 2015b. *Hvorfor musikk? En musikkpedagogisk idéhistorie* [Why music? Ideas in the history of music education]. Oslo: Gyldendal.

———. 2015c. "Intrinsic Value of Musical Experience: A Rethinking; Why and How?" In *Philosophy of Music Education Challenged: Heideggerian Inspirations*, edited by Frederik Pio and Øivind Varkøy, 45–60. Dordrecht: Springer.

Varkøy, Øivind, and Inger Anne Westby. 2014. "Intensity and Passion: On Musical Experience, Layers of Meaning, and Stages." *Philosophy of Music Education Research Review* 22, no. 2 (Fall): 172–87.

Weber, Max. 2011. *The Protestant Ethic and the Spirit of Capitalism*. Translated by Stephen Kalberg. New York: Oxford University Press.

Žižek, Slavoj. 2011. *Living in the End Times*. London: Verso.

9 | The Sacred Sphere: Its Equipment, Beauty, Functions, and Transformations under Secular Conditions

Maria B. Spychiger

The construct highlighted in this chapter, the sacred sphere, relates in its most obvious materialization to spaces and locations, historic and contemporary. They are highly shaped and have intense meanings. Designated objects, musical sounds, substances, lyrics, stories, particular figures, and persons with their actions and interactions belong to it. The creation of the sacred sphere has dramatically driven forward artistic activity, education in the required skills, and the development of beauty. The chapter begins with a model of the sacred sphere in order to enter this lively, artful, busy, and inspiring area. Its basis is the phenomenon of the human mind creating second worlds. They represent mental realities additional to the factual world. In individual lives as well as societies of faith, the sacred sphere functions as a connecting zone between the worlds. Music is discussed as a prominent agent of sacred spheres. The second part of the chapter deals with the question of what the sacred sphere is when a society is secular, or if an individual's second, fictional worlds are not religious but may be found in literature, philosophy, film, music, science, and so forth. Unlike its role in systems of faith, education is then no longer in charge of creating and holding up a religious second world, rather it is the societal key to providing access to second worlds of all kinds in human culture.

A Connecting Device

The suggested model extends a template from the psychology of the person-environment relationship, called the *ecological-semiotic function circle*. It was introduced by psychologist Alfred Lang (1993) and is an adaptation of the biological function circle once developed by Jakob von Uexküll (1864–1944).

Biological and Psychological Function Circle

Uexküll, a pioneer of ecology, focused on the environmental embeddedness of all living creatures, the ever-dependent structure of life, and the multiplicity and interplay of species' niches, and factored this into a first biological model which he

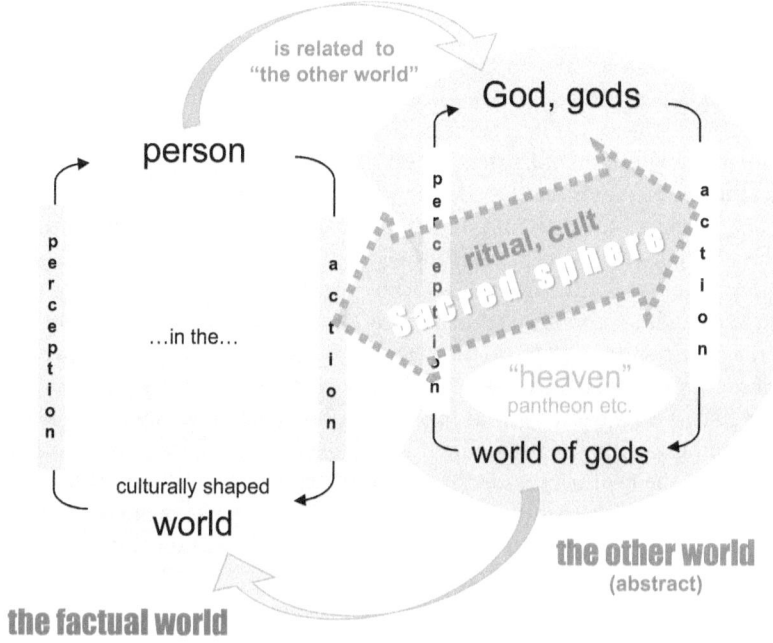

Figure 9.1. Extended model of the semiotic-ecological function circle, *Second-World Model*, with the sacred sphere as connecting space.

called the *function circle* (Uexküll 1909). The later psychologically adapted function circle, as provided by Lang, emphasizes the extended capacity of the human species to generate and promote culture, which is a result of its intense symbolic activity and use of signs.

Lang's circle is shown on the left side of figure 9.1. It comprises four clockwise connected positions. Opposite to one another, say at 12 and 6 o'clock—as the clock metaphor may help to stress that the model relies on movement and time—are the person (12), and the world (6). The two are interrelated by the person's action (at 3) on the right side of the clock, and perception (at 9) on the left. Lang applied the terms "IntrA" to the inside of the person, "ExtrO" to its action, "ExtrA" to the outer world in which the person lives, and "IntrO" to the person's perception of that world. Lang always emphasized the fact that the world inhabited by the human species is engendered and shaped culturally. Humans do not live naturally in a primordial sense, rather, and by their own intervention, they have substantially changed the living conditions and the face of the planet. The semiotic capacities of the individuals enable the species to create a constantly changing and developing cultural world.

The right side in figure 9.1 shows the extension of Lang's psychological function circle. It tries to capture the notion that humans elicit further symbolic and abstract worlds. They are products of the human mind, invisible by their nature. In an evolutionary perspective, this addition first has the scope of a religious world and is labeled "the otherworld."

The Sacred Sphere 143

Extension of the Ecological-Semiotic Function Circle

The otherworld can take on multiple nonreligious qualities, which may play out in all kinds of artistic narratives, film, music, literature, sculpture, and so on, in digital worlds as well as in scientific thinking. We will proceed to this later in this chapter. The spotlight of figure 9.1 is on the sacred sphere.[1] Its function is to connect the two elements developed so far, the factual world and the otherworld.[2]

Sacred spaces cover all the qualities and capacities that the human mind is capable of experiencing, from complete silence to eccentric arousal. In religious societies, the otherworld is divine. Dedicated locations, such as churches or temples, aim to provide an atmosphere[3] of connection between human and divine worlds. In the Jewish-Christian faith, the place where God lives has been projected into space, or, more poetically speaking, imagined as *in heaven*. Numerous painters have given visual expression to this projection, most famously perhaps Michelangelo on the ceiling of the Sistine Chapel in the Vatican. Heaven is the home of God. Over the centuries, especially so in the twentieth, millions of people have seen Michelangelo's painting, and know many of its parts. Among the plentiful creatures and ornamental details, the finger of God points toward Adam, almost touches his hand, and literally hands life over to him.

The painted ceiling holds the Jewish-Christian myth of creation. Other religions have projected the numinous into space as well; for example, the Egyptian female goddess Nut spans the sky above the earth, like a heavenly bow or band. Throughout the ages and cultures, the human mind implicates the capacity to build fictional worlds parallel to the factual world. It does this unceasingly and connects to them; otherwise, individuals feel deprived and incomplete.[4] Humans *do* live with those mental worlds in addition to the sensual, material world. They constantly transcend the factual world.

Functions and Components of the Sacred Sphere and its Spaces

Persons who are, by their faith, bonded to an otherworld attribute specific functions and properties to it. Their orientation and goal is toward that place not on earth, to which they deeply expect to go, and to live on, after they have died (or, as the old term says, "passed away"). The decades of life may serve as the preparation for that transition. Sacred locations provide the atmosphere of being in touch with the otherworld.

A Protecting, Communal, and Educational Area

As inspired by the image of the Egyptian goddess Nut, the primary and central function of the sacred sphere is to transfer the feeling of protection and security that emanates from the otherworld. At least as important, is that knowledge and cognizance also spring from the otherworld and are conveyed by the sacred sphere to those who participate and communicate in it.

The locations of the sacred sphere are extremely interesting. The objects are manufactured to high artistic standards; the music is often of the best a society has. The most distinguished organizations and creative minds are assigned to building that space. The best craftsmen and artists carry out the aesthetic tasks of creating outstanding buildings, with their multiple sacred objects, sculptures, paintings, and music (see also Spicer 2013). The role of music in summoning the sacred atmosphere when the people who belong to the faith come together is perhaps outstanding: listening to music and the communal musical activities, immaterial by its nature and nonverbal, but often combined with language in singing activities, may have the effect of altering the individual state of consciousness to a collective experience.[5] Within the Christian faith, the liturgical event of *Communion* may represent a culmination of this type of spiritual experience.

The artistic level of sacred spaces determines the educational requests in these activities. The masters working for them have often taken on the role of bringing up the next generation of artists. The educational process in the sacred space is dedicated, however, to the respective religion first. The music, the architecture as a whole, the creatures, the objects, the paintings, the lyrics, and the stories, all of this serves to convey and teach the corresponding gospel and to transcend from the immanent into the otherworld. These processes may eventually lead to secularization, since educational acts—the deep reflection of topics, their documentation, the related discussions and social interactions, the acquisition of practical competences toward artistic expression, literacy, architectural knowledge, administrative management, and so on—extend the mind. The corresponding activities are culturally nourished, as are the materials required for building, furnishing, and artistically decorating sacred spaces that come from the factual world. Accordingly, the learner is brought to topics outside the sacred sphere. The educational process tends to progression by its nature.

Further Characteristics and Upcoming Questions

Special objects, such as bells, books, candles, flowers, goblets, musical instruments, and so forth are required for carrying out specific actions within the sacred sphere. The numerous figures and creatures that belong to a faith, captured in sculptures or paintings, play a large role in creating the atmosphere and meaning. The members of the faith relate and bond to them; they are part of their lives. The sacred sphere is the place to meet with them in a near-materialized way.[6]

The objects of the sacred sphere and the architectural surroundings accumulate great wealth and—often—beauty. Considering the immense importance of the sacred sphere in a society of faith, and its ongoing creation, the question may now be asked: How does the sacred space play out in a person, and in a society, if only a minor role is attributed to religion? Or, borrowing the title of Charles Taylor's (2007) seminal book: How does this work in a secular age? Does the sacred sphere also play out in the life of people who are not religious and do not adhere to a faith? Or, more sociologically speaking: Having the psychological reality of the otherworld in mind, and the investment of the species in being connected to it, does the sacred sphere persist in a secular age? Ethical guidelines, all ranges of feelings from sweetness to fear, thoughts, talents, and aesthetic abilities are encouraged and invested in the sacred space. In return for these efforts, one may experience wellbeing and a sense of completeness, feelings of protection, perhaps even the recovery from an illness. In this context, and regarding the significance of the sacred space, the question just asked is perhaps already answered: It is unlikely that such investment and meaning would suddenly disappear and cease to exist, without substitution.

Before coming to conclusions, however, more concrete explorations of the sacred sphere need to be undertaken and reflected upon. The presence of music in the creation of the sacred sphere is at the core of the more specific question of whether music plays a unique role in influencing the mind toward spiritual feelings,[7] not only in people of faith, but also in those who live secular lives. This latter situation will be discussed later, in the section titled "Secular Sacred Spheres." Spiritual experience and participation in the divine world rely on transactions in the sacred sphere.[8] Also, the religious key concept of sacrifice can be well understood by conceptualizing the sacred sphere: sacrifices are brought from the factual to the otherworld—whereas the endowments of blessing, grace, mercy, and love come from the other direction.

Creatures and Figures, Events and Experiences in the Sacred Sphere

The creatures within the sacred space perhaps cause the most puzzling and stimulating reactions among its equipment. They are agents of the sacred sphere's connectivity; they link the factual and the otherworld. Accordingly, they themselves are semifactual or semiother.

Sacred-Sphere Figures in Cultural Context

Angels, saints, ancestors, particular animals, demigods of all kinds—manifold figures exist in the various religions.[9] Some distinct figures persist because they have been painted, carved, or sculpted, such as—to give just a random example—Kokopelli, a figure from pre-Columbian religion, found in the southwestern United States, mostly in rock-art sites. He is a semi-human creature. His body's shape is fully human, with the addition of a hump, which, as the story goes, may carry songs, seeds, or other fertilities. He is a musician: in all portrayals he is playing his flute, mostly while walking. In some images, he has a feathered headdress, in others not. Also, his penis may be pictured or not; if yes, it is always erect. Thousands of versions of the Kokopelli figure exist (Slifer and Duffield 1993). Kokopelli is like an emblem of music manifesting itself in musical instruments together with the performer's body.[10]

He has counterparts in European regions: Pan is a musician, also a flute player, and Orpheus is an artist of the lyre and a composer. They all relate to natural spaces and are representatives of the adoration of fertility. Remarkably, Kokopelli is alive in our time. Both in his homeland and far beyond he is a known and beloved figure, featured on T-shirts and coffee cups and as a charm. Most people do not know about his religious background. He is a twenty-first-century trickster with public recognition, a presence in private lives, most likely playing a role in personal mood-management. The American secular Kokopelli has equivalent colleagues in the Old World as well: Till Eulenspiegel, Pierrot, clowns and jesters, including new ones like Harry Potter, they all share this status of being secular figures with sacred-sphere qualities; they are semihuman, coming from, and belonging to, a different, surreal world, which once had, or may still have, religious traits. The term *hybrid*, as introduced by Bruno Latour (2008), may help to further clarify their constitution as composite beings. In our context of the sacred sphere, they are a mix of the sacred and the factual world and as such qualify exactly for a life in the connecting sphere. They originate from there, or, in other words, are a product of that state of the human mind, as will be worked out in the section titled "The Sacred Sphere as a Cognitive Condition."

Ritual Acts

The cults of a religion regulate the activities carried out in the sacred sphere. In the Christian faith, the sacraments are representative of the invisible world of God and bring the relevant meanings and stories to mind. The involved persons participate in this world through the related ritual actions and obtain assurance of belonging to it. Baptism, the Lord's Supper, and confession are such receiving rituals.

It is interesting that sacred spaces can emerge from mobile sacred objects, called devotionals (including Kitsch objects). With them, ritual acts, dances, and so on can take place outside dedicated sacred locations. The makeup of the sacred sphere depends at least as much on a more abstract semiotic bundle, of which music is one element. Locally bound or not, musical instruments are a very important part of the sacred sphere. The *ney* in the Sufi culture, the *shofar* in the Jewish culture, the organ in the Christian culture, and many others could be named. The sounds produced through these objects, along with the ritually assigned human voice, are central to the actions in the sacred sphere. The exclusive use of the voice is most prominent in the Islamic culture, whereas the Christian religion was the source of an outstanding cultural musical development. It includes not only the processes of musical composition, but also the techniques of building elaborated instruments and the skillful art of playing them.

Many people in our days, attached to a faith or not, experience religious feelings captured in religious music, whereas others may state that they experience beyondness in a spiritual sense while listening to music that is not religious at all.[11]

Toward Secularity

A Secular Age, the already mentioned publication by Charles Taylor in 2007, is a highly recognized contemporary source of orientation with regards to religious questions. The author argues that only in modern times have human beings reached the capacity for a feeling of completeness, or fullness (in his words), independent of faith and another world. The philosophical and technological development after the eighteenth-century enlightenment provided opportunities other than the desperate hope for relief from the misery of life in a world beyond. "Modern secularity in my sense," Taylor states, "has been coterminous with the rise of a society in which for the first time in history a purely self-sufficient humanism came to be a widely available option" (Taylor 2007, 18).

Happiness may become the goal of life in the here and now; and the split between the "factual" and the "other" world possibly fades away. In terms of the two worlds, as shown in figure 9.1, Lang's preceding model would then not need the extension as undertaken. Thinking on this further, the sacred sphere would in modern and late-modern times either not exist—which is unlikely—or simply indwell in the one circle.

By the logics of psychological thinking and observation, Taylor's connection between modernity and the secular option seems to be obvious. But other authors disagree. For example, the German philosopher Hans Joas (2012) points to the fact that secularization is by far not a general development in our time, and that there are even European countries that do not fit the picture (such as Poland, Ireland, perhaps also the German federal state of Bavaria). It seems to me that the identification of a sphere between worlds (as shown in fig. 9.1), and the prevalence of secular spheres of meaning that resemble the meaning of sacred spaces, go along with Joas's skepticism.

Secular Sacred Spheres

We now turn to experiences of this type in nonreligious contexts. The sacred sphere is set to provide experiences of connectedness.[12] The underlying hypothesis is that a touch of spirituality is maintained, and that the surrounding atmosphere can be compared to the sacred sphere, although the equipment and the interactions are secular.

Psychological Need and Cultural Development of Interior Mental Worlds, and Related Exterior Spaces

If there are secular sacred spaces, where are they and what are their characteristics? In the course of evolution, the human species improved its options of physical movement in parallel with broadening the capacities of the mind. Long-term memory and symbolic activity let the individual human being, and the species as a whole, constantly move in worlds of meaning that are not materially present. This is what Lang (1993) had in mind when he labeled Uexküll's ecological function circle semiotic if applied to the human species.

The nonreligious mind does not relate to a divine otherworld. That second world from the model in figure 9.1 may, under this condition, for the most part disappear behind the factual world and attach to it. The marked double-arrowed area, which stands for the sacred sphere, should then be built back into the factual-world component but remain visible. Several other such sacred-sphere areas, now thought of as secular sacred spheres, should be added, in order to represent the multiple attachments, or connections, that a person has to all kinds of further worlds—film, music, literature, social relationships, manifold areas of knowledge, expertise, aptitude, and passion. The worlds of meaning in late modernity are individual, with fluid and multiple contents, and often mediated by technical devices.

Old systems of the sacred sphere may have become fully independent of the religious world, but perhaps, and namely in the arts, feel similar to religion itself. The emphatic statement of a young person in an interview on the personal meaning of music may give an example: "What you need to understand about me is that *music is my religion*" (Spychiger 2013).

Societal and Individual Worlds of Meaning

The "further worlds" are semiotically constructed entities of meaning in various stages of perfection. The arts hold a key position in generating them, as philosopher Ernst Cassirer (1874–1945) showed in his seminal work on symbolic form (three volumes which he wrote and published in 1920–1930; see also Cassirer [1944]). Susanne Langer (1942) deepened Cassirer's concept of symbolic form especially with regards to the presentational symbol. An individual's emotions reach far into these other worlds. Humans relate to, even bond with, figures in the sacred sphere if they are religious, and they do so with the figures in the secular sacred sphere if they are not religious. The longing to be whole, as deduced from the nonsecular two-component model (fig. 9.1), is a human disposition. The human mind (which Donald [2001] called "so rare" in the title of his book) invents fantastic things, ongoing and fluid, as well as preserved in stories, music, and other forms.

Furthermore, humans also constantly reflect on factual world topics. Weather, food, geographic details and obstacles, danger, death, social interaction, short-term and long-term relationships, sexuality and reproduction, are all subject to this cognitive activity of reflection and anticipation. Designers of architectural objects that represent important systems of the contemporary factual world may have absorbed sacred concepts and feelings in a similar way as the aforementioned young man did his music. For example, the significance of sport, as well as the financial system, and also the arts, manifests itself in impressive and beautiful buildings. They resemble temples and cathedrals in their magnificence. The best architects are dedicated to their construction, just as it was with the sacral buildings of the past. Looking at, and visiting, sports stadiums and banks may elicit aesthetic feelings similar to the experience in historic temples, mosques, and cathedrals.[13] It may well be compared to what philosopher of music education Bennett Reimer (1988) described as the experience of *beyondness*, or what John Dewey (1934 [1980], 145) called "the intrinsic assurance of worth."

Continuing this train of thought, we may assume that the genesis of worlds of meaning is a bootstrapping process between individual interior knowledge and systems of thought and exterior material manifestation. The connecting device is at work, be it with religious connotation or not, administering meaning. Humans can exist without faith and still reach fulfillment (or wholeness). To adhere to a religious system is not an anthropological constraint, but the creation of mental worlds parallel to the factual world is one.

The Sacred Sphere as a Cognitive Condition

After identifying worlds of meaning independent of religious systems, a psychological perspective on the development of the individual will now be provided. I assume that cognitive conditions determine the type of meaning that a mind creates. The descriptive cognitive condition may also be understood as state of mind or state of consciousness.

Worlds of Meaning in Terms of Jean Piaget's Stage Model of Cognitive Development

We may look at the magic components of imagination in accordance with the stages of cognitive development, as theorized by Jean Piaget (1896–1980). As Piaget's stages (Piaget 1952) are often understood as steps from low to high, and metaphorically from dark to light, we should be careful with such appraisements (see Spychiger 2014), but nevertheless hope to benefit from Piaget's insight into the human cognitive organization.

Preoperational thinking, stage two in Piaget's model, which is also the phase of magical thinking, is the interesting sequence of cognitive development, and human mental condition, for our purposes. It concerns the preschool age, when children are highly active with their newly obtained capacity to use language. It serves communication as much as it nurtures the creation of fantastic realms, including the imagination of all kinds of figures, such as dwarfs, giants, witches, fairies, and magicians. Objects of the factual world at this stage have souls, feelings, and even the power to have an impact on the course of events. Remarkably, this unrealistic world is not separated from the factual world; rather, children have a basic, vital, and communicative relationship with it. While not immediately immersed in it, they may call this relationship play, as the adults do, and perceive it as such. But the nonseparation of magical and nonmagical thinking is common and uncomplicated at this age. The relationship is different in adulthood. Believing in miracles, playing games very intensely, being heavily involved with objects (such as dolls, or toy cars) might be taken for a deficient sense of reality. Religious systems, with their magic, may in this context be interpreted as socially accepted and organized Piaget stage-two worlds, and so can other, nonreligious worlds of meaning, such as the arts or the entertainment industry.

Stage two in Piaget's model is followed by stage three, the concrete-operational, and stage four, the formal-operational stage. Increasing mastery of the factual world, along with insights into the status of the other worlds, are outcomes of these cognitive progresses. The preconditions to separate the experienced world into abstract concepts of nature and culture, mind and matter are reached developmentally. Post-Enlightenment modernity, or the secular age, would then be representative of these levels of cognitive development. The secularization thesis links this peculiar entanglement with the requirement of separating the magic and the factual from one another. The ability to do so is assigned to growing up, to reaching adulthood and obtaining maturity.

"We Have Never Been Modern" (Bruno Latour)

On the other hand, a number of philosophers have questioned this developmental view. In the first decade of the new millennium, sociologist Bruno Latour expressed disbelief that there is a continuous, progressive process of modernization (Latour 2008). Taylor (2007) also distances himself from a direct alliance between maturity and scientific thinking: "The sense that we have reached maturity in casting aside faith can be played out in the register of disengaged reason, and the need to accept the deliverance of neutral science, whatever they be.... Indeed, the sense may be that we have to avoid a too simple reliance on science in the search for meaning" (588–89). Following Taylor's explanations, maturity displays itself when a person acknowledges the relative (versus absolute) validity of our convictions and has become capable of enduring temporary loss of meaning (Taylor 2007, 582, 589).

Latour's (2008) appraisals of the situation are more radical. He uses the term *hybrid* in order to recapture nature and culture together, objecting that the revolutions of modern times did separate nature and society. He names science, technique, administration, economy, and religion, which in his view have led to the violent and bloody destruction of a large number of natural environments and cultures. Modernization is impossible, he states; or, as worded in the title of his book: we have never been modern. The human mind has not followed the separation of life and the scientific law of nature. Magical thinking maintains its place in humans' cognitive organization.[14] In sum, the answer to the question raised—whether the sacred sphere persists in a secular age and in secular people(s)—is *yes*. The connecting and meaning-making function of the sphere is valid for both types, the sacred and the secular sacred. Meanings originate from feelings of fulfillment. In whatever way and context they come about, they may feel *holy* if they are strong.[15]

The role of education in these processes needs to be addressed in more depth. Education is, in religious contexts, the provider of the related knowledge and of the ability to express and transfer religious experience. The sacred space promotes the religious atmosphere and makes it accessible to all senses. The beauty and expressiveness of the sacred space is as much to please the divine world as the factual and altogether serves to keep the dynamics between the factual and the otherworld positive. The better its connecting function is achieved, the more the members of the faith feel *whole*.

Education and Music Education as Means of Access to Worlds of Meaning

The cultural background of the religious community's world is captured in the sacred space that it creates. Also, sacred spaces are always spaces of cultural education across all its domains, such as literature, music, dance, sculpture, painting, and architecture. As mentioned earlier, in the section titled "Functions and Components of the Sacred Sphere and Its Spaces," the role and task of education in and toward the sacred is comprehensive, and the debate on the role of religion in education is virulent and has gained a global dynamic in our time (see Beaman and Van Arragon 2015). Thinking from the other side, that is, from the perspective of education in the factual world, including secular otherworlds, brings us to the multiple worlds of meaning. Education promotes and extends meaning and enables cultural participation. It brings content and information into the world of the individual learner that were previously not on his or her horizon. Education provides a process of practice in order to furnish learners with competencies. It unlocks cultural spaces and functions in order to design and shape them.

Embeddedness and Domain-Specificity of Musical Learning and Education

Musical learning, and music education, is a good example of how learning takes place in context and how it does not merely occur by mediating competencies educationally (see also Goguen 2004). Musical learning is embedded or, with regard to the semiotic-ecological function circle, is a *learning ecology* (see also O'Neill 2017). Accordingly, music education and related teacher education is a discipline of its own, with all its various topics and fields. The related learning processes are specific to this domain and so are musical activities and experiences, as is their potential to build up worlds of meaning.[16] In addition, these worlds and their related processes of learning take place in social relationships (see O'Neill 2017). Altogether, they cannot be replaced with experiences in domains other than the musical; for example, music is not learned by painting, just as the blacksmith did not learn his craft by working with wood, but with iron.

Much of musical expression and art originate from the sacred sphere. Knowledge about, and introduction to that sphere may, and should be, part of a formal learning process, since it belongs to the culture in which they live. Students can be exposed to sacred places and learn about the musical instruments that belong to it, and about the people who present and play them. Such educational endeavors unlock the sacred sphere and make the relating culture accessible. Moreover, locations can be opened up to musical learning activities for students; for example, churches are often ideal music rooms and may serve as rehearsal and performance locations for children's choirs and many types of music-making groups.

A Searching Area

Understanding the sacred and secular-sacred sphere as a searching area may conceptualize the construct with a term that is equally modern and associated with a traditional religious attitude (see also Frenschkowski 2006). A searching area embraces the learner in an inspiring educational environment. It coordinates and brings education together with the question of the existence of sacredness in secular times, and on a new level of autonomy. Education will always be at the forefront of change if it functions as the gateway to new and old worlds of meaning. It should do so in all kinds of societal and cultural domains, as reflected in the faculties of universities and school subjects. With regard to the individual—children, youngsters, adults at all stages of life—the door to worlds of meaning opens when opportunities for learning and experiencing are provided.[17] To name just a few: learning to play an instrument and discovering music in its theoretical construction and depth of meaning; learning to swim and coordinate the invisible body functions with the element of water; diving into storybooks, or YouTube worlds—these and many more processes may represent such connecting experiences. Children who are brought from deprived homes to learning environments will then have access to second worlds that they otherwise would not know, could not participate in, and would never be able to contribute to. The connecting *agency* (a term by Latour [2005]) of the sacred sphere is very prominent in such examples.

In a further step, it may be necessary to think of the psychologically difficult, even precarious question of guidance. The religious sacred sphere does have a tradition of guidance, with humans asking and expecting it from the otherworld. But in the modernity of North Atlantic societies, such guidance is no longer generally expected. Rather, it falls onto the societal structures, groups, and the individual. The explosiveness of this situation is reflected in the problems of leadership with which the systems of the society (as depicted by Luhmann 2001) are almost constantly confronted. Crises are frequently diagnosed, more so as the technologically enhanced connectivity between the various societal systems progresses. Such challenging situations are known across the systems in politics, sports, religion, finances, law, environmental protection, and others.

Does education as a societal system fulfill its tasks? The educational system is always at risk and may currently be in a crisis. According to Reichenbach, "Education does not have the role of guiding the interplay of the societal domains and their ability to construct and conceive meaning, it nevertheless is the societal system that is in charge of providing alternatives to the centricity of human action and thinking, namely, alternatives to the swamplands of thoughtlessness, indifferentism, incapacity, and self-contempt"[18] (Reichenbach 2015, 17). In terms of my model, Roland Reichenbach's harsh words may well translate into education's responsibility for guiding individuals toward that sphere, in our days secular-sacred, that creates worlds of meaning. It may also be a sphere for self-conscious perception of the kind the young man in the interview spoke of: "music is my religion." It belongs to education, and its endeavors to be aware that there is a difference between the factual and the other world(s), and that their connectedness is a mental process, and that such processes need promotion, need to be nourished. The peaceful coexistence of the worlds within and between persons and peoples—the ultimate dream forever—can then surface and become topic of discussion and focus of work.

MARIA B. SPYCHIGER is Professor of Empirical Music Education at the University of Music and Performing Arts in Frankfurt (Main), Germany. Her research interests include the psychology of music and music education, in particular the effects of music, the musical self-concept, the nature of aesthetic experience, and the phenomenon of learning from mistakes.

Notes

1. The more traditional English word for sacred is *holy*, originating from *whole*. As Marco Frenschkowski (2006, 35) amplifies, "holy" is the fundamental category of the religious. It emerges when the numinous is completed with an ethical aspect and therefore becomes, in Paul Tillich's terminology, the *ultimate concern.*

2. As for the labeling factual and otherworld, the German language has specific terms: *Diesseits* and *Jenseits*. They may translate to "this side" and "the other side," or the "here-world" and "beyond-world."

3. The concept of atmosphere is understood the way Gernot Böhme (1995) introduced it, as an entity of its own, which is perceived and experienced aesthetically.

4. Discussing this point, Charles Taylor relates to the work of Albert Camus, who, especially in *The Myth of Sisyphus*, describes "this desire for unity, this longing for resolution" (Taylor 2007, 584).

5. See Janelle Colville Fletcher and Margaret S. Barrett, "Shaping Identities through Religious Music Engagement," chapter 4 in this volume.

6. See Øivind Varkøy, "Mysterium Tremendum et Fascinans," chapter 8 in this volume.

7. Many others have discussed this; for a profound examination, see Hans Küng (2006).

8. See Frank Heuser, "Music Education as Sacred Practice," chapter 10 in this volume.

9. With regard to the Christian faith, and for a profound analysis, see Adela Y. and John J. Collins (2008).

10. This thought is inspired by Philip Alperson's (2008) paper "The Instrumentality of Music."

11. See Thorgersen and Wachenfeldt, "When Hell Freezes Over," chapter 14 in this volume.

12. For a contemporary discourse on connectedness that includes ethical and spiritual dimensions, see Hüther and Spannbauer (2012).

13. The new building of the European Central Bank in Frankfurt (Main), Germany, designed by the *Coop Himmelb(l)au*, is a prominent current example. It was completed and opened in 2015. It is a light glass construction, standing by itself, close to the river Main. It is visible from far away. With its sparkling blue façade, it reaches for the sky

and elicits an impression of transcending itself to the various shades of the blue sky. The name "Himmelb(l)au" of the architects' office is a play on the words *heaven* (Himmel), *blue* (blau), and *building* (Bau). In this way, it heavily relies on terms related to the sacred sphere.

14. The example I chose out of the millions of possible others is from a feature broadcast by a Swiss radio station, which had a story on an association for garden gnomes. It turned out that the members of this group shared the belief that there are two kinds of gnomes: ensouled and not ensouled. Accordingly, one could say that many of the St. Nicholases are fake but that there is also a real one. On the one hand, St. Nicholas does not exist; on the other, he does. The two worlds, the preoperational, magic-animated one, and the operational, scientific-enlightened one, coexist.

15. The word *holy* may translate into "awesome," "very important," "wonderful," "great," "amazing," and so forth, if expressed in secular terms; in the frame of the individualized sacred sphere, perhaps also "personal," "intimate," or "private." The initial word *holy* is often used in secular contexts as well.

16. From the perspective of research on identity, or self, scientific knowledge and practical and artistic competencies are domain-specific (Spychiger 2017).

17. See Frank Heuser, "Music Education as Sacred Practice," chapter 10 in this volume.

18. The full original citation in the German language is "Bildung fängt nicht dort an, wo Erziehung aufhört, vielmehr stehen beide in der Aufgabe, den Menschen aus seiner Zentrizität herauszuholen, aus dem Sumpf der Gedankenlosigkeit, der Interesselosigkeit, des Unvermögens und der Selbstverachtung" (Reichenbach 2015, 17). For the notion of the German term *Bildung*, see chapter 11 in this volume by Alexandra Kertz-Welzel.

References

Alperson, Philip. 2008. "The Instrumentality of Music." *Journal of Aesthetics and Art Criticism* 66, no. 1 (Winter): 37–51.

Beaman, Lori G., and Leo Van Arragon, eds. 2015. *Issues in Religion and Education: Whose Religion?* Leiden, Neth.: E. J. Brill. http://dx.doi.org/10.13154/er.v2.2015.LIV-LX.

Böhme, Gernot. 1995. *Atmosphäre*. Frankfurt: Suhrkamp.

Cassirer, Ernst. 1944. *An Essay on Man: An Introduction to a Philosophy of Human Culture*. New Haven: Yale University Press.

Collins, Adela Y., and John J. Collins. 2008. *King and Messiah as Son of God: Divine, Human, and Angelic Messianic Figures in Biblical and Related Literature*. Grand Rapids, MI: Eerdmans.

Dewey, John. (1934) 1980. *Art as Experience*. New York: Perigee.

Donald, Merril. 2001. *A Mind So Rare: The Evolution of Human Consciousness*. New York: W. W. Norton.

Frenschkowski, Marco. 2006. "Ist Phantastik postreligiös? Religionswissenschaftliche Beiträge zu einer Theorie des Phantastischen." In *Nach Todorov: Beiträge zu einer Definition des Phantastischen in der Literatur*, edited by Clemens Ruthner, Ursula Reber, and Markus May, 31–51. Tübingen, Ger.: Francke.

Goguen, Joseph A. 2004. "Musical Qualia, Context, Time and Emotion." *Journal of Consciousness Studies* 11, nos. 3–4 (May): 117–47.

Hüther, Gerald, and Christa Spannbauer, eds. 2012. *Connectedness: Warum wir ein neues Weltbild brauchen*. Bern: Hans Huber.
Joas, Hans. 2012. *Glaube als Option: Zukunftsmöglichkeiten des Christentums*. Freiburg, Ger.: Herder.
Küng, Hans. 2006. *Musik und Religion: Mozart, Wagner, Bruckner*. Munich: Piper.
Lang, Alfred. 1993. "Zeichen nach innen, Zeichen nach außen—eine semiotisch-ökologische Psychologie als Kulturwissenschaft." In *Welt der Zeichen—Welt der Wirklichkeit*, edited by Peter Rusterholz and Maja Svilar, 55–84. Bern: Paul Haupt.
Langer, Susanne. 1942. *Philosophy in a New Key: A Study in the Symbolism of Reason, Rite, and Art*. Cambridge, MA: Harvard University Press.
Latour, Bruno. 2005. *Reassembling the Social: An Introduction in Actor-Network-Theory*. New York: Oxford University Press.
———. 2008. *Wir sind nie modern gewesen*. Translated by Gustav Roßler. Frankfurt: Suhrkamp.
Luhmann, Niklas. 2001. *Das Erziehungssystem der Gesellschaft*. Frankfurt: Suhrkamp.
O'Neill, Susan. 2017. "Young People's Life: Learning Ecologies, Identities, and Connectedness." In *The Oxford Handbook on Musical Identity*, edited by Raymond MacDonald, David J. Hargreaves, and Dorothy Miell, 79–104. Oxford: Oxford University Press.
Piaget, Jean. 1952. *The Origins of Intelligence in Children*. Translated by Margaret Cook. New York: International Universities Press.
Reichenbach, Roland. 2015. *Bildung, Reformation, Kitsch*. Unpublished speech given at the University of Vienna, May 27.
Reimer, Bennett. 1988. *A Philosophy of Music Education*. 2nd ed. Englewood Cliffs, NJ: Prentice Hall. (1st edition 1970.)
Slifer, Dennis, and James Duffield. 1993. *Kokopelli: Flute Player Images in Rock Art*. Santa Fe, NM: Ancient City.
Spicer, Andrew. 2013. "'To Show That the Place Is Divine': Consecration Crosses Revisited." In *Images and Objects in Ritual Practices in Medieval and Early Modern Northern and Central Europe*, edited by Krista Kodres and Anu Mänd, 34–52. Newcastle: Cambridge Scholars.
Spychiger, Maria. 2013. "'Musik ist meine Religion': Musik als säkulare und individualisierte Bedeutungsträgerin und die spirituelle Dimension des musikalischen Selbstkonzepts." In *Musik und Religion: Psychologische Zugänge*, edited by Jacob A. van Belzen, 183–98. Wiesbaden, Ger.: Springer.
———. 2014. "Sprachbilder und geometrische Figuren für die Musikpädagogik? Eine pädagogisch-psychologische Reflexion über die Stufenmetapher." In *Impulse zur Musikdidaktik: Festschrift für Mechtild Fuchs*, edited by Georg Brunner and Michael Fröhlich, 59–80. Innsbruck, Austria: Helbling.
———. 2017. "Musical Self-concept as a Mediating Psychological Structure: From Musical Experience to Musical Identity." In *The Oxford Handbook on Musical Identity*, edited by Raymond MacDonald, David J. Hargreaves, and Dorothy Miell, 267–87. Oxford: Oxford University Press.
Taylor, Charles. 2007. *A Secular Age*. Cambridge, MA: Harvard University Press.
Uexküll, Jakob von. 1909. *Umwelt und Innenwelt der Tiere*. Berlin: Springer.

10 | Music Education as Sacred Practice: A Philosophical Exploration

Frank Heuser

As she stepped to the pulpit after reading a passage from the Gospel of St. John to the congregation, the Episcopal priest closed her eyes for several seconds. The ensuing moments of silence clearly denoted that the parish was about to enter a sacred space. The short period of stillness just prior to the sermon signaled that what followed would be a special time, one in which the words spoken by this person might somehow be exactly those that each of the many parishioners present needed to hear at that moment on their own spiritual journey. By beginning the homily with the statement "May these words be Your words, and if not, may these clever people hear what You need them to hear," the priest indicated that the congregation would be entering a sacred space. This suggested that even if the sermon was not actually the inspired words of a deity, the thoughts offered might provide each listener with various degrees of comfort, special insights into their current spiritual struggles, and possibly a moment of transcendence.[1]

For individuals with religious convictions, places of worship provide a physical location for spiritual meditation that serves as a "sacred space." As Iris Yob (2011) points out, however, the feelings of awe and wonder that can be experienced in such settings are not limited to houses of worship or other clearly defined sacred places and often occur in natural settings of incredible beauty. She suggests that the spiritual feelings of "deep joy and sense of being overwhelmed and humbled" extend to all individuals regardless of creed and are "a natural facet of being human." Although the concepts embraced by the words *sacred* and *spiritual* tend to be conflated with religious meanings in popular discourse William Paden (1991) insists that the term *sacred* need not refer "either implicitly or explicitly to an a priori religious reality" (10) and the sacred is not exclusively a religious designation. Veikko Anttonen (2000b) supports this view, stating that long before the term became associated with religion, it was used to express distinctions "between those things that possess a special cultural value and those that do not demand particular attention or specific rule-governed behavior" (43). He suggests that "things set apart as 'sacred' transcend the individual consciousness" (2000a, 275) and form culturally dependent cognitive categories. He elsewhere states that in contemporary society, "people have greater intellectual and moral freedom to create their own 'sacred' moments within their secular cosmology" that "can be comprehended in terms of the category of the sacred" (Anttonen 2000b, 42). Anttonen's statements parallel the thinking of Maria Spychiger (this volume), who suggests that a "sacred space" or, in her words, a "sacred sphere" allows individuals to build alternative mental worlds that extend the mind and alter the "individual state of consciousness to a collective experience." Such "sacred spaces" facilitate forms of culturally determined behavior, allowing individuals to "relate to and even bond with" others as they engage in their own secular but personally meaningful sacred practices. Embracing a worldly view of the sacred has allowed me, as a professor in a public university who inducts future music educators into the teaching profession, to engage my own students in discussions that might enable them to resolve conflicts between their personal spiritual convictions and the realm of secular educational practices.

Recognizing that *sacred* can have meanings that differ from the religious implication usually associated with the Sacred allows individuals to employ the term in secular settings.[2] Doing so in modern Western cultures, where a secular framework dominates most educational practice, requires an understanding of the interplay between secularity, spirituality, and religion. In many ways, the spaces entered when engaging in musical activities also provide opportunities to embrace the sacred. The conductor consciously pausing for several moments prior to performing the Barber *Adagio,* or the pianist sitting quietly on the bench before beginning Debussy's *La Cathédrale Engloutie,* send a signal to their audiences paralleling that of the Episcopal priest before her sermon. Both silently signify that the ensuing time will be special, will be sacred. If approached with the right frame of mind, what the audience hears holds the potential for transcendent spiritual experiences that might not be possible without the reverential stance expected of Western concertgoers. Although young people are often spiritual seekers, the ritualized moments of silence demarking different types of sacred time and space seem exceedingly rare and are not a common part of our sound- and media-filled culture (Smith and Denton 2009). This silent demarcation of a time for something special is one of the commonalities shared by religion, many spiritual practices, and music. The action is a small sacred rite that, as Dale Cannon suggests, functions to sharpen focus and "orient the mind in accordance with" the traditions of a given practice (Cannon 1995, 52). Like music, religious or what some prefer to think of as spiritual practices are a ubiquitous aspect of all human cultures (Durkheim 2008). Just as universal deep truths can be revealed through various faith practices, the mindful learning of music might serve as a locus of self-exploration that provides pathways to the spiritual. Music invites social interactions connecting individuals to their inner selves, to each other and their community, and often facilitates feelings of oneness with a larger entity that we identify as transcendent spiritual experience.

In this chapter, I explore how some of the learning customs employed in music education parallel many practices present in spiritual traditions and suggest ways that awareness of such parallels might enhance instructional processes. The enhancement is realized by examining the emergence of secularity in the West, surveying definitions of spirituality that might enable educators to engage safely in instructional practices of a seemingly spiritual nature, and exploring suggestions that spirituality and religion are not universally viewed as separate entities. Because music has always been connected with religious and spiritual activities and can so readily consume and transform individuals, while thereby connecting them with fellow humans, it seems unnatural that the spiritual potential of music is not explored during music learning. Understanding that secularity does not necessarily negate the presence of the spiritual may lead to critical examination of instructional traditions and allow music educators to become comfortable exploring spiritual aspects of their teaching.

Secularism in Western Culture

Secularity is one of the defining characteristics of modern Western and particularly North Atlantic culture. If one believes Christopher Hitchens, Richard Dawkins, Sam Harris, and Daniel Dennett (2019), who are known as "the Four Horsemen of New Atheism," matters of religion and spirituality no longer hold meaning for members of contemporary society. Recent books such as the *God Delusion* (Dawkins 2006) and *God Is Not Great: How Religion Poisons Everything* (Hitchens 2007) denouncing organized religion have topped best-seller lists. Other evidence for secularization abounds. Former houses of worship such as St Andrew's Church in Hartlepool, England, or the church of Santa Barbara in the northern Spanish town of Llanera now serve communities as popular bars, restaurants, and even skateboard parks (Caulfield 2015; "Former Church" 2011; Kassam 2015). The boundaries of what was considered good taste are challenged by vernacular forms of art that some view as degrading, rather than celebrating, the human spirit (Casey 2004). Even mentioning that spirituality or religion might guide public discourse can bring a barrage of hate from atheists seeking to protect the world from such matters and often approaches the same level of passion one expects from zealots (de Waal 2013). It seems that most aspects of public life in Western culture are now firmly rooted in the secular, rather than the theological or spiritual.

The unbelief accompanying secularism has become pervasive in an age when scientifically acquired information is regarded as the gold standard for all human knowledge. This conviction implies that other forms of inquiry cannot equal the understandings developed through the sciences. The powers of human reason central to the scientific method can make the accomplishments of philosophical inquiry and theological revelations seem inferior. In *Science as a Vocation*, Max Weber (1946) states that the "fate of our times is characterized by rationalization and intellectualization and, above all, by the 'disenchantment of the world'" (155). Disenchantment refers to the rationalization and devaluation of mysticism in modern society resulting from an overwhelming presence of scientific endeavors. The modern context has profound consequences for the psychological and spiritual organization of the "modern self" and has contributed to the end of religion as a significant institutional and social force.

Charles Taylor (2007) suggests that before the sixteenth century the world was instead "enchanted," and one in which religion as promoted by the Roman

Catholic Church was unchallenged, and any form of unbelief or atheism was impossible. Although this view has support from a number of scholars (Edwards 1988; Febvre 1982; Hamilton 2003), Taylor ignores views of other researchers who dispute that uniformity of belief was a universal characteristic of the Middle Ages. For example, David Wootton (1985) reports that some medieval authors expressed skepticism about the immortality of Christ, denied the existence of an immortal soul, and confronted Christian beliefs. John Arnold (2005) suggests that until the Renaissance "there was no one medieval lay faith but a spectrum of faith, belief and unbelief" (230).

Regardless of alternative points of view, Taylor argues for the emergence of secularity from a medieval world with universal Christian beliefs. He suggests that since the Renaissance, indifference and hostility toward theological ideas have become associated with the rise of secularism, which is viewed as a positive development in the evolution of thought toward modernity. The new secular age undermined the need for religious explanations of the world and, ultimately, for hierarchical organized religion in Western society. In Western thought, secularization is considered a rational and natural point of view, and it is believed that the need for religious consolation will diminish as people enjoy ever-greater levels of material well-being. Celebrating human cognitive capacities seems to eliminate any need for considering spirituality in the educational enterprise.

Taylor (2007) argues against Weber's secularization thesis by suggesting that the world has not seen the disappearance of religion but is instead experiencing a diversification and an expansion of faith-based practices. In his view, the move toward secularity has been an ongoing evolutionary process through which existing approaches to religious life are questioned, undermined, and replaced by new ones, the primary impetus being expanding views of what is important for human life. Whereas most accounts of Western modernity center on declining theological beliefs as the essence of secularism, Taylor focuses on the kinds of religious practices that make sense in a humanistic and increasingly secular age.

For Taylor (2007), a "secular age" is a world in which unbelief in God has emerged as a viable option for many people. In his view, "there has been a titanic change in our western civilization. We have changed not just from a condition where most people lived 'naïvely' in a construal (part Christian, part related to 'spirits' of pagan origin) as simple reality, to one in which almost no one is capable of this" (12).

Taylor identifies three stages of secularity. The first is marked by the gradual disappearance of religious involvement from the public sphere. In this stage there was a move from "enchanted reality" toward the "disenchanted reality," as described by Weber. Taylor deliberately employed the phrase "enchanted reality" to evoke the premodern condition of a world in which unbelief was inconceivable. The second stage of secularity involves declining personal religious practice and the marginalization of religion in public discourse, as all affairs of the state become expressed in nontheological terms. The third stage is what Taylor actually means by "a secular age." This form of secularity represents a shift "from a society where belief in God is unchallenged and indeed unproblematic, to one in which it is understood to be one option among others" (3) He asks how a society that was recently explicitly Christian has become one in which individuals are now faced with the choice of belief or unbelief. This forms a cultural background that Taylor calls the "immanent frame" (542).

In Taylor's view, the division between an "immanent" or secular frame of reference and a spiritually focused frame of reference resulted from changes after the Reformation that took place as laypeople assumed societal functions that had been the province of clergy. The change permitted a social life distinct from the spiritual, and it became increasingly possible to rationalize religious institutions as being separate from those of the state. The role of the church evolved from that of nurturing ideals of Christian perfection to that of cultivating worldly goals such as peace, prosperity, and social justice. Eventually the immanent order came to be viewed as all that there is, and the ideal of a transcendent or higher order came to be regarded as a human invention. Rather than existing in a dyadic relationship with the transcendent, the immanent order has become central to the way North Atlantic modernity interprets the world. Although such an inflexible distinction has never been part of any other human culture, Westerners tend to apply it universally, and the "immanent frame" has become the context in which we decide for or against belief. Secularism has supplanted religion as the underlying principle influencing all aspects of modern Western culture. By rejecting a world where human values are derived from theology, modernity has seemingly turned its back on the possibility of transcendence, of building relationships based on theological insights and practices rather than individually derived understandings, and of exploring values that might lead to the discovery of deeper meanings in life. Rather than living in relation within a community and learning to respond to the mutual pulls and tugs occurring as we explore our responsibilities toward each other, individuals now rely on the "immanent frame" as the way to define the world so that it suits their own needs. Taylor does point out, however, that the "immanent frame" does not preclude the acceptance of faith, or of a wide variety of views that may be considered spiritual or sacred in nature.

Rather than supporting the prevailing narrative of modernity as being the triumph of reason over the tyranny of the Roman Catholic Church, in *The Theological Origins of Modernity*, Michael Allen Gillespie (2008) suggests that the contemporary world is much less secular than conventional wisdom asserts. Instead of being disengaged from theological discourse, he regards modernity as a different way of exploring questions that were once understood as theological. In Gillespie's view, modernity was set in motion as religious belief became a private issue that allows people to practice as they choose as long as personal beliefs do "not challenge secular authority, science or reason" (Gillespie 2008, x). From his perspective, modernity builds on the work of Renaissance humanists who attempted to retrieve philosophical practices of antiquity to deal with the increasing degradation of the human spirit resulting from the success of the scientific enterprise. The philosophical struggles accompanying the birth of science were reactions to a worldview that saw human understanding as scientifically rather than theologically derived. None of the humanists in this struggle professed atheism; but they did place emphasis on human reason and cognitive faculties, rather than on a divine being.

Although secularity seems to have emerged from opposition to what some regard as a unified theological framework, various forms of unbelief have long lived in dialectic with religion and other traditional spiritual practices. Gillespie suggests that the modern enterprise is not an attempt to eliminate religion, but rather an effort to redefine its nature and position in human culture. Acknowledging the ongoing dialectic between religion and unbelief allows us to view secular modernity not as a radical break with Christian heritage, but rather as the emergence of a fundamentally new mode of life that allows for multiple spiritual and sacred practices.

Defining the Territory: Spirituality or Religion

Concepts of religion and spirituality, which in many traditions are often considered synonymous, can be examined as distinct forms of human belief and activity. In the same way as there are multiple modes of formalized worship, there can be many approaches to experiencing and expressing spirituality both within and outside organized practices. The Dalai Lama (1999), who serves on the Board of World Religious Leaders, carefully distinguishes religion from spirituality:

> Religion I take to be concerned with faith in the claims to salvation of one faith tradition or another, an aspect of which is acceptance of some form of metaphysical or supernatural reality, including perhaps an idea of heaven or *nirvana*. Connected with this are religious teachings of dogma, ritual, prayer, and so on. Spirituality, I take to be concerned with those qualities of the human spirit—such as love and compassion, patience, tolerance, forgiveness, contentment, a sense of responsibility, a sense of harmony—which brings happiness to both self and others. (22)

In his view, there is a difference between engaging in specific religious practices and exploring the spiritual dimensions of daily life with intentionality in the search for ultimate meaning. Other authors considering the nature of spirituality support this view. In *The Mystic Heart*, Wayne Teasdale (1999) states that "being spiritual suggests a personal commitment to a process of inner development" (17) rather than devotion to a specific religious pathway. In their research on spiritual development among university students, Astin, Astin, and Lindholm (2011) suggest that spirituality is concerned with "inner, subjective life" (4) affective experiences, and concerns about the meaning and purpose in life rather than in religious dogma. Building on research by Kendler, Gardner, and Prescott (1997), who suggest that personal spirituality is a concept distinct from religion, Lisa Miller (2015) maintains that spirituality involves "an inner sense of living in relationship to a higher power" (6). As Kenneth Pargament (1999) states, spirituality "is becoming differentiated from religion as an individual expression that speaks to the greatest of our capacities" (6).

A multitude of views are present in the ongoing debates over differences between religion and spirituality. Whereas Pargament feels that spirituality is a part of religion, Hans Stifoss-Hanssen (1999) believes that it should be considered a "wider concept than religion" (26) and that definitions require continuous refinement. Sahaya G. Selvam (2013) argues that although acknowledging differences between religion and spirituality may be necessary in secularized Western societies, such distinctions do not represent how these concepts are understood from a global perspective. He offers a comprehensive multidimensional model of religion and spirituality that suggests a continuous spectrum of perspectives in the human search for meaning, ranging from the upwardly directed and profoundly "Sacred" found in deep communion with higher states of being to the rather mundane sense of "sacred" that becomes possible through outwardly directed daily routines. This allows for constructs such as "religious-spirituality" or "secular-spirituality" and provides a taxonomy for examining religion and spirituality throughout the world, which implies that some practices may be appropriate for use in secular settings.

Dale Cannon (1995) identifies six generic modes of being religious, which include ritualized activities, rational examination, deep reflection, dedicated practice, social engagement, and mystical seeking. Such culturally determined behavioral categories (Spychiger, this volume) are not limited to religion and can be interpreted through a framework of secular-spirituality. Cannon's generic modes resemble a number of the learning customs and procedures employed in music education and offer openings for music teachers to understand possible parallels between musical and religious practices. The repetitive activities seen in faith communities include the continuous revisiting of sacred literature, regular participation in community rituals, developing and reinforcing a common repertoire of collective wisdom, and working with others toward mutual goals. These practices can be seen as analogous to the musician periodically revisiting repertoires to discover deeper insights, engaging in ritual acts of public performance, learning common techniques or repertoires central to a given musical genre, and performing with others to create something that transcends the music-making abilities of any individual. Although music can readily connect individuals with fellow humans, teachers are understandably cautious about addressing matters of spirituality in secularized settings. Such hesitancy is completely justified if spirituality is connected to a specific religion. Embracing an all-encompassing rather than strictly religious view of spirituality allows educators to take advantage of special moments in teaching to discuss issues of meaning and transcendence without fear of violating boundaries separating church and state. The implication is that teachers might become comfortable exploring issues of connectedness, community, and relationships with others that are known best through empathy, intuition, and emotion without fear of treading on the forbidden territory of religious creeds.

Sacred Practices in Music Education

Music teachers may innately understand the power music has to touch individual souls and unite them in common purpose. In secular situations, however, creating a sacred space in which young people might explore their spiritual essence can seem dangerous, especially in settings where contrasting belief systems are present. We avoid such risks by limiting teaching to that which is easily measurable, rather than to the important and magical aspects of music that might offer far greater meaning to the learner (Pratt 1990). As teachers, we must acknowledge that everyone has the potential to use one's many rich capacities, such as "intuition, empathy, emotion and faith" (Palmer 1983, 52) to connect with the world beyond themselves in as many ways as possible. Even though students in North Atlantic countries are products of a secularized postmodern culture, many young people are "spiritual seekers" struggling to find meaning in their subjective lives (Smith and Denton 2009).

Rather than accepting traditional religious beliefs without question, youthful seekers actively explore a multiplicity of customs and practices. Perhaps unreceptive to organized religions, they nevertheless consider themselves as spiritual beings and readily experiment with a variety of meaning systems to intentionally develop a blend of practices (Lindholm et al. 2011). The numerous possibilities presented by the modern world have opened them to exploring an array of truths and to selectively developing an eclectic blend of beliefs and practices to meet their personal needs. They are spiritual nomads, engaged in a "perpetual quest for greater insight and more authentic and fulfilling experiences" (Smith and Denton 2009, 73).

Recognizing that students in our music classes are seekers with profound longings for deeper experiences to connect with each other, their teachers, and their community suggests that educators can actively seek ways to cultivate each individual's spiritual essence. Both music classrooms and private studios offer opportunities through which this might be accomplished. In particular, music learning settings provide openings to explore the profound nature of the guru-disciple relationship and to engage in nonverbal thinking processes. The interdependency required among learners during ensemble instruction can help students experience connectedness and feel the profound support that is possible only through active participation within a community devoted to common purpose.

In *Bowling Alone,* Robert Putnam (2001) described the disconnection individuals feel and the impact isolation has on cultural and social structures in US society. With the digital communities that have sprung up since the book was published, there is fear that online media are further replacing actual human-to-human interactions (Carr 2010; Turkle 2011). The educational offerings available over the internet illustrate how easy it is to accomplish numerous learning activities without actually meeting a teacher or fellow students. Although this efficient mode of transmitting knowledge does present possibilities for music education, we must ask just how the ensuing separation of teacher from learner, as well as student from student, affects one of the most important byproducts of the learning process: human relationships.

One of the great values of music instruction has always been the close interactions that evolve between teacher and student. Whether in ensembles or the private studio, the master/apprentice relationship between music teacher and music learner often approaches that of the sacred and can become like the bond that develops between a disciple and his or her revered spiritual guru. The Sanskrit word *guru* means "teacher" or "master." A guru is a highly respected person who possesses saintly qualities and helps disciples on their journey toward enlightenment. The concept of the guru can be traced to the early *Upanishads* (Sri Aurobindo 1996), where the idea of the divine teacher embodied in an individual being living on earth emerged from early Brahmin traditions. In Hindu belief, the guru is an enlightened master whose authority is derived from experience and who instructs disciples in matters of spiritual development and religious traditions. Next to parents, the esteemed guru is the most venerable influence on an individual's life. It is essential that music teachers acknowledge that their relationships with learners can develop into the type of a deep connection that arises between a guru and a disciple.

Much formal music study requires that a learner participate in an apprenticeship under the guidance of a mentor whose musical knowledge, much like that of a spiritual guru, is derived from experience. The respected teacher models skills a student needs to acquire, refines their musical progress by nurturing verbal feedback, and initiates the novice into a community of musical practice. Because studying music requires that learners engage in some type of public performance, it is natural for teachers to become deeply invested in their students. The preparation involved in the learning process requires that the teacher have patience, musical skills, pedagogical insights, and the ability to create the best possible individual pathway for each student. Just as the guru-disciple relationship described by Paramahansa Yogananda in *The Autobiography of a Yogi* (1946) enabled him to establish his own spiritual identity, the young musician's mentor must recognize that each student needs to establish an individual identity as a musician. In such a relationship, the learner has complete trust in the abilities of the teacher to guide him or her through the many possible challenges that arise over the years they work together. In the best circumstances, a deep bond develops between mentor and apprentice that nurtures the need both have for connectedness to others. As the mentor finds ways to help the novice develop proficiency and explore the expressive essence of the music she is studying, the learner experiences what it means to have faith in another human being. As the maturing musician masters an increasingly difficult repertoire and begins to find satisfaction in exploring creative musical possibilities beyond the simple pleasure of performing, she learns what it means to sense unity with others and the surrounding world. At its best, the Western approach to music learning, with its model of one-on-one master-apprentice style instruction or of an inspirational teacher-conductor guiding an ensemble to a great performance, provides the learner with direct insights into the awe, mystery, humility, and compassion that might be awakened through guru-disciple relationships.

Because it can be a deeply trusting guru-like relationship, music teachers must make sure that interactions with students are ethical. The teacher should not assume the role of a master, demanding unquestioning obedience as the student is carefully molded into a replica of the instructor, but rather that of a compassionate nurturer whose goal is musical fulfillment for and independence of the learner. For the private instructor, this means that hopes for fame as a teacher who consistently produces competition winners must be balanced by respecting the desires many students have to play only for personal gratification. It is humbling to discover that music may not be the career choice for a learner who has incredible potential. Likewise, ensemble teachers must learn to treat students as fellow travelers with whom they make music and explore layers of meaning, rather than as mere sound producers that allow the director to conduct concerts or win competitions. All too often, ensemble teachers try to achieve better performances by exerting extrinsic pressures on students, or by replacing current members with more accomplished performers. A more ethical approach to improving performance quality requires the gentle nurturing of the students one is blessed to teach. Because students have faith in a good music teacher, it is essential that the mentor actually model what it means to be a responsible and ethical citizen in our communities and culture. Thus, the teacher with whom the student interacts must reflect the adult we would like each student to become. In this way, the music teacher might mirror the spiritual essence of a venerated guru.

Encounters with the solitary self are a central aspect of many faith traditions. Ranging from the third-century Desert Fathers, who retreated to barren wilderness areas of Egypt and paved the way for Christian monasticism (Gorg 2011), to modern-day seekers attending electronics-free retreats for the purpose of withdrawing from digital discourse (Baek 2013), surrendering to places of sacred silence can bring profound spiritual insights. Providing opportunities for students to become silent and listen deeply is of course one of the many goals of music education. Although no one would suggest isolating music students into monastic cells, their voluntary retreat into practice rooms provides a way of experiencing nonverbal encounters with their own inner being. As they practice, the quality of musical output is reviewed, assessed, and revised without using spoken words. Yes, an inner verbal dialogue with the interior self may direct hoped-for improvements, but also many subtle comparisons are taking place on only the musical level, which allows the learner to make adjustments in fine-motor skills and phrasing that contribute to deeply communicative music making. As the ability to communicate emotional content improves, the musician learns to connect more intimately with colleagues in ensemble settings, where interactions between individuals are often accomplished through subtle musical and visual, rather than verbal, cues. As performance competence is refined, music making becomes a path for connecting the cognitive, emotional, and spiritual self to others. Skills that were initially cultivated in the sacred solitude of the practice room enable individuals to escape their isolation and experience the awe and mystery that takes place as music making allows their inner self to become deeply connected with others.

Music teachers must recognize that mentorship is comparable to the role of a guru and thus must honor their work as a form of sacred, albeit secular, practice. Approaching their craft in this manner demonstrates an understanding that the human connections established during music creation can give rise to learning experiences through which barriers between individuals might shrink into insignificance (Cheah 2009; Riiser 2010). A music educator concerned with nurturing the spiritual will treat teaching as a sacred space, thereby creating an environment honoring and respecting individuals while cultivating a sense of mutual interdependence as a central value of the learning community. In such settings, students become emotionally as well as physically comfortable and can feel moments of transcendence that allow them to regard themselves, their fellow students, and the world with more trust than might otherwise be possible. The working together of teacher and student through musical learning processes results in a whole that is greater than any of the individual pieces and can be a magical force promoting openness and spiritual growth. As bell hooks (2010) has said, the classroom is "a place where paradise can be realized, a place of passion and possibility, a place where spirit matters, where all that we learn and all that we know leads us to greater connection, into greater understanding of life lived in community" (151). hooks's words seem particularly appropriate to the sacred practices that seem so much a part of music learning settings.

Conclusion

Music can be a powerful way for individuals to connect with their spiritual selves. Regardless of one's view toward religious practices, many forms of music, ranging from deeply moving symphonic performances to the haunting melodies of a Native American flutist, can transport listeners into awe and wonder. Because music so readily provides peak emotional experiences (Maslow 1968) through which people might be transformed and more closely connected with each other, it makes sense to include the spiritual potential of music in the process of music education. This might be safely accomplished by carefully incorporating some of the secular aspects of Cannon's (1995) modes of being religious into learning environments. It is the secular characteristics, not the religious interpretations of Cannon's categories, that are suitable for use in educational settings.

All too often in secular society, the human spirit is absent from our music classrooms and teaching studios. Yes, the body and cognitive self may be present, but the feelingful "spiritual essence" of the learner is frequently left at the door, as instruction focuses exclusively on preparing students for performances or achieving predetermined learning outcomes. As a result, the transformative potential that might be experienced through music making remains unexplored. Because secular approaches to contemporary political and social life emphasize a complete separation of church and state, music teachers are understandably hesitant to deal with spiritual issues in school environments. But those interested in exploring the spiritual in educational settings should be better equipped to do so, with the knowledge that secularity and spirituality have a history of coexistence. Although the interplay of the secular, spiritual, and religious can be contentious, they continue to influence the contemporary world.

Embracing a multidimensional view of religion and spirituality, as suggested by Sahaya G. Selvam (2013), allows teachers to help students develop the capacity to see beyond themselves, to become more than they are, to see mystery and wonder in the world around them, and to experience private and collective moments of awe, wonder, and transcendence. By understanding that the human desire to experience higher awareness is not necessarily attached to, and can be separate from, religious faith, the music teacher might safely create sacred spaces and thereby explore the often unacknowledged spiritual essence of the human condition.

Although Charles Taylor identifies three modes of secularity, religious involvement has not disappeared from the modern world. A peculiar aspect of what Jürgen Habermas (2006) refers to as postsecularity is that many areas of the world maintain an interest in religion and make real efforts to explore aspects of human nature that transcend logical and empirical ways of knowing. It seems that religion and spirituality will continue to live in communion with secularity, in spite of the desires of doubters and skeptics. For music educators, opening our classrooms to the spiritual does not require violating the principles of separating church and state. It means that we must assume the role of a caring and benevolent guru whose concern is not the imposition of specific beliefs on students, but rather the creation of places in which learners can explore who they are and who they might become through experiences of transcendence, joy, and community. Thomas Merton (1979) suggests that "the purpose of education is to show a person how to define himself authentically and spontaneously in relation to his world—not to impose a prefabricated definition of the individual on himself" (23). When instructional practices carefully and sensitively create sacred spaces for experiencing moments of transcendence, secular forms of spirituality can assume an important role in our music teaching.

FRANK HEUSER is Professor of Music in the Herb Alpert School of Music at the University of California–Los Angeles. His research interests include developing ways to improve music pedagogy and medical problems in the performing arts.

Notes

1. In this chapter, *transcendence* refers to experiences in which individuals move beyond their usual limits, boundaries, and consciousness. Transcendence might include feeling a deep connection with music and other individuals and may or may not result in sensing connections with higher planes of existence.

2. The majority of references to "sacred" in this chapter refer to times, spaces, and activities that are special and different from the rather mundane tasks of daily life. Although these sacred times and activities might be approached with reverence, they are not necessarily of a religious or hallowed nature. When referring to higher states of being or consciousness, *Sacred* will be used.

References

Anttonen, Veikko. 2000a. "Sacred." In *Guide to the Study of Religion*, edited by Willi Braun and Russell McCutcheon, 271–81. London: Bloomsbury.

———. 2000b. "Toward a Cognitive Theory of the Sacred: An Ethnographic Approach." *Folklore* 14 (December): 41–48.
Arnold, John H. 2005. *Belief and Unbelief in Medieval Europe*. London: Bloomsbury.
Astin, Alexander, Helen W. Astin, and Jennifer A. Lindholm. 2011. *Cultivating the Spirit: How College Can Enhance Students' Inner Lives*. San Francisco: Jossey-Bass.
Aurobindo, Sri. 1996. *The Upanishads*. Twin Lakes, WI: Lotus.
Baek, Raphaella. 2013. "At Tech-Free Camps, People Pay Hundreds to Unplug." *All Tech Considered*, July 5. NPR. http://www.npr.org/sections/alltechconsidered/2013/07/05/198402213/at-tech-free-camps-people-pay-hundreds-to-unplug.
Cannon, Dale. 1995. *Six Ways of Being Religious*. Belmont, CA: Wadsworth.
Carr, Nicholas. 2010. *The Shallows: What the Internet Is Doing to Our Brains*. New York: W. W. Norton.
Casey, Damien. 2004. "Sacrifice, Piss Christ and Liberal Excess." *Arts and Opinion* 3, no. 3. http://www.artsandopinion.com/2004_v3_n3/pisschrist.htm.
Caulfield, John. 2015. "Is Nothing Sacred? Seattle Church to Become a Restaurant and Ballroom." *Building Design and Construction*, March 23. http://www.bdcnetwork.com/nothing-sacred-seattle-church-become-restaurant-and-ballroom.
Cheah, Elena. 2009. *An Orchestra beyond Borders*. London: Verso.
Dalai Lama. 1999. *Ethics for the New Millennium*. New York: Riverhead.
Dawkins, Richard. 2006. *The God Delusion*. New York: Houghton Mifflin.
de Waal, Frans. 2013. "Has Militant Atheism Become a Religion?" *Salon*, March 25. http://www.salon.com/2013/03/25/militant_atheism_has_become_a_religion/.
Durkheim, Émile. 2008. *The Elementary Forms of Religious Life*. New York: Oxford University Press.
Edwards, John. 1988. "Religious Faith and Doubt in Late Medieval Spain: Soria circa 1450–1500." *Past and Present* 120 (August): 3–25.
Febvre, Lucien. 1982. *The Problem of Unbelief in the Sixteenth Century: The Religion of Rabelais*. Cambridge, MA: Harvard University Press.
"Former Church Set to Become Restaurant." 2011. *Hartlepool Mail*, April 6. http://www.hartlepoolmail.co.uk/news/community/former-church-set-to-become-restaurant-1-3256059.
Gillespie, Michael Allen. 2008. *The Theological Origins of Modernity*. Chicago: University of Chicago Press.
Gorg, Peter. 2011. *The Desert Fathers: Saint Anthony and the Beginnings of Monasticism*. San Francisco: Ignatius.
Habermas, Jürgen. 2006. "Religion in the Public Sphere." *European Journal of Philosophy*, 14, no. 1: 1–25.
Hamilton, Bernard. 2003. *Religion in the Medieval West*. Oxford: Oxford University Press.
Hitchens, Christopher. 2007. *God Is Not Great: How Religion Poisons Everything*. New York: Hachette.
Hitchens, Christopher, Richard Dawkins, Sam Harris, and Daniel Dennett. 2019. *The Four Horsemen: The Conversation That Sparked an Atheist Revolution*. New York: Random House.
hooks, bell. 2010. *Teaching Critical Thinking*. New York: Routledge.
Kassam, Ashifa. 2015. "Empty Spanish Church Transformed into 'Sistine Chapel' of Skateboarding." *The Guardian*, December 17. https://www.theguardian.com/world/2015/dec/17/empty-spanish-church-transformed-into-sistine-chapel-of-skateboarding.

Kendler, Kenneth S., Charles O. Gardner, and Carol A. Prescott. 1997. "Religion, Psychopathology, and Substance Use and Abuse; a Multimeasure, Genetic-Epidemiologic Study." *American Journal of Psychiatry* 154, no. 3 (March): 322–29.

Lindholm, Jennifer A., Melissa L. Millora, Leslie M. Schwartz, and Hanna Song Spinosa. 2011. *A Guidebook of Promising Practices: Facilitating College Students' Spiritual Development*. Los Angeles: Regents of the University of California..

Maslow, Abraham H. 1968. "Music Education and Peak Experience." *Music Educators Journal* 54, no. 6: 72–171. https://doi.org/10.2307/3391274.

Merton, Thomas. 1979. *Love and Living*. New York: Farrar, Straus, Giroux.

Miller, Lisa. 2015. *The Spiritual Child*. New York: St. Martin's.

Paden, William E. 1991. "Before 'the Sacred' Became Theological: Rereading the Durkheimian Legacy." *Method and Theory in the Study of Religion* 3, no. 1: 10–23.

Palmer, Parker. 1983. *To Know as We Are Known: Education as a Spiritual Journey*. San Francisco: Harper and Row.

Pargament, Kenneth I. 1999. "The Psychology of Religion and Spirituality? Yes and No." *International Journal for the Psychology of Religion* 9: 3–16. https://doi.org/10.1207/s15327582ijpr0901_2.

Pratt, George. 1990. *Aural Awareness: Principles and Practice*. New York: Oxford University Press.

Putnam, Robert. 2001. *Bowling Alone*. New York: Simon and Schuster.

Riiser, Solveig. 2010. "National Identity and the West-Eastern Divan Orchestra." *Music and Arts in Action* 2, no. 2: 19–37.

Selvam, Sahaya G. 2013. "Towards Religious-Spirituality: A Multidimensional Matrix of Religion and Spirituality." *Journal for the Study of Religions and Ideologies* 12, no. 36 (Winter): 129–52.

Smith, Christian, and Melina Lundquist Denton. 2009. *Soul Searching: The Religious and Spiritual Lives of American Teenagers*. New York: Oxford University Press.

Stifoss-Hanssen, Hans. 1999. "Religion and Spirituality: What a European Ear Hears." *International Journal for the Psychology of Religion* 9, no. 1 (November): 25–33. https://doi.org/10.1207/s15327582ijpr0901_4.

Taylor, Charles. 2007. *A Secular Age*. Cambridge, MA: Belknap.

Teasdale, Wayne. 1999. *The Mystic Heart: Discovering a Universal Spirituality in the World's Religions*. Novato, CA: New World Library.

Turkle, Sherry. 2011. *Alone Together: Why We Expect More from Technology and Less from Each Other*. New York: Basic.

Weber, Max. 1946. "Science as a Vocation." In *Max Weber: Essays in Sociology*, edited and translated by Hans H. Gerth and C. Wright Mills, 129–58. New York: Oxford University Press.

Wootton, David. 1985. "Unbelief in Early Modern Europe." *History Workshop* 20 (Autumn): 82–100.

Yob, Iris M. 2011. "If We Knew What Spirituality Was, We Would Teach for It." *Music Educators Journal* 98, no. 2: 41–47.

Yogananda, Paramahansa. 1946. *Autobiography of a Yogi*. New York: Philosophical Library.

11 | *Advocatus Diaboli*: Revisiting the Devil's Role in Music and Music Education

Alexandra Kertz-Welzel

Opinions differ on music and music education's relationship to religion. Some scholars might be excited about the opportunities music education offers for religious education, for instance in examining similarities between religious and intense musical experiences (Freer 2011) or the possibilities of using musical works such as Johann Sebastian Bach's *St. Matthew Passion* as a way of teaching Christian values. These connections between music education and religion are particularly fascinating in countries where religious education is not part of the public-school curriculum. For other scholars, however, it might rather be surprising or even frightening to see this relationship, and it may seem preferable to maintain the distinctions between religion and music as school subjects, perhaps fearing that the power of music could be harnessed for the religious indoctrination of students.

The relationship between music, education, and religion is not unproblematic,[1] and the dangers of misusing music for religious persuasion are significant. In this chapter I scrutinize the connections between music, education, and religion from a philosophical point of view, following notions of critical theory as exemplified in the critique of German music education by Theodor W. Adorno (1973). At the core of the investigation is the attempt to illustrate the problems arising from pursuing utilitarian and religious goals in music education. Metaphorically speaking, this will be a search for the devil in music and music education. I utilize the devil as a metaphor and guide, as he is presented as a dialectical character in German literature, particularly in the play *Faust* (2005 [1808]) by Johann Wolfgang von Goethe and the novel *Doctor Faustus* (Mann and Woods 1999 [1947]) by Thomas Mann. Our journey will take us from general considerations of the dialectical nature of the devil to places where you would expect him—and others where you would not. It will be an exercise in dialectical thinking, calling for a critical awareness of the relationship between music, education, and religion.

The chapter starts with a short description of who the devil is in general and with regard to two literary works. The next section explores where the devil can be found, no matter whether in music, education, or music education. The notion of Kitsch in relation to music education will particularly be scrutinized, before moving on to examining German music education during the Third Reich and Adorno's critique. The final section develops alternative perspectives and calls for music educators and scholars to become the devil's advocate by being more critical toward the link between music education and religion. While exploring the dialectical nature of moral and religious intentions in music education, this chapter provides only glimpses at certain dimensions of the topic, not aiming at a comprehensive examination.

Who Is the Devil?

The devil is the personification and the symbol of evil. He is a fallen angel or an evil spirit. He is God's enemy. He tries to seduce people and wants their damnation. Some characteristics of the devil are obvious, as exemplified in many works of art: He is a dark angel with wings or he has cloven hooves, horns, and a trident. He might spread a sulfuric stench. He often seems to impersonate an animal, with ghostly or human features. He tries to seduce people who struggle with their human limitations and are desperately looking for truth and fulfillment. Since he is repulsive and fascinating at the same time, he has been an important topic in literature. As exemplified in the works of German writers Johann Wolfgang von Goethe (1749–1832) and Thomas Mann (1875–1955), the devil can be a highly intelligent, cynical, and fascinating counterpart to God.

Goethe's play *Faust*, completed in 1808, is the most famous work of literature exemplifying the devil's fascinating seductive power. It has had a significant impact on his general image: The devil promises to help Renaissance scholar Heinrich Faust gain the knowledge and fulfillment he is looking for. He therefore agrees to a contract with the devil, who offers Faust a moment of complete fulfillment and happiness; in return, Faust has to accept eternal damnation. In essence, *Faust* is the exemplary myth of humankind, symbolizing the longing for transcending human limitations toward complete knowledge, sensual fulfillment, and eternal happiness. Mephisto, as the devil is called in Goethe's play, is a charismatic, intelligent, and cynical character. His most striking feature is his dialectical nature, indistinguishably uniting good and bad. This makes him dangerous and seductive for human beings. This feature is best characterized by the following famous quote: "Part of that Power, not understood, / Which always wills the Bad, and always works the Good" (Goethe [1808] 2005).[2] Mephisto implies here that he is not bad at all, because while he aims for evil, he does good—and vice versa. The devil minimizes his influence, implying that he is not able to do any real harm. This deceit can pose a serious danger to human beings by leading them to underestimate the devil's real power, realizing the misjudgment only when it is too late. This dialectic of the devil is one of the devil's most significant and most seductive features.

The other important literary work serving as a point of reference for this chapter is Thomas Mann's novel *Doctor Faustus* (Mann and Woods 1999 [1947]). Mann locates the Faust legend in the context of the first half of the twentieth century, amid the politics of Germany's Third Reich, and new developments in the history of music. At the center of the novel are the life and work of the fictitious German composer Adrian Leverkuehn, whose goal is to create music never heard before. He enters a Faustian bargain, where the devil offers him a completely new way of composing, in exchange for his soul, his happiness, and the experience of love. Music plays an important role in Mann's novel, notably also from the influence of German philosopher and musicologist Theodor W. Adorno (1903–1969) advising Mann in musical matters. The devil, and an understanding of music as strict dodecaphony, are metaphors employed to explain why Germans obediently followed Hitler, willingly subjecting themselves to his totalitarian ideology. Dialectics is one of the main principles exemplified in the novel, both in music, in society, and in people's lives. The devil in particular reveals his dialectical nature in more than one situation in this novel, as one of his most striking statements illustrates: "A highly theological matter, music—just as is sin, just as I am" (Mann and Woods 1999 [1947], 257). According to the devil, nothing is what it seems, good is evil and evil is good. There seems to be hidden dialectical structures in everything, including music.

The devil's dialectical character, as defined by Goethe and Mann, is exactly the kind of devil this chapter refers to. He is no longer characterized by a sulfuric stench or cloven hooves. Rather, he has human features, hiding behind the appearance of good. In terms of general dialectics, it is not clear what good and what evil is, because it is often contorted and confused. Even the obviously good can turn out to be evil, or vice versa. The devil's dialectical nature can best be summarized by a quote from John Milton's poem "Paradise Lost" (1667): "Out of good, still to find means of evil" (Milton 1667, li. 165). This observation opens up interesting perspectives for music education's connection to religion and good teaching intentions.

Where Is the Devil?

Searching for and identifying the devil has a long tradition in the history of music, aesthetics, and music education (Lippman 1992). The devil is not always, however, where one might expect him to be, for instance in dissonant music or sensual sounds. The real evil that, metaphorically speaking, seduces and destroys people can be found much more often in false theoretical constructs and notions, for example about music education and its goals.

In Music

Music has often been seen as a part of God's creation (e.g., in the Bible), as a symbol for the sublime order of the universe (e.g., Pythagoras, Boethius), as supporting the stability of the state (e.g., Plato), or arousing and cleansing emotions in order to foster moral behavior (e.g., Aristotle). If these positive notions of music represent harmony, heavenly order, and well-being, one might assume that the devil must be the complete opposite: disturbing the harmony of the universe (e.g., through dissonances), destroying the order of the state (e.g., through wrong tonalities or instruments), or arousing sensuality (e.g., through rhythmically charged music and movement). These notions have been connected to "devilish" music throughout the history of music and aesthetics. Entertaining music, dance music, popular music, dissonant music, music that does not follow certain rules or does not use appropriate instruments, have all been labeled evil or degenerate. "Evil" music was always suspected of fostering immoral behavior, as discussions about degenerate music concerning dissonant music and jazz during the Third Reich, or Elvis Presley's style of dancing, have underlined. North and Hargreaves (2008) describe this kind of music as "problem music."

Metaphorically speaking, however, is the devil really "in" certain kinds of music? Has music the power to incite immoral behavior? Although no empirical evidence has been found that the devil resides in any particular music more than another (see North and Hargreaves 2013), regarding music education, the assumption that some genres of music might be evil, and should thus be avoided, has had a significant impact on the history of music education in schools internationally. Music education has sought not only to protect students from evil or devilish music by avoiding certain repertoires, it has also aimed to foster moral behavior *through* music. The history of pedagogical dreams, from Plato to Schiller's concept of aesthetic education with the purpose of humanizing people through aesthetic experiences, has had a huge impact on music education philosophies and approaches to the present day (Kertz-Welzel 2005a).

But, although the notions of "humanizing" people or fostering moral behavior through the power of music might appear to be worthwhile endeavors, such intentions raise significant concerns and problems. Transforming people through music, even with the intention of humanizing them, can be, and has been, misused by the powerful, whether on huge political stages or in the confines of classrooms. Fostering certain kinds of behavior through music can be seen as similar to training people to fit within a specific ideal of humanity or to completely subject themselves to certain worldviews. Milton's statement "out of good, still to find means of evil" can therefore be a helpful guideline to thoroughly investigate where the devil really is. On closer inspection, that which appears too good to be true, may reveal itself as little more than Kitsch.

In Kitsch

Kitsch is a term used to describe simple and sentimental artistic creations that provide immediate emotional and psychological comfort; an escape in times of trouble. Kitsch is emotionally charged and aims to "banish the demons of life such as problems, misery, or death" (Giez 1994, 49) in a naive and superficial way. Although the notion of Kitsch concerns particularly artistic creations, it can also be applied to various other fields. Kitsch, therefore, is a well-known topic in education, as Swiss educational researcher Reichenbach (2003) explains. It can concern various aspects, such emotionalism in educational processes, as well as preferences for simplicity—for instance, in denying the hardships of learning. *Schmalz*, that is, exaggerated enthusiasm, is an important aspect of Kitsch in education, leaving little room for doubt or criticism. Pedagogical heroism can also be understood as part of Kitsch, suggesting that a teacher always has to be happy, to enjoy teaching, and to be constantly available to help students. Pedagogical heroism can also be related to an understanding of the teacher as therapist or counselor. In general, Kitsch in education tries to reduce the complexity of teaching and learning. It refuses to accept that the reality of teaching is often problematic or frustrating and that it takes a lot of perseverance and resilience to be a successful teacher or student.

German music education scholar Maria Spychiger (2011) has identified Kitsch in music education, for instance, in sentimental notions about the outcomes of music learning. Particularly the so-called transfer effects—as in utilitarian views such as music fostering creativity, intelligence, and social or moral behavior—were, for her, indicators of emotionally charged educational illusions or Kitsch. Such notions are often used to justify music education as part of the school curriculum. For Spychiger, however, Kitsch does not strengthen music's position in the school curriculum. If another school subject might better support utilitarian goals, then, music education could be dispensable. For Spychiger, justifying music education through utilitarian goals as related to Kitsch is not helpful. Her point also concerns attempts to teach morality. She considers it to be a kitschy overextension and oversimplification, because music alone cannot promote moral behavior (Spychiger 2011, 8). Although music certainly has an impact on people and fosters individual, perhaps even moral, development, it is not correct to conclude that music education as a school subject should concentrate on these goals. Utilizing music education to support moral or religious education reduces it to an educational means. Doing so not only marginalizes important musical goals of music education but also can lead to a possible misuse for indoctrination or manipulation, perhaps supporting a character ideal focused on uncritical trust in authorities and obedience that benefits politicians, dictators, or certain kinds of teachers. Following notions of Kitsch in music education could be dangerous, exemplifying Milton's assertion "out of good, still to find means of evil" on the dialectical nature of good intentions.

In fact, seemingly comforting and innocuous Kitsch may, metaphorically speaking, more commonly be a home for the devil than sensual sounds or dance movements. Spychiger (2011) argues, therefore, for teachers' critical awareness of Kitsch in their subject matter and teaching materials in order to identify hidden ideologies and inappropriate goals. Spychiger underlines the danger of Kitsch in music education

> is its power in the moral domain. Morality is linked to emotion, and music carries and easily triggers emotions.... We are especially in a crucial zone and walk on a thin line. If moral goals and ends are linked to music's power, such as personality development through musical activity, or if music's short term power is used for arousing emotions for moral cause.... Music education as an academic discipline should be aware of these relationships and should stand as a kind of a domain of anti-kitsch. (10)

Although Kitsch might appeal to the public through establishing emotional goals for music education, music education is an academic discipline. As such, music education is not destined to fulfill emotional needs or transform human beings and the society but should rather prepare students to gain musical competencies and skills and also to be reflective and self-determined, as, for instance, the northern European notion of *Bildung* indicates (Kertz-Welzel 2017). Utilizing music education for transformational processes can be misused. It is not surprising that dictators have always supported attempts to change people and society by means of education, including music education. Kitsch, for them, was and is a very handy concept in favor of their dreams of a new world, new society, and new human beings. An extreme example for such an attempt is certainly Adolf Hitler (1889–1945) and the misuse of music education during the Third Reich.

In Musische Erziehung

For the National Socialists, music education was an important school subject. Through songs promoting their ideology and various musical activities inside and outside schools, they hoped to plant their ideas of a new world and society in young minds (Kertz-Welzel 2004). Based on Plato's notions about the transformational power of music for individuals and the state, the Musische Erziehung aimed at a renewal of societies and its people. As emphasized in German scholar's Ernst Krieck's programmatic book *Musische Erziehung* (1933), published in the same year that Hitler rose to power, *Musische Erziehung* presents a fundamental critique of Western culture and its intellectual approach, emphasizing feeling and experiencing over thinking. Music education is thus envisioned as part of a holistic education. Music's emotional power is supposed to heal the damage caused by an overemphasis on intellectual activities and renew the harmony of body and soul. Furthermore, having intense aesthetic and emotional experiences by means of joint music making is supposed to strengthen peoples' commitment to a community and its leader.[3] Connected to the notion of community and strong leadership is the longing for a simplicity of life, overcoming the cultural compulsions of an intellectual approach.

The ideals of *Musische Erziehung* clearly aimed beyond mere musical goals of music education. It rather promoted a new way of life, thereby promising a renewed society and whole human beings. This promise of healing and reconciliation is certainly a promise well known in education and music education and would, according to Reichenbach (2003), qualify as Kitsch. But it might even present more than Kitsch and could be similar to religious teachings, as criticized by Adorno (n.d.), because it envisions a renewed and healed world, society, and individuals. These intentions can easily be used for certain aesthetic or political ideologies (Kertz-Welzel 2005a).

It is not surprising that many music educators supported Hitler and the National Socialists because both shared the same dream for transforming people and society and supported a general renewal. People often tend to uncritically follow leaders who share and support their dreams. It is, therefore, also not surprising that in Mann's novel *Doctor Faustus*, Hitler is cast as the devil. Hitler exemplifies many characteristics of the devil mentioned before and is convincing and seductive, using music and music education to renew society and liberate people. Proclaiming the best intentions, while at the same time misusing people's trust for his own ideological purposes, Hitler exemplifies the dialectics of the devil—and the dialectical nature of music education approaches such as *Musische Erziehung*. This illustrates not only Milton's statement "out of good, still to find means of evil," but also the more general dialectics of the devil and his ability to turn things around, as presented by Goethe and Mann. After all, *Musische Erziehung* exemplifies the longing that music education functions as a supplement for religion, supporting the call for renewal, simplicity, and obedience. These goals were challenged by a powerful thinker, German philosopher and musicologist Theodor W. Adorno.

Adorno's Critique of *Musische Erziehung*

Theodor W. Adorno (1903–1969), who was Thomas Mann's musical adviser for his novel *Doctor Faustus*, criticized German education and music education for the Faustian bargain they entered into during the Third Reich. According to Adorno, the success of the National Socialist ideology in Germany was possible only because the educational system failed to educate self-determined and mature citizens who would resist any kind of fascist ideology (Adorno 2005). Adorno saw music education as part of this process. But music education's susceptibility to the National Socialist ideology also exemplified, for him, more general problems (Kertz-Welzel 2005b). First, *Musische Erziehung* represents an anti-intellectual approach. It devalues thinking and critical consideration in favor of intense musical experiences, particularly in community. For Adorno, favoring emotions over thinking does not foster the development of self-determined and mature human beings. Furthermore, the transformation of society through music education, and thereby the solving of political, economic, or social problems, as attempted by *Musische Erziehung*, is not possible for him. Rather, other means are necessary, such as political and social actions. The second aspect Adorno criticizes is the overemphasis on community and leadership: making music in a group is fun and often provides profound musical experiences. But, the danger lies in getting lost within a community, forgetting how to think or act independently. Becoming accustomed to permanently following a conductor's or leader's directions does not support the development of an independent mind. The third critical issue Adorno raises is the fact that music education is not supposed to be some kind of religious teaching and to offer salvation, focused on oversimplified holistic intentions such as healing, renewal, or transformation through the power of music. For Adorno, music education should be focused on music and musical understanding. Transforming human beings and society is not part of its mission and can better be described as misuse of music education for ideological purposes and indoctrination (Adorno 1973). Overall, for Adorno, the actual transformative power of music can be understood only in terms of *Bildung*.

This general German educational term describes a kind of formation and cultivation that puts education for maturity and self-determination at the core of schooling. In music education, *Bildung* has specific implications, also fostering the ability for aesthetic judgment. But the focus is first and foremost on music; fostering maturity might occur as a positive side effect. This is different from employing music education with the aim to transform people or the society.

Adorno is certainly not an unproblematic author, particularly in his notions about popular music. But research has shown that some of his concepts offer useful contributions to new perspectives in some fields, for example the sociology of music (DeNora 2003). His ideas about music education could also be utilized for developing new and critical perspectives on notions about music's transformative power, education, and society. When looking for the devil in music and music education, we might well find him where music education promises salvation and transformation, but, in the end, supports the misuse of people, trying to turn them into a certain kind of character, living according to somebody else's rules. When this happens, music education clearly promotes ideologies. Paintings of hell often imply something like that, with people depicted as being forced to do things imposed on them, condemned to suffer for eternity.

Conclusion

The devil has many faces in the realm of music and music education. He can certainly not only be found in Kitsch or *Musische Erziehung*, but also in many attempts to use music as a means for transforming human beings. It is obvious, however, why connecting music education to religious intentions can be fascinating: many musicians and teachers themselves have experienced the transformative power of music and the similarity of aesthetic to religious experience. But Adorno's perspective can be useful for reconsidering music education's purpose. For him, music education should be primarily about music. Music itself already has an impact on the personality, also supporting personal development. But this is not the foremost goal of music education—rather, it is a side effect. In the German and northern European tradition, when describing the impact music education has on personal and character development, the notion of *Bildung* is widely used (Heimonen 2014; Varkoy 2015). It indicates that music education can be about more than just music, and that the cultivation and formation of individual maturity, self-determination, and aesthetic judgment is important. This perspective certainly challenges naive assumptions about music, education, and religion.

In view of the devil and the power this metaphor has, challenging assumptions about music, education, and religion, it might be useful to argue for the position of the *advocatus diaboli*, the devil's advocate. The devil's advocate takes a critical position, questions everything, and tests the quality of concepts and the validity of arguments in order to find out whether there are better answers. In music education, the task of the devil's advocate would be to scrutinize common beliefs about music education, helping to establish an attitude of being critical and not trusting positive visions. It is important to realize that there are always dialectical structures; one should be careful when something looks too good and is focused on healing instead of concentrating on the music itself. In view of Milton's "out of good, still to find means of evil," one should realize that there are clearly not only positive aspects, but also bad ones, where the devil is hidden and puts educational success in danger.

As musicians and teachers, we often face the devil. Aesthetically, we play with evil all the time, experiencing and transcending our limits as Faust did, sometimes even entering Faustian bargains, accidently or on purpose. The good and evil, failing and succeeding, are part of the business of teaching and being a musician. But the devil's advocate demands a critical and truthful attitude toward our weaknesses, knowing that we have emotional needs, perhaps enjoy Kitsch, and would like to transform human beings and the society through the power of music. The devil's advocate acknowledges our needs and does not judge prematurely. He or she tries to understand, to raise awareness for respective issues and to try to open up new perspectives. The power of the devil often feeds itself from unconscious and unreflected actions, as well as the hidden dialectics of many things we encounter. The devil's advocate can help to overcome naive assumptions and find new ways of acknowledging our weaknesses and emotional needs, but also to stay focused on the real goals of music education. It will help to improve music education theory and practice by focusing on what is our main business, music, but also welcoming the transformative "side-effects" as indicated by *Bildung* and its implications for personal development.

Everybody who believes in the educational power of music and also the need for critical reflection can be an *advocatus diaboli*. It is crucial, however, to realize the dialectics of music and music education and to be aware of the problems that fascinating music education approaches have, in order to avoid the misuse of music education for ideological and indoctrinating purposes. The field clearly has a need for devil's advocates. They are the only ones who can beat the devil at his own game, which is dialectics.

ALEXANDRA KERTZ-WELZEL is Professor and Department Chair of Music Education at Ludwig-Maximilians-Universität in Munich, Germany. She is author and editor of several books, including *Globalizing Music Education: A Framework* (IUP, 2018).

Notes

1. For more information on this topic, see chapters 17 and 18 in this volume.
2. The German original is as following: "Ich bin ein Teil von jener Macht, die stets das Böse will, und stets das Gute schafft."
3. During the Third Reich, everybody was expected to be part of special groups such as the Hitler Youth, where ideological training was often supported by musical activities such as singing or playing in an ensemble.

References

Adorno, Theodor W. 1973. *Dissonanzen: Einleitung in die Musiksoziologie.* Frankfurt: Suhrkamp.

———. 2005. "Education After Auschwitz." In *Critical Models: Interventions and Catchwords*, translated by Henry W. Pickford, 191–204. New York: Columbia University Press.

DeNora, Tia. 2003. *After Adorno: Rethinking Music Sociology.* Cambridge: Cambridge University Press.

Freer, Patrick. 2011. "Spirituality and Music Education [from the Academic Editor]." *Music Educators Journal* 98, no. 2: 8–9. http://scholarworks.gsu.edu/cgi/viewcontent.cgi?article=1024&context=music_facpub.

Giez, Ludwig. 1994. *Phaenomenologie des Kitsches.* Frankfurt: Fischer.

Goethe, Johann Wolfgang von. (1808) 2005. *Faust.* Gutenberg version. http://www.gutenberg.org/files/14591/14591-h/14591-h.htm#IV.

Heimonen, Marja. 2014. "Bildung and Music Education: A Finnish Perspective." *Philosophy of Music Education Review* 22, no. 2: 188–208.

Kertz-Welzel, Alexandra. 2004. "The Singing Muse: Three Centuries of Music Education in Germany." *Journal of Historical Research in Music Education* 26, no. 1: 22–24.

———. 2005a. "In Search of the Sense and the Senses: Aesthetic Education in Germany and the United States." *Journal of Aesthetic Education* 39, no. 3: 102–14.

———. 2005b. "The Pied Piper of Hamelin: Adorno on Music Education." *Research Studies in Music Education* 25, no. 1: 1–12.

———. 2017. "Revisiting Bildung and Its Meaning for International Music Education." In *The Oxford Handbook of Music Education Policy*, edited by Patrick Schmidt and Richard Colwell, 107–21. New York: Oxford University Press.

Krieck, Ernst. 1933. *Musische Erziehung.* Leipzig: Armanen-Verlag.

Lippman, Edward A. 1992. *A History of Western Musical Aesthetics.* Lincoln: University of Nebraska Press.

Mann, Thomas, and John E. Woods. 1997 (1947). *Doctor Faustus: The Life of the German Composer Adrian Leverkuehn as Told by a Friend.* New York: Vintage International. Page references are to the 1999 edition.

Milton, John. 1667. *Paradise Lost.* London: Simmons.

North, Adrian C., and David J. Hargreaves. 2008. *The Social and Applied Psychology of Music.* New York: Oxford University Press.

———. 2013. "Pop Music Subcultures and Wellbeing." In *Music, Health, and Wellbeing*, edited by Raymond MacDonald, Gunter Kreutz, and Laura Mitchell, 502–12. New York: Oxford University Press, 2013.

Reichenbach, Roland. 2003. "Pädagogischer Kitsch." *Zeitschrift für Pädagogik* 49, no. 6: 775–89.

Spychiger, Maria. 2011. "Kitsch in Music Education." Paper presented at the Twenty-Third Mayday Group Colloquium, University of Utah, Salt Lake City, June 16–20.

Varkoy, Oivind. 2015. "Bildung: Between Cultural Heritage and the Unknown, Instrumentalism and Existence." In *The Routledge International Handbook of the Arts and Education*, edited by Michael Fleming, 19–29. London: Routledge.

Part 4
Emancipation, Regulation, and the Social Order

12 | The Humanist Defense of Music Education in Civil and Religious Life: *The Praise of Musicke* (1586) and *Apologia Musices* (1588)

Hyun-Ah Kim

Throughout the literary corpus of Renaissance humanism and the Reformation there is a consensus that music is a divine gift, albeit a double-edged sword, that is, an art that affects human beings for good or ill. Emphasizing the effects of music, major humanist educators and reformers such as Thomas Elyot (1531), criticize what they see as the abuse of music. Although the criteria of musical abuse were not always clear-cut, their polemics called into question the value of music in civil and religious life, which, in turn, caused a series of musical apologetics. As reflected in these polemical and apologetic writings on music, the intersection of music, religion, and education was at the core of the humanist discourse on music. Influenced heavily by the ancient philosophy and theology of music, the humanists discussed music as an integral part of education and religious practice in both positive and negative terms.

This chapter explores some of their critical perspectives on the relationship between music, education, and religion, with reference to two Elizabethan musical treatises that epitomize the humanist apologetics of music: the anonymous *Praise of Musicke* (1586) and John Case's *Apologia musices* (1588). These treatises refuted the musical polemics in England that persisted throughout the Reformation era. Different as the two treatises are in many respects, they nonetheless share the goal of reviving the study of music, against the common charge that music harbors symptoms of vanity and vice. Both marked a milestone in the apologetics of music that concerned the value of music not only for its own sake, but also as a means to moral, religious, and spiritual ends. Most important of all, they offer critical insights for reconsidering the nexus of music, education, and religion from a historical perspective that bridges the gap between antiquity and modernity. Yet they remain hardly examined, apart from the issue of authorship.

The aim of this chapter is thus twofold: first, to evaluate the significance of the two treatises in relation to the history of apologetic literature on music as an integral part of moral education and religious practice; and second, to illustrate how religious worldviews support or hinder the teaching and learning of music, personal and social development, and ethical beliefs and sensibility.[1] Furthermore, it suggests a historical perspective that offers critical reflections on the relationship between religion, education, and musical practice.

The humanist defense of music education is not new in content or perspective. Under the inspiration of musical antiquity, however, it supports the ethical framework of education, within which music plays an essential role, against the religious authorities that restrict existing musical practice for fear of musical abuses. The humanist perspective on music education is antiquarian, yet in no way lacking interest in improving the contemporary world. It points to the benefit of a historical approach for rethinking the place of music education in modern secular society, where music is primarily a source of entertainment. Although many religious institutions or organizations have used music as a means of edifying in various forms, music is generally regarded as auxiliary rather than essential to the goals of education and religion in the public domain. Because this gap exists between the humanist notion of music as a didactic entity and the popular perception of music in our time, therefore, it will be instructive to ponder the humanist musical apologetics that present the most compelling arguments for the timeless value of music as integral to moral education and religious practice.[2]

The English Context of Musical Polemics

From the early sixteenth century onward, the humanist reformers and educators frequently criticized the musical practices of English churches. Their criticism resulted in the reduction of choral foundations at cathedrals and collegiate churches during liturgical reforms under the reign of Edward VI (1547–53). Until the late 1570s English chorister education—the seedbed of future musicians—focused on learning and morals rather than on music. Later reformers tended to be more radical in censuring existing musical practices. They confirm the earlier Reformed view that church music is not for the entertainment of the congregation but for the edification of the church, since singing is prayer, to be conducted with spirit and with understanding. Their moralistic polemics against musical abuse became even stronger in the mid-1570s when public theaters were first established in England (Wickham, Berry, and Ingram 2000). In his *Schoole of Abuse* (1579), for instance, Stephen Gosson condemns pipers [organists], alongside poets and players, as the "caterpillars that devour a Commonwealth." Provoked by Gosson's *Schoole of Abuse*, Thomas Lodge (1853 [1579]), a playwright and poet, wrote the treatise "Defence of Poetry, Music, and Stage Plays," which was issued privately in 1579 but withdrawn immediately. The most vehement contempt poured on the immorality of theatrical performances, including play, music, and dance, is found in Puritan polemical writings. Their criticism is not only concerned with the theatrical performance of music but, more fundamentally, with musicians who are the agents of this devilish and idle pastime.[3] Unlike the common charges of the Puritan hostility toward theatrical performances, however, the Puritans were not always negative about play, as far as it was useful for their propaganda. Percy Scholes (1969 [1934]) demonstrates that secular music, including opera, flourished during the Commonwealth, and the Puritans enjoyed dancing and recreational music in moderation, as long as the sanctity of Sunday was not violated.

Phillip Stubbes (c. 1555–c. 1610), for example, in his *Anatomie of Abuses* (1583), which was the most popular moralistic critic in the 1580s, denounces the musicians who are "most licentious, and loose minded"—"most inclined to all kind of insolence and lewdness."[4] Furthermore, Stubbes boldly urges the musicians who "draw[ing] so many thousands to Hell," to give up their occupations— "pipers, fiddlers, minstrels, and drummers." Stubbes's concern lies in the harmful effects of music on children particularly. Under the question "How to have children learned in all wickedness," Stubbes warns that "if you would have your daughter whorish, bawdry, and unclean, and a filthy speaker, and such like, bring her up in music and dancing, and my life for yours you have won the goal." Although "music is the good gift of God" that "delights both man and beast, revives the spirits, comforts the heart," Stubbes argues, it "estranges the mind" and "stirs up filthy lust," especially when "used in public assemblies and private conventicles as directories to filthy dancing." "Such sweet music," according to Stubbes, "at the first delights the ears, but afterward corrupts and depraves the mind, making it weak . . . inclined to all licentiousness of life whatsoever." Insofar as music serves for a religious or spiritual purpose in a right manner, however, it is highly appreciated: "But if music openly were used (as I have said) to the praise and glory of God, as was intended by it at the first, or privately in a man's secret chamber or soul for his own solace or comfort to drive away the fantasies of idle thoughts, solicitude, care, sorrow and such other perturbations and molestations of the minds, which is, the only ends where to true music tends, it were very commendable and tolerable."

Most of all, for the Puritans like Stubbes, the primary function of church music was pedagogical, and they requested more didactic worship in which the whole congregation should participate through intelligent singing. Their attempts to introduce new legislation on the liturgy continued in Parliament from the early 1570s onward. The most heated debates on the liturgy were in 1586 and 1587 when moves were made to change the Book of Common Prayer (Foster 2014). Although they allowed the moderate use of music for secular occasions and sang psalms with lute accompaniment privately, the Puritans, powerful in the royal court and universities in the 1580s, rejected instrumental and choral music used in the liturgy, excluding any form of professional music. This fundamentally negative view of instrumental and choral music used in the churches is rooted in Neoplatonic ideas of music, prevalent in the patristic theology of music that heavily influenced the Reformed theologians.[5] It was in this context that *The Praise of Musicke* and the *Apologia musices* were published as serious responses to the Puritan attack on the abuse of music prevalent in religious ceremonies and secular recreation. These two treatises marked the first systematic apologetics of music as essentially beneficial for humans, which was anticipated by Matthew Gwinne's (1558?–1627) oration, *In Laudem Musices Oratio* ("oration in praise of music") at his inaugural lecture in 1582 following his appointment as lecturer in music at Oxford.[6] Both were published by Joseph Barnes (c. 1546–1618), the first printer to the University of Oxford, whose leadership and scholarship were then dominated by the Puritans.

The Praise of Musicke (1586)

The Praise of Musicke was dedicated to Sir Walter Raleigh (c. 1552–1618), a favorite courtier of Elizabeth I, who was one of the most prominent in the queen's circle in the 1580s. According to the printer Barnes, the goal of publishing this treatise, recommended "by men of good judgment and learning," is "to revive that study which laid, as dead, for a time" (*The Praise of Musicke*, folio *ijr). Anonymous as it remains, the authorship of *The Praise of Musicke* is of significance in relation to the impact of humanist education on music during the English Reformation. Both "good learning" (*bonae litterae*) and "eloquence" (*eloquentia*) were at the core of the cultural and intellectual life that the humanists cultivated throughout the sixteenth century.[7] Musicians at the royal chapels and collegiate churches and cathedrals were readily exposed to this high culture of the day. In such a context, masters of the choristers taught not only music but also morals and grammar, whose main sources were proverbs and classical and Christian *sententiae*, as demonstrated by Flynn's (1995) study that, nevertheless, overlooked the impact of the humanist moralism and learning on chorister education. The number of schools and university colleges increased dramatically in late sixteenth-century England, a phenomenon that was "a tribute to the success of Protestantism with the ruling elite and was one way in which reformation was to be propagated" (Foster 2014, 2). The number of musicians pursuing academic qualifications had also increased under this sociocultural influence, and some of them even received doctorates in music. Although conferring a doctorate in music was not entirely based on academic merits but required submission of musical compositions, the candidates belonged to academic circles (Carpenter 1955).

In this context, an eloquent apologetics of music like *The Praise of Musicke* could be written by a *learned* musician. A case in point is John Merbecke (c. 1505–c. 1585), choirmaster and organist of St. George's Chapel, Windsor, who was a prolific writer and compiler of vernacular Christian literature, including the first concordance of the English Bible, published by a royal printer, Richard Grafton, in 1550. His literary output attests to the impact of *new learning* disseminated by the humanists within the contemporary chorister education, which was in line with the reform of grammar schools (Kim 2008). As hinted at by *The Praise of Musicke*, the author is a musician by profession, trained at the Chapel Royal and educated at Oxford, who must have been disturbed more than anyone else by the existing polemics against music and musicians (*Praise of Musicke*, folios *ijv, *iijr, 136). The content of *The Praise of Musicke* proves the academic competency of the author, versed not only in music but also in the letters of both classical and Christian antiquity central to humanist education. During the premodern period, musicians employed by cathedrals and collegiate churches had various tasks, including teaching and scribing as well as singing. Under the influence of humanist education and religious reforms in England and elsewhere, chorister schools became more intellectually oriented than it had ever been before. In this cultural and intellectual milieu, the choirmasters of cathedrals and collegiate churches compiled commonplace books (*loci communes*) for teaching morals and religion at the chorister schools (Schubert 2010). In the early seventeenth century, masters of the choristers were still responsible for the moral training of the boys, for which they gathered quotations, proverbs, and the like. Andrew Melville, master of the song school at Aberdeen between 1636 and 1640, for example, compiled a commonplace book for this purpose (Aberdeen University Library MS 28).

The Praise of Musicke defends music, especially against those who want to remove choral and instrumental music from the church performed by occupational musicians. Yet his defense is not uncritical of the current abusive situation: "alehouse, vagabond and begging minstrels I defend not" (31). According to the author, it is the lewd musicians whose behavior has made many—ancient and contemporary alike—consider excessive training in music to be the cause of their depravities, a view that became commonplace through the famous classical proverb "Tibicinis vitam vivis":

> "Tibicinis vitam vivis" (you live the life of a flute-player) was a taunt levelled at a man who lived in great comfort, but at other people's expense. Aristotle was thinking of men of this class when he enquired in his *Problems* [*Problemata*, 920 b29–36] why it is that as a rule those connected with the stage are hardly ever respectable. He gives three reasons: either their professional skills absorb a great part of their lives and they have no time to spare for the principles of philosophy, or they live a life of unbroken luxury and self-indulgence, or their poverty by itself drives them to vice. (Erasmus 1992, 33:147–48)

Although this reasoning is not a condemnation of music itself, nonetheless, the criticism of immoral musicians tends to undermine the value of music itself. The author thus asserts emphatically that music "is great if we do not partially and unequally burden her with those faults whereof she is guiltless, the artificer may offend, men's affections are corrupt, times unseasonable, places inconvenient, the art itself notwithstanding in her own proper and lawful use innocent and harmless" (*The Praise of Musicke*, 36).

The Praise of the Musicke consists of the twelve chapters listed below. From the first chapter through the eighth, it argues for the various functions of music in civil life, drawing on the classical mythology of music. The rest of the treatise, which is more intensive than the earlier chapters are in argumentation, discusses the "lawful use of music in the church" on the basis of ecclesiastical authorities.

1. The Antiquity and Origin of Music: First generally, then more particularly set down
2. The Dignity of Music: Proved both by the rewards and practice of many and most excellent men
3. The Suavity of Music

4. The Effects and Operation of Music
5. The Necessity of Music
6. The Use of Music generally in the Course of Our Life
7. The Particular Use of Music in Civil Matters, especially in Sacrifices, Feasts, Marriages and Burials
8. The particular Use of Music in Warlike Matters
9. The Lawful Use of Music in the Church, confirmed by the Practice of the Church
10. The Lawful Use of Church Music, Proved by Authorities out of the Doctors
11. Sentences of the Scripture, for the Use of Church Music
12. A Refutation of Objections against the Lawful Use of Music in the Church

While arguing for the benefits of music in practical terms, *The Praise of Musicke* is not a mere justification for the utility of music, but presents a learned argument for the intrinsic value of music by appealing to the classics, the Bible, and the patristic writings—the literary and intellectual basis of Christian humanism. The author's interest does not lie in the physical elements of music alone, although the beauty and utility of music as audible sound are basic to his argument. The tone of this treatise is didactic in a manner typical of the humanist moralism that concerns moderation, temperance, and virtue, focusing on the emotional and ethical benefits of music in terms of "delectation, discipline, and happy life" (*The Praise of Musicke*, 71; Aristotle 1981, VIII, 5). The author stresses the classical views that "music belongs to virtue" and is "profitable to the correction of life and manners," and "musicians" are called "as the masters and correctors of manners" and "moderators or teachers of temperance" (*The Praise of Musicke*, 67–68, 70). For this very pedagogical reason, music was "first brought into the church, and used in divine service," claims the author (*The Praise of Musicke*, 70). Regarding the choral music that the Puritans rejected especially because it obscures the Word of God, the author points out that the fault is in those who sing in such a way, not in the art (*vitium hominum non artis*) (*The Praise of Musicke*, 141). In a defense of the use of both choral and instrumental music in the church based on the key musical writings of the church fathers and the Reformed theologians, the author illustrates how music has served for the edification of the church from ancient time to his days. "If," however, "there were no other reason" to keep the music in the church, adds he, it would be "of sufficient force to persuade the lawful use of music as a pleasant bait," for music "allures people into the church who otherwise would not come, and makes them stay there till the divine service be ended" (*The Praise of Musicke*, 151).

Apologia Musices (1588)

John Case was "one of the most learned and substantial of the 'non-fictional' Latin writers of Elizabethan England" (Binns 1990, 366). A highly esteemed scholar and teacher at Oxford University, he was more renowned overseas than in his homeland as an expert of Aristotelian philosophy and logic. Case's literary works are significant in relation to Renaissance Aristotelianism, yet they have received little attention from modern scholarship (Wood 1691, 259). Case has frequently been regarded as the author of *The Praise of Musicke*, and his *Apologia musices* has been considered simply a Latin translation of *The Praise of Musicke* (Barnett 1969, 256–57). As I have demonstrated elsewhere, however, it is highly unlikely that Case was the author of *The Praise of Musicke*. *Apologia musices* is rather different from *The Praise of Musicke* in content, structure, and tone, despite their common goal in arguing for the inherent value of music and the benefits of music education (Kim 2017b).

Apologia musices, dedicated to Sir Henry Unton (c. 1557–96) and Sir William Hatton (1560–97), is a defense of "music, both vocal and instrumental as well as mixed," as indicated by its full title, *Apologia musices tam vocalis quam instrumentalis et mixtae*. The treatise argues against the Platonic preference for vocal music over instrumental, the ethics of music that underlay the Reformed musical polemics. It consists of eight chapters and begins with an encomium of music by explaining its divine origin and multifaceted characteristics, on the basis of musical antiquity. The second chapter concerns the definition and multiplicity of music and discusses the ethos of musical modes that lies at the heart of Renaissance musical theory and practice.[8] The third deals with the question why music is beneficial for all kinds of life, which Case divides into three categories: mechanical work (farmers, soldiers, and artisans); in civil and political action (polite citizenry, nobility, and senators); and in contemplation (philosophers, scholars, and priests). The fourth chapter explores whether the inner forces and powers of the soul are more affected by vocal and instrumental music than by the objects of other senses, focusing on the harmony (concord) discussed by Marsilio Ficino (1433–99), a physician, priest, and musician who founded the Platonic Academy in Florence (see Kim 2017a). In the fifth chapter, Case argues that the art of music is more necessary for a "theoretical and contemplative life" than for an "active and practical life" by illustrating various biblical and Christian figures. The sixth focuses on the effects of instrumental music in contemplating the divine. The seventh chapter treats the political use of music, which is common and universal, according to Case, emphasizing the importance of considering its audience, arrangement, methodology, and motivation. Perhaps this chapter best shows Case as a teacher of Aristotelian logic, in defending music used in theaters, banquets, and marriages, and other private recreations. In the last chapter, which comprises twenty-one questions and answers to them, Case argues for the necessity of music in various circumstances and discusses the use of theatrical, instrumental music and dance, which is often associated with effeminacy in the musical polemics (see Austern 1993).

Case's approach to music is fundamentally religious and philosophical, although he supports a variety of musical activities in secular occasions and recreations. According to Case, "the human mind arose from the First Cause and from music," and it is "perfected and blessed when returned to the First Cause and to Music" (Case 1588, I, 2).[9] "Having originated from God," therefore, it is "unfair and even injurious to God, to us, and to nature, if we banish music from heaven, from the temple, from the market, from the public and private use of it as a profane and spurious science" (I, 3). Moreover, Case stresses the classical concept of music as "a teacher of virtue," asserting that music is not only "the sweetness of virtue" (I, 5), but "it itself is virtue" (VII, 51). In rebuking those who reject music as a corrupter of morals and denounce music as a plague on republics, Case demonstrates that music was used by the greatest teachers in antiquity "as a medicine for the plague" and concludes that "God is the author of music, its nurse is universal nature, and its instrument is the device of the whole universe" (I, 5–6). Hence, "nothing is more unjust and unfair to judge music as spurious and profane which is called the preserver of justice, the guardian of temperance, the moderator of morals, the fuel and flame of religion. It conserves justice, for the status of state (as Plato affirms) is dependent upon the mode of harmony" (I, 4). As a subject for education, music is "a science, since it has definite subject, harmony, it has definite properties, clearly by its modulating the soul of the mortal." More precisely, music is "the science of harmony (*scientia concentuum*), since it consists of number, proportion, concordant things, vocal and instrumental." Most important of all, that "it is granted to the worship of God and to the consolation of human life," which "shows music to be a divine science, because it flows from God" (II, 9–10).

In light of Aristotelian philosophy, Case maintains that music has excellent power for "quietness," "the instruction of life," and "contemplation" (V, 31). Music is "necessary for those who pray" (V, 30), for it "moves the soul's internal power and potentials more than do any other objects of the senses" (IV, 25–26). In conclusion, Case thus affirms that "music is the most divine science of the mind, therefore it is most apt to move the mind, which is why it is necessary for contemplation" (*Est musica divinissima scientia mentis, ergo aptissima ad movendam mentem, ergo ad contemplationem necessaria*) (V, 35). But this affirmation is not without a warning about musical abuse in both the public and private realms. Seeking pleasure in music is nothing wrong, but only if performed in moderation and decorum—"to which virtue belongs" (VII, 55). Case differentiates delighting in music from the study of music that exhausts and consumes the spirit. That is to say, music itself is most beneficial for all, but "an exceedingly intensive study of music can be harmful, because it entails labor and work, by which the sharpness of the soul grows feeble most, therefore, those studying music too much keenly often become insane" (VIII, 69).[10] In this regard, *Apologia musices* differs strikingly from *The Praise of Musicke*, which does not hold any negative view on the study of music. Case confirms Aristotle's caution on professional musical training, which is in line with Plato's disapproval of the poets and musicians who are "uneducated" and prone to mere exhibitionism of their skills in performance (Aristotle 1981, 1341a; Plato 1967, 700–701).

Critical Reflections

The Praise of Musicke and *Apologia musices* both highlight the essence of music in ethical and religious terms on the basis of how music was defined and used in classical and Christian antiquity. They do not, however, defend music unconditionally; *The Praise of Musicke*, as the author emphasizes, is "so far from allowing of the abuse" (*Praise of Musicke*, 129), while Case wrote *Apologia musices* in defending the *musica* and *concentus* that originated from God (in the mythology, *sonus*, the king of harmony, has two sons, *concentus* and *accentus*. The former was born of *musica*; the latter, of *grammatica*) (Case 1588, A2r–v; cf. *Praise of Musicke*, 38). For the authors, music is fundamentally an ethical and religious-philosophical concern that characterizes contemporary humanist writings on music. The humanist educators and reformers admit the fact that music is the source of pleasure—an innocent pleasure that is "the characteristic of all music." (Plato, *Laws*, book 7, 802c1961, 802).[11] Yet they are not unaware that the science of music becomes cheapened when used for pleasure's sake alone, as Franchinus Gaffurius (1492) argues that for Socrates, Plato, and the Pythagoreans, music is for moderating the soul under reason, and it was a discipline either for the divine worship or for the *paideia*[12] or for the well-being of the state and community, not for theatrical purposes.

It was under this impetus of the ancient musical philosophy that the humanists strove to revive the science of music as an integral part of moral education and religious practice. Their perception of music as an ethical entity that constitutes both education and religious practice is not so common in our contemporary world, where music stands out most in the field of entertainment rather than in that of education.[13] As this essay has discussed, the humanist moralist approach to music as essential to education and religion lies at the heart of the Reformation theology of music in general and the Reformed tradition in particular, which underlies the Puritan musical polemics. Although both *The Praise of Musicke* and *Apologia musices* do not reject music in the theater, their basic arguments for theatrical music are ethical and political in stressing the utility of different music at different occasions. Case treats theatrical music from the viewpoint of the political use of music and makes a distinction between "heavenly or Dorian music" and the "civil or Phrygian"; the former is more necessary for the "contemplative life" while the latter for the "active life" (Case 1588, VII).

Generally speaking, modern musicians rarely function as well-rounded educators, committed to moral education, unlike the premodern choirmasters. The reason is fundamentally that the departmentalization in academic disciplines is nowadays implemented in the name of professionalism, which tends to deter a more holistic education that takes interdisciplinary approaches. Such a specialist, albeit narrow, approach is not a phenomenon that pertains to modern musicianship and music education exclusively. A similar tendency to fragmentation is common in other segments of post-Enlightenment society (Kapp 2012 [1961]; Macintyre 2006). Besides, it is no longer customary to consider the value of music or musician in relation to virtue as it used to be in premodern academia. Some contemporary philosophers have discussed virtue as it relates to music. But their arguments are largely confined to musical practice in secular terms, not to the ethical dimension of music and musician within the pedagogical context of religious institutions (Kapp 2012 [1961]; Macintyre 2006). Moreover, music is an object of aesthetics rather than of ethics in current philosophical scholarship, while an interest in the nexus of music and social justice has been growing, in the field of both music education and theology (Benedict et al. 2015; O'Connor, Kim, and Labriola 2017). Perhaps (and rightly so), modern ethicists, secular or religious, have more serious issues than music to tackle in facing urgent environmental, political, and economic problems globally and locally, although they are not unaware of the age-old tie of music, education, and ethics. Crucially, music has developed in its own right in modern secular society, without institutional moorings. In such a context, the value of music is no longer attached to the classical ethics of virtue that, coupled with Christian virtues, lay at the core of the early modern humanist education.[14] It may well be for this reason that the relations between music, religious practice, and moral education are so seldom considered in current scholarship, unlike the ancient and early modern musical discourses, which *The Praise of Musicke* and *Apologia musices* illustrate through the lens of classical, patristic, and biblical studies cultivated by the humanists.[15] Fundamentally, therefore, dealing with music in relation to virtue is directly associated with the question of the autonomy of music both as a science and as a practice, a question that will undoubtedly bring a great challenge to musicians.

As we have discussed so far, these two treatises tackle some fundamental questions about music, that is, how to define and interpret music and why music is important to both individuals and society for moral and religious education. The ultimate concern of *The Praise of Musicke* lay in ecclesiastical music, and the author argued for a theologically valid use of music within the Reformed tradition, whereas *Apologia musices* discusses music from a more universal and philosophical perspective. Both, however, are based on the notion of music as the origin and manifestation of virtue, typical of the humanist education in music, yet without being overtly moralistic or demonizing innate pleasure in music. Rooted deeply in the classical interpretation of music, the treatises apply the ancient teaching of music to their contemporary musical practice in redefining music and its role in education and religious practice. In doing so, they reinforce the essence and role of music as the basis of moral and religious education. Case's apology of music presents one of the most lucid interpretations of music as a science from a theoretical perspective, whereas *The Praise of Musicke* is a musician's encomium of music and, more concretely, a musician's defense of his own art and profession against religious authorities hostile to them. It should also be noted that these two treatises were published when the social status of musicians, even those employed by the courts and cathedrals, was low, and the majority of musicians suffered from perennial financial hardship, social discrimination, and various restrictions in society at large (March 2010). Both treatises are illuminating in this regard, for their apologia of music ultimately concerns the place of the musician as an important agent of education and religious practice.[16] One way or another, thus, they lead the reader to the classical and historical approach to musical learning as essential for the moral education that was at the center of religious practice and spiritual formation during the early modern period, but it has seldom been considered in any depth in our time.

HYUN-AH KIM is Postdoctoral Research Fellow of the Theological University of Kampen in The Netherlands and Research Fellow of the European Melanchthon Academy of Bretten in Germany. She is a specialist in Christian music and on Reformation musical history and theology.

Notes

1. On the relationship between religion and music education, see Hoffman 2011.
2. For a discussion of problems using music as a means for particular goals ethical, religious or political, see Alexandra Kertz-Welzel, this volume. In it, Kertz-Welzel treats the case of the National Socialists, who propagated their ideology through various musical activities and education, following Plato's notions about the transformational power of music for individuals and the state. See also Kertz-Welzel 2004.
3. On devilish music, see Kertz-Welzel, this volume.
4. The original treatise has no consistent pagination in the original treatise. I have modernized all the quotations from *The Anatomie of Abuses* and *The Praise of Musicke*.
5. On the Neoplatonic characteristic of the Reformation polemics against instrumental music, see Kim 2015.
6. This lecture was printed in Ward 1740, app. XIV, 81–87.
7. On English humanism, see Bradshaw and Duffy 1989; Cartwright 2006; Martindale 1985; Pincombe 2001; Weiss 1967; and Woolfson 2002.
8. For a recent study on the *mode ethos*, see Palisca 2013.
9. Translation of citations from *Apologia musices* in the present chapter is mine.
10. Case 1588, VIII, 69.
11. Plato, *Laws* 802.
12. On the *paideia* (culture; education), see Jaeger 1969, 1986 [1945]).
13. On the nexus of music and ethics, see Alperson 2014; Cobussen and Nielsen 2012.
14. For a pioneering study for the modern revival of virtue ethics, see Macintyre 2007 [1984].
15. See, for example, Brown 2014, esp. 112–13. Brown considers the extent to which emotions are involved in music in its relation to religion, and highlights music as tied with entertainment, while overlooking the significance of moral philosophy underlying religious views on the (in)appropriateness of music in the context of religious rituals. On religious music in relation to the ethics of music, see Kim 2013, 220–46.
16. For a modern example of how the visual images of musicians are controlled by religious-political authorities in the fear of their negative effects on education, see Naqvi, this volume.

References

Alperson, Philip. 2014. "Music and Morality." In *Ethics and the Arts*, edited by Paul Macneill, 21–31. Dordrecht: Springer.
Aristotle. 1981. *The Politics*. Translated by T. A. Sinclair. Harmondsworth: Penguin.
Austern, Linda. 1993. "Alluring the Auditorie to Effeminacie: Music and the Idea of the Feminine in Early Modern England." *Music and Letters* 74, no. 3: 343–54.
Barnett, Howard. 1969. "John Case—an Elizabethan Music Scholar." *Music and Letters* 50, no. 2: 252–66.

Benedict, Cathy, Patrick Schmidt, Gary Spruce, and Paul Woodford, eds. 2015. *The Oxford Handbook of Social Justice in Music Education*. Oxford: Oxford University Press.
Binns, James. 1990. *Intellectual Culture in Elizabethan and Jacobean England: The Latin Writings of the Age*. Leeds, UK: Francis Cairns.
Bradshaw, Brendan, and Eamon Duffy, eds. 1989. *Humanism, Reform, and the Reformation*. Cambridge: Cambridge University Press.
Brown, Frank B. 2014. "Musical Ways of Being Religious." In *Oxford Handbook of Religion and the Arts*, edited by Frank B. Brown, 109–29. Oxford: Oxford University Press.
Carpenter, Nan. 1955. "The Study of Music at the University of Oxford in the Renaissance (1450–1600)." *Musical Quarterly* 41, no. 2: 191–214.
Carr, David. 2006. "The Significance of Music for the Promotion of Moral and Spiritual Value." *Philosophy of Music Education Review* 14, no. 2: 103–17.
Cartwright, Kent. 2006. *Theatre and Humanism: English Drama in the Sixteenth Century*. Cambridge: Cambridge University Press.
Case, John. 1588. *Apologia musices tam vocalis quam instrumentalis et mixtae*. Oxford, UK: Joseph Barnes.
Cobussen, Marcel, and Nanette Nielsen, eds. 2012. *Music and Ethics*. Aldershot, UK: Ashgate.
Elyot, Thomas. 1531. *The Boke named the Governour*. London: T. Berthelet.
Erasmus, Desiderius. 1992. *Collected Works of Erasmus*. Edited and translated by R. A. B. Mynors. Toronto, ON: University of Toronto Press. 33: 147–48.
Flynn, Jane. 1995. "The Education of Choristers during the Sixteenth Century." In *English Choral Practice 1400–1650*, edited by John Morehen, 180–99. Cambridge: Cambridge University Press.
Foster, Andrew. (1994) 2014. *The Church of England 1570–1640*. London: Longman; New York: Routledge.
Gaffurius, Franchinus. 1492. *Theorica musicae*. Milan: Philippium Mantegatium.
Gosson, Stephen. 1570. *The Schoole of Abuse*. London: T. Dawson for Thomas Woodcocke.
Gwinne, Matthew. 1740. "In Laudem Musices Oratio (1582)." In *The Lives of the Professors of Gresham College*, John Ward, App. XIV: 81–7. London: J. Moore.
Hoffman, Adria R. 2011. "Rethinking Religion in Music Education." *Music Educators Journal* 97, no. 4: 55–59.
Jaeger, Werner. 1969. *Early Christianity and Greek Paideia*. Oxford: Oxford University Press.
———. 1986 (1945). *Paideia: The Ideals of Greek Culture*. 2nd English ed. 3 vols. Translated by G. Highet. London: Oxford University Press.
Kapp, Karl. 2012 (1961). *Toward a Science of Man in Society: A Positive Approach to the Integration of Social Knowledge*. The Hague: M. Nijhoff.
Kertz-Welzel, Alexandra. 2004. "The Singing Muse: Three Centuries of Music Education in Germany." *Journal of Historical Research in Music Education* 26, no. 1: 22–24.
Kim, Hyun-Ah. 2008. *Humanism and the Reform of Sacred Music in Early Modern England: John Merbecke the Orator and "The Booke of Common Praier Noted" (1550)*. Aldershot, UK: Ashgate.
———. 2013. "*Homo Ludens*, Music, and Ritual: The Play/Non-play Characters of Religious Music." *Questions Liturgiques /Studies in Liturgy* 94, no. 3: 220–46.
———. 2015. *The Renaissance Ethics of Music: Singing, Contemplation, and Musica Humana*. London: Pickering and Chatto.

———. 2017a. "Music of the Soul (*Animae Musica*): Marsilio Ficino and the Revival of *Musica Humana* in Renaissance Neo-Platonism." *Reformation and Renaissance Review* 19, no. 2: 122–34.

———. 2017b. *The Praise of Musicke, 1586: An Edition with Commentary*. New York: Routledge.

Lodge, Thomas. 1853 (1579). *A Defence of Poetry, Music, and Stage-Plays*. London: Shakespeare Society.

Macintyre, Alasdair. 2006. "The End of Education: The Fragmentation of the American University." *Commonweal* 133, no. 18: 10–14.

———. 2007 (1984). *After Virtue: A Study in Moral Theory*. 3rd ed. Notre Dame, IN: University of Notre Dame Press.

March, Christopher. 2010. *Music and Society in Early Modern England*. Cambridge: Cambridge University Press.

Martindale, Joanna, ed. 1985. *English Humanism: Wyatt to Cowley*. London: Croom Helm.

O'Connor, Michael, Hyun-Ah Kim, and Christina Labriola, eds. 2017. *Music, Theology, and Justice*. Lanham, MD: Lexington.

Palisca, Claude V. 2013. "The Ethos of Modes during the Renaissance." In *The Emotional Power of Music: Multidisciplinary Perspectives on Musical Arousal, Expression, and Social Control*, edited by Tom Cochrane, Bernardino Fantini, and Klaus Scherer, 103–15. Oxford: Oxford University Press.

Pincombe, Mike. 2001. *Elizabethan Humanism: Literature and Learning in the Later Sixteenth Century*. London: Longman.

Plato. 1961. *Laws*, 2 vols. Translated by Robert G. Bury. Cambridge, MA: Harvard University Press.

The Praise of Musicke: Wherein besides the antiquitie, dignitie, delectation, and vse thereof in ciuill matters, is also declared the sober and lawfull vse of the same in the congregation and Church of God. 1586. Oxford, UK: Joseph Barnes.

Scholes, Percy. 1969 (1934). *The Puritans and Music in England and New England: A Contribution to the Cultural History of Two Nations*. Oxford, UK: Clarendon.

Schubert, Peter. 2010. "Musical Commonplaces in the Renaissance." In *Music Education in the Middle Ages and the Renaissance*, edited by Russell Murray Jr., Susan Weiss, and Cynthia Cyrus, 161–92. Bloomington: Indiana University Press.

Scruton, Roger. 2002. "The Decline of Musical Culture." In *Arguing about Art: Contemporary Philosophical Debates*, edited by Alex Neill and Aaron Ridley, 119–34. New York: Routledge.

Stubbes, Phillip. 1583. *The Anatomie of Abuses*. London: Richard Jones.

Ward, John. 1740. *The Lives of the Professors of Gresham College*. London: J. Moore.

Weiss, Roberto. 1967. *Humanism in England during the Fifteenth Century*. 3rd ed. Oxford, UK: Basil Blackwell.

Wickham, Glynne, Herbert Berry, and William Ingram, eds. 2000. *English Professional Theatre, 1530–1660*. Cambridge: Cambridge University Press.

Wood, Thomas. 1691. *Athenae Oxonienses*. London: Printed for Thomas Bennet.

Woolfson, Jonathan, ed. 2002. *Reassessing Tudor Humanism*. New York: Palgrave Macmillan.

13 | The Curious Case of *Good Morning Iran*: Music and Broadcast Regulation in the Islamic Republic

Erum Naqvi

On January 18, 2014, a national television show called *Good Morning Iran* made international headlines when it aired about ten seconds of footage showing Iranian musicians on broadcast television. Authorities later attributed the footage to an editing error. The surprise occurrence broke a thirty-year taboo on broadcasting music on state television. Since the early days of Iran's 1979 revolution, public music practices have been regulated by several state-appointed bodies in the Islamic Republic.[1] In line with regulatory practices that apply to broadcast television, all musical footage is edited when aired on national television. But the content that is edited is not the material that is heard—that is, the sounds. Rather, it is material that is seen, specifically, imagery of musicians playing instruments. Footage is typically dubbed over with static images of nature or flowers, or filmed so that carefully placed objects (such as vases of flowers) obscure musical instruments being played.[2] In some cases, performances (such as concerts) that are reappropriated for broadcast by state media are screened with blurred footage of instrumentalists performing.[3] Broadcast music regulation falls within a larger and more dynamic picture of regulation across the public contexts in which music has a presence in Iranian culture, including live performance, education, and distribution. All are subject to various rules. This chapter explores music regulation in two ways: first, in terms of public policy and its potential motivations and, second, in terms of conceptual implications about the understanding of musicality in Iran. Specifically, what are the intersecting concerns that affect music regulation policies in Iran for public broadcasts? And, if *Good Morning Iran*'s editorial blunder implies that removing the imagery of musicians playing instruments somehow makes the music less musical, and therefore less controversial, what does this say about the understanding of musicality in Iran? How is this case informed by pedagogical, musicological, and conceptual insights about the music genres that are utilized in Iranian broadcast television?

Music Regulation Policies in Iran: Religion, Politics, and Nationhood

Musical practice has a long and varied history in Iranian culture. Court musicians in ancient palaces, villagers in remote areas, and devotional Sufi mystics in the Middle Ages constitute Iran's musical past. Urban classical performers, rural folk artists, and pop starlets populate the face of Pahlavi-era musical culture. Artists in diaspora, scholars of Iranian classical music at the center and margins of education policy, youths performing underground rock, rap, and electronica in Tehran's basements, and artists going viral on social media platforms feature in Iran's contemporary musical world. Today, all forms of music blare from car radios in downtown city streets. Traditional music is broadcast on national television, performed in public concerts, and heard from speakers placed in in public parks. Music thrives in both private and public spaces, despite a complex and ever-evolving relationship with regulators since the 1979 revolution (Semati 2017; see also Nooshin 2005, 2017). In the most general terms, since Iran's post-revolution constitution was publicized as a theocratic (specifically, Islamic) one, it may seem that a central motivation for regulation is a perceived conflict between musical practice and Islam. Yet the relationship between music and Islam is ambiguous and heavily disputed among scholars in many cultural contexts, resulting a highly pluralistic picture of views about music's permissibility in an Islamic culture. Moreover, this is no simple claim to make about Iran, not least because of the historical, political, and cultural intersections that also underpin the role of music in Iranian society as it stands today.

Theologians' evaluations—both endorsing and rejecting music in Islam—often differ on the basis of differing interpretations of two primary sources of information about Islamic practice: the Qur'an, Islam's central religious text, and the *hadith*, a body of historical literature considered to capture sayings and practices of early followers of the religion. The text of the Qur'an does not contain an explicit statement about music's ethical status. Consequently, scholars often refer to passages in the Qur'an about other forbidden and endorsed cultural practices, disagreeing about whether they implicitly encompass musical practice within their scope. Others supplement Qur'anic interpretation with claims based on references to music from the broader hadith literature, which contains conflicting claims about the permissibility of music. Shiloah (2001) puts it that way, in his analysis of music in Islam:

> The first and most sacred source in our case is the *Qur'an*. Both those in favor of music, and those opposed had recourse to it, which is perplexing because nothing in the *Qur'an* concerns music explicitly. Hence the parties to the dispute address themselves to exegetes who suggest either implicit prohibition or admissibility.... Recognizing the weakness of these arguments, disputants found stronger support in the authoritative sources of the *hadith* (Traditions of the Prophet).... Antagonists would cite different *Qur'anic* verses in support of their respective theses but, when they had recourse to the *hadith*, opposite conclusions are quite often drawn from the same tradition. (31–32)[4]

To complicate matters further, various sects of Islam endorse different portions of hadith literature over others, while some (collectively known as "Quranists," or "Scripturalists") reject the authority of the hadith altogether (Bankowska 2007). Beyond disagreements over music's permissibility, scholars also disagree about the musiclike activities that actually count as "music," about which ethical claims are being made. For example, in most (if not all) branches of Islam, chanting and poetic or songlike recitation of the Qur'an are endorsed as a part of religious practice. In some branches—such as Sufism, highly popular in Iran's history—devotional practices include more robust musical performance (Daniel and Mahdi 2006, 191). To accommodate these activities, some theologians consider singing (and sometimes drumming, which is also used by a number of Islamic sects in devotional practice) to fall outside the concept of music, including only instrumental music as the strictly "musical" activity that need be addressed with respect to its permissibility. Other theologians cut up the conceptual landscape according to the cultural purposes to which musical activities are put, carving out space for both singing and instrumental performance by arguing that when they arise in culturally permissible contexts such as devotional and certain social activities, they too fall outside the concept of music.[5] In other words, many argue that only musical performance associated with "sensuous" recreational activities counts as the music that falls under ethical scrutiny.[6] In summarizing the methodologies used to address the status of music in Islam, al Faruqi (1985) aptly attributes the pluralism in the claims about music's ethical status to intersections between differences of opinion about (1) sources, and which are considered legitimate; (2) the strength of association between musical and other, more explicitly endorsed or prohibited, nonmusical cultural activities; and (3) terminology, that is, the activities from the gamut of musical practice that strictly fall under the concept music and those that do not (3–5).

With all this in mind, it is important to remember the extent to which various theological and scholarly views on the status of music in Islam are mentioned in practice or policy vary radically across nations and cultures. Iran's postrevolution constitution contains explicit statements about the permissibility of a number of cultural practices, in some cases citing Qur'anic passages, but it does not include formal claims about music ("Constitution" n.d.). This absence is perhaps itself a function of the noted ambiguity of music's status among historical Islamic sources. In addition, while Iran's postrevolution constitution was publicized as largely theocratic, and based on Islamic criteria, Iran's newly established leader Ayatollah Khomeini's early speeches about his political ethos also emphasized cultural and national motivations aimed at targeting Western imperialism (Siamdoust 2017, 4). When considering music regulation policies enacted in postrevolution Iran, it is telling that ideological concerns about nationhood feature heavily.

Music was initially banned on state-run broadcast media in 1979. Yet its permissibility began to fluctuate almost immediately, beginning with the airing of state-sanctioned political anthems, revolutionary songs, and military music (Siamdoust 2017, 87–90). Shortly thereafter, Iranian classical music—known as *musiqi-e-sonnati* (traditional music) or *musiqi-e-assil* (original or authentic music)—considered an "authentic" expression of Iranian culture, was also exempted from more stringent restrictions that applied to other genres of music, particularly in broadcast and educational contexts. In fact, many argue that Iranian classical music underwent a fruitful revival period in this time, in which the art form evolved and thrived, amassing popularity on a much wider scale than had ever been the case in its history (Nooshin 2014, 289–92). Some argue this moment in Iran's history is best captured by a "return to roots" (rather than a strictly religious) ideology centered on removing foreign cultural influences from musical culture following heavy prowesternization policies in Pahlavi-era Iran (Nooshin 1999, 2014, 2015). As Nooshin (2015) puts it:

> The Revolution was akin to a national independence struggle, in this case against neo-colonial control, effected by a populist uprising which brought together nationalists, religious groups, and a wide spectrum of political organizations. Only after the Shah fled Iran in January 1979 and the subsequent return of Ayatollah Khomeini from exile, did the religious factions gain the upper hand, leading to the declaration of the Islamic Republic on 1 April 1979. The nationalist nature of the revolution had profound implications for Iranian classical music, which despite the restrictions that took effect almost immediately, experienced an extraordinary grass-roots renaissance. (33)

In Iran's political sphere, views on the permissibility of music (as in wider Islamic scholarship) are similarly ambiguous, though are often skewed toward political platforms, concerns with national cultural identity, or some combination thereof. For example, on a speech in July 1979, Khomeini equates music with opium and categorizes it as problematic to the health of a nation. Siamdoust (2017, 7) translates his comments: "Opium brings a sort of apathy and numbness and so does music. If you want your country to be independent, from now on you must transform radio and television into educational instruments—eliminate music."

Later, in 1988, Khomeini attributes the numbing effect to only some music, including among the objectionable forms music from various other nations (in this instance, mentioning Saudi Arabia), and music of certain genres that were prioritized by state broadcast media in Iran's prerevolution regime, particularly pop music (Siamdoust 2017). Reformist president Mohammad Khatami's policies loosened regulations that apply to domestic pop music, resulting in a reemergence of underground local pop music culture into the public sphere during his term in office (1997–2005). And, in reinstating several regulations during his term in office, populist and conservative president Mahmoud Ahmadinejad prioritized policies that prohibited "Western" music on state-run broadcast media from 2005 to 2013, before restrictions are somewhat eased again under reformist president Hassan Rouhani (elected in 2013 and for a second term in 2017; Nooshin 2008). Today, the official policy of the Ministry of Culture (Ershād), which is responsible for issuing permits for the performance, recording, and distribution of music in Iran, similarly reflects a position that is bound up as much in political and national solidarity as it is in religious and moral concerns, as Siamdoust's summary translation of Ershād's central criteria indicates:

> The submitted work must conform to certain standards, including: (1) Should not elicit indecent behavior. (2) Should not promote secularism. (3) Should not insult the Islamic Government, high clerics, Islam itself, well-known figures, or

distinguished historical personalities. (4) Must have musical as well as lyrical integrity. (5) Must encourage the spirit of national consensus, unity, and solidarity. (6) Lyrics with critical content must, in their essence and symbolically, strengthen social esteem as their main theme. (7) Must guide youth, ebullient forces, and, in general, all social classes towards optimistic future invested with open vistas and hope. (Siamdoust 2017, 101)

Interestingly, Iran's state broadcasting media corporation, Islamic Republic of Iran Broadcasting (IRIB)—responsible for the production and transmission of twelve national, ten international, and thirty regional television channels, as well as almost forty radio channels, and Iran's national newspaper, *Jaam-e Jam*—runs independently of Ershād, with in-house music production agencies and centralized broadcasting criteria. A notable difference that operates in this domain is the prohibition of displaying imagery of instruments being performed on television (Siamdoust 2017, 104–5). This requirement is puzzling given its absence from larger discussions about the permissibility of music within Iranian culture, and also from other public domains in which music functions in Iran, not least the thriving contemporary live concert performance scene (Naqvi 2017). Some theorists attribute the reasoning behind this policy to Khomeini's views on music (Mohammadi 2003, 37), although Iranian state media is accountable to the state's current leaders and ultimately to Iran's highest ranking politician, the Supreme Leader Ayatollah Ali Hosseini Khamenei. With the ambiguities and fluctuations in the perspectives about appropriate policies for music's public face among Iran's leaders, one thing that can be expected is a tendency to err on the side of caution with respect to how much "music" is in the music that is broadcast on public television (Siamdoust 2017). The implication follows, as suggested at the outset of this inquiry, that removing imagery of musicians performing instruments somehow makes a musical broadcast less musical, and therefore less controversial. The insight tallies closely with concepts of musicality that have traditionally prevailed in Iranian classical music—the high musical art of Iranian culture—and the most long-standing genre of music outside political and military music to maintain a presence on broadcast media since the revolution. Both traditional pedagogical practices and discussions by scholars and artists of the art form imply a central focus on witnessing embodied acts of dexterity in performance as a hallmark of this musical genre, particularly in instrumental performance. Arguably, these are bound up as much with visual as they are with sonic dimensions of performance.

Dexterity in Classical Performance: Pedagogical and Conceptual Insights about Musicality in Iran

Iranian classical music, referenced in Iran as *musiqi-sonnati* (traditional music), or *musiqi-assil* (original or authentic music), was historically the music of Persia's royal courts. It was transmitted aurally from master (*Ostād*), typically a distinguished court musician, to apprentice (During, Mirabdolbahi, and Safvat 1991; Farhat 1990; Nettl 1978, 1992; Nooshin 1999, 2015; Shiloah 2001; Wright 2009; and Zonis 1973). In the early twentieth century, the tradition acquired a formal place in Iran's university system and a handful of Ostāds transitioned from the royal courts to the public educational sphere, codifying the art form and shaping the scholarly, artistic, and instructional norms for the tradition (Miller 1999; Nettl 1978, 2002, 2009; Nooshin 1999). Today, the title of Ostād denotes at once, and without distinction, a musician, scholar, and teacher of the classical genre (During et al. 1991).

Unlike other genres of Iranian music, which are more commonly associated with recreational practices like dancing, *musiqi-e-sonnati* is typically performed for contemplation. It is based on a rigorous implicit structural framework called the *radif*, which is intuitively internalized by aspiring musicians during their musical training. The radif demarcates approximately five hundred motivic fragments (called *gusheh*s) that are divided into twelve groups (called *dastgāh*s), each representing a small sonic area of the instrument being performed. In traditional performance, which is typically of a dastgāh, a musician explores the designated sonic area by intuitively calling to presence and weaving together the fragments associated with that *dastgāh* in loosely ascending sonic order at high speed, and with high ornamental complexity, using a process of spontaneous extemporization known as *bedāhe-navāzi*. The opening and closing passages of a performance are typically more structured and bookend a freer portion of extemporization that is typically unmetered (During et al. 1991). The traditional performance ideal is spontaneous articulation in the moment (*dar lahzeh*) of a musical expression that stays within the structural limitations of the radif while exploring and extending it without obvious repetition. Owen Wright (2009) suggests that "in Persian music, mastery requires competence across the spectrum, but with the most prized ability being that which can negotiate an individual path through and around familiar territory" (38). A common metaphor for this performance style is the nightingale, famed in Persian legend for its supposed ability to ceaselessly articulate very subtly different melodies without ever repeating itself (Nettl 2013; Nooshin 1998, 2015). Musical appreciation centers in large part on attention to the embodied display of dexterity in performance. Highly traditional instruction is similarly centered on a bodily-motion-oriented pedagogy (During et al. 1991; Nooshin 1998, 1999).

The most traditional instruction takes place through a lengthy process of absorption centered on bodily mimicry. Ideally, there is no explicitly theoretical training and very little discussion about the motifs being learned, despite the theoretical and structural complexity of the radif.[7] Rather, the student watches the teacher extemporize in small interludes based on the radif's core structures and copies what the teacher does, until, eventually, the radif is intuitively absorbed. The emphasis on motor memory as a pedagogical device is one reason students are traditionally discouraged from writing notes down as aids to the memory, as this famous historical anecdote about drum master Djamchid Chemirāni recounts:

> Djamchid Chemirāni talked very little in the class. At times, he would remind us about some necessary points, but, generally, he tried to make it possible for the student to grasp things directly by himself. . . . One day a student, before leaving the

classroom and unaware of being watched by the teacher, began to jot down something on a pad of paper. Djamchid Chemirāni walked over to him quickly, asked him to hand over the pad, and added with a smile: "It's better to forget than to write down!" (During et al. 1991, 211–12)

The general consensus among Ostāds is that once the radif has been implicitly internalized (a process that can take several years), the student will be able to able to extemporize by spontaneously reproducing and rearranging phrases in a manner that is informed by the radif's structure, without needing to explicitly think about the act of doing so (Farhat 1990; Nettl 1992; Nooshin 2015; and Zonis 1973). Ostāds generally perceive this to be achievable when the musician internalizes the radif so deeply that it becomes something like a seemingly innate musical grammar, and many Ostāds suggest that the traditional instruction method instills the syntax of the radif in a way similar to the way in which a child learns her first language.[8] Ostād Tala'i remarks that

> in learning the *radif*, there is a point of meeting known as internalization. This occurs when a performer, after so many times of learning the music by heart and then forgetting it, by sheer perseverance, reaches a level where the *radif* becomes more than just a set of notes or even a set of melodies. Here the performer is so familiar with the concepts and elements of the *radif* as to never forget them. He may even believe that the *radif* is a product of his own "psyche." ... After the internalization process, which may take several years to achieve, the performer goes beyond mere apprenticeship. Based upon what is remembered of the *radif*, he is now able to rearrange and reproduce the phrases in a new way. This happens without thinking or even being aware of what is happening (Tala'i 2000, 1).

It follows that concepts of creativity are often tied to embodied aspects of performance in this genre, stressing in particular the intersection of speed, dexterity, and generative processes, as Nooshin's (1998) technical analysis of radif based extemporization suggests: "An important factor is the speed with which decisions regarding such detailed aspects of the music have to be made in the performance situation, suggesting that in terms of compositional techniques, much of what happens in improvised performance occurs at some unverbalised level of conception" (101). Nooshin continues: "Through the learnt repertoire, musicians build up a store of aural and sensori-motor patterns which can be used directly in performance or form the basis for the generation of new patterns" (108; see also Naqvi 2015, 71).

The emphasis on displays of dexterity as a central aspect of the classical art form is evident in both pedagogical accounts and in documentation of early music appreciation. Notably, descriptions tend to emphasize visual aspects of performance—like hands in motion—as much as sonic components of performance, such that both what is seen and what is heard seem to fall under the concept of music in this genre. *Zarb* [goblet drum] master Zia Mirabdolbaghi implies as much: "the only thing at play was the 'stuff' of music, that is the sound of the master's zarb, the movements of his fingers, and the repetition of many different rhythms" (During et al. 1991, 211). Ruhollāh Khāleqi's (1906–65) description of an instrumental performance is similarly telling in this regard. He is compelled by what he sees the performer do as much as the sounds he hears, if not more so:

> All eyes were riveted on the maestro's hands. Rapidly the mezrābs [hand-held hammers for playing the santur] struck the strings. They were so finely and evenly regulated that they seemed to be drawing lines in the air perpendicular to the santur. Shifting around between the rhythmic pieces and melodies for chanting, Somā' Hozur probably played for more than half an hour, spellbinding everyone. Had today's santur players been there that night, they could have found out for themselves the meaning of the words skill and mastery. How can I describe the pieces I heard from Somā' Hozur? Let me only write one sentence and leave it at that: years later, when little Habib [Somā' Hozur's son and apprentice] grew up and became Habib Somā'i, his santur had the effect of the master's (Ruhollāh Khāleqi, quoted in During et al. 1991, 227).

The insight—about witnessing the visual aspects of a performance—evokes conceptual analyses of other forms of improvisation, particularly where emphasis is placed on an experiential encounter with an act of creation as it transpires. Philip Alperson (1984) argues that for improvisation (characterized as musical practice in which the acts of composing and performing explicitly converge), audience members' aesthetic appreciation extends beyond sound structures that are generated to encompass the activity of their making in the performing moment. For this reason, Alperson argues that even when listening to audio recordings of live performances, embodied facets are implicated in our appreciation: "in such cases, though, these artifacts can and often do function as recordings from which we read off, as it were, the original action" (26). The sentiment is echoed by Lee Brown, who suggests that what interests audiences of jazz improvisations is a combination of musical structure and performing activity (Brown (1996, 2011). In the Iranian classical context, because musical structure is somewhat fixed by the radif, the locus of appreciation shifts toward the skill with which the musical expression is articulated, an important facet of all live performance.[9] Specifically, witnessing the skill of performers as they manipulate their instruments and articulate sounds entails appreciating *how* they do what they do. It is important to note that this type of appreciation is deeply intertwined with visual components of performance—say, of seeing a drum player's fingertips unfurl and strike a drumhead in swift succession, proceeding intricately toward the center of the drum's skin as sounds emanate from it.[10]

The historical significance of this aspect of performance anchors what is at stake in many debates that have surrounded Iranian classical music's evolution. For example, pedagogical disputes about the practices of Iranian classical music have, for the better part of a century, centered on the extent to which traditional performance is affected by the integration of instructional tools like written notation, explicit discussion of sound structures, and composition techniques that shift the emphasis to an understanding of musicality as the skillful manipulation of the instrument as the driving force in extemporization (Miller 1999; Naqvi 2015). These debates extend back to the early twentieth century when a group of Ostāds spearheaded by Ali Naqi Vaziri (1887–1979), founder of the National Academy of Music, sought to modernize Iranian classical music with the introduction of experimental instructional and compositional techniques informed by Western classical music. This ideology was met with opposition by a number of Ostāds favoring highly traditional instruction practices and performance ideals, resulting in the founding of a rival institute called the Center for Propagation and Preservation of Iranian Music, or simply, *Markaz* (meaning "center") in 1968 (During et al. 1991; Nooshin 2014). Similarly, in the production of new music, experimentation, developments, and evolutions in the genre are similarly often contextualized relative to the introduction of sonic novelty, explicit thinking about sound structures, and the educational practices that facilitate them.[11]

Conclusion

Iran's classical music has expanded somewhat beyond the traditional paradigm outlined here, encompassing—among other things—the introduction of larger sonic scopes, new instruments, source material that extends beyond the radif, and experiments in improvisational techniques, particularly in the contexts of live performance and the development of new music (overseen by Ershād), as well as in terms of education ideologies, resulting in a somewhat pluralistic picture of musical practice across the genre.[12] Broadcast music that is overseen by the IRIB, however, leans toward conventional rather than experimental faces of traditional music. The reasons for prohibiting imagery of musical instruments being played are likely, as I have suggested, a multifaceted accommodation of policymakers' perspectives, informed by intersecting concerns with religion, politics, and nationhood. Historical norms that prevail over traditional music and its appreciation in Iran, however, indicate why this regulatory act is of musical significance, particularly when it comes to instrumental music. When musicality is conceptualized in terms of embodied dexterity, it does not seem curious but rather fitting to say that removing imagery of musicians does, in fact, make the music less musical, even if the sounds the musicians utter are left untouched. And it prompts the conclusion that both within and beyond the Iranian context, the visual component of performing activity is closely woven into the fabric of what it means to say that something is musical.

ERUM NAQVI is Faculty Writing Fellow in the Social Science and Cultural Studies Department at the Pratt Institute. Her research interests include comparative ontologies of creativity, questions about embodied understandings of artistic works and performances in music of the West and in classical and modern cultures of the Middle East, and issues of gender and sexuality and expressions of activism in various kinds of social and political regimes.

Notes

1. For a summary of these from 1979 to 2000, see Youssefzadeh (2000).
2. See, for example, Dehghan (2014), Ernst (2014), and Mostaghim and Sandels (2014).
3. A concert by popular singer Salar Aghili was aired like this by Islamic Republic of Iran Broadcasting (IRIB) on February 12, 2012. See "Strange Airing" (2016).
4. See also Otterbeck and Ackfelt (2012, 229–30).
5. See al Faruqi (1985, 8) for a chart mapping cultural activities and the associated musiclike practices that are excluded from counting as music under this approach. See also Otterbeck and Ackfelt (2012, 230).
6. See also Shiloah (2001, 33).
7. Nooshin (2015) refers to this as the "non-verbalized teaching" (77). See also Naqvi (2012).
8. "The radif teaches musical syntax. Knowing the words well is not enough. Even if we learn by heart the whole content of a dictionary, it is not enough; we must know the syntax of the language, and that is actually what the radif teaches" (Ostād Safvat quoted in During et al. 1991, 216). See also "Our yardstick [*melāk*] is the *radif*. It is our book from which the grammar is described" (Ostād Lotfi quoted in Nooshin 2015, 123).
9. Lydia Goehr (1989, 1992, 2007) argues that the conceptual dominance of the work concept in Western classical music overshadows attention to the embodied aspects of musical performance in nineteenth-century aesthetic theory and its legacy.
10. See, for example, *The Art of the Piano* (2009) at 29:40 and "Daf & Tombak" (2011).
11. See Nooshin's (2015) analysis of a new improvisation technique created by contemporary artists and educators Ostāds Amir Eslami and Hooshyar Khayam.
12. On new classical music experimentation and recordings, see Nooshin (2015). On the live performance context, see Naqvi (2017).

References

Alperson, Philip. 1984. "On Musical Improvisation." *Journal of Aesthetics and Art Criticism* 43, no. 1: 17–29.

The Art of the Piano: Great Pianists of the 20th Century. 2009. YouTube video, 1:46:44, posted by "PedroTaam," January 26. https://youtu.be/vpiMAaPTze8.

Bankowska, Aleksandra. 2007. "Scripturalism in Islam: The History of the Quranic Movement." *Hemispheres: Studies on Cultures and Societies* 22: 5–31.

Brown, Lee. 1996. "Musical Works, Improvisation, and the Principle of Continuity." *Journal of Aesthetics and Art Criticism* 54, no. 4: 353–69.

———. 2011. "Improvisation." In *The Routledge Companion to Philosophy and Music*, edited by Theodore Gracyk and Andrew Kania, 59–69. New York: Routledge.

"Constitution of the Islamic Republic of Iran." n.d. Foundation for Iranian Studies. Accessed January 22, 2019. http://fis-iran.org/en/resources/legaldoc/constitutionislamic.

"Daf & Tombak." 2011. YouTube video, 7:23, posted by "Ronen Braverman," July 9. https://youtu.be/VjogLVtBAd0.

Daniel, Elton L., and Ali Akbar Mahdi. 2006. *Culture and Customs of Iran*. Westport, CT: Greenwood.

Dehghan, Saeed Kamali. 2014. "Iran Broadcaster Breaks Rule over Musical Instruments Played on TV." *The Guardian*, January 22. http://www.theguardian.com/world/2014/jan/22/iran-broadcaster-rule-musical-instruments-tv.

During, Jean, Zia Mirabdolbaghi, and Dariush Safvat. 1991. *The Art of Persian Music*. Translated by Manuchehr Anvar. Washington, DC: Mage.

Ernst, Douglas. 2014. "Iranian TV Shows Musical Instruments for 10 Seconds—and Religious Controversy Ensues." *Washington Times*, January 23. http://www.washingtontimes.com/news/2014/jan/23/iranian-tv-shows-musical-instruments-ten-seconds-a/.

Farhat, Hormoz. 1990. *The Dastgāh Concept in Persian Music*. Cambridge: Cambridge University Press.

al Faruqi, Lois Ibsen. 1985. "Music, Musicians, and Muslim Law." *Asian Music* 17, no. 1: 3–36.

Goehr, Lydia. 1989. "Being True to the Work." *Journal of Aesthetics and Art Criticism* 47, no. 1: 55–67.

———. 1992. *The Imaginary Museum of Musical Works: An Essay in the Philosophy of Music*. New York: Oxford University Press.

———. 2007. *Elective Affinities: Musical Essays on the History of Aesthetic Theory*. New York: Columbia University Press.

Miller, Lloyd. 1999. *Music and Song in Persia*. Salt Lake City: University of Utah Press.

Mohammadi, Ali. 2003. "Iran and the Modern Media in the Age of Globalization." In *Iran Encountering Globalization: Problems and Prospects*, edited by Ali Mohammadi, 24–46. New York: Routledge.

Mostaghim, Ramin, and Alexandra Sandels. 2014. "Iran State Breaks Decades Long Taboo on Showing Instruments." *Los Angeles Times*, January 23. http://www.latimes.com/world/worldnow/la-fg-wn-iran-tv-music-instruments-20140123-story.html.

Naqvi, Erum. 2012. "Teaching Practices in Persian Art Music." In *The Oxford Handbook of Philosophy in Music Education*, edited by Wayne Bowman and Ana Lucia Frega, 181–91. New York: Oxford University Press.

———. 2015. "Comparative Ontology and Iranian Classical Music." PhD diss., Temple University.

———. 2017. "Gigging 'Classical' in Iran." *Popular Communication* 15, no. 3: 221–32.

Nettl, Bruno. 1978. "Classical Music in Tehran: The Process of Change." In *Eight Urban Musical Cultures*, edited by Bruno Nettl, 146–85. Champaign: University of Illinois Press.

———. 1992. *The Radif of Persian Music*. Champaign, IL: Elephant and Cat.

———. 2002. *Encounters in Ethnomusicology: A Memoir*. Warren, MI: Harmonie Park.

———. 2009. "On Learning the *Radif* and Improvisation in Iran." In *Musical Improvisation: Art, Education and Society*, edited by Gabriel Solis and Bruno Nettl, 185–99. Champaign: University of Illinois Press.

———. 2013. *Becoming an Ethnomusicologist: A Miscellany of Influences*. Lanham, MD: Scarecrow.

Nooshin, Laudan. 1998. "The Song of the Nightingale: Processes of Improvisation in *Dastgāh Segāh* (Iranian Classical Music)." *British Journal of Ethnomusicology* 1998, no. 7: 69–116.

———. 1999. "Iran: The Art of Ornament." In *World Music: The Rough Guide: Africa, Europe, and the Middle East*, edited by Simon Broughton, Mark Ellingham, and Richard Trillo, 355–63. London: Penguin.

———. 2005. "Underground, Overground: Rock Music and Youth Discourses in Iran." *Iranian Studies* 38, no. 3: 463–94.

———. 2008. "The Language of Rock: Iranian Youth, Popular Music, and National Identity." In *Media, Culture, and Society in Iran: Living with Globalization and the Islamic State*, edited by Mehdi Semati, 69–93. New York: Routledge.

———. 2014. "Two Revivalist Moments in Iranian Classical Music." In *The Oxford Handbook of Music Revival*, edited by Caroline Bithell and Juniper Hill, 277–99. New York: Oxford University Press.

———. 2015. *Iranian Classical Music: The Discourses and Practice of Creativity*. London: Ashgate.

———. 2017. "Whose Liberation? Iranian Popular Music and the Fetishization of Resistance." *Popular Communication* 15, no. 3: 163–91.

Otterbeck, Jonas, and Anders Ackfelt. 2012. "Music and Islam." *Contemporary Islam* 6, no. 3: 227–33.

Semati, Mehdi. 2017. "Sounds like Iran: On Popular Music of Iran." *Popular Communication* 15, no. 3: 155–62.

Shiloah, Amnon. 2001. *Music in the World of Islam: A Socio-Cultural Study*. Detroit, MI: Wayne State University Press.

Siamdoust, Nahid. 2017. *Soundtrack of the Revolution: The Politics of Music in Iran*. Stanford, CA: Stanford University Press.

"Strange Airing of Salar Aghili Concert." 2016. Parsine.com, February 22. http://www.parsine.com/fa/news/273880/.

Tala'i, Dariush. 2000. *Traditional Iranian Classical Music: The Radif of Mirza Abdollah*. Costa Mesa, CA: Mazda.

Wright, Owen. 2009. *Touraj Kiaras and Persian Classical Music: An Analytical Perspective*. New York: Routledge.

Youssefzadeh, Ameneh. 2000. "The Situation of Music in Iran since the Revolution: The Role of Official Organizations." *British Journal of Ethnomusicology* 9, no. 2: 35–61.

Zonis, Ella. 1973. *Classical Persian Music*. Cambridge, MA: Harvard University Press.

14 | When Hell Freezes Over: Black Metal—Emancipatory Cosmopolitanism or Egoistic Protectionism?

Ketil Thorgersen and Thomas von Wachenfeldt

In the early 1990s, churches burned in Norway and fellow musicians killed each other in the name of Satan. Revolting against Christianity and praising the Antichrist, a new (anti)liturgical satanic music genre was defined: black metal.

True Mayhem: Black Metal as a Musical Expression and Ideological Concept

This chapter aims to investigate and discuss black metal as music education and (anti)religious enculturation. The discussion will relate to philosophies in which art and education are discussed as cosmopolitan in order to understand how black metal constructs itself as elitist and protectionist, and at the same time open and explorative (Papastergiadis 2012; Spivak 2012). Black metal is a subgenre of heavy metal that is particularly widespread in the northwestern parts of Europe, where it originated, and it has since spread over the world. Heavy metal evolved in the late 1960s from a combination of rock and roll and blues, with more focus on the extreme aspects of sonic and visual elements. It was also a time when rock music, through bands like Black Sabbath, began a flirtation with occult symbols and lyrics about Satan and evil (Bayer 2009). The musical field of heavy metal has, from these beginnings, evolved into a range of subgenres—some more mainstream and some more extreme. The most extreme genre that has reached larger audiences is black metal.

Black metal as a genre had not acquired full autonomy during the 1980s, in many respects being very similar to speed metal and thrash metal. From these roots, the new and more heavy- and groove-oriented death metal genre spread and was popularized among the youth first and foremost in the Western world. Around 1991, the defining characteristics of black metal and its differences from the closely related genre death metal were not entirely clear. In an interview from that year, Øystein Aarseth (a.k.a. Euronymous) (1968–93), one of the main characters within the growing black-metal community, stated that his band Mayhem performed "true" death metal and black metal, clearly distinguishing between the two (Kristiansen 2011). He defined the genre according to the topics of the lyrics, as he also explained in a Swedish radio show, *Musikjournalen* (1993): "Black Metal is satanic, heavy, in a way. It can be ordinary Heavy metal or just noise, but what's important is that it is satanic—that's what makes it Black Metal." Aarseth also stressed that death-metal bands such as Entombed, Therion, and Deicide—mainly from Sweden and Florida in the United States—were nothing but posers, and some of them received more or less serious threats from Aarseth and his kinsmen in and around what was referred to as the Black Circle. The Black Circle (in Norwegian, Den Sorte Sirkel) was an assembly around Aarseth, consisting of young orthodox black-metal musicians from Norway and Sweden, whose bands (for example, Burzum, Enslaved, Emperor, Marduk, and Dissection) are still today considered sacrosanct and have reached a sort of apotheosis within the field. Death and black metal were, according to Aarseth, not music for the masses but should be reserved for a designated and devoted elite. Uffe Cederlund, a guitarist with Entombed, illustrates the point in a comment on the cancelation of Entombed's performance in Oslo around 1993 for security reasons: "I can understand the reaction. Things got too big and too mainstream. It went on to be like H&M."[1] Therefore, it seemed to the members of the Black Circle as a necessity to try to recapture the low budget lo-fi sound that characterized the bands from the first wave of black metal[2] from the 1980s and strengthen the ideological aspects of the lyrics and imagery. The move can be seen as a first step to define the genre—not only musically but also ideologically. The genre's gatekeeper was first and foremost Aarseth but included the individuals in and close to the Black Circle.

The black metal that developed in the early 1990s became a continuation of and a reaction to the aesthetics of the first wave, with the music and lyrics defined by its focus on the celebration of Satan, darkness, and evil. The sound was extreme but varied from technically advanced and produced to low-fi and almost punk sounding. Some scholars have analyzed black-metal ideology as being more of an intellectual game and play than being "for real," but as the religious historian Faxneld (2014) stresses, such a simplification is dangerous. In the black-metal milieu there were, and probably still are, people who live according to the ideals of destruction, oppression, and antihappiness and live to make life as miserable as possible for themselves and others. This characterization does not, however, represent the majority of black-metal fans and musicians, who live and believe some variety of an ideology by which they pursue the good life through worshipping the devil and evil.

In the summer of 1991, Aarseth opened a record store named Helvete (Norwegian for "Hell") in Oslo.[3] The store's opening triggered a set of events that have forged the definition of black metal. As the name suggests, the records in Helvete were from the most extreme metal bands from around the world. Helvete became a focal point for the black-metal musicians who would subsequently become the most revered in the genre. Aarseth had also for some time built up his own record label, Deathlike Silence Productions, which was intended for the most extreme bands of death and black metal. The year 1991 can in many respects be considered the turning point of a paradigm shift in the world of extreme metal music.

Only a few months earlier, the singer in Mayhem, Per Ohlin (a.k.a. Pelle Dead, 1969–91), who had also sung in the classic Swedish death-metal pioneers Morbid, committed suicide in a house rented by the band in Kråkstad, outside Oslo (Kristiansen). Aarseth and Ohlin had become a powerful think-tank duo in which the former may be considered as the entrepreneur and the latter as the visionary and philosopher. Both Mayhem and Morbid had earlier included some humorous elements in their music and lyrics, but humor was from 1991 abandoned in favor of a far more sinister image. The lyrics written by Ohlin had two salient topics: Slavonic folklore and death—all nestled in a satanic context.[4] The stage was decorated with pig skulls and Ohlin cut himself on stage and wore rotten clothes at concerts—expressions that have served as a role model for many of today's more serious and "true" black-metal bands. Both Aarseth and Ohlin were musically rooted in the first wave from the early 1980s, but when these bands adopted Satan and satanism as an image or a symbol for individual freedom, Aarseth and Ohlin pushed the concept of satanic metal-music to a completely different and far more lethal level.

One band that passed all credibility tests of the Black Circles, both musically and ideologically, was the one-man band Burzum, with Kristian Vikernes (a.k.a. Count Grishnackh) on drums, bass, guitars, vocals, and keyboards.[5] Vikernes and Aarseth became close friends and Burzum became the second band to release an album with Aarseth's record company, Deathlike Silence.[6] Vikernes also played the bass on Mayhem's genre defining (or redefining) record De Mysteriis Dom Sathanas (1993), when the original bass player Jørn Stubberud (a.k.a. Necrobutcher) left the band after the vocalist Ohlin's suicide and the ensuing controversies.[7] But something happened between Aarseth and Vikernes. People in and around the Black Circle described a power struggle between the two radical and charismatic individuals. Vikernes challenged Aarseth as the leader of the inner core of the Scandinavian black-metal movement. The struggle climaxed with Vikernes killing Aarseth on August 10, 1993. Vikernes claimed that he did it in self-defense when Aarseth threatened to murder him. He was sentenced to twenty-one years in prison, the maximum punishment in Norway at the time, for murder and three church burnings.[8]

These intense years for the Black Circle, between 1990 and 1993, and the events that took place in Norway around Aarseth, Ohlin, and Vikernes, laid the foundations and defined the musical, ideological, and religious conditions for the black-metal genre. Still to this day, the label "true Norwegian black metal" is considered a viable quality marker in the extreme metal community. The music that developed from Venom and Bathory (see note 2) and was refined and defined through the hands of Aarseth and Vikernes created the black-metal sound that persists to the current day: characterized by open minor chords, often played with tremolo in mediantic progressions, producing an epic atmospheric sound accompanied by, as Aarseth puts it, "machine gun drumming" (Musikjournalen 1993). The musical distinctions from death metal that were established around the time are that black metal is, in general, characterized primarily by melodies and soundscapes over heaviness, groove, and technical excellence. The events in the early 1990s paved the way for a new and strong genre that developed and spread over the world. The genre is where many young people learn to play with music, and also with evil.

Metal Is the New Black[9]—Cosmopolitanism, Education, and Present-Day Black Metal

Vikernes killed and burned churches for his black-metal ideology—but how are musicians today constructing black-metal musicianship at the intersection of art, popular culture, religion, and ideology? And could black metal, as a learning practice, somehow inform music education as school practice with its tight bonds between musical agency and its critical (anti)religious base? There is at least something in the culture of black-metal musicianship that promotes musical and intellectual excellence. Today's black-metal bands are filled with technically proficient musicians whose compositions often display a knowledge of diverse musical traditions such as folk music, film music, and classical music. Hundreds of bands in the Nordic countries serve as the primary contexts for many young people's musical learning, guided by ideals of excellence that require hard work and determination—combined with a certain mind-set (Faxneld 2015).

Black metal is, as previously stated, a genre in which the music is inseparable from the message—a message that is most often described as satanic. Key figures such as Aarseth have stated that their performances are rather religious than musical, but the idea that satanism can be defined as a religion is disputable (Faxneld 2015). Satanism may better be understood as a collection of ideologies or ideological practices defined by their anti-Christian or antireligious focus—often portraying Satan, Lucifer, the Anti-Christ, or whatever the entity is called, as they rebel against false happiness and oppression of authoritarian systems such as churches, the national state, and so forth. Lucifer symbolizes individual freedom and the fulfilment of the fullest human potential, and it is therefore sometimes also referred to as a self-religion (Dyrendal 2008; Faxneld 2014). Organizations such as Anton LaVey's Church of Satan have not had any major impact on the black-metal scene, probably because leading black-metal musicians have described LaVey's philosophy or religion as being too humanistic and hedonistic (Hagen 2011). The satanism that black metal constructs is rather a mix between occultism, anti-Christianity, self-religion, and various kinds of pagan and pre-Christian belief system. The religious view is enclosed by a certain popular cultural character, which religious studies scholar Partridge (2005) calls occulture—the blend of popular culture and occultism. In a way, black metal can be understood as the liturgical music of this "religion." Black-metal musicians, including those whose views are presented later in this chapter, are often practicing some version of this religion as a part of their existential artistic practice.

Regardless of its global popularity, black metal seem elitist and judgmental. It might be strange, therefore, to employ ideas of cosmopolitanism as a means of understanding it. Cosmopolitanism as academic theory departs from the idea that cosmopolitanism is a state of mind that invites, welcomes, and explores cultural diversity and simultaneously expresses and represents a cultural heritage, questioning that heritage at the same time, aiming to "avoid reductionism and self-interested simplification" (Schmidt 2013, 27). Related to cosmopolitanism is the ancient (utopian) philosophical idea that peoples and cultures of the world cannot (or should not) be divided by state borders or other (de)limiting structures. In music education, Partti (2012) argues that cosmopolitanism is more a state of mind than an embrace of an "identity of a musical jack-of-all-trades, with abilities to master various musical genres, styles, and instruments" (101). Trying to understand black metal in this light is therefore particularly interesting, because at first glance the genre appears to be the very antithesis of such an open and welcoming attitude. But, in addition to a culture of exclusivity and elitism, black metal reaches globally, disregards borders and sedimented regulations or laws, is inherently critical, and aims to emancipate people from institutional chains.[10]

Cosmopolitanism should not be understood as aiming to make everything and everyone the same, only that everyone and all cultures and cultural expressions should be acknowledged, respected, and freed from the taken-for-granted bonds that tie down the ability to see oneself and others as they are and what they may become (Delanty 2006). Cosmopolitanism most often comes from and represents a privileged position—a mind-set available to those with the symbolic and economic capital that can enable them to be cosmopolitan (Bates 2014; Spivak 2012). Schmidt (2013) argues that cosmopolitan ideas can help free music education from the "us-them" dichotomy that hinders freedom and creativity by situating "us" in a too familiar frame. Cosmopolitan education should rather facilitate an openness toward the unknown and a critical and reconstructive view of personal cultural heritage—an education that actively works to explore, share, scrutinize, respect, and celebrate difference. Black metal is not overtly open to other cultures, but its adherents actively explore the unknown and seek to interact with other cultural mediations.

The case of black metal becomes particularly interesting when one assumes the view that art, as (a set of) cultural practice(s), has cosmopolitan potential, or even that art in itself is cosmopolitan (Papastergiadis 2006). By understanding black metal as an educational and religious practice, theories of cosmopolitanism could provide opportunities to understand black-metal practices in spaces of different and simultaneous modalities and rhizomatous causalities. Art needs to be seen as action with a social and spatial function. "It is important to stress that as art addresses its place in the world, it is simultaneously redefining both its social project and its aesthetic framework" (Papastergiadis 2006, 9). Artistic practices are hence considered images that create innovative spaces where new possibilities can be realized, and aesthetic education is any action that creates such new spaces by reterritorializations and disruptions of the familiar. Black metal definitely aims to disrupt the security and comfort of the familiar and to deterritorialize and reterritorialize not only the musical landscape but the world as we know it.

The Opening of the Gates—to Enter the Dark Realms

At this point in our chapter, we turn to empirical findings of interviews with five active young male black-metal musicians, all actively making music. Participants were sought through various black-metal-music internet forums; they ranged in age between seventeen and twenty-six at the time of data collection in early 2015. They were all male, a selection reflecting the scene, even if several active and respected female musicians are in the scene as well. Participants lived in various regions of Sweden and Finland and played a variety of instruments. The interviews focused on how these young musicians culturally and musically appropriate the black-metal genre. All quotes in this section are with the five respondents interviewed during spring 2015 unless otherwise specified.

All participants described how they ventured into black metal via some musical experience that gave them a feeling of authenticity. In their early to mid-teens they had what might be termed a peak experience through encounters with black metal—a feeling of finding what they were looking for. As one participant reflected, "I guess I was around thirteen years old when I heard Mörk Gryning [in English: Dark Dawn] and I thought, Hell, that sounded good! I want to play that."

They had all played other kinds of music before but were attracted by the elements of darkness, fear, and evil in the music. The Swedish band Watain, which is often seen to represent a more accessible version of black metal, is mentioned by several as providing this feeling of finding what they were looking for. Their routes into the genre musically were described as being the same as in any other genre of rock: You find some friends who share your taste in music, you listen to the music you want to sound like, then you incorporate it by copying and through help from formal and informal teachers or peers. Somewhere along the way, you begin writing your own songs. What these young musicians emphasized was that black metal is not solely about the music or about the musicianship in itself. When pressed on the issues of musical parameters and learning, they answer in precise ways that clearly demonstrate their musical knowledge and competence. Nevertheless, conversations quickly drifted to their ideas of artistic meaning and how they aim to invoke a particular set of emotions and experiences in their audiences. For these musicians, black metal is seen as a genre of music that is particularly concerned about the aesthetic communication between artist and audience.

The participants regarded individuality and freedom from dogmas as the highest human ideal. Their attitudes also involved a contempt for all kinds of organizations or structures that attempt to limit the individual's growth or individuality. The Christian church was considered the main villain here, but Islamic and Judaic practices were also considered oppressive. Satan is hence uplifted as a symbol for rebellion against taken-for-granted truths and blind obedience, with

God seen as autocratic oppressor. Satan is positioned as the hero and the voice for those who dare to be deviant, for those who see through the ignis fatuus that blurs the vision of the masses. As a participant expressed it, "That's why I believe that the general theme [of black metal] is satanism and to follow the devil as well, because he is sort of pillar for—for the individual—to not budge under anyone or to be dominated by anyone, but to be your own master. And you find your own path. And anyone who opposes this can go to hell."

The music thus serves to clarify reality through terrifying and liberating existential aesthetic experiences. As one participant explained, it is important to be informed, to educate yourself to be able to be a black-metal musician and deviant thinker: "I think that knowledge will take you damn far in the spiritual work. It feels as though mankind has entered a kind of stupor—a large boulder of idiocy. And for every scripture I read, it's like taking a chisel and hitting away a piece of that idiocy."

Aligning with what was presented earlier, the satanism they worship and express musically is a mash-up of ideas that is influenced by magic, occultism, antireligion, and classic satanism(s). They all expressed their own personal satanism as some sort of new-age satanism: "I find good parts from these already made concepts . . . but I disagree with a lot usually, and I find the best from everything to form my own opinions."

The musicians considered their genre as exclusive, but at the same time all of them played, or had played in the past, other genres as well. They respected skilled musicians of any genre but simultaneously did not really care, since other music was not that important to them. Elements from certain genres such as folk music and classical music were incorporated into the musicians' compositions and arrangements to achieve their musical goals—in much the same way as they borrowed religious elements from various faiths, myths, and rituals. The music was intended to convey the (often brutally) honest flipside of life (death) through a combination of lyrics of death and evil, uncomfortable sounds, unexpected composition, visual effects such as corpse paint, blood, skulls, and occult images—and sometimes even the smell of blood, dirt, or dead meat—excluding pleasantries such as love and happiness that were seen to blur the vision, as well as nonperennial issues such as politics.

Keeping Up Appearances

Some essential components rise from the interviews on style: the corpse paint and stage performance, the jargon that emphasizes a kind of "noble evil," and an almost pretentious existential and philosophical way of reasoning about life and how artists and music should be, act, and sound to be granted authenticity within the field. The ideals of the complete black-metal "*Gesamtkunstwerk*" open up the darkest parts of the human psyche and behavior and serve as an existential alternative to the happiness and salvation propagated by most institutionalized religion. One seventeen-year-old participant explained it this way: "When you play black metal, in my view, you should always keep up appearances. It is not a requirement for a black metal artist that, when they take off the corpse paint and walk off the stage, they are who they advertise themselves to be. But everything should suggest that you are. So what you are as a civilian is not so important as long as the audience believes that you could eat their child."

Others claimed that they performed occult rituals, experimented with magic, and attended black masses, but at the same time regarded the evil as good—both for themselves and for others, and that the unpleasant aesthetic communication is necessary in order to reach this evil good. The mind-set can partly be understood by drawing parallels with other kinds of art, as described by another participant: "If death metal is like a splatter movie, then black metal is like a psychological thriller." For these participants, the distinction between real and theater was not necessarily clear, nor necessary. In this way, black metal can be seen to point toward cosmopolitanism at the same time as it is giving it the finger.

Black metal constructs a cosmopolitan darkness on the one hand and at the same time tries to look backward into a primordial past that never was, or at least in many respects that has been constructed and formulated by historians and ideologists during the romantic era (von Wachenfeldt 2015). These young men have chosen a path to express themselves and to engage in identity construction. They are striving for freedom from evil or through evil in different ways. The music—or art—becomes (part of) their access to, and constructions of, the religious and spiritual potential of their lives.

Untying the Double Bind of Western Music Education

So what lessons could black metal pedagogy teach Western music education? Black metal pedagogy could inspire formal music education through its binary focus on existential aesthetic communication and artistic excellence. A celebration of the free will, creativity, and critical thinking and ultimately a quest to reach one's full potential. At the same time, black metal represents some of the more destructive, protective, antidemocratic, and selfish ideas in current popular culture; simultaneously both cosmopolitan and anticosmopolitan.

As previously shown, black metal inspires musical excellence, focuses a complete artistic experience grounded in burning existential issues, and uses music to critique dominating and oppressive structures. As a metaperspective, black metal might be interpreted as a kind of Luciferian principle in society. The word *Lucifer*, constructed from the Latin *lux* (light) and *ferre* (bring), can be interpreted as the archetype of deviousness and illumination, the chaotic principle, the trickster, who disturbs the divine order by fooling the gods and brings knowledge to the human race.[11] The Luciferian principle pervades the search for knowledge and enlightenment among the young musicians whose voices are heard in this chapter, but it is also revealed in the chaotic sonic and artistic expressions. If we add, as the musicians do, the original meaning of Satan, the accuser, the mind-set of the informants is somewhat clearer. The individuals within the field of black metal act in many ways as prosecutors, pointing out the hypocrisies of the Western humanistic and democratic narrative—a narrative that in some aspects derives from Christianity with intellectual totalitarianism, egalitarianism, and conformism, popularly labeled political correctness. In daily life, we probably experience several characters who question the prevailing order and therefore pave the way for change. On the other hand, some of the informants manifest a rather reactionary and nostalgic view that rather connects with classical Western cultivation and romantic idealism.

The rewards of black metal are reached through a focus on awareness of the communicative aspects of music. These musicians describe themselves as asking what the music can do for them in their lives, how the music achieves such an effect, and how they can affect both the audience's feelings and, in a longer run, their insights. Aesthetic communication where existential exploration of personal and others' scarier sides through critical examination of themselves and others are what drives the artistic play of these musicians. As argued elsewhere (Ferm and Thorgersen 2007; Thorgersen 2013, 2016), communicative aesthetic aspects of music should be one of the driving forces in music education rather than an afterthought to the technical, theoretical, and musicological content that is most often the vehicle in music education. Perhaps paradoxically, music becomes more important for these black-metal musicians precisely because the music serves as a tool of Satan, a tool to reach a higher (or lower) goal. The common argument that music becomes less important when used to achieve some other means such as learning mathematics or reading, here the relation seems to work the other way around. Because of the existential nature of the meaning black-metal musicians seek to communicate and explore, the music becomes essential as a tool for them to understand themselves, the world, the afterworld, and good and evil. Music education could probably learn from the black-metal mind-set by focusing on what music does to and for the pupil and society, on what feelings, insights, and effects they want to achieve and how to achieve these. To do so, the education would need to constantly focus on analysis, experimentation, and critique by revising the known.

Art should, according to Deleuze and Guattari (1994), provide new and unexpected versions of the world that breaks away from the existential flow. The awareness of existential breaks is essential among black-metal musicians, and therefore black metal could perhaps help music education to reveal and escape the double bind of gendered, white, middle-class, and hegemonic music cultural capital (Spivak 2012). The work process described by the musicians in this study can be seen as serious play. As Bjørkvold (1989) points out, when children play, they effortlessly both act a role and live an alternative reality. They are both aware of what the "real world" is and unaware of what is outside the play. The concept of play connects black metal to ideas of the sublime that helps us understand art as something that allows us to explore the dangers and nastiness we might need to face through a safe filter (Burke 1757). Black metal therefore fits into a long tradition of understanding art as playful experimentation with what is hard to deal with in other ways. To facilitate such a sublime playfulness, one that is both real and an act at the same time, is a major challenge for music education, but it nonetheless is an important one. If music education is compared with other arts such as visual arts education, music education on all levels often comes across as fairly uncontroversial and conformist. But music is important because it moves people in unexpected and subtle ways, and it cannot rest on its laurels and still expect to stay important. Black-metal pedagogy provides examples of how music can move out of the comfort zone by exploring other sides of being human than the pleasant and conformist.

While introducing elements from black metal into mainstream music pedagogy could of course be both dangerous and foolish, the challenges posed by black-metal pedagogy should not be so easily dismissed. Music education needs to rise to the occasion in a world that is more and more complex, while media is ever more tailored to reflect a simplified, preconceived view of the world. Music education needs to embrace cosmopolitanism, in that it reaches out culturally, reaches back and forth historically, and reaches into the complexity of what constructs each individual culturally, socially, and historically. The disrespectful use of, and at the same time acknowledgment of, influences from folk music, classical music, visual, mythical, ritual, and musical folklore, as well as other kinds of popular culture, should inspire music educators to evoke student's motivation to look outside their preferred musical tastes to create what is truly theirs. To change is painful; learning is change: therefore, pain and discomfort should be an essential aspect of musical learning. Black metal should replace formal music education—when hell freezes over.

KETIL THORGERSEN is Associate Professor in the Department of Humanities and Social Sciences Education at Stockholm University in Sweden. His research interests are in music education, the philosophy of music education, and musical learning at the intersection of autodidactic learning and learning within formal institutions.

THOMAS VON WACHENFELDT is Associate Professor in the Department of Creative Studies, Umeå University in Sweden. His research interests include the tension between formal and informal learning and how ideologies affect the perception of musicality and education within the field of traditional folk music in Sweden.

Notes

1. Hennes and Mauritz, a popular Swedish clothing company that sells cheap clothes to the international masses. The source is private correspondence with Uffe Cederlund, July 29, 2015.
2. The first wave of black metal is a fairly loose concept. The bands connected with the first wave are usually the English Venom, Swiss Hellhammer (later Celtic Frost), Danish Mercyful Fate, and the Swedish one-man band Bathory.
3. In 1992, Jon Nødtveidt of Dissection opened a branch of the record store Helvete in Gothenburg, Sweden, but it closed after a fairly short time (Slayer Mag Diaries 1993).
4. The influence of Eastern European culture is still present in the aesthetics and imaginary of Mayhem. Aarseth was politically engaged in Rød Ungdom (Red Youth)

and a self-proclaimed Stalinist/Maoist, and he was "very fascinated by countries like Albania, North Korea or Kampuchea" (Kristiansen 2011, 210). The current singer, Attila Csihar—who joined after Ohlin's suicide and left the band between 1994 and 2004 and then rejoined—is from Hungary. The cover of Mayhem's latest album, *Esoteric Warfare* (2014), made by the Polish artist Zbigniew M. Bielak, has an unmistakable appearance reminiscent of the old Soviet Union.

5. Vikernes later changed his forename to Varg, meaning wolf. In recent years, both names were replaced with a new name: Louis Cachet.

6. The first band was Sweden's Merciless.

7. Aarseth was the one who found Ohlin dead. Instead of immediately calling the police and ambulance, Aarseth drove five kilometers, bought a disposable camera, and took pictures of the dead body. He also used pieces from the skull as a necklace (Johannesson and Jefferson Klingberg 2011).

8. Vikernes never took responsibility for the church fires and claims that they were carried out by younger people who wanted to impress him and Aarseth to gain entrance to the Black Circle (Midtskogen 2009).

9. "Is the new black" here refers to the notion that black is always in vogue in the fashion industry. See, for example, https://www.urbandictionary.com/define.php?term=the%20new%20black.

10. The dialectics of Satan and satanism in music education is treated in more detail in chapter 11 in this book, where Alexandra Kertz-Welzel discusses what evil could be in music education from a critical perspective. It is interesting that she brings up the critical stance of the devil's advocate as a way to fight the devil—a view that might complement or contradict what we are arguing in this chapter.

11. Compare this construct with the half god and trickster Loki—also from *lux*—who is the chaos factor in Norse mythology, and also the Greek titan Prometheus, who stole the fire (enlightenment/knowledge) from Olympus and brought it to humanity. Both of them were punished and shackled by the gods (Loki was tortured by a snake and Prometheus by an eagle). The characters represent a disturbance of the oligarchical principle, where the power is held by the few over the many. It is easy to draw parallels with today's economic and therefore ideational power of a small percentage of mankind, where the antinomian, idealistic, and primordial views within the field of black metal is a threat to conformism and commercialism.

References

Bates, Vincent C. 2014. "Rethinking Cosmopolitanism in Music Education." *Action, Criticism and Theory for Music Education* 13, no. 1 (March): 310–27. http://act.maydaygroup.org/articles/Bates13_1.pdf.

Bayer, Gerd. 2009. *Heavy Metal Music in Britain*. Farnham, UK: Ashgate.

Bjørkvold, Jon-Roar. 1989. *Det musiske menneske: Barnet og sangen, lek og læring gjennom livets faser*. Oslo: Freidig.

Burke, Edmund. 1757. *A Philosophical Enquiry into the Origin of Our Ideas of the Sublime and Beautiful*. London: R. and J. Dodsley.

Delanty, Gerard. 2006. "The Cosmopolitan Imagination: Critical Cosmopolitanism and Social Theory." *British Journal of Sociology* 57, no. 1 (March): 25–47.

Deleuze, Gilles, and Felix Guattari. 1994. *What Is Philosophy?* London: Verso.

Dyrendal, Asbjørn. 2008. "Devilish Consumption: Popular Culture in Satanic Socialization." *Numen* 55, no. 1: 68–98.

Faxneld, Per. 2014. *Satanic Feminism: Lucifer as the Liberator of Woman in Nineteenth-Century Culture.* Oxford: Oxford University Press

———. 2015. "Kom, Ondska, bliv mitt goda: Black metal-nyreligiositet och motdiskursens ordning." *DIN: Tidsskrift for Religion og kultur* 17, no. 1: 62–94.

Ferm, Cecilia, and Ketil André Thorgersen. 2007. "Aesthetic Communication in Music Education—Student's Awareness." Paper presented at the ISPME conference. London, ON, Canada.

Hagen, Ross. 2011. "Musical Style, Ideology, and Mythology in Norwegian Black Metal." In *Metal Rules the Globe: Heavy Metal Music around the World*, edited by Jeremy Wallach, Harris M. Berger, and Paul D. Greene. Durham, NC: Duke University Press.

Johannesson, Ika, and Jon Jefferson Klingberg. 2011. *Blod, eld, död: en svensk metalhistoria.* Stockholm: Alfabeta.

Kristiansen, Jon. 2011. *Metalion: The Slayer Mag Diaries.* New York: Bazillion Points.

Midtskogen, Rune. 2009. "'Greven' angrer ingenting." *Dagbladet*, August 4. http://www.dagbladet.no/2009/07/04/magasinet/innenriks/kriminalomsorg/kirkebrann/drapsdom/7051663/.

Musikjournalen. 1993. Stockholm: Sveriges Radio. https://www.youtube.com/watch?v=XOXb06JC3JA.

Papastergiadis, Nikos. 2006. *Spatial Aesthetics: Art, Place and the Everyday.* London: Rivers Oram.

———. 2012. *Cosmopolitanism and Culture.* Cambridge, UK: Polity.

Partridge, Christopher. 2005. *The Re-enchantment of the West.* Vol. 1, *Alternative Spiritualities, Sacralization, Popular Culture and Occulture.* London: T&T Publishers

Partti, Heidi. 2012. "Learning from Cosmopolitan Digital Musicians: Identity, Musicianship, and Changing Values in (In)formal Music Communities." Helsinki, Fin.: Sibelius-Akatemia.

Schmidt, Patrick. 2013. "A Rabi, an Imam, and a Priest Walk into a Bar . . . or, What Can Music Education Philosophy Learn from Comparative Cosmopolitanism?" *Philosophy of Music Education Review* 21, no. 1: 23–40.

Spivak, Gayatri Chakravorty. 2012. *An Aesthetic Education in the Era of Globalization.* Cambridge, MA: Harvard University Press.

Thorgersen, Ketil. 2013. "Musik som estetisk kommunikation i fritidshemmet." In *Meningsskapande fritidshem: Studio som arena för multimodalt lärande*, edited by Malin Rohlin, 57–80. Lund, Sweden: Studentlitteratur.

———. 2016. "Music Education as Manipulation: A Proposal for Playing." Unpublished manuscript.

von Wachenfeldt, Thomas. 2015. *Folkmusikalisk utbildning, förbildning och inbillning en studie över tradering och lärande av svensk spelmansmusik under 1900- och 2000-talen, samt dess ideologier.* PhD diss., Luleå University of Technology.

Part 5
Agency and Social Change

15 | Radical Musical Inclusion in Higher Education: The Creation of Foundation Music

June Boyce-Tillman

Between[1]

Between the God and the Goddess
And the mosque and the synagogue

Between the bullet holes in the tumbled statue
And the grass blades on the landfill

The shaman and the cleric
The hysteric and choleric

The slaying and the praying
And the coping and the hoping

In the fractured rapture
In the hole in the soul

At the crack
The lack

Might
Bite

The Contradiction of "or"
Meets
The Paradox of "and"

Rebirth.

June Boyce-Tillman

The mixing that results from diversity challenges higher education's espousing of Plato in its tendency to set up certainties and proven hypotheses in search of the perfect form.[2] The opening poem suggests that certain truths lie between established areas of truth, thus continually challenging fixed systems. The classical musical aesthetic has similarly set up monolithic standards of perfection as the ultimate goal of music education, based on Hanslick.³ The present chapter asks for a dialogue between this aesthetic and other value systems. It examines, in detail, a music project in the UK that has entered the process of "queering" current curriculum models by drawing on the university's Christian foundation.⁴

Introduction

This chapter explores the development of music within a UK university with a religious foundation, using the Christian narrative as a source for interrogating dominant cultural narratives. My position in relation to the case study is as a professor in the university and an Anglican priest with a feminist liberation theological position. My professorship is in applied music, and I have considerable experience of music in education, liturgy, and healing contexts. In this essay, my concern was with representing something of the Anglican religious foundation of the university through musicking. I was the instigator of the project and its leader for some ten years. However, as cooperation was at its heart, I carried out unstructured interviews with other members of the team in the course of my leadership and beyond. My concern from the outset was to queer the certainties of the Anglican Christian tradition and thus open up a radically inclusive community, resembling an ideal for the Church—embracing those of all faiths and none. Behind the initial idea is a radical, completely inclusive ecclesiology of music.

A raft of musical activities, set up outside the formal higher education curriculum in this institution, established an inclusive value system; which "queered" the classical musical aesthetic and enabled all students to find their own place within the musicking community and subverted the heteropatriarchal church structures underpinning the classical aesthetic and opened the way for the dialogue of difference (Boyce-Tillman 2014). Queer theology challenged these through "a passion for organizing the lusty transgressions of theological and political thought. This is an encounter with indecency, and with the indecency of God and Christianity" (Althaus-Reid 2002, 200). Foundation Music in Winchester University was generated from the contemporizing of the ancient religious foundation, which led to a queering of the values of the world of Western classical traditions related to a new ecclesiology. In this chapter, this new ecclesiology will be illustrated through the Space for Peace event, which will be approached through an autoethnographic methodology. In doing so, I examine how the acceptance of unresolved paradox might fill the *hole in the soul* in a postsecular society.

The Background and Context of Foundation Music

The University of Winchester is an Anglican foundation from the mid-nineteenth century.⁵ Since my appointment there in 1989, the university has been engaged with understanding what this foundation might mean in the contemporary world. Foundation Music—an extracurricular raft of musical activities—was named because of its relation with the Anglican Foundation and had the following aims:

a. To enrich the student experience by a variety of musical ensemble experiences (embracing cultural diversity and including student-led and student-initiated ensembles)
b. To forge links with the local community through high-profile performance events involving local community groups[6]
c. To represent the ethical principles of the Anglican foundation of the university by serving the needs of the local community through such events as raising money for local charities and performing for vulnerable groups such as inmates at Winchester Community Prison
d. To support the liturgical life of the university and beyond[7]

Student involvement grew very quickly. Foundation Music now includes about six hundred students across the whole university. It has at least twenty-five ensembles, including classical choirs, the Sounds of New Gospel Choir (taught orally), African drumming, jazz bands, and barbershop ensembles.

Collegiality

The first aim was to create an inclusive community. A small community has an important role within the wider university community, particularly for vulnerable students—to help them with *the coping and the hoping* that characterize university life. For example, one student who had failed a teaching practice, thus ending her aim to become a teacher, said that in this difficult transition period at least on a Monday night the King Alfred Singers was still the same. Foundation Music provided a supportive community of learners, in line with Christian principles. The inclusive nature is represented by the absence of auditions and a nurturing leadership style that sees mistakes as simply part of a learning journey (Morgan and Boyce-Tillman 2008). Foundation Music can be seen as a return to the values of a theology that includes the feminine—the *goddess* of the opening poem—concerned with human flourishing.[8]

The administrative structure was collegial, "queering" power-based structures. I set up what Charles Handy (1995) called a "shamrock" structure, in which each ensemble was self-contained and related directly to the center. In such a structure, individual initiatives could be quickly enacted, because there was no hierarchy of committees to be navigated.[9] The development of new ideas was, therefore, close to the passion of those who had generated them, so that the *rapture is not fractured.*

The Common Good

The second and third aims were to serve the wider public good. The ensembles accept a number of local engagements, including weddings, charity concerts, evensongs in the cathedral, and my large-scale pieces. The engagements challenge class, ethnic, and gender divisions and engender debates in the realm of ethics and morality. Rowan Williams (2012) suggests that the intelligent citizen needs to develop "humane imagination" and "empathy" (271). Music is well placed to deliver these qualities, for it can encompass the feelings of *the hysteric and the choleric* (Laurence 2008). One student's regular engagement with the Singing for Wellbeing choir, for example, has led her to develop her empathetic skills for a career as a community musician.

Anglican Heritage

The fourth aim, centered on Anglican-Christian ritual, links Foundation Music with a particular religion, which various students approach through different perspectives. The approach can be critical, as Estelle Jorgensen suggests;[10] Miettinen suggests that education *should* challenge students to think differently.[11] In the interests of hospitality to other faith traditions and representing the rise, in the postsecular twenty-first century, of various spiritualities, an interfaith ritual was also developed and named Space for Peace (Boyce-Tillman 2011, 2012, 2016; Illman 2012; King 2009; Laurence and Urbain 2011, 185–201; Taylor 2007). Space for Peace explores the interface between various religious traditions, as in the opening poem.

Justice Seeking

Bearing in mind the emphasis on justice in the Christian narrative, I challenged the prevailing classical music ideology from the perspective of my immersion in feminist theological and musical critiques of heteropatriarchy (Boyce-Tillman 2007, 2014). My social constructionist position included examining the impact of political, social, research, and knowledge production on the way in which music has been constructed (Foucault 1980): "the open mesh of possibilities, gaps, overlaps, dissonances and resonances, lapses and excesses of meaning when constituent elements of anyone's gender, of anyone's sexuality aren't made (or can't be made) to signify monolithically" (Sedgwick 1994, 7). This position sees music as a means of social action.[12] Much of the literature on Christianity in higher education sees justice seeking as following the values represented in the Jesus narrative, epitomized by the phrases *between the bullet holes in the tumbled statue and the grass blades on the landfill*.[13] Warren Carter (2001) deals with this in detail as he explores how the early Christian church was a community alternative to the dominant culture. Jesus was a challenger of the underpinning values of the political systems of his day. Christianity "respects our common places of pluralism and encounter. It recognises that persons of belief must be called to account for their faith and be prepared to justify themselves; but primarily, seeks to pursue a public vocation that is more interested in the well-being of humanity than narrow or partisan self-interest" (Graham 2015, 52). Within Foundation Music, students can explore and develop their own meaning-making systems spiritual and religious domains and relate to their own sense of identity.[14]

Radical Musical Inclusion

I have drawn on the fields of philosophy, spirituality, ecclesiology, and social psychology to construct a theory of radical musical inclusion in the field of dialogue using music.[15] In "the plurality of self and other is peace" (Levinas 1969, 203). Accomplishing this goal needs more than intellectual tools to provide an "incarnating encounter" (Illman 2012, 60; Illman 2009), if viewed from a Christian perspective. Within the self, the dialogue between the alterities is a source of creativity,[16] as in the opening poem. For fifteen years, I worked to develop musicking structures for bringing together diversity, culminating in 2015 in *From Conflict to Chorus—An Intermezzo for Peace*. The work was based on letters, poems, and songs from World War I and included the Singing for Well-Being choir (which included people who had received a diagnosis of dementia) as well as children with profound and multiple learning difficulties, a soloist with visual and learning impairment, community choirs, a professional orchestra, Hampshire schools, and university choirs). The challenge with some of these groups is the random sounds that they may introduce. A composer integrated their sounds into the performance. As part of the orchestra, guns were reconstructed into a large human-figure sculpture, which the children played in the composition. The guns (decommissioned) converted into a musical instrument were a powerful symbol of peace for everyone present.

In such an event, the organizer (previously composer) becomes a frame builder. Composing becomes the building of a scaffold on which everyone can realize their full potential, not (as in the Western classical aesthetic) as someone imprinting one's own creation on a group of people, some of whom may well be excluded if they cannot carry out the instructions—where at the crack the lack might bite (Holzman 2008).

Through such events, Foundation Music seeks to embody social justice and develop students who will be prepared to challenge the status quo. Responding to my more experimental musical works, students often say that I taught them always to think outside the box—never to be trapped by the myths we live by (Midgely 2003). Several have gone on to positions as community music enablers (L. Higgins 2012).

My concern is to challenge, interrogate, and transform the dominant classical music paradigm, into which I had been initiated at Oxford University.[17] I had already been closely involved in community musicking, as celebrated by Christopher Small (1998)—who wanted to include the context and the underpinning value systems within the analysis of musical events—a system based on process rather than product. The development of community music challenged the value systems governing the Academy, whose pursuit of musical excellence was based on the Platonic premise that truth is the same for everyone at all times (L. Higgins 2002, 19; Sacks 2002, 19). This premise had thus far resulted in a hierarchical view of singing groups and traditions, with the oral and informal at the bottom (Morgan 2013).

The dominant singing traditions—often called classical—values products over process, individual achievement over community building, challenging entry routes divorced from nurture, and unity within its structures, rather than encompass diverse traditions and styles. In the early twenty-first century, two living aesthetics are associated with singing in UK society: "The classical perspective on singing emphasizes performance, perfection, and virtuosity—the standard or 'taproot' aesthetic that has been recognized in music education since its inception in the mid-1800s. The second aesthetic for singing stresses community building, diversity, group collaboration and relationship (Pascale 2005, 167).

Foundation Music supports effectively a wide variety of musical styles led by people of a wide variety of experience and expertise. These include orate and literate traditions—so challenging the classical European traditions[18]—with different leadership styles and performance traditions—*the shaman and the cleric* are brought together (Ong 1982). Working with a small paid staff meant developing students' musical leadership skills as well as working with the wider community through an effective community engagement policy.

Kathleen McGill (1991) sees improvisatory techniques as drawing on femme-identified oral and collaborative culture. She links that culture with women's desire for forms that enable social cooperation. Women favor forms that do not "enact difference in oppositional terms"; instead, she sees women as favoring forms in which difference becomes "multiple, inclusive and highly adaptive" (McGill 1991, 68–69). My pieces are cocreated and coconducted with the performers and "queer" the established forms of classical construction, such as the cantata or symphony. Collaborative and cooperative ways of leading also "queers" the individualized styles of leadership within the Western classical musical tradition and restores the values of the goddess cultures (Jantzen 1998).[19]

Uniformity and Unity

This thinking led me to embrace diversity by producing works with communal value systems, as well as performing the standard classical repertoire, so that *the contradiction of "both" meets the paradox of "and."* The dominant traditions—whether musical or theological—have often set up a Platonic position based on uniformity of belief or practice. I engendered a respectful encounter with difference, which may be a new experience for undergraduates: "Deep learning is a phenomenon that has been quite widely researched and discussed. . . . [Students] become more critical of the accepted wisdom in the traditions from which they come and learn to live with questions and uncertainties with regard to their faith and ethics" (Garner, Burgess, and Eshun 2015, 93). The encounter can include a critique of the church (Forrester 2004, 6).[20] By encountering different musical traditions, students' own value systems are often challenged, and they move along on their own spiritual journey—to explore the "betweens" within it.

An Ecclesiology of Music

I have had a lifelong experience of the Anglican parish tradition in the UK, including the parish church choir, which attempted to embrace all who wanted to join. Church choirs (and indeed churches) were, in theory at least, inclusive, but in practice often exclusive, particularly in such areas as gender, disability, and sexuality. My musical philosophy uses an ecclesiological frame (Boyce-Tillman 2016). The four pillars of the traditional church were

- Unity
- Holiness
- Catholicity
- Apostolicity

Drawing on the work of Elisabeth Schussler Fiorenza (2000) and Robert Goss (2002), Tiffany Steinwert (2003) "queered" the church's pillars in order to produce a truly inclusive model of church. Unity needs to be challenged in its guise of doctrinal uniformity (expressed traditionally in creedal statements). In my musical thinking, the challenge has taken the form of including a variety of styles (orate and literate) in the same piece to produce a unity that is not uniformity, both *the shaman and the cleric*.

Holiness moves from individualized piety to justice seeking. My musical events are concerned with justice, such as *The Great Turning* (2014)—with its concern for respect for the earth and ecology—including *the grass blades on the landfill*. The *slaying* is brought together with the *praying*.

Catholicity is traditionally worked out in a form drawing on Roman imperialism—both in the so-called Roman Catholic Church and in the Protestant traditions, especially in their colonial enterprises; it needs to be about the accepting of difference—both *the mosque and the synagogue*. My musical policy has been one of radical musical inclusion.

Apostolicity ceases to be concerned with a patriarchal lineage and becomes committed action (Steinwert 2003). In musical terms, Foundation Music principles are reflected in the immense stress on well-being and commitment through musicking and encouraging students to assume leadership roles—to become the *shamans* and *clerics* of music.

Foundation Music is a queer ecclesiology expressed through musicking.

Space for Peace

This ecclesiology is most clearly expressed in the project Space for the Peace, in which a variety of religious and secular traditions are brought together. Its embracing of diversity sets the freedom of carnival within a cathedral space—a return of the Dionysian, as the middle section of Space for Peace has been described as a musical sweet shop because people can go around and sample a variety of delights as different groups simultaneously sing music from their own tradition (Bakhtin 1993). As we have seen, the church has traditionally been very controlling, not only in its dogma but also in its liturgies with their fixed literate form. The central free improvisatory section has the sounds merging in and out with one another. In this sense, it is like Charles Ives's *Fourth of July*, but here it is not controlled by the composer but by the performers and the audience. The celebratory improvisational approach enables performers to explore the possibilities of their own chosen style and work out their relation to other styles. Process is now merged with product. The performance produces unforeseen consequences, such as when the rabbi approached the imam near the end of the piece and sang with him a shared verse—the *mosque* met the *synagogue*.

Many comments after the performance of Space for Peace showed that a heteroglossaic space had been created by the inclusion of a multiplicity of voices. This term originated with Bakhtin (1993) in his analysis of the novel, where it is used to mean the presence of, and perhaps conflict between, different types of speech. The cathedral proved a space that was well suited to mixing difference effectively. The opening of the event was more conventional, with choirs singing individual chants that fitted together as a quodlibet and led those present gently into the idea of the carnivalesque.[21] It reflects a democratization of the liturgy/concert, which frees up a space to give the possibility of greater freedom and celebration of diversity. It is a democratic project designed to foster cooperation (not least between the university and the local faith communities). It is potentially a transformative event, because of the musickers' power to construct a spirituality that embraces paradox and contradictions. Garner, Burgess, and Eshun (2015) report one person's reaction: "*Space for Peace* was one of the high points of my life. . . . It came to me that peace is possible" (93).

Throughout the piece, the energy is felt to build, with the stones creating echoing loops from the complex soundscape (Boyce-Tillman 2010).[22] Near the end of the event, everyone, in a candle-lit procession, centers on a single note on which they sing a word for peace, giving the texture of a drone extolled by Perković and Mandić in Serbian Orthodox chanting. Over this, singers and instrumentalists improvise. Here, this immense diversity descends into a clear expression of unity. Unity and diversity are embraced within a single musical event. It is a small and simple act of hope, as described by Badarne and Ehrlich.

Liberal Education

Where does this approach of both valuing and accommodating difference fit within a university with a Christian foundation? Higher Education in the UK had a Christian foundation from the beginning, at medieval Oxford and Cambridge—with three underlying principles:

- Love of Knowledge
- Formation in a strong community of learners
- Usefulness to society

The universities, however, were never exclusively Christian. Although they had chapels and regular Christian worship, they were always hospitable to other faiths, notably the pagan traditions of Greece and Rome. A strong community of learners was based on collegiality and the formation of students within a hospitable, ethical, and godly community. The third was the serving of the public good—a vocational vision with the pursuit of Knowledge that is useful to society.

Holmes (1997), stressed the formation of persons, which he linked with the idea of a liberal education. He wanted education seen, not as the transfer of a compendium of useful Knowledge, but as the shaping of persons, suggesting that teachers should continually interrogate the effect that they are having on their students, rather than the information they are imparting. Exploration of the betweens of a culture encourages students to bring their own identities into the lecture hall and to form an internalized Wisdom. The main role of a university is to enable the wider society to understand itself more deeply, so that Wisdom and Knowledge are intertwined. John Henry Cardinal Newman (n.d.a), the Anglican cleric who converted to Catholicism and became an Oxford academic, conceptualized a pluralist, inclusive curriculum that linked Knowledge with experience and saw the university as having has "a greater role than just doling out qualifications—that of shaping the whole individual."[23]

This is the Wisdom approach to learning, as expressed in Winchester University's motto—Wisdom ond Lar (Wisdom and Knowledge). Cardinal Newman gave a series of lectures in 1852 reflecting on the purpose of a university. He clarified the relationship of faith to Knowledge: If then a University is a direct preparation for this world, let it be what it professes. It is not a Convent, it is not a Seminary; it is a place to fit men [sic] of the world for the world. . . . It is not the way to learn to swim in troubled waters, never to have gone into them" (Newman n.d.b). Therefore, the notion of embracing diversity in a collegial community engenders a Wisdom that prepares people for the work of life—central to a liberal education.

Faith, Meaning, and the Formation of the Person

The integration of faith and learning must ultimately take place at the level of worldview, which Holmes calls "a systematic understanding" (Holmes 1987, 57). Part of the value of universities to society is that they can be independent places of debate and deliberation in the interests of the long-term ethical and intellectual ecology of a civilization (Ford 2007).[24] The "predicament of the modern mind" is that it is "at a loss to know what life is all about" (Holmes 1987, 3, 4). Holmes links this predicament with secularization, suggesting that universities could be a place where meaning is created rather than discovered.[25] Here the place of *paradox* needs deep exploration. He sees how a religious worldview can give purpose and coherence to people's lives in an age of egotism and materialism, in the form of insight into other people's positions.[26]

John Dewey saw an important place for the aesthetic experience in a fragmented world as providing a coherently meaningful experience (Westerlund

2002). Here music can play the part of an open space in which meaning is not tied too tightly to a single worldview.[27] It can set up situations for discovery of meaning. The music "does not offer meaning but triggers the effort to produce the meaning" (Voegelin (2010, 165). A considerable literature explores not only the connection between music and faith traditions but also sees music (and, indeed, the arts as a whole) as a new faith tradition in itself (Boyce-Tillman 2016), which, in the twenty-first century, has emerged as an atheist spirituality. This spirituality acknowledges the useful functions of religion, which de Botton (2012) sees as fostering community and providing coping strategies for pain and suffering, concluding "There might be a way to engage with religion without having to subscribe to its supernatural content" (5–6). De Botton's hope is that the arts might be as effective as religion in their ability to guide, humanize, and console. The arts inform the search for meaning without engaging in metaphysical belief systems. There is a similarity between religious thinking and artistic knowing within the context of a postsecular society.

Wisdom as Decision Making

Through Foundation Music, students can negotiate their own routes, gaining experience through decision making. Students select a route through the ensembles that feels right for them: Wisdom combines "knowledge, understanding, good judgement and far-sighted decision-making" (Ford 2007, 1). Wisdom is based on making choices. Our university curricula offer so few choice-making opportunities. Rowan Williams (2001) critiques an educational system "more and more dominated by an instrumentalist model."[28] While Knowledge may be situated in the controlled environment of the defined modules, with their declared learning outcomes and the demands of the state, Wisdom is engendered by negotiating routes through the wider community of university life. It is perhaps best explored through extracurricular activities: "Students take responsibility for their own learning when they participate in out-of-class activities and events that enrich the educational experience" (Kuh et al. 1994, xi). This result is reflected in many of the narratives collected from students who have been part of Foundation Music.

Sean Steel (2015) looks for a restoration of a Dionysian spirituality within education (in an article primarily concerned with US education) through the medium of music.[29] He relates Dionysian spirituality to "the loss of self-awareness that occurs in the best musical experiences" (78), which might be true of music freed of the controls of a curriculum. Musicians can lead us in joyful choruses (K. Higgins 2011). Foundation Music provides a "chorus school" for the university as a whole, which draws freely on its expertise for a multitude of university celebrations.

The principles underpinning Foundation Music at a UK university are seen as queering current curriculum models by enabling informed choices.[30] Learning often occurs in a community context, not in individual lessons, and inexperienced learners are quickly incorporated into ensembles, in a way more common in community practice and informal learning contexts than in classical music traditions.

Conclusion

This chapter discussed the relationship between music and religion in a higher education institution in the UK, based on a queer theology that challenges prevailing value systems. It has related music and meaning making through embracing various spiritualities; the *hole in the soul* of a postsecular world might be filled by the embracing of *contradiction* and *paradox*. It has seen how the story of Jesus might be seen as queering the values of the dominant society in areas such as class, gender, sexuality, disability, and ethnicity; these areas can be addressed by including orate as well as literate traditions. Knowledge may be seen as situated in the more controlled environment of the defined higher education curriculum modules dominant in the UK, but Wisdom is seen in this context to be engendered by the capacity to make choices offered by the extracurricular activities of Foundation Music.

The underlying philosophy of Foundation Music celebrates the meeting of possibilities and opportunities—the "betweens" of the opening poem—without obliterating their differences. By queering the dominant musical paradigm, this chapter has opened up music as a tool for reconciliation and creativity and a place where spiritualities can be celebrated. The results of the case study with Foundation Music demonstrate that cultural and personal *rebirth* may lie in this process.

JUNE BOYCE-TILLMAN read music at Oxford University and is Professor of Applied Music at the University of Winchester. Her interests are in music education, theology, liturgy, feminism, composition and dialogue, and healing and wellbeing through music. She has published widely on music education, including an edited book on spirituality and music education. Her doctoral research into children's musical development has been translated into five languages. She is an international performer, especially on the work of Hildegard of Bingen. Her one woman shows concentrate on spiritual themes and the lives of the mystics. She is a hymn writer—*A Rainbow to Heaven*—whose work is used internationally. She has written about and organized events in the area of interfaith dialogue using music. She lectures internationally and is concerned with radical musical inclusion, composing large-scale works for cathedrals such as Winchester, Norwich, and Southwark involving professional musicians, community choirs, children and adults with disabilities, and schoolchildren. She is editing a series on music and spirituality for Peter Lang, which includes her book *Experiencing Music-Restoring the Spiritual* and the edited collection *Queering Freedom: Music, Identity and Spirituality: Perspectives from Ten Countries*. She founded the Centre for the Arts as Well-being and the Tavener Centre for Music and Spirituality at the University of Winchester, UK. She is an Extra-ordinary Professor at North West University, South Africa. She is an Anglican priest and an honorary chaplain to Winchester Cathedral.

Notes

1. The notion of accepting paradox and the break with rationality is part of Øivind Varkøy's chapter 8 chapter in this volume. Laura Mietinnen's chapter 16 in this volume suggests that a crossing of separate identities gives an opportunity for new understanding and growth.
2. This is explored in more detail in Morgan and Boyce-Tillman (2008).
3. See Erum Naqvi, chapter 13 in this volume.
4. Winchester University was founded in the nineteenth century by the Anglican Church to train teachers of religious education for the church schools in the Winchester Diocese. Although it has developed into a university with a wide range of courses, the governors of the university have endeavored to remain true to the aims of the original foundation of what was then a college.
5. The Church of England or Anglican Church is the established Christian church in England. I have used the word *Anglican* in relation to Winchester University but *Christian* in relation to the values of the Christian church in general. In this chapter the particular Christian values I am embracing are community, inclusion, hospitality, empathy, virtue-ethics, justice-seeking, meaning making including spirituality, and serving the public good.
6. One of these—an intergenerational project—is described by Iris Yob in chapter 17 in this volume.
7. Liturgical singing as a way of belonging is described by Fletcher and Barrett in chapter 4 and Perković and Mandić in chapter 6 in this volume.
8. See also Christ (1997). The point is explored in more detail in Boyce-Tillman (2007).
9. This placed me in the role of facilitator as described by Miettinen in Chapter 16 in this volume.
10. Chapter 1 in this volume.
11. Chapter 16 in this volume.
12. As Kallio, Westerlund, and Alperson suggest in their introduction to this volume.
13. The original poem drew on a statue of the Virgin Mary now peppered with bullet holes and the attempt of the earth to revitalize itself in the small blades of grass poking through the ruins.
14. The topic is explored by Miettinen in chapter 16 and by Fletcher and Barrett in chapter 4 in this volume.
15. See Boyce-Tillman (2016); Illman (2010); Urbain (2008).
16. This relates to the notions of performed selves described in the work of Bauman by Miettinen, chapter 16 in this volume, and in relation to Judith Butler in Westerlund, Kallio, and Partti, chapter 3 in this volume.
17. See the discussion of Hanslick by Naqvi in chapter 13 in this volume.
18. See Naqvi's examples of improvisation in chapter 13 in this volume.
19. Explored in much more detail in Morgan and Boyce-Tillman (2008).
20. Jorgensen considers the same point in chapter 1 in this volume.
21. A quodlibet is a piece where several tunes fit together effectively. This one is made up of seven short chants—some traditional and some by the author.
22. These elements of communitas form a central part of Victor Turner's (1974, 1982) idea of liminality, and of constructs discussed in many chapters in this volume, such as the otherworld of Spychiger in chapter 9, and an in-between or a liminal zone described by Miettinen in chapter 16.
23. See also Deboick (2010).

24. This vision is not unlike the concept of *Bildung* expressed by Thorgersen and von Wachenfeldt, chapter 14 in this volume.
25. Or, as Spychiger (chapter 9 in this volume) suggests, searched for.
26. See Fletcher and Barrett, chapter 4 in this volume.
27. This can be seen as an antidote to religious fundamentalism.
28. From *Historical Sketches*, Volume III, "The Rise and Progress of Universities," Chapter I, Section 6, http://www.cardinalnewmansociety.net/university.html.
29. This could be linked with Bakhtin's idea of the carnivalesque, as discussed earlier in this chapter. See also Varkøy, chapter 8 in this volume.
30. Varkøy, in chapter 8 in this volume, suggests enabling such choices is necessary for personal development.

References

Althaus-Reid, Marcella. 2002. *Indecent Theology*. London: Routledge.
Bakhtin, Mikhail. 1993. *Rabelais and His World*. Translated by Hélène Iswolsky. Bloomington: Indiana University Press.
Boyce-Tillman, June. 2007. *Unconventional Wisdom*. London: Equinox.
———. 2010. "Even the Stones Cry Out: Music Theology and the Earth." In *Through Us, with Us, in Us: Relational Theologies in the Twenty-First Century*, edited by Lisa Isherwood and Elaine Bellchambers, 153–78. London: SCM.
———. 2011. "Making Musical Space for Peace." In *Peace and Policy Dialogue of Civilization for Global Citizenship*, Vol. 15, *Music and Solidarity: Questions of Universality, Consciousness and Connection*, edited by Felicity Laurence and Olivier Urbain, 185–201. New Brunswick NJ: Transaction.
———. 2012. "Music and the Dignity of Difference." *Philosophy of Music Education Review* 20, no. 1 (Spring): 25–44.
———. 2014. *In Tune with Heaven or Not: Women in Christian Liturgical Music*. Frankfurt: Peter Lang.
———. 2016. *Experiencing Music—Restoring the Spiritual: Music as Wellbeing*. Frankfurt: Peter Lang.
Carter, Warren. 2001. *Matthew and the Margins: A Socio-Political and Religious Reading*. Sheffield, UK: Sheffield Academic.
Christ, Carol P. 1997. *Rebirth of the Goddess: Finding Meaning in Feminist Spirituality*. London: Routledge.
Deboick, Sophia. 2010. "Newman Suggests a University's 'Soul' Lies in the Mark It Leaves on Students." *The Guardian*, October 20. http://www.theguardian.com/commentisfree/2010/oct/20/john-henry-newman-idea-university-soul.
De Botton, Alain. 2012. *Religion for Atheists: A Non-believer's Guide to the Uses of Religion*. London: Hamish Hamilton.
Fiorenza, Elisabeth Schussler. 2000. *Jesus and the Politics of Interpretation*. New York: Continuum.
Ford, David. 2007. *Christian Wisdom*. Cambridge: Cambridge University Press.
Forrester, Duncan. B. 2004. *The Scope of Public Theology* 17, no. 2: 5–19.
Foucault, Michel. 1980. *Power/Knowledge: Selected Interviews and Other Writings, 1972–77*. Edited by Colin Gordon. Hemel Hempstead, UK: Harvester Wheatsheaf.
Garner, Mark, Richard Burgess, and Daniel Eshun. 2015. "Submitting Convictions to Critical Enquiry: A Challenge for Higher Education." *Occasional Papers on Faith*

  in Higher Education, no. 1 (April): 62–76. London: Whitelands College, University of Roehampton, and Colleges and Universities of the Anglican Communion. https://cuac.anglicancommunion.org/media/153639/Occ-Papers-on-Faith-in-HE-no-1.pdf.

Goss, Robert E. 2002. *Queering Christ: Beyond Jesus Acted Up*. Chicago: Pilgrim.

Graham, Elaine. 2105. *Apologetics without Apology: Navigating Our Way in a Globalized and Multi-faith World*. Occasional Papers on Faith in Higher Education, no. 1 (April): 29–42. London: Whitelands College, University of Roehampton, and Colleges and Universities of the Anglican Communion. https://cuac.anglicancommunion.org/media/153639/Occ-Papers-on-Faith-in-HE-no-1.pdf.

Grey, Mary. 2015. "Joy in Enough." Keynote presentation at A Cosmological and Ecological Approach to Healing, Holy Rood House Summer School, Thirsk, UK, June 29.

Handy, Charles. 1995. *The Age of Unreason: New Thinking for a New World*. London: Arrow.

Higgins, Kathleen Mary. 2011. *The Music of Our Lives*. New ed. Toronto: Lexington.

Higgins, Lee. 2012. *Community Music: In Theory and in Practice*. Oxford: Oxford University Press.

Holmes, Arthur F. 1987. *The Idea of a Christian College*. Grand Rapids, MI: Eerdmans.

Holzman, Lois, ed. 2008. *Vygotsky at Work and Play*. London: Taylor and Francis.

Illman, Ruth. 2010. "Plurality and Peace: Interreligious Dialogue in a Creative Perspective." *International Journal of Pubic Theology* 4, no. 2: 175–92.

———. 2012. "Incarnating Encounters." In *Mapping Religion and Spirituality in a Postsecular World*, edited by Giuseppe Giordan and Enzo Pace, 43–62. Leiden, Neth.: Brill.

———. 2009. "Momo and Ibrahim—'Thus-and-Otherwise': A Dialogical Approach to Religious Difference." *Journal of Contemporary Religion* 24, no. 2 (May): 157–70.

Jantzen, Grace M. 1998. *Becoming Divine: Toward a Feminist Philosophy of Religion*. Manchester, UK: Manchester University Press.

King, Ursula. 2009. *The Search for Spirituality: Our Global Quest for Meaning and Fulfillment*. Norwich, UK: Canterbury.

Kuh, George D., K. B. Douglas, J. P. Lund, and J. Ramin-Gyurnek. 1994. *Student Learning outside the Classroom: Transcending Artificial Boundaries*. ASHE-ERIC Higher Education Report no. 8. Washington, DC: George Washington University.

Laurence, Felicity. 2008. "Empathy." In *Music and Conflict Transformation: Harmonies and Dissonances in Geopolitics*, edited by Olivier Urbain, 13–25. London: I. B. Tauris.

Laurence, Felicity, and Olivier Urbain. 2011. *Peace and Policy Dialogue of Civilization for Global Citizenship*, Vol. 15, *Music and Solidarity: Questions of Universality, Consciousness and Connection*. New Brunswick, NJ: Transaction.

Levinas, Emanuel. 1969. *Totality and Infinity: An Essay in Exteriority*. Pittsburgh, PA: Duquesne University.

MacIntyre, Alasdair. 2007. *After Virtue: A Study in Moral Theory*. 3rd ed. Notre Dame, IN: University of Notre Dame Press.

McGill, Kathleen. 1991. "Women and Performance: The Development of Improvisation by the Sixteenth-Century Commedia dell'Arte." *Theatre Journal* 43: 59–69.

Midgley, Mary. 2003. *Myths We Live By*. London: Routledge.

Morgan, Sarah. 2013. "Community Choirs—A Musical Transformation" Unpublished paper.

Morgan, Sarah, and June Boyce-Tillman. 2008. *A River Rather than a Road: The Community Choir as Spiritual Experience*. Oxford, Peter Lang.

Newman, John Henry. n.d.a. *Historical Sketches*. Vol. 3, *The Rise and Progress of Universities*, ch. 1, sec. 6. Society for the Study of Cardinal Newman. Last modified April 10, 2009. http://www.cardinalnewmansociety.net/university.html.

———. n.d.b. *Some Major Ideas and Themes from Newman's Reflections on the University*. Society for the Study of Cardinal Newman. Last modified April 10, 2009. http://www.cardinalnewmansociety.net/university.html.

Ong, Walter. 1982. *Orality and Literacy: The Technologizing of the Word*. London: Methuen.

Pascale, Louise. 2005. "Dispelling the Myth of the Non-singer: Embracing Two Aesthetics for Singing." *Philosophy of Music Education Review* 13, no. 2: 165–75.

Sacks, Jonathan. 2002. *The Dignity of Difference*. London: Continuum.

Sedgwick, Eve Kosofsky. 1994. *Tendencies*. New York: Routledge.

Small, Christopher. 1998. *Musicking: The Meanings of Performing and Listening*. Middletown, CT: Wesleyan University Press.

Steel, Sean. 2015. "The Birth of Dionysian Education (Out of the Spirit of Music)," pt. 2. *Philosophy of Music Education Review* 23, no. 1 (Spring): 67–81.

Steinwert, Tiffany. 2003. Unpublished paper presented in Carter Heyward's class on queer theology, April 28. Cambridge, MA: Episcopal Divinity School.

Taylor, Charles. 2007. *A Secular Age*. Cambridge MA: Belknap.

Turner, Victor. 1974. "Liminal to Liminoid in Play, Flow, and Ritual: An Essay in Comparative Symbology." *Rice University Studies* 60, no. 3: 53–92.

———. 1982. *From Ritual to Theatre: The Human Seriousness of Play*. New York: PAJ.

Urbain, Olivier, ed. 2008. *Music and Conflict Transformation: Harmonies and Dissonances in Geopolitics*. London: I. B. Tauris.

Voegelin, Salome. 2010. *Listening to Noise and Silence: Toward a Philosophy of Sound Art*. New York: Continuum.

Westerlund, Heidi. 2002. "Bridging Experience, Action, and Culture in Music Education." *Studia Musica* 16: 191. Helsinki: Sibelius Academy Music Education Department.

Williams, Rowan. 2012. *Faith in the Public Square*. London: Bloomsbury.

16 | Religious Identities Intersecting Higher Music Education: An Israeli Music Teacher Educator as Boundary Worker

Laura Miettinen

When a music teacher steps into a classroom, she or he is immediately surrounded by various cultural influences and demands relating to the students, the curriculum, the school, and educational policy. In the midst of it all, the teacher also tries to stay true to her own personal and professional beliefs, values, and ethical principles of how to be a good teacher. If the students represent different religious beliefs and backgrounds, which is most likely the case given the cultural diversity and plurality of most contemporary societies, the teacher is also required to be aware of different—and at times conflicting—religious values in the daily work of teaching and learning music. Although religion plays an essential role in many musical traditions, it has seldom been addressed as a topic in music education research (Hoffman 2011; Jorgensen 1997, 2011). As regards professional teacher identity, earlier discussions on the relationship between musicianship and educatorship (e.g., Elliott 1995), as well as the more recent identification of the musical and the pedagogical as the dominant aspects of music educators' identity formations (e.g., Ballantyne, Kerchner, and Aróstegui 2012; Bouij 1998; Hargreaves et al. 2007; Pellegrino 2009, 2014), have shed light on certain key aspects and mechanisms in music teachers' identity work. In my view, however, the discussion should be opened up to include wider understandings of teachers' identification processes in order to meet the complex educational needs of increasingly diverse societies. Thus, I suggest, along with other researchers, that if teachers are to navigate the personal and professional challenges and demands that arise from culturally and religiously diverse classroom settings, it is also necessary to attend to their personal experiences of "what it feels like to be a teacher in today's schools, where many things are changing rapidly, and how teachers cope with these changes" (Beijaard, Meijer, and Verloop 2004, 109).

In this chapter, I explore the intersectionality of religious identities and higher music education through such a personal account, focusing on the role of religion in the professional identification processes of an Israeli music teacher educator working with ultra-Orthodox Jewish female teacher students in Israel. I examine more closely the identity work of one music teacher educator and the ways that religion, as belonging to the more personal aspects of identity, can play a part in the professional identification process and in the interplay between the teacher and her students in a religiously oriented teaching context. Here, *intersectionality* is understood as a crossing of different identities and perspectives that creates a potential space for new understandings and growth within music teacher education (Abril 2014). In the ultra-Orthodox Jewish educational context, religious values and norms define the starting points for what is taught and how and what is considered appropriate or inappropriate teaching content. The situation can require a considerable amount of work and self-reflection from a music teacher educator who is not ultra-Orthodox, in negotiating and reshaping her own ideals of what the content and purpose of music teacher education should be. There are two questions that guide my analysis and interpretation in this chapter: How does the music teacher educator describe her own position in the music education class in terms of her professional and religious identity? And how does she experience her relationship with students from this perspective? The data consist of two semistructured interviews carried out in 2014 and 2015, analyzed using the methodology of theoretical reading analysis (Kvale and Brinkman 2009). Following this method, I constructed an analytical lens through which to view the data using Zygmunt Bauman's (2000; 2004) notion of *identification*, as discussed in his theory of Liquid Modernity, and Akkerman and Bakker's (2011) theorization of *boundary crossing* (see also Suchman 1993). Looking at the data through these concepts, I aim to understand more thoroughly how the teacher is seeing herself as a professional and a person in relation to her students, how she identifies the boundaries between herself and the students, and what kind of shared space their interaction creates.

My own position as a researcher in the context of this study is that of a music teacher and educator. I am also a cultural outsider, in that I have no prior relationship with the community that I am investigating. As in any research, I am aware that my own preconceptions and assumptions on the topic and context might interfere with my interpretation of the research data. Thus, I am conscious of the requirement for reflexivity throughout the research process.

Meeting "Rina" and Her Views on the Ultra-Orthodox Community

Rina[1] is an Orthodox Jewish music teacher educator who is teaching musicology and music education subjects in a special music teacher program for Jewish ultra-Orthodox female students in Israel. Rina tells me that she was brought up within a national religious Judaism that has "close affinity" to ultra-Orthodox Judaism in, for instance, dress code (especially women's) and in the observant view on the interpretation and application of the laws and ethics of the Torah (e.g., keeping the Sabbath). As she grew up, however, she made a conscious choice to follow "a more liberal kind of Jewish religiousness—much more aligned with secular Judaism than with ultra-Orthodox [Judaism]." I asked her to describe from her point of view the ultra-Orthodox Jews as a community and the stereotypes that the surrounding Israeli society have of them. Rina explained that the ultra-Orthodox community segregates itself from Israeli society in various ways, for instance, by having its own educational system and being exempted from military service. In Rina's experience, one of the reasons for the segregation is that the ultra-Orthodox want to protect their way of life by protecting themselves from the influences of the surrounding society. The ultra-Orthodox ideology consists of respecting and following the religious tradition and studying the holy Jewish scriptures. Rina sees the ultra-Orthodox as a community-oriented group within which the members of the community offer help to each other altruistically. These supportive practices also have a downside, as other members of Israeli society tend to see the ultra-Orthodox Jews as nonconformists and anti-Zionists (they do not recognize the state of Israel), which often results in conflicts between the ultra-Orthodox and other community groups.

Since many ultra-Orthodox men do not participate in the workforce, but are instead supported by the community so that they may pursue religious studies—which is regarded as the highest form of religious participation—Rina sees the role of women as crucial in "holding it all together." The women simultaneously maintain the roles of wife, mother, and primary provider for the family. According to Rina, the ultra-Orthodox women have "a very strong ethos of perfectionism"; they are upholding the high moral standards of the community by following the rules of modesty and dress code. Ultra-Orthodox women's work often takes them outside of their homes or immediate neighborhoods, sometimes even outside their community, and they seek vocational training in order to find gainful employment. In their community, teaching is seen as a traditionally female vocation, and thus many of the ultra-Orthodox women train to be teachers (see Blumen 2002). However, teaching and performing music presents many restrictions for the ultra-Orthodox. For instance, women are not allowed to sing in the presence of men. There are also strict rules on repertoire: listening to any kind of Western church music (or other religious, non-Jewish music) is forbidden. Vocal music (both religious and secular) is seen as suspicious because of the lyrics: if the text of the song has immodest content (e.g., love, desire, lust), it cannot be listened to or performed. In addition, the repertoire of Western popular music can also be restricted because of the immodesty of the lyrics and the "impure" atmosphere, influences, and contexts of its musical styles. Despite these musical restrictions, being a music teacher has become an accepted career choice for an increasing number of women within the ultra-Orthodox community.

Conflicts and Contradictions: Fluid Identification and Religious Restrictions

When I ask Rina to describe herself as a music teacher educator in relation to the ultra-Orthodox female students, she tells me that although she sees herself as an observant Orthodox Jew, she also thinks of herself as a feminist and a liberal. These seemingly contradicting qualities that she recognizes in her worldview sometimes create conflict, but at the same time the contradiction is her strength: being able to step in and out of the strictly traditional and conservative outlook of the ultra-Orthodox community gives her a broader perspective and makes her identification process fluid.

According to Bauman (2004), in the present liquid times, an individual possesses not only one monolithic, fixed identity that is unchangeable from birth, but is rather constantly reconstructing oneself through *identification*, a process that happens repeatedly over time. Bauman's notions of liquid identity and identification refer to the crossing of different identity markers such as gender, age, class, nationality, ethnicity, and religion across time and place. This intersectionality of different identity markers creates a constant flow of identities; the individual's adherence to particular identity markers at a particular time also depends on the prevailing circumstances and interaction with others. Such a fluid identification can be recognized in Rina's account of how she sees herself as a teacher educator in relation to the ultra-Orthodox students. She also describes herself as a person who likes to challenge traditions, who is asking questions instead of providing answers, and who is able to admit that she is not always right as a teacher. These statements challenge the authoritarian status of a teacher often assumed by the ultra-Orthodox community. Here, Rina compares her own religious and moral outlook with the ultra-Orthodox doctrine:

> I'm very postmodern in my Judaism, which means that I allow much of my religion to go through myself as authority and [I am] less dependent on structured society, authority. I—don't have to ask a rabbi [about] everything that I do. I have my own kind of criteria and my own independent dialogue with God. Now these women who are in their society, where it's about social roles, and women are not supposed to, [to] a certain extent, have a direct dialogue with God—it's supposed to go through their husbands—I can be a threat to that kind of society. Their values are more black and white—so, even simple things, like pedagogy. My pedagogy is postmodern. I do not come with answers. They've never experienced that before. You know, the teacher has the answers.

The strict religious rules and norms of the ultra-Orthodox community influence its members' everyday actions and interactions. Rina feels that she has to restrict aspects of or even change her identity in various ways in order to be able to teach the class. Her appearance and her way of speaking are the visible and audible ways of signaling assimilation: when entering the campus, she has to obey the modesty rules of ultra-Orthodox women by wearing a long skirt, a shirt that covers her arms and neckline, and a head covering. She tells me that this makes her very uncomfortable, and she does it very reluctantly. Despite the discomfort that the restrictions make her feel, she does not want to give up teaching in the ultra-Orthodox program. When I ask her why, she tells me that her motivation springs from the feelings of satisfaction and gratification:

> First of all, it's a lot of satisfaction—because I believe that I'm contributing something that they're not getting from anywhere else. That's from the feedback that I get from students—my musicianship is very much listening-based and I see myself very much as a kind of amplifier. That's the metaphor I use for me—and I think one of

the things I do best is getting everything ready for people who may be more talented than me to go on stage. That's the main focus of my musicianship. So, being able to do this—with various populations—it's gratifying to me.

Rina's amplifier metaphor captures her way of seeing her educatorship as based more on being a facilitator or provider than a musician per se and explains how this identification gives her continuous pleasure and motivation in her work. Taking a certain position and making a statement, "This is who I am as a teacher," helps Rina to identify the strengths of her personality and position herself in relation to her students and the official educational framework of the program. In their literature review of research conducted on teachers' professional identities, Beijaard et al. (2004) argue that teachers construct their professional identities from different aspects, which can either be central or more peripheral to their sense of self. These sub-identities relate to the contexts and relationships that the teachers face, but it is most essential that the sub-identities do not conflict, because "the more central a sub-identity is, the more costly it is to change or lose that identity" (122). Balancing between her sub-identities and the demands of the program, Rina is in the middle of an ongoing identification process during which she tries to answer questions like "Who am I at this moment?" and "Who do I want to become?"—making the process fluid and constantly in flux. The fluid process of intersecting sub-identities, or, as Bauman (2000, 83) puts it, "the intrinsic volatility and unfixity of all or most identities," creates a constant struggle within a person, whose desires for the future are based on the fleeting impressions of the present. As important as it is to concentrate on the teacher's identification processes in order to obtain more information on what happens educationally in a religiously oriented and culturally diverse classroom, it is also necessary to take a closer look at the interaction between the students and the teacher, particularly where and in what ways this connection can be established.

Being a Boundary Worker

In the course of six years as a teacher in the program, Rina has learned sensitivity in recognizing the lines that cannot be crossed in terms of discussed topics, acceptable musical repertoire, and her own self-expression and behavior. She is able to move beyond the boundaries that the ultra-Orthodox doctrine sets up, partly because she herself has grown up in a similar religious context and thus has a deeper understanding of the cultural values that are immanent in the community. She is respectful of the boundaries but she personally feels that her task as a music teacher educator is to challenge the students to think differently, and even critically. In their literature review of boundary crossing in the field of educational learning theory, Akkerman and Bakker (2011) describe this as motion that takes place between two activity systems—in this case the cultural and religious backgrounds, values, and beliefs of the teacher and the students—that have potentially similar interests but that belong to different cultures (139). Rina and the ultra-Orthodox female students share an interest in teaching and learning music and music education, but they differ in their cultural and religious emphases and orientations.

According to Akkerman and Bakker, "[T]he boundary in the middle of two activity systems thus represents the cultural difference and the potential difficulty of action and interaction across these systems but also represents the potential value of establishing communication and collaboration" (2011, 139). Rina herself identifies the potential difficulty as a gray area or a borderline where she can be playful and experimental; at the same time she has to be very careful in recognizing the limits and in knowing where the red line is. She has to sense when she cannot go further without crossing the line and in that way visibly rebel against or contest the prevailing societal order. When I ask her whether she always knows where the lines should be drawn, she admits that it is not always easy to identify them. She says that she has an "inner commitment" to respect the limits of ultra-Orthodoxy, in part because of her own religious background, which is very close to ultra-Orthodox Judaism. Therefore, she also says she knows the cultural language of the ultra-Orthodox and has a more nuanced understanding of the ways of the community. She describes entering the gray area in her teaching as "playing with fire" and adds that she sometimes stumbles. For instance, one time in class she accidentally started playing a CD with a vocal version of Schubert's Ave Maria instead of an instrumental version. After noticing the mix-up, she did not stop the CD. After the class, one student approached her and told her that listening to that vocal piece crossed the line for her and she said that she hoped Rina would not do it again. According to Rina, this crossing the line was caused by the lyrics in the vocal version, revealing that the piece was church music. Had she played the piece without the lyrics, it might have been easier for the student to ignore the immodest connotations of the piece. This story shows the ultra-Orthodoxy's ambiguous attitude toward its musical restrictions and how contextual (and also personal) implementing them can be.

The preceding examples show the need to keep in mind that when we talk about religious identities (of the students and of the teacher) in a religiously governed context, a variance within the group will always play itself out in classroom situations. Although the degree of strict adherence to religious rules can vary among the ultra-Orthodox students, there is an authoritative frame, a complex matrix of religious and cultural influences and demands, within which both the teacher and the students have to navigate. According to Rina's own descriptions of her teaching, her mechanisms for coping with the authoritative frame include good negotiation skills, using humor as a tool for creating a more relaxed and trustworthy atmosphere, and being open to new situations that may arise. In class, she navigates between what she feels is important to her as a music educator—for example, introducing popular music to the students—and what she recognizes as nonnegotiable on the religious authority's side: the repertoire consists mostly of popular instrumental music pieces, and when she wants to introduce some important pop songs to the class, she makes sure to choose songs with lyrics that do not contain immodest content. Rina also finds peer-support from her ultra-Orthodox teacher colleagues very important in her ability to deal with the borderline issues that come up in class. She discusses her plans regularly with her superiors, with whom she feels close and whom she trusts and respects. Rina uses peer-support and guidance as a mirror that reflects how far she can go without damaging the trust that she feels the heads of the program and her ultra-Orthodox colleagues and students have granted her.

According to Rina, the ultra-Orthodox women who graduate from the program and who have trained to be musicians are not usually able to continue their careers professionally because of the community's rules: women usually get married young and start families soon after, which means having as many children as is physically possible. Rina says that although some of her secular teacher colleagues might see this attrition as frustrating, she does not consider it to be a failure: "That's the life that they have chosen, or the life they were born into. I think, anybody who invests as much time as they want in developing musicianship has a gift, for life, no matter what life they choose. So as much as I try to challenge them and open them and play with the boundaries, it's very important to me not to be the kind of person saying, 'I have a better life than you. Come, live my life.'"

In the light of her accounts and her own description of herself as a cultural insider-outsider, Rina can be described as a boundary worker, a person whom Akkerman and Bakker describe as someone who "not only act[s] as bridge between worlds but also simultaneously represent[s] the very division of related worlds" (2011, 140). This kind of positioning at the boundary calls for self-confidence and a willingness to engage in dialogue, both traits that Rina herself thinks she possesses. It can be argued that Rina's representation of herself and the flexibility and negotiation skills that she claims to have are manifestations of identity work at the boundary constructed from intersecting identities that are constantly flowing. Thus, these intersecting identities can be seen as a source of boundary-crossing competence (Walker and Nocon 2007) or intercultural competence (e.g., Deardorff 2006), a set of skills and abilities that Rina needs when working at the boundary.

Creating a Third Space at the Boundary

In accordance with ultra-Orthodox mandates for segregation between the sexes, Rina's classroom is reserved for women. She describes it as a "beautiful space—where so many things can happen—so that's the space that I try to hold onto." In the process of boundary crossing, the "space" can be perceived as a kind of *third space* (Bhabha 1994; in education, e.g. Gutiérrez 2008; Hulme, Cracknell, and Owens 2009; Klein et al. 2013; Otsuji and Kinoshita Thompson 2009; Stevenson and Deasy 2005), which is created between the two existing activity systems as they interact, thus revealing the ambiguous nature of boundaries: the boundary both divides and connects sides. The third space in between can also, however, be seen as a liminal zone, a space into which people at the boundary can step and where all the existing practices and conceptions from both sides can be left behind in order to come up with new understandings and ways of interacting.

According to Akkerman and Bakker (2011), this stepping into the in-between space creates "a need for dialogue, in which meanings have to be negotiated and from which something new may emerge" (141).

Rina explains this third space and what it means to step into it with a powerful story about a class she had to teach after a massacre near the ultra-Orthodox school where the program operates. At first, she did not know how to face the situation and the students, but then she decided to bring in a familiar song, and they all started singing it together: "[F]or that moment—it's like—we're all in this together and we have a common language. And we can just be human together." For Rina, that was one very powerful way of breaking the boundary between herself and the students in that shared space in spite of cultural and religious differences. Looking at this experience from Bhabha's postcolonial perspective as an articulation of culture's hybridity and "the cutting edge of translation and negotiation," the in-between space can be explored as a place where "we may elude the politics of polarity and emerge as the other of our selves" (1994, 56). Thus, creating a third space at the boundary provides room for the mutual learning of how to negotiate between identities and understandings in a shared space. Ideally, this negotiation can lead to new in-between practice, a boundary practice (Akkerman and Bakker 2011, 144) where the principles of shared meanings and understandings can flourish, creating potential for true intercultural exchange within music education.

Co-constructing New Understandings of Being Human *Together*

Through analyzing the case, I have attempted to show that the notions of identification and the theorization of boundary crossing are applicable when examining an educational context from the perspective of identity formation. In this case, the perspective has been that of a teacher, thus showing only one side of the story. The analysis can still provide us with information and experiential knowledge on the kind of boundary work that is going on in a culturally complex situation. In the light of this research, creating and maintaining a third space in the classroom depends on the teacher's abilities to interpret the situations accordingly and sense in what direction they could be developing. In this particular case, the interaction and willingness to be flexible rest heavily on the shoulders of the teacher, thus placing a great emphasis on her personality: identifying herself as liberal, open, and sensitive, but also respectful and reflective, helps Rina to open up pathways to her students that can lead to experiencing togetherness through processes in which music is very much involved. More research is needed in order to examine the mechanisms of how mutual interaction and power relations inform the process.

Adding to the previous discussion on music teacher education and identity (see Bernard 2005, 2007; Bouij 2007; Dolloff 2007; Roberts 2007; Stephens 2007) and in reflecting on the potential that this research could provide for higher music education and music teacher training, the emphasis is on two partially interrelated aspects of teacherhood: identification and interaction. In a classroom where the teacher and the students represent different cultural and religious backgrounds, it might be valuable to focus not primarily on the differences but rather on the shared experiences of being human together. Through critical reflection and self-examination, which should start already during their music teacher education studies, future music teachers might be able to pinpoint the strengths of their personalities and catch a glimpse of those sub-identities that resonate with them more strongly than others. As a result, the ongoing practice of reflexivity might inform the choices of the pedagogical approaches that the music teachers choose to employ in teaching. Also, since teacher educators are usually modeling the way they want their students to be as teachers, how the music teacher educator acts and behaves are powerful tools in advancing basic humanistic educational values such as human rights and equality in class. While in this chapter I have discussed how religious values can influence music teaching and learning, it is also necessary to bear in mind that although religion might constitute one of the fundamental aspects in shaping one's sense of self, a person's freedom to *not* adhere to a religious belief has to be recognized as a basic right as well and taken into account when designing culturally sensitive music teacher education.

As a result of the intersectionality of different identities and perspectives both in music teacher education and in music classrooms, a mindfully guided interaction can create a space where people can meet each other and become aware of their cultural and religious preconceptions. In this space, they can start to critically co-construct new understandings of themselves, each other, and the world. Allsup and Westerlund (2012) envision the shared spaces as laboratories where the music educator, in addition to being a musical expert, "is guided to exercise the wider educational and ethical considerations of his craft as well as given tools for experimenting, all in the service of his future students' musical and personal growth" (144). Thus, the co-construction of new understandings and the "imaginative encounters between what is and what might be" are inherently ethical in nature (144). The process that begins in the shared space can also be described as the process of cultural hybridity, which "gives rise to something different, something new and unrecognizable, a new area of negotiation of meaning and representation" (Rutherford 1990, 211). Music making is one of the creative tools through which the connection between people can be realized in the process of cultural hybridity. This shared creative and reflective process can in turn advance culturally sensitive, ethically oriented learning wherein cultural differences can be recognized and contested, discussed, and embraced together.

LAURA MIETTINEN is Doctoral Researcher in Music Education at the Sibelius Academy, University of the Arts, in Helsinki, Finland. Her research focuses on music teacher educators' intercultural competences and identity formation, cultural diversity in music education, and educational psychology.

Notes

This publication has been undertaken as part of the Global Visions through Mobilizing Networks project funded by the Academy of Finland (project no. 286162).

1. Rina (pseudonym) has given her consent for publishing the findings of the data in academic articles used for my doctoral dissertation. Furthermore, she and I discussed the fact that, despite every effort from my side to secure her anonymity, there is a possibility of someone identifying her in the text from her teacher position in the program. She does not consider this representation or possible recognition to be problematic.

References

Abril, Carlos R. 2014. "Invoking an Innovative Spirit in Music Teacher Education." In *Promising Practices in 21st Century Music Teacher Education*, edited by Michele Kaschub and Janice Smith, 175–88. Oxford: Oxford University Press.
Akkerman, Sanne F., and Arthur Bakker. 2011. "Boundary Crossing and Boundary Objects." *Review of Educational Research* 81, no. 2: 132–69.
Allsup, Randall E., and Heidi Westerlund. 2012. "Methods and Situational Ethics in Music Education." *Action, Criticism and Theory for Music Education*, 11, no. 1. http://act.maydaygroup.org/articles/AllsupWesterlund11_1.pdf.
Ballantyne, Julie, Jody L. Kerchner, and José L. Aróstegui. 2012. "Developing Music Teacher Identities: An International Multi-site Study." *International Journal of Music Education* 3, no. 3: 211–26.
Bauman, Zygmunt. 2000. *Liquid Modernity*. Cambridge, UK: Polity.
———. 2004. *Identity: Conversations with Benedetto Vecchi*. Cambridge, UK: Polity.
Beijaard, Douwe, Paulien C. Meijer, and Nico Verloop. 2004. "Reconsidering Research on Teachers' Professional Identity." *Teaching and Teacher Education*, 20, no. 2: 107–28.
Bernard, Rhoda. 2005. "Making Music, Making Selves. A Call for Reframing Music Teacher Education." *Action, Criticism and Theory for Music Education* 4, no. 2. http://act.maydaygroup.org/articles/Bernard4_2.pdf.
———. 2007. "Multiple Vantage Points: Author's Reply." *Action, Criticism and Theory for Music Education* 6, no. 2. http://act.maydaygroup.org/articles/Bernard6_2.pdf.
Bhabha, Homi K. 1994. *The Location of Culture*. London: Routledge.
Blumen, Orna. 2002. "Criss-Crossing Boundaries: Ultraorthodox Jewish Women Go to Work." *Gender, Place and Culture* 9, no. 2: 133–51.
Bouij, Christer. 1998. "Swedish Music Teachers in Training and Professional Life." *International Journal of Music Education* 32, no. 1: 24–32.
———. 2007. "A Comment to Rhoda Bernard: Reframing or Oversimplification?" *Action, Criticism and Theory for Music Education* 6, no. 2. http://act.maydaygroup.org/articles/Bouij6_2.pdf.
Deardorff, Darla K. 2006. "Identification and Assessment of Intercultural Competence as a Student Outcome of Internationalization." *Journal of Studies in International Education* 10, no. 3: 241–66.
Dolloff, Lori-Anne. 2007. "'All the Things We Are': Balancing Our Multiple Identities in Music Teaching." *Action, Criticism and Theory for Music Education* 6, no. 2. http://act.maydaygroup.org/articles/Dolloff6_2.pdf.
Elliott, David J. 1995. *Music Matters*. Oxford: Oxford University Press.

Gutiérrez, Kris D. 2008. "Developing a Sociocritical Literacy in the Third Space." *Reading Research Quarterly* 43, no. 2: 148–64.

Hargreaves, David. J., Ross M. Purves, Graham F. Welch, and Nigel A. Marshall. 2007. "Developing Identities and Attitudes in Musicians and Classroom Music Teachers." *British Journal of Educational Psychology* 77, no. 3: 665–82.

Hoffman, Adria R. 2011. "Rethinking Religion in Music Education." *Music Educators Journal* 97, no. 4: 55–59.

Hulme Rob, David Cracknell, and Allan Owens. 2009. "Learning in Third Spaces: Developing Trans-Professional Understanding Through Practitioner Enquiry." *Educational Action Research*, 17, no. 4: 537–50.

Jorgensen, Estelle R. 1997. *In Search of Music Education*. Urbana: University of Illinois Press.

———. 2011. "How Can Music Education Be Religious?" *Philosophy of Music Education Review* 19, no. 2: 155–63.

Klein, Emily J., Monica Taylor, Cynthia Onore, Kathryn Strom, and Linda Abrams. 2013. "Finding a Third Space in Teacher Education: Creating an Urban Teacher Residency." *Teaching Education* 24, no. 1: 27–57.

Kvale, Steinar, and Svend Brinkmann. 2009. *InterViews: Learning the Craft of Qualitative Research Interviewing*. 2nd ed. Thousand Oaks, CA: Sage.

Otsuji, Emi, and Chihiro Kinoshita Thompson. 2009. "Promoting 'Third Space' Identities: A Case Study of the Teaching of Business Japanese." *PORTAL Journal of Multidisciplinary International Studies* 6, no. 1. doi: http://dx.doi.org/10.5130/portal.v6i1.834.

Pellegrino, Kristen. 2009. "Connections between Performer and Teacher Identities in Music Teachers: Setting an Agenda for Research." *Journal of Music Teacher Education* 19, no. 1: 39–55.

———. 2014. "Examining the Intersections of Music Making and Teaching for Four String Teachers." *Journal of Research in Music Education* 62, no. 2: 128–47.

Roberts, Brian A. 2007. "Making Music, Making Selves, Making It Right: A Counterpoint to Rhoda Bernard." *Action, Criticism and Theory for Music Education* 6, no. 2. http://act.maydaygroup.org/articles/Roberts6_2.pdf.

Rutherford, Jonathan. 1990. "The Third Space: An Interview with Homi K. Bhabha." In *Identity: Community, Culture, Difference*, edited by Jonathan Rutherford, 207–21. London: Lawrence and Wishart.

Stephens, Jonathan. 2007. "Different Weather." *Action, Criticism and Theory for Music Education* 6, no. 2. http://act.maydaygroup.org/articles/Stephens6_2.pdf.

Stevenson, Lauren M., and Richard J. Deasy. 2005. *Third Space: When Learning Matters*. Washington, DC: Arts Education Partnership.

Suchman, Lucy. 1993. "Working Relations of Technology Production and Use." *Computer Supported Cooperative Work* 2: 21–39.

Walker, Dana, and Honorine Nocon. 2007. "Boundary-Crossing Competence: Theoretical Considerations and Educational Design." *Mind, Culture, and Activity* 14, no. 3: 178–95.

17 | Religion and Music in an Education for Social Change

Iris M. Yob

Religion, music, and education intersect in many contexts and in a variety of ways, each of which can illuminate them as three fundamental arenas of human thought and their role in human endeavor. The point of intersection I will explore here is when the express purpose is to create social change, that is, to bring about improvement in the human condition through community service or service learning, in what has become known as the Higher Education Community Engagement Movement (see Hartley 2009). College and university partnerships with local communities to address real needs, opportunities, and challenges have been reframed and even more widely envisioned in a recent publication by the United Nations Educational, Scientific and Cultural Organization (UNESCO 2015): *Rethinking Education: Towards a Global Common Good?*. The document proposes a variety of learning resources, activities, and learning assessments beyond the traditional classroom based on the humanistic values of "respect for life and human dignity, equal rights and social justice, cultural and social diversity, and a sense of human solidarity and shared responsibility for our common future" (38).

Because these developments are affecting education throughout the world, instances of UNESCO's recommended approach to teaching and learning warrant our scholarly scrutiny. To that end, I will describe and critically analyze three community service projects in higher education as a primary set of cases for exploring the roles of religion and music in contributing to social change. Here the context is concrete and dynamic: we see the three arenas in action and in their interaction, the contributions they can make, and the conflicts they can engender. The three cases present particular moments when something is said or done that seems especially revelatory. Our task here is to discover what they reveal and whether common threads emerge among them.

Three Cases

The criteria for selection of these three cases—from a wider sample over a variety or contexts, cultures, and countries—were, first, they were situated in Western, traditionally Christian contexts. This criterion allowed for comparison and contrast in effects within the same religious tradition. Second, the cases were sufficiently well developed and the instructors were able to provide rich information for analysis. Third, all the cases showed signs of effectiveness as andragogic approaches or in making a significant and positive difference in the area of need they were addressing, or both. That is, in each case, the faculty leader reported changes in motivation, depth of learning, and career choices of the students involved in the project or could point to the impact of the project on the people in the particular community they served. Much of this effectiveness was presented through anecdotes, although, in two cases, a more rigorous collection and analysis of data about some elements of the project had been undertaken and reported (Brenner 2011; Brenner 2014) or has led to ongoing grounded research studies (Boyce-Tillman, interview, 2013). Both the anecdotal evidence and the more thorough research findings are in line with the current body of research on learning through community service (see Finley 2011). While a set of three examples is barely sufficient to reveal clear patterns of similarity and difference in the role of religion and music in their settings, it is sufficient to suggest some consistencies and departures that are informative for our present purposes.

The first example is from the University of Winchester in the United Kingdom, a university under the governance of the Church of England, where June Boyce-Tillman has taken her students on numerous outreach programs addressing specific needs and concerns in the community, but here we will look at just one example in detail. The university is located close to an estate for low-income housing. Entrepreneurs have purchased properties in the estate, which they rent to students at the university, and by doing so have introduced a different demographic into the community: noisy students, who keep odd hours, party late into the night, and socialize in large groups. Students also tend to take shortcuts across property lines to get to class. As well, the university has outgrown its space, and so student commuters look for parking spaces in the estate. As Boyce-Tillman describes the situation for the locals, "Not only are they invaded by students, but they're invaded by cars" (Boyce-Tillman, interview, 2013). The net result has been a growing resentment between "town" (the local residents) and "gown" (the university community). With the help of funding from the Higher Education Initiative, established to support this kind of interface between the university and the community, Boyce-Tillman and her students developed a singing program in the estate. They guided schoolchildren in interviewing local leaders to discover the music they had enjoyed singing and put together an intergenerational concert. Working with the community around singing, she and her students have been able to begin to break down the town-gown divide.

In the second example, the most developed and long-standing activity of the three, Brenda Brenner of Indiana University in the United States addresses needs in an impoverished school that was deemed to be failing for not showing improvement in test scores on basic skills such as reading. The school serves the needs of often itinerant, underemployed, or unemployed immigrant and distressed families and provides more free school lunches and supplemental meals for the children than any other school in the county. Many of the parents are illiterate, or did not complete high school, and are suspicious if not hostile toward school and schooling in general. Within the district served by the school are the homeless shelter, the shelter for abused women and children, the trailer parks, and low-end housing projects. Some of the parents are incarcerated and the children are with caretakers. The office of school principal has a high turnover rate. With her students, Brenner conducts a violin program in the school, beginning with the first graders. The program began in 2008 and it now serves over 250 children in the earliest two grades, giving violin lessons as part of the curriculum with optional private music lessons beyond to fourth grade for those who request them. Altogether, about 36 undergraduate and graduate music students are now engaged in the program as violin teachers. The children have access to violins and classes are conducted throughout the school year, with a concert presentation in the university's grand music hall at the end of the year. Emphasis is placed on making music through a series of carefully graded steps in ear training and technical accuracy in holding the instrument, fingering, bowing, and so on.

The third example involves both music and dance. Christa Coogan of the University of Music and Performing Arts Munich in Germany, finds support for community outreach in the Bologna Accord, an agreement to develop a set of common understandings and elements to facilitate cross-national equivalencies in higher education, including the principle of "education through responsibility" (*Bildung durch Verantwortung*). Among other things, she has connected with children at a local school with learning disabilities. Many of the children are from immigrant families, some of whom had been subject to abuse and torture. Using an Orff Schulwerk approach, Coogan and her students offer a form of music and dance therapy beginning with body percussion, with the girls moving on to Orff instruments and the boys to Djembes and hand drums, leading eventually to improvisation. Meanwhile, these seventh-grade children also attended several concerts during the year from a percussion band, a funk band, and a dress rehearsal of the Bavarian State Ballet. Recently, Coogan, her student assistants, and the children combined forces with a community band, the Express Brass Band, where the children tried out various instruments, one even to the extent of playing the tuba for their performance. Coogan calls the culminating event "a lecture/demonstration/showing/performance" (Coogan, interview, 2013).

What do these instances reveal about the nature of religion and music in education for social change?

Religion

The involvement of religion in education is inevitable, since religion is an inescapable part of the cultural, social, and political environment, but its role can be ambiguous and sometimes subtle. In these three cases, we see three different attitudes to and relationships with Christianity that can highlight both the positive contributions to an education for social change and the challenges it can bring. In Boyce-Tillman's university, the Anglican religion is foundational but gradually secularizing; in Brenner's case, the university is avowedly nonreligious, in that it endeavors to maintain "the wall of separation between church and state," an expression used in the United States to describe the intention of the first amendment to the constitution; and in Coogan's institution, religion is simply ignored. Despite these differences, some patterns of similarity in religion's effect are also evident.

Religious duty is specifically spelled out in the Gospels, in which it is reported that Jesus said that after loving God, the next great commandment is that "You shall love your neighbor as yourself" (Mt 22:39; Mk 12:31, 33; Lk 10:27 (NRSV), summarizing in a few words what had been written in Jewish law and teaching and what is now foundational in Christian teaching as well. In these words, we find evidence of what may be the common principle running throughout these three cases: an equalizing, democratizing principle that regards and treats others with the same regard and care that we would reserve for ourselves.

One of the positive contributions of Christian religious influences observed in these cases is a motivation to serve others. Boyce-Tillman, who is also an Anglican priest, draws directly on her faith not only in her choosing to be involved in outreach efforts but also in her commitment to sustain those efforts through long hours of hard work. Because of her belief in the crucifixion and resurrection, she explained that although injustice is rife, "the Christian narrative is about the worst thing that human beings can do is always redeemable.... To see the dark things of life, if that's how you want to see them, as also a source of vitality and hope." To which she added, "I'm hopeful because I believe that there is a resurrection principle, there is a redeeming principle at the very heart of the matter" (Boyce-Tillman, interview, 2013).

Although Christianity might provide a foundational motivation for serving others, the persistence of the ethical framework does not always correspond with an equally persistent observance of other aspects of religious thought and behavior. Coogan, for instance, at first described her outreach efforts as stemming from a sense of "religious duty," although later she reminisced that for her it is not a matter of "wearing your religion on your sleeve" but a way of living, setting an example, being "open to all kinds of moral and spiritual quests," Coogan specifically questioned her students about this and none of them believed that religion had any influence on their decision to work with these disadvantaged children (Coogan, personal communication, 2014). Brenner endorsed the fundamental value of social justice that her faith advocates and that she said "is a big part of what I believe in"; but she also admitted that, "I am not a religious person." It is "not my belief in God or another spirit or anything like that that is driving what I do." In essence, the ethical framework of her faith propels her, as it does Coogan, into community service even after she no longer subscribes to most of the other teachings and practices of her faith (Brenner, interview, 2014).

Boyce-Tillman recognized this trend in Christianity. She said, in effect, that the Anglican tradition is manifest in two ways: its traditional practices of Christian worship and its ethical outreach on social justice issues, its role in abolishing slavery in the past being a significant example. An interesting development, in her avowedly religiously affiliated university, is a drift from the religious to the more social domain. To illustrate, Boyce-Tillman added that in the university in the 1960s, Anglicanism was manifested in requirements for students to attend chapel every day. Students who had not attended daily prayer had to appear before the principal to explain their absence. Now its Anglicanism is manifested in its updated ethical code expressed in six values: respect for individuals, diversity, intellectual freedom, spirituality, creativity, and community outreach, all of which reflect more focus on social justice than religious tradition (Boyce-Tillman, interview, 2013).

The fact that the religious domain is fading for some, perhaps many, is identified by the school of thought known as post-Christianity, which recognizes that Christianity is not as dominant as it once was even in previously identified Christian cultures. The change may be seen as an after effect of the Enlightenment, which put greater trust in empirical evidence than in the magical and mystical and introduced alternative accounts of origins and destiny. Also, the encounter with different religions and worldviews in a globalized world has introduced new questions, even doubts, about former beliefs, and an array of options for making meaning.

One question that emerges from these three accounts is how well the ethical code will flourish if it becomes totally cut off from its theological foundation. Up to now, however, the religious duty of caring for one's neighbor has not diminished and, in fact, flourishes in Christian countries around the world, even where Christian beliefs and commitments to church attendance are waning (see Walden University 2013). The paradox is illustrated by the "death of God" movement (Altizer 2002; Dennett and LaScola 2013; Vahanian 1961; Van Buren 1966) occurring simultaneously with the "social gospel" movement (Evans 2001; Malina 2001; White and Hopkins 1976), which pursues the social justice implications of Christian teachings, and "feminist theology" (see Chopp and Davaney 1997; Clifford 2001; Loades 1990), which addresses injustices against women as it reinterprets and reforms theology and church practice.

Meanwhile, although the religious basis of ethical behavior, with its prescriptions, guidelines, and justifications about how one should live might be weakening, it is at times being replaced by spiritual awareness, which tends to be more subjective, individualized, and personal. Brenner's (interview, 2014) understanding is one kind of expression of this spirituality. In her mind, spirituality is broadened beyond religious parameters to include the realm of music, and although her spirituality is based on the music, so too in part is her motivation to serve the needy children in the neighborhood. She explained in an interview, "a lot of my spirituality comes from music. I feel spiritually uplifted by music, by making music. . . . I really want the children to have that experience" Working with the young violinists she described as "an entirely spiritual activity . . . it is so incredible to get these kids all playing together" (Brenner, interview, 2014). Again we see the erosion of traditional religion, and here it is replaced by something else, music, as a source of spiritual experience.

Christianity, however, like most human endeavors, can turn on its fundamental principles and become a source of injustice or inequity rather than a power for good. In her state-supported university where any expression of faith can become a matter of concern, Brenner gives a couple of examples that are informative.

She reports how one of her students came to the school carrying a cello case adorned with a religious slogan. Brenner identified him as "hyper-Christian," that is, those that "come from a very far right background, . . . have very staunch beliefs about this, that, or the other." In contrast, she said of herself, "I mean that to me, it kind of turns me off. I don't wear T-shirts about what my faith is or anything like that" (Brenner, interview, 2014).

Classrooms typically present a range of religious affiliations and commitments, presenting a particular challenge at all levels of schooling. Accusations are frequently leveled at schools for teacher bias one way or another, demanding of teachers a continuous dedication to reflection on religious difference and their own preferences in expressions of religious faith. Here was an instance in which teacher and student parted ways. On the teacher's part, she can argue that overt Christian proselytizing is not allowed in the school setting. On the student's part, he could argue that a slogan pasted to his instrument case was hardly proselytizing. Nevertheless, there it was for all to see. Brenner's approach was simple and straightforward. Although explicit sensitizing to religious difference in the public-school setting is addressed in other classes, she decided in her class to address her concern about this religious slogan by immersing everyone in the classroom in music, believing it to be an umbrella under which diversity is possible. More important, she believes music making itself can provide a larger unifying focus that overcomes divisiveness. Without drawing attention to the slogan, she let the music absorb and neutralize any negativity or tension that might have been created. In this way, the student's religious commitment was unchallenged and attention to it was diverted to the music itself (Brenner, interview, 2014).

Brenner employed the same approach even more deliberately in another incident of religion-based tension. She recalled an occasion when she had paired a Palestinian student from the West Bank with an Israeli for the community-service activity. The Palestinian was fearful that she could not work well with her partner. Brenner's response to her was clear: "You are going to have to work next to him. . . . You know, it's about the music. . . . It is not about your religious or political beliefs and you have to be a role model to go in there and work together and come together for the sake of the music" (Brenner, interview, 2014). When religion seemed to be not living up to its own best principle of loving one's neighbor as one loves oneself, she turned to music to support the social justice she was working toward. She could do so because her class was a safe space, and although students' real fears and concerns are not ignored, she believes the purpose of the exercise was to make music and teach music to children, and the aesthetic activity again served as a diversion and counterinfluence.

Brenner has an almost mystical connection with music, seeing it as something almost otherworldly and able to transcend all kinds of religion, religious history, and traditions of intolerance. Carrying her belief with her into the classroom makes music making for her and those who are influenced by her a transformative experience. She told of troubled children in her classes becoming good pupils, estranged college students overcoming their intolerances, and disengaged parents becoming involved in their children's education through making music.

For her, and to some extent for each of the three professors in these cases, music takes the impulse to do good that a religion might prompt, overcomes religion's potential problems, and makes it effective in changing lives.

Music

The question arises, What is it about music-making that, for Brenner at least, makes it even more powerful than religion in overcoming differences between people and transforming lives? Or, more broadly expressed, What is it about music that makes it such a powerful force for social change?

In each of the three cases we are examining, everyone is making music. In Indiana, Brenner, her university students (including historically estranged people), and the children in poverty play violin together, and when renowned violinist Joshua Bell, a graduate of Indiana University, was in town visiting his alma mater, he played with the children too (Brenner, interview, 2014). At Winchester, Boyce-Tillman, her students, and the people from the housing estate—from children through to the elders—joined in the intergenerational singing project (Boyce-Tillman, interview, 2013). In Munich, Coogan, her dance students, the special-needs children, and the community band played music together and the children danced. At the public performance, children from the audience joined those on stage to dance or to beat-box with the microphone (Coogan, interview, 2013).

One exception in our examples is worth noting, and that is when Coogan took her special-needs children to listen to and watch the performances of others. During her project, they attended three events together. Since her group was made up of learning-disabled seventh graders, one can imagine that the funk band would be a big draw, but the group also attended a percussion concert and a ballet rehearsal. A month after their own performance, the group attended another ballet rehearsal, which attracted some other children from the school who had not been part of the project. Coogan reported that "they came to this rehearsal of their own accord and asked if we will offer a project next year so that they can participate" (Coogan, interview, 2013). Although music making has shown itself to be powerful in reaching and changing lives, from this account we should not overlook the power of music listening (and watching) as well.

Performing or attending to music together seems to be a key to making transformative connections among people in all these examples. But, again, what is it about music that has this power to engender hope, overcome hostility, and change lives? One path to uncovering why or how this comes about may be in the mystical or spiritual connection with music suggested most transparently by Brenner but incipient in the reports of the other two music educators.

Several theories about music may help explain the effect. Along these lines, one thinks of Susanne Langer, and subsequently Bennett Reimer in music education, with her delineation of the arts, including music, as presentational symbolism depicting the inner life of feeling (Langer 1942). By participating in music making, one can learn not only new performance skills but also, beyond words, one can be in touch with humankind's dreams and fears and find therein hope, courage, joy, and a bonding with the larger world. Langer's theoretical foundation has recently been picked up by writers in psychoanalysis. Siegfried Zepf (2013), for one, has argued that the feeling of at-oneness with others that singing and playing together encourages is a particularly powerful part of the symbolism of music, irrespective of what music is being engaged. In simple terms, Zepf would suggest that music allows the Palestinian and Israeli to play together, overt religious differences to be annulled, and the blights of poverty, disability, hostility, and alienation to be overcome in one's sense of mutual well-being and connection with others. To "understand" (since this understanding is not essentially a cognitive or literal understanding) a wider array of feeling awareness can lead to coping, managing, and perhaps overcoming the negative. There is no evidence that this is so, but one can hope, and there is no evidence that it is not so, but if it is possible, Zepf suggests, "one must be willing to listen and engage oneself in this music" (343). However, when one thinks of the first and second graders being taught the violin, or the learning-disabled children in the music and dance project, or even the children and elderly from the housing estate, the presentational symbolism of music seems to be too esoteric and sophisticated an explanation to be helpful in explaining the power of music for participants who would seem to lack the maturity or ability to engage in music for "understanding."

Flow theory from positive psychology describes how engagement in an activity, especially a creative activity, can be totally absorbing for its own sake as one strives for mastery. This theory may explain how music-making can awaken an intrinsic motivation that overrides other forces in the lives of the participants, possibly propelling them to a different way of being in the world. Praxial theorists pick up on flow theory and point to the first-person involvement in the act of music making (and as we have seen in Coogan's case, the act of music listening as well), where the whole self is engaged. As a self, the individual is actively working with others, constructing understandings of oneself and others and finding personal meaning. This "wordless understanding," as David Elliott (2000) notes, "feeds back to us in the form of positive, powerful, beautiful, moving, meaningful, motivating musical experiences" (87). One would hope that such understanding would bring about change in the music makers' lives, but flow theory focuses particularly on the music-making itself without making too bold a claim about its influence on extramusical experience.

Both theories, then, offer a partial explanation for the power of music as a transformative force. To them we can add another possible source of the power of music for social change. From the intergenerational singing project with the residents of the housing estate, to her many other musical outreach programs, Boyce-Tillman has been determinedly inclusive in music-making. She has deliberately reached across religious faiths, socioeconomic strata, and generations to involve them all in music making toward a greater good. Her ensembles can include everybody, whether community or village choirs, university choirs, children's choirs, folk groups, cantors, imams, church choirs, the disabled, dementia patients, or whoever else might sing or perform in the local area. In reflecting on this inclusiveness, Boyce-Tillman used the expression "the ultimate democratization of music" (Boyce-Tillman, interview, 2013); that is, music-making is democratized by including the voices of all and excluding no one, and although she does take a lead in conducting parts of a program during some of her large productions, individual groups choose which music to perform and when in the program they will perform it.

In the social-change context, this democratization has particular significance. Social change is not just about changing others, but changing us all, since we all are part of a social system and contribute for good or ill to that system. Thought leaders and researchers in social change across many disciplines have proposed that the focus should move from "working *for* others" to "working *with* others" in shared decision making, learning from each other, and bringing about a more lasting collective change (see Maton 2008; Mitchell 2008; Peterson 2009). In a community-service project, in which professors, students, and community members are working together, not only is the music-making democratized but the situation also opens the possibility that all will be affected by the change efforts and so will be more likely to be successful in producing broad and real transformation.

In Boyce-Tillman's intergenerational singing project, the children of the estate interviewed the elders about their favorite music, and with the help of her students she led them in singing together these favorite songs (interview, 2013). In the music and movement classes led by Coogan, there was time and space for improvisation (Boyce-Tillman, interview, 2013). Democratization in music-making and the transforming power of music may seem at first glance to rely on people engaging with their own kind of music. Although that is true in most cases, each of the three cases we are looking at has some interesting exceptions. As a music education community, we have come to recognize that, more often than not, classical music is the privilege and choice of the elite in society, but as Leonard Tan (2014) has argued, that will become increasingly true if we exclude, even for the best of reasons, others from understanding and appreciating it too. Coogan took her learning disabled seventh graders to a funk concert, but she also took them to the Bavarian State Ballet rehearsal, and it was a later ballet visit that attracted other children to her project. Brenner's first and second graders who study violin with her are learning to play a classical instrument and tune their ears to classical music—definitely not the music of their homes or neighborhood. The transformative power of classical music making with these children in poverty is as real as that of the popular music making of the children Coogan works with. From these cases, it is possible only to speculate about the reasons, but having met and talked with the instructors in all cases, I wonder whether the power of these music-making experiences lies not so much in the kinds of music chosen for performance but in the inclusiveness of making or taking music together, during which everyone has a part and a contribution, and all are engaged and valued.

Just as religion can turn on its own best principles of social justice, so too can music. Apart from exclusionary practices in the choice of repertoire, music-making can also institutionalize its own hierarchies of oppression with authoritarian conducting and management practices (Allsup and Benedict 2008), where performers have no rights and no say in what, when, and how to perform or by employing sexist or racist practices in choosing individuals for particular roles or whose music is performed (Gould 1994, 2005; Green 1994; Koza 1994). Coogan and Boyce-Tillman work very hard on preparing for and executing their projects, but they facilitate rather than dictate the performances by allowing their participants choice and personal preferences. One of Coogan's students encountered a tuba for the first time when the group worked with a local band and embraced the new instrument to the extent that he asked for and was granted the opportunity to play a few notes in the public performance (Coogan, interview, 2013). Boyce-Tillman researched her participant's favorites and focused her performances on their music and personal enjoyment (Boyce-Tillman, interview, 2013).

Again, there is a significant exception. In teaching violin, Brenner adopts a very traditional and conservative approach. The children must hold the instrument in the proper way, bow and finger correctly, stand with the correct posture, and tune their ears to new and unfamiliar sounds. No exceptions and no personal preferences are invited in these matters, which comes as no surprise. These children are willful, chaotic, unruly. The university students who come to teach them are shocked into asking, "What is it with these kids?!" In this case, Brenner is responding to a real need these children have: predictable, consistent discipline. She insists and the music-making insists, and the children respond and prosper. One of her stars was a young first grader who had already built a personal file an inch thick recording his behavioral problems before he settled into his music and consequently the school environment. He was gaining the attitudes and self-discipline skills needed in a democratic society. Upholding democratic practices requires both vigilance and adaptability when social change is the intent (Brenner, interview, 2014).

Education for Social Change

Reflection on the three cases does not yield a clear-cut definition of "social change," or perhaps even a sense of what in particular one looks for when the change has actually been accomplished. Although the participants in these cases did not define social change, two themes emerged in their descriptions that throw some light on what they consider social change to be. One theme addresses human need systemically; the other individually. The first theme concerned the issue of social justice. The three participants each responded to what was clearly an inequity or an apparent lack of fairness that they wanted to address—whether for the poor and immigrant children in the affluent United States, the special-needs children in Germany, or the neighboring housing estate taken advantage of by the university community in England. With their student teams, they endeavored to give others the best they could in a musical experience to equalize opportunity and redress the injustice.

A second theme was empowerment. Putting music within reach of the poor, disadvantaged, different, or disenfranchised built their sense of self-worth and self-efficacy. Music gave them a scaffolding for success and for building confidence. They were proud of their accomplishments, gained through listening, playing an instrument, improvisation, movement to music, drumming, or singing—pride that these professors believed could spill over into other aspects of their lives. When the advantaged and the disadvantaged, the rich and poor make music together, it "challenges the hierarchical, nondemocratic structures which bedevil our society," Boyce-Tillman (interview, 2013) declared, and by "reversing the disempowerment system, that would be construed as social change."

Social-change activity can work on either front: social justice (creating equity and fairness) or empowerment (building self-efficacy, self-esteem, and personal value), and maybe both simultaneously. Notably, both equity and self-efficacy are linchpins in democracy. An implication one might draw is that if social justice works on outward conditions by providing real opportunities for the disadvantaged and empowerment works on inward conditions by improving an inner sense of self-worth, then maybe there is a distinct need to do both to maximize the impact of social-change efforts. From the accounts we have reviewed here, music education outreach activity is able to accommodate both for collective music making and can be both an equalizer for the group and an inner energizer for the individual. That is, it can be broadly inclusive of everybody while at the same time giving each individual an opportunity to stand up and be heard.

Conclusion

Although religion, music, and an education for social change have been examined here as separate fields of endeavor, in the lived experience they merge and mutually affect and implicate each other. One can readily suppose that effective efforts for social change through community engagement can be enhanced when religion, music, and education work together to uphold the fundamental element of democratization. Treating the other as one would wish to be treated, recognizing equal value and worth in all people regardless of their religious affiliation or expressions of faith, being inclusive when providing access to music and music making, and supporting self-efficacy and equity in the communities they serve can all be means to promote the common good and bring about positive social change. Music education faculty and students can be particularly effective in doing so.

IRIS M. YOB is Professor Emerita of Education at Walden University. Her research interests are in the philosophy of education, particularly the philosophical aspects of religious and spiritual education, education in the arts and music, and education for social change and the common good.

References

Allsup, Randall Everett, and Cathy Benedict. 2008. "The Problems of Band: An Inquiry into the Future of Instrumental Music Education." *Philosophy of Music Education Review* 16, no. 2 (Fall): 156–73.

Altizer, Thomas J. J. 2002. *New Gospel of Christian Atheism*. Aurora, CO: Davies Group.

Brenner, Brenda. 2011. "Finding Our Shared Humanity: Cross-Cultural Connections in Music." Paper presented at the Seventh International Conference for Research in Music Education, Exeter, UK, April 12–16.

———. 2014. "The Fairview Violin Project: A Model for Culturally Relevant Music Instruction." Paper presented at Conference of the European Association for Music in School, University of Nicosia, Nicosia, Cyprus. May 21–24

Chopp, Rebecca S., and Sheila Greeve Davaney. 1997. *Horizons in Feminist Theology: Identity, Traditions, and Norms*. Minneapolis: Augsburg Fortress.

Clifford, Anne M. 2001. *Introducing Feminist Theology*. Maryknoll, NY: Orbis.

Dennett, Daniel C., and Linda LaScola. 2013. *Caught in the Pulpit: Leaving Belief Behind*. Durham, NC: Pitchstone Publishing.

Elliott, David J. 2000. "Music and Affect: The Praxial View." *Philosophy of Music Education Review* 8, no. 2 (Fall): 87.

Evans, Christopher H., ed. 2001. *The Social Gospel Today*. Louisville, KY: Westminster John Knox.

Finley, Ashley. 2011. *Civic Learning and Democratic Engagements: A Review of the Literature on Civic Engagement in Post-secondary Education*. Washington, DC: American Association of Colleges and Universities.

Gould, Elizabeth. 1994. "Getting the Whole Picture: The View from Here." *Philosophy of Music Education Review* 2, no. 2 (Fall): 92–98.

———. 2005. "Nomadic Turns: Epistemology, Experience, and University Women Band Directors." *Philosophy of Music Education Review*, 13, no. 2 (Fall): 147–64.

Green, Lucy. 1994. "Gender, Musical Meaning, and Education." *Philosophy of Music Education Review* 2, no. 2 (Fall): 99–105.

Hartley, Matthew. 2009. "Reclaiming the Democratic Purposes of American Higher Education: Tracing the Trajectory of the Civic Engagement Movement." *Learning and Teaching* 2, no. 3 (Winter): 11–30.

Koza, Julian. 1994. "Aesthetic Music Education Revisited: Discourses of Exclusion and Oppression." *Philosophy of Music Education Review* 2, no. 2 (Fall): 75–91.

Langer, Susanne K. 1942. *Philosophy in a New Key: A Study in the Symbolism of Reason, Rite, and Art*. Cambridge, MA: Harvard University Press.

Loades, Ann, ed. 1990. *Feminist Theology: A Reader*. London: SPCK.

Malina, Bruce J. 2001. *The Social Gospel of Jesus: The Kingdom of God in Mediterranean Perspective*. Minneapolis: Augsburg Fortress.

Maton, Kenneth I. 2008. "Empowering Community Settings: Agents of Individual Development, Community Betterment, and Positive Social Change." *American Journal of Community Psychology* 41, nos. 1–2 (March): 4–21.

Mitchell, Tania D. 2008. "Traditional vs. Critical Service-Learning: Engaging the Literature to Differentiate Two Models." *Michigan Journal of Community Service-Learning* (Spring): 50–65.

Peterson, Tessa Hicks. 2009. "Engaged Scholarship: Reflection and Research on the Pedagogy of Social Change." *Teaching in Higher Education* 14, no. 5: 541–52.

Tan, Leonard. 2014. "Towards a Transcultural Theory of Democracy for Instrumental Education." *Philosophy of Music Education Review* 22, no. 1 (Spring): 61–77.

UNESCO. 2015. *Re-thinking Education: Towards a Global Common Good?* Paris: United Nations Educational, Scientific and Cultural Organization.

Vahanian, Gabriel. 1961. *The Death of God: The Culture of Our Post-Christian Era*. New York: George Braziller.

Van Buren, Paul M. 1966. *The Secular Meaning of the Gospel*. New York: Macmillan.

Walden University. 2013. *Social Change Impact Report*. http://www.probonoaustralia.com.au/news/2013/12/social-change-impact-report#.

White, Ronald C., and C. Howard Hopkins. 1976. *The Social Gospel: Religion and Reform in Changing America*. Philadelphia: Temple University Press.

Zepf, Siegfried. 2013. "What Are We When We Listen to Music." *Canadian Journal of Psychoanalysis* 21, no. 2: 326–50.

18 | Dancing on the Limits: An Interreligious Dialogue

Belal Badarne and Amira Ehrlich

Contemporary Israeli society is characterized by sociopolitical tensions and norms of socioreligious segregation. In education, the tension can be seen through mandates to segregate populations according to socioreligious affiliation, mirroring the broader geopolitical profiles of many Israeli neighborhoods, towns, cities, and entire regions. Almost three decades ago, Semyonov and Tyree (1981) noted that, in Israel, "Persons are not distributed to communities randomly but in part on the basis of their religious and ethnic background" (654), testifying that most specifically, "Segregation between Arabs and Jews is overwhelming" (654)—observations that remain uncomfortably relevant today. Carter (2007, 82) warns of the consequences of such educational segregation: "Few opportunities exist for meaningful interaction between members of these two major groups. Furthermore, the majority of families—both Jewish and Arab—send their children to segregated schools, a practice that tends to promote rival views and little understanding of the other groups concerns. Ultimately, it can promote violence."

Despite appearances, our experiences suggest that intercultural interactions between Jews and Arabs in Israel *do* take place through daily encounters at supermarkets, gas stations, and other central public locations of interaction. Dialogue between socioreligious groups can be a part of day-to-day life, but it often lacks depth of intention. The local reality resonates with Gay's (2010) description of contemporary US demographics, where "daily interactions with one another are sporadic and superficial" and where "knowledge about cultural diversity is filtered largely through mass media" (143). In Israel, most specifically, dialogue between religious Jews and Muslims is rare, and often explicitly avoided even on the practical level of daily encounters. In challenging the divisive local practices, this chapter presents a rare dialogue between two religiously observant music educators who are searching for new possibilities for mutual understanding and identification through documenting, exploring, and exposing the ways in which we negotiate our own knowledge and our religiously observant communities' knowledge of doctrines in our daily practices of music education.

Framing the Challenge

Israeli public education is structured very much through categories of religious affiliation. Schools are mandated by the government and populations are allocated through socioreligiously segregated institutions. Jewish religious, Jewish ultra-Orthodox, Jewish secular, Muslim, Christian, and Druze all have schools of their own, differing in core curriculums, which leads to separate matriculation examinations, overseen by separate inspectorates and supervisors. Ministry dictates, alongside community norms and expectations, bring an influx of religious considerations to educational curriculums and policies.

When it comes to music, both Muslim and Jewish traditions include ambivalent and sometimes paradoxical attitudes toward musical practice. Historically associated with social permissiveness and licentious behavior, music has been discredited by religious leaders and spokespersons of both religions for generations. Nevertheless, both religions include music as integral to sacred practice. Musical forms of worship in both religions are justified in ancient sacred scripture descriptions of sacred musical events and dictates (Alalbany1996; al-Bitawi 2009; Bedford 2001; Schwartz 2013; Sendrey 1974; Shiloah 1992, 1997).

Music educators working within religious communities cannot avoid tensions that often arise between religious doctrines and musical practice. For example, practice of voice training of Jewish ultra-Orthodox women cannot ignore the basic cultural equation of a women's voice with lewdness (Babylonian Talmud, Brachot 24a). Similarly, any musical activity taking place within the Muslim community cannot deny the basic Islamic decree of music as *harram*—an unholy pursuit. Neo-Hassidic Jewish sectors, on the other hand, rely heavily on mystical traditions in which music is embraced in practices of religious worship and addressed as nothing less than a main gateway to the soul. As religiously observant music teachers working within religious communities, we often find ourselves caught between our commitment to upholding doctrines and our passion for setting professional standards of musicianship. Where religion sets a limit, we try to maximize gray areas without going too far and thus define ourselves as "dancing on the limits."

Setting the Stage for Interreligious Dialogue

The framework of this research effort is one of interreligious interaction. Such collaboration, based on dialogue and sharing, between a Muslim and a Jew in Israel is not a commonly documented occurrence. Full appreciation of our study effort and rationale begins, therefore, in recognition of who we each are and what enabled our collaboration. Having grown up within opposite religious poles of the Israeli social spectrum—Belal in the Muslim city of Arraba and Amira in a Jewish religious neighborhood of Jerusalem—we first met as graduate students in Levinsky College's master of education program in music education. Following our MEd certification, each of us pursued doctoral studies in music education. By the time we had met, each of us had developed an extensive practice of music education within our respective religiously observant communities. Belal works as an elementary school teacher in a Muslim public school and is involved in general education and teacher professional development in his community, as well as in Christian Arab, Druze, and Bedouin communities throughout Israel. Belal also performs regularly with both amateur and professional ensembles of many types and styles, in his community, around Israel, and abroad. Amira worked as a music coordinator and teacher in a Jewish National Religious boys' high school for music for more than a decade. At the time of writing this chapter, we were both employed as music teacher educators at Levinsky College, where we first met: Belal in the Safed program for music teacher certification, geared to Arab populations of the north; and Amira working in the ultra-Orthodox woman's music teacher education program.

As a "site of engagement" (Scollon and Scollon 2004, 8), the Levinsky College campus acts as a safe place, insulated from daily sociogeographical-political tensions. In other words, the college campus is a rare place where a religious Jewish woman and Muslim man can sit down, drink coffee—or share pita bread—and converse. Such a sight may seem impossible or ludicrous in many other locals and contexts in Israel. As a state college, Levinsky must affiliate with a religious definition in alignment with institutional categories mandated by the Ministry of Education. As a result, officially speaking, Levinsky is a Jewish college. Nevertheless, throughout the various college faculties, one encounters both integrated non-Jewish students and segregated programs geared to other or more specific socioreligious sectors. Levinsky's faculty of music education, for example, prides itself in its segregated Jerusalem campus for Jewish ultra-Orthodox women on one end of the cultural spectrum and its Safed campus, predominantly oriented to Arab (Muslim, Christian, and Druze) populations of the north on the other. At the same time, the main campus in Tel Aviv is open to all students of any socioreligious identity who are able to register in mainstream programs where everyone studies together. Our work as music teacher educators involves both segregated socioreligious groups and integrated groups.

Approach and Methods

As a collaborative work, this chapter expresses our commitment to promoting interreligious and intercultural communication within contemporary Israeli society. In doing so, we adopt a cultural framework that positions the participants of a study as social actors acting within social spaces. In this way, Belal and Amira are understood as cultural change agents, working from within their communities to expand cultural and musical norms of their socioreligious sectors. In the interest of enhancing intracultural and intercultural understandings, we follow Rogoff's (2003) notion of culturally informed research as a means of exposing regularities and patterns of change that underlie the everyday lives of ourselves and of others.

The dialogical nature of this study seeks to explore enabling and constraining forces that shape cultures of music education. Data was collected primarily through conversation. Throughout the 2013–14 academic year, we engaged in a series of five in-depth conversations of approximately four hours each. Three such conversations took place on Levinsky College's main campus in Tel Aviv. Two other conversations took place elsewhere, as we each took the time to visit each other's respective socioreligious symbolic location: Amira visited Belal at the Safed campus in February 2014; and although—as a Muslim man—Belal cannot easily access the Jerusalem's woman campus, we did meet for one conversation in a coffeehouse in central Jerusalem in July 2013.

All conversations were recorded and later transcribed. As we shared transcriptions via email, we commented further on each other's data and supplemented public-domain video examples of our respective practices. Correspondence via email, and later also via WhatsApp, provided an opportunity to expand our conversations and generate additional data.

Data analysis was conducted collaboratively, applying Scollon et al.'s (2012) notion of "grammar of context" to the content of our conversations. Doing so involved descriptions and interpretations of: (1) scene, (2) key, (3) participants, (4) message forms, (5) sequence, (6) co-occurrence patterns, and (7) manifestations. As our conversation continued and unfolded, we each offered interpretations of each other's data and kept track of recurring themes that seemed to emanate from *both* of our practices. When we reviewed the data and analyses, we combined and collapsed similar themes into five major categories, through which we will present our findings.

Dancing on the Limits

Music education in Israel has historically been associated with three main motivations: (1) socialization, (2) acculturation, and (3) individualization (Cohen and Laor 1997). In the double commitment that we experience as religious music teachers devoted to religion and to music, we embody all three motivations, albeit they may entail contradictory aspects. Although we hope to contribute to the sectarian identities of our communities, we work to expose students to musical worlds that lie beyond their reach. We respect community norms and religious restrictions, but we take advantage of gray areas, encouraging students to develop a personal style of observance that embraces an openness that may appear to some community members as dangerous or subversive.

The five themes of experience identified through the analysis of our dialogue are (1) sublimation, (2) stretching the limits, (3) educational morals, (4) gender difference, and (5) the prominence of teacher image. Salient illustrations are shared from each theme, presented in turn. The illustrations and anecdotes are written together and often take turns telling about our partner, rather than of ourselves. What follows should not be read as a comparison but rather imagined as a conversation where, as one of person shares a story, a thought, or an incident, his or her interlocutor responds by sharing something from his or her own experience that resonates with what has been shared. As in conversation, what emerges includes and highlights nuances of difference alongside similarities.

Sublimation: "For the Joy of God"

The role of music in both Jewish and Arab doctrine is contentious. Muslim and Jewish traditions include doctrines and restrictions on contexts of musical practice, to some extent a residue of historical associations of music with social permissiveness and licentious behavior. Nevertheless, both religions include music as integral to sacred practice.

Working within religiously observant communities in Israel, we have often faced suspicions of an innate relationship between music and licentious behavior. Both of us have encountered musical moments in which dance evoked by live music reached ecstatic proportions. Belal recalled playing with his wedding ensemble at a devoutly religious event. As the music intensified, men engaged in energetic dance, even climbing up on tables and removing their shirts. Belal remembered feeling embarrassed at the sight—knowing that he and his music were inspiring such behavior. Discussing this scene, a local sheikh told Belal that, "as long as it is for religious joy, it is acceptable."

Recently, one of Belal's wedding ensemble musicians brought him a newly printed religious pamphlet dedicated to outlining the dangers of music. We wonder whether this new publication is a response to an expansion of musical activity or change in style of musical activity in Belal's community. The rise and spread of digital media and the impact of Western popular styles may be functional in eliciting such a response. Perhaps it is only a matter of time and frequency, as pamphlets of this sort have been commonly circulated in many Muslim communities for hundreds of years.

Amira shared a similar experience, where such ecstatic dance was not only permitted and accepted but even encouraged by some. In her work with a religious Jewish adolescent boys school for music, jazz- and rock-inspired arrangements of Jewish Hassidic melodies were quite commonly performed. At one school concert, such a performance brought students from the audience to the stage. On stage and beneath the stage, students danced vigorously, just as adolescent boys would dance at a rock concert. The students saw nothing wrong with this and later admitted that this kind of dancing and music seemed a most natural part of their school music experience, describing it as "for the joy of God." At that particular moment, however, some school staff members felt disturbed by what they later described as "an immodest dance style" and tried to direct students back to their seats.

Amira showed Belal video footage of the incident, pondering, in retrospect, what kind of negotiation that school staff could be engaging in to bridge gaps between encouraging natural musical excitement "for the joy of God" and upholding religious norms of modest behavior. Through mutual analysis of this moment, Amira recognized the enactment of a standard of sublimation: where libido energies and bodily expression are reframed as a passion for God. In this case, teenage energies were being channeled through religious ecstasy but maintained an overt bodily expression not easily accepted by all observers as "religious."

How about This? Stepping beyond the Limits

Belal often mentioned tensions between Islamic bans on music and his own practice. Islamic tradition allows male vocal music and drumming but no other instruments. While working with a religious ensemble that performed in religious Islamic weddings, Belal decided to incorporate a keyboard synthesizer as an extension of a rhythm instrument. As he brought in the synthesizer, Belal demonstrated a chord-based rhythmic pattern and asked the group whether they thought it was acceptable as an extension of "drumming." Gradually, Belal began to decorate the harmonic rhythmic pattern with melodic elaborations, every now and then seeking approval from the other musicians by asking, "How about this?" Before long, the "vocal-drumming" ensemble was playing instrumental countermelody and harmonic accompaniment and no one seemed to mind. By being familiar with the history of what is traditionally called forbidden, Belal—as an active and trusted member of his community—was able to stretch the limits and effect transformation in what had previously been established as acceptable.

Similarly, Amira was able to bend some of the rules of National Religious and ultra-Orthodox musical norms, in which music with English lyrics or popular genres are generally avoided in educational contexts because they are considered immodest in content and context. Amira's acquaintance with the details and motivations behind this religious restriction allowed her to broaden the spectrum of musics that she incorporated into her lessons in both Jewish communities where she worked. Choosing instrumental jazz and rock music and selecting songs with modest lyrics, Amira challenged traditions of simply avoiding popular music as a study subject or ensemble pursuit. In doing so, Amira took care to share her ideas with colleagues whom she considered more strictly religious than herself, sometimes even asking religious authorities like a school rabbi, often playing musical examples and asking, "How about this?"

As a result of Amira's work, the National Religious boys' school for music eventually increased the incorporation of Afro American pop music performed in school-public concerts. Sometimes titles of songs were translated into Hebrew, striving to enhance possible religious connotations. Love songs were often presented as songs of love for God rather than of romantic love, and instrumental arrangements (where lyrics could be omitted) were prioritized over vocal renditions. Tim Rice and Elton John's "Can You Feel the Love Tonight," for example, was translated into Hebrew as "There Is Love in the World" (rather than the secular translation of "There Is Love in the Air")—resonating connotations of Hebrew Nationalist poet H. N. Biyalik and of neo-Hassidic rabbinic writings.

For Educational Purposes—It's OK

When music is employed for educational purposes, many limits, apparently, can easily be stretched. On a pilgrimage journey, Belal was once pleased to find an oud of great quality and an interesting-sounding drum. Without thinking twice, Belal purchased the instruments for his collection. As he reboarded the pilgrimage bus, Belal was confronted by his fellow pilgrims: "Instruments are forbidden in Islam," they cautioned. Belal was quick to explain that he is not merely a musician, but a music educator, and excused the instruments as tools for his educational work. The drum was then allowed on the bus, under the pretense that "for education—it's OK." The oud, however, was sadly left behind, since the core of the instrumental restriction focuses on melodic and harmonic instruments but is more lenient toward percussion.

Amira recalled many similar instances that echoed the contention that "for education—it's OK." In fact, this very statement, uttered by a school rabbi, allowed Amira to take male students to live concerts of classical music, even at the risk of exposing them to a female soloist or women sitting next to men in the audience. Attendance at concerts that included female vocal soloists was subsequently prohibited, limiting the concert programs that the students were allowed to attend. Amira remembered an incident that challenged the rabbi's own lenience, when a female violin soloist performed her concert in a sleeveless evening gown. Students who attended the event complained to their rabbi, and the notion of allowing male students to attend public concerts "for educational purposes" came under closer scrutiny in the following months.

Women, Music, and Empowerment

The role of women in music, on stage and off, is a major issue in many religious discourses on music, the epitome of which echoes in the Jewish Talmud's equation of women's voice to lewdness. Jewish and Muslim norms of women's modesty equate public performance, especially vocal performances by women, to bodily exposure. Although the marginalization or exclusion of women in music in these religiously observant communities may seem to hold firm, we have witnessed and been active in subverting this common expectation in our respective communities. Our understanding of musical practice work to debunk the equation of musical performance to bodily exposure. We work to develop female practices in which a woman can play and sing in public in modest dress and with modest body language.

Belal teaches girls alongside boys in his community's elementary school. In Muslim communities, it is more common for men to pursue music than women. Girls before puberty may engage more easily with music, but there is a gendered community tradition of girls singing and boys playing instruments. Sharing stories of his experience, Belal admitted, "In Muslim society men can afford to do things that women can't." Nevertheless, Belal works to empower the girls, mostly through including them in musical ensembles as vocalists. There has been some resistance to girls practicing and advancing in music for fear of immodesty, but nevertheless Belal shared stories of leading religious figures of his community sending their daughters to him for music lessons. Belal takes pride in the progress of young women singers who started out in his elementary school music classes, even if few of the girls choose to persist in music, professionally or as amateurs. In the professional realm, Belal insisted on incorporating a female vocalist in his ensemble's recent recordings. The singer, a wife and mother of children in the community, requested that only audio and no video footage be made posted online. Adhering to this request enabled Belal to include this female singer in his recordings and enabled her voice to be heard.

Listening to these recordings, Amira became envious of this sensitive agreement that enabled the woman's participation in such a professional recording. The ultra-Orthodox Jewish women whom Amira works with do not perform for male or mixed audiences and limit even their audio recordings to women listeners only. In fact, there was no ethical way for Amira to share the music sung by these female students with Belal. The extremity of sexual segregation in the Jewish ultra-Orthodox musical context results in the formation of a female subculture where female empowerment is enacted solely within female spaces. Amira interpreted her experiences with the ultra-Orthodox women whom she teaches as empowered through such a musical subculture.

As we discussed our respective experiences of female empowerment, religious icons came to mind. Amira told Belal of the biblical character of Miriam, whose drumming, singing, and dancing is depicted in the "Song of the Sea" (Ex 15, 20–21), wondering whether Islamic myth included any such parallel. Belal shared two quotes of Islamic holy books that describe women as drummers:

> Oh Messenger of Allah, I vowed that if Allah returned you safely that I will beat the duff in front of you. The Prophet (peace be upon him) replied: "If you vowed to do it, then do it, if not then don't." So she took the drum and started to beat it. Abu Bakr came to my house while two small Ansari girls were singing beside me the stories of the Ansar concerning the Day of Buath. And they were not singers. Abu Bakr said protestingly, "Musical instruments of Satan in the house of Allah's Apostle!" It happened on the 'Id day and Allah's Apostle said, "O Abu Bakr! There is an 'Id for every nation and this is our 'Id" (Sahih Al-Bukhari Hadith—2.72).

Sharing these religious narratives, we embrace the empowerment of women in music in our communities as grounded on religious precedent and share pride in female graduates of our respective practices.

Good Boy Arraba; Good Girl Jerusalem

As our sharing of key encounters continued, we noticed the prominence of the music teacher image emerging as a most dominant theme. We began to acknowledge a major affordance of our experiences as embodying the dual identities of community insiders committed to a religiously observant life and also our participation in professional communities of music. As religiously observant teachers, we realized we were privileged to have the trust of our communities, even as we worked to challenge the borderlines of religious dictates in pursuit of enacting our own professionalism. Personal knowledge of religious dictates and their histories allowed us to maneuver wisely in bending and stretching religious limits. Musical professionalism and personal musical knowledge inspired us to expand communities' musical experiences, sometimes instigating acts toward cultural change.

In analysis, we agreed that this intricate balance depends much on our ability to maintain a positive religious image in our communities. Paraphrasing the Israeli colloquial idiom describing a man of good morals as a "good boy Jerusalem,"

Belal described his image in his community as a "good boy Arraba." Elaborating on this, Belal described himself as adhering to external Muslim affiliations, publicly participating in prayer, and modeling community standards of moral behavior. Belal testified to many collaborations with community religious figures and interpreted his having as students the children of key religious authorities as proof of their trust in him.

In Amira's case, the function of teacher image is intertwined with a deep sensitivity and openness to adopting community dress codes. Amira shared pictures of herself dressed in ultra-Orthodox attire, according to which she adorns a traditional head covering hiding all her hair and wearing collared and long-sleeved shirts, long skirts, and stockings. Amira described her professional life as demanding several different wardrobes, and she dresses each day to fit the campus she is destined to attend. Her personal daily wardrobe does not include any type of head covering, and she alternates between trousers, skirts, and dresses and includes open sandals in the summer. While acceptable in the nuance of the religious community where she lives, not all these clothes are considered suitable for the educational contexts in which she works. All her employers acknowledge the gap between her daily dress customs and appreciate the sensitivity taken in dressing "correctly" for work. Amira interpreted this arrangement with her employers as indicative of moral trust.

We both confessed that what some of our alumni do musically and culturally, we ourselves must continue to abstain from in order to continue to influence future generations. Belal is proud of graduates who have established international musical careers. In one case, a graduate's musical choices that gained him international recognition angered his hometown of Majdal Shams. Belal recognized that his own openness as a music professional allowed him to expose students to many musical styles and genres that go beyond community acceptance. As a teacher, Belal is committed to a musical openness that later allows graduates to choose for themselves. Although Belal himself takes caution not to anger his community, "dancing on the limits," he realizes that opening students up to broad musical influences can lead them to make their own choices of limits as they become professionals in their own right.

Amira shared in Belal's sentiments for his graduates, having experienced similar results with some of her own alumni. Musically speaking, we found interesting parallels in the integration of eastern and western influences in Jewish and Arab alumni ensembles. As music educators, we acknowledge the personal and cultural authenticity emerging in graduates' musical careers and take pride in the new soundscapes we hope to have introduced to students we have encountered in our community practices.

Small and Simple Acts of Hope

The findings of this study tell a tale of multicultural cross influence in contemporary Israeli society. Music is shown to act as a social practice, as an educational pursuit, and as a religious outlet within traditionally religious communities of

Muslims and Jews alike. As music teachers living within these communities, we sometimes act as participant observers, oscillating between being insiders and being outsiders within our communities. Ultimately, we do not see ourselves—and are not seen by our communities—as actively working to subvert religious standards or doctrines. When successful as teachers, we are able to reinterpret traditional religious dictates, expanding musical presence and practice in our communities. In doing so, we intricately expose gaps between traditional religious dictates, philosophical mindsets of each religion, and contemporary practice.

The effects of our work are evident in the life, career, and artistic choices of our alumni. In this respect, our impact coincides with a zeitgeist of global change and cross-cultural sharing that has been encouraging new and mixed soundscapes and increased musical interest and activity within religious communities in Israel. We believe that the gentle expansion of community limits on music can affect cultural conceptions and practices and can have an effect on the cultural mindsets of segregated communities. Much further research is needed to confirm this belief and to explain how making it real might work.

Within our respective communities, we have noticed that any impact on students expands further when it influences students' parents and families. In this small and focused way, more and more community members become aware of the possible educational authority that musicians and music educators can, and perhaps should, have in the interpretation of music-related doctrines. Our commitment to cooperation with respective religious authorities enforces this possibility, proving to our communities that we are not making doctrinal decisions on our own and that our intensions are not subversive.

We hope our commitment and exemplification of collaboration in interreligious dialogue will act as an example and resonate hope in advancing understanding within and between our communities. It is hard to imagine massive change in current standards of socioreligious segregation in Israeli society. The chance that any of our respective alumni would coincidentally meet up and collaborate musically is close to null. Formal contact between Jewish and Arab music educators is also almost nonexistent in the current structures established by the Israeli Ministry of Education. Nevertheless, we frame our example of collaboration within the context of small and simple acts of hope, the likes of which can be found often in the fine print of our experiences of this reality.

BELAL BADARNE is Lecturer at the College of Sakhnin for Teacher Education and in Kaye College in Be'er Sheva and a music educator and researcher currently responsible for the Arts and Music in Bedouin Society for the Ministry of Education in Israel.

AMIRA EHRLICH is Lecturer and Program Coordinator of Graduate Studies in Music Education at Levinsky College of Education, Tel Aviv, and Academic Program Director of the Mandel Leadership Institute's Program for ultra-Orthodox women in Jerusalem.

References

Alalbany, Muhammad N. 1996. *Tahrim alat Attarab* [Prohibition of musical instruments]. Aljbail, Saudi Arabia: Aldalil Library.
Bedford, Ian. 2001. "The Interdiction of Music in Islam." *Australian Journal of Anthropology* 12, no. 1: 1–15.
Bitawi, Geber K., al- 2009. *Alghinaa Wlmusica Ashaabiya min Manthur Islami* [Song and folk music from Islamic perspective]. Nablus, West Bank: Alnajah University.
Carter, Gene R. 2007. "Learning Together, Living Together." *Educational Leadership* 65, no. 2: 82–84.
Cohen, Veronica, and Lia Laor. 1997. "Struggling with Pluralism in Music Education: The Israeli Experience." *Arts Education Policy Review* 98, no. 3: 10–15.
Gay, Geneva. 2010. "Acting on Beliefs in Teacher Education for Cultural Diversity." *Journal of Teacher Education* 61, nos. 1–2: 143–52.
Rogoff, Barbara. 2003. *The Cultural Nature of Human Development*. New York: Oxford University Press.
Scollon, Ron, and Suzanne W. Scollon. 2004. *Nexus Analysis: Discourse and the Emerging Internet*. London: Routledge.
Scollon, Ron, Suzanne W. Scollon, Suzanne B. K. Scollon, and Rodney H. Jones. 2012. *Intercultural Communication: A Discourse Approach*. 3rd ed. Malden, MA: Wiley-Blackwell.
Schwartz, Dov. 2013. *Kinor Nishmati* [Viol of my soul]. Ramat Gan, Isr.: Bar Ilan University.
Semyonov, Moshe, and Andrea Tyree. 1981. "Community Segregation and the Costs of Ethnic Subordination." *Social Forces* 59, no. 3: 649–66.
Sendrey, Alfred. 1974. *Music in the Social and Religious Life of Antiquity*. Plainsboro, NJ: Associated University Presses.
Shiloah, Amnon. 1992. *Jewish Musical Traditions*. Detroit: Wayne State University Press.
———. 1997. "Music and Religion in Islam." *Acta Musicologica* 69, no. 2: 143–55.

Music, Education, and Religion: An Invitation

Alexis Anja Kallio

As a conclusion to *Music, Education, and Religion: Intersections and Entanglements*, this chapter reflects upon the considerable ground covered within these pages but also considers new paths for the future. Attending to each aspect of the intersections in turn, I first question just what we mean when we write about religion in what has been characterized as a secular, or postsecular, age. As the introduction states, definitions of the religious and the secular are multiple and multifaceted, a rich and diverse tapestry of beliefs, practices, and meanings. Such complexity is also true of other issues and ideas raised in the chapters of this book, which I turn to next in a consideration of culture, considering how it is manifest through understandings of identity and community. As we navigate this world (and others) in relation with others, I finally question the direction in which we are headed, particularly focusing on the ideals of social justice as they are raised in this book. These discussions serve as an invitation to reflect on how far we have come and also to imagine the directions that future scholarship at the intersection of music, education, and religion may take.

Music Education and Religion in a (Post-)Secular Age

In his highly acclaimed work, Charles Taylor (2007) argues that in comparison with contemporary societies such as Islamic countries, India, and Africa, and the history of humankind thus far, the North Atlantic world is distinctly secular, and Western Europe also demonstrates significant shifts "away from God" (2). He describes life in this secular age as characterized by a divide between church and state, relegating understandings of "religion, or its absence [as] largely a private matter" (2). In this age, actions are guided by rationality rather than belief or superstition, and individuals are faced with diverse (non)spiritual beliefs to choose from—of which, belief in God is "frequently not the easiest to embrace" (3). Contrast this decade-old description of an almost wholly secularized milieu with the insights offered in the preceding chapters, where lived experiences of religiosity, spiritual belief, or disbelief are far from straightforward in today's social, musical, and educational contexts. For instance, Percović and Mandić (chap. 6) contextualize their chapter within an Orthodox revival in post-Soviet Serbia. Moro (chap. 5) describes the careful cultivation of religiomusical communities in diaspora. Naqvi (chap. 13) highlights the potency of music in an Iranian context that is highly regulated according to interpretations of religious ideas and ideals. Fletcher and Barrett (chap. 4) illustrate how music in an Australian Catholic school setting can foster a variety of religious beliefs and values. Even in Taylor's supposedly secular United States, "Resurgent fundamentalists and evangelicals are flexing their political muscles, . . . religious conflict and controversiality is sharpening, . . . Church-state tension is increasing and religiopolitical ideologies or variations of civil religion are polarizing" (Robbins and Anthony 2017, 1). As stated in the Introduction, religion is far from dead and buried.

The binary once assumed between religious belief and secularity is drawn into question, as illustrated by the boundary-crossing teacher in Miettinen's chapter (16), who expresses her own religiosity as "a liberal kind of Jewish religiousness . . . aligned with secular Judaism." Väkevä (chap. 7) presents a case in which the religious meanings of a particular piece of music coalesce with cultural memories and traditions, similarly obfuscating the divide between the sacred and secular. The climate in which such a myriad of (non)religious adherences and expressions are made possible has been analyzed by scholars in terms of "desecularization, resacralization, de-Christianization, and the emergence of a post-secular society" (Moberg, Granholm, and Nynäs 2012, 2). The shifting power structures between religious institutions and other public systems warrant attention as new identities, agencies, and communities are made possible, also through music. As Boyce-Tillman explains (chap. 15), a university with a Christian foundation might "fill the *hole in the soul* of a postsecular world" by embracing diversity, and the paradoxes and contradictions of spirituality through musicking. Heuser (chap. 10) employs metaphor in drawing similarities between sacred rituals and those of musical practice, exploring the establishment of a sacred space in secular contexts. Varkøy (chap. 8) implores educators at attend to all layers of musical meaning, including spiritual and existential layers. However, chapters by Westerlund, Kallio, and Partti (chap. 3) and Väkevä (chap. 7) caution that the inclusion of secular or religious musical material as part of teaching and learning does not necessarily result in the inclusion of secular or religious students and may even result in assimilatory processes of indoctrination. Alperson (chap. 2) also reminds us that "religion has been a source of grievous harms," harms that can indeed be inflicted through music, as is also described in Kertz-Welzel's chapter (11). Thus, attending to the "deeper perspectives in music" (Varkøy, chap. 8) may not always result in desirable consequences (see also Thorgersen and von Wachenfeldt, chap. 14). Without offering prescriptive solutions, the conversations that may be read between the chapters of this book establish a foundation from which scholars may further explore the multifaceted roles and functions that religion and spirituality may fulfil in postsecular, liquid modern (Bauman 2000) music education. As Orsi (2005) states, "Religion does not make the world better to live in (although some forms of religious practice might); religion does not necessarily conform to the creedal formulations and doctrinal limits developed by cultured and circumspect theologians, church leaders, or ethicists; religion does not unambiguously orient people toward social justice. . . . Religion is often enough cruel and dangerous, and the same impulses that result in a special kind of compassion also lead to destruction, often among the same people at the same time" (191).

Thus, rather than conceiving of belief and skepticism as polar opposites, or even as either end of a continuum, and acknowledging that (a)religious practices and expressions manifest in any number of positive or negative ways, the intersections between music, education, and religion offer an invitation to explore "a more integrated way of being" (Boyce-Tillman 2014, 11) and the political processes that are embedded within, and produced through, such experiences and identities.

Demarcating Difference

As described by Habermas (2010) in his writings on postsecularism, a growing public consciousness of religion is brought about, in part, by increasing immigration and encounters with religious others. These encounters bring various challenges as to whether they further reinstate the hegemonies of majority knowledge orthodoxies and social realities or encourage us to "reimagine and rearticulate power, change, and knowledge through a multiplicity of epistemologies, ontologies and axiologies" (Sium, Desai, Ritskes 2012, iii). The field of music education in particular is overwhelmingly White, which is not to dismiss or disavow the quality of work that has been and is being done, but serves as a call to reconsider and disrupt the systems that enable the privileges that so many of us in the Academy enjoy. A first step is a recognition of how Others are recognized and defined, and how we define ourselves in relation.

Deliberations over the distinction and recognition of both individual and communal identities have long been the focus of sociological research, and identifying Others is increasingly complex amidst the ebbs and flows of a globalizing world (Giddens 1991). This complexity is aptly described by Estelle Jorgensen in the opening chapter of this book, positioning herself as a "citizen of the world," an identity an increasing number of us assume, living outside our home countries (if indeed "home" as a distinct location still exists) and engaging with diverse cultural artifacts and practices every day, in activities as diverse as what we eat for lunch to what we listen to on our music playlists. The destabilization of identities and cultures by such liquid modern conditions (Bauman 2000) has significant implications for how we can, or should, engage with Others in upholding the ideal of cultural pluralism. Embracing cultural diversity in music and education settings entails not only a recognition of "the kinds of difference, and the forms difference might take" (Moro, chap. 5), but also the navigation of tensions that may arise when "multiple, incongruent and . . . noncomplementary worlds" meet (Westerlund, Kallio, and Partti, chap. 3). Where identity and culture *have* been the focus of sociological attention in terms of ethnicity, nationality, race, social status, and even musical tastes, scholarship has largely neglected identities in relation to religious belief (Flanagan 2016). In reflecting on the connections between music, education, and religion in terms of identity and culture in this volume, I here take the opportunity to critically question just what we are writing about when we refer to cultural identity or culture, and what work remains to be done.

In their update to Kroeber and Kluckhohn's (1952) seminal work, *Culture: A Critical Review of Concepts and Definitions,* Baldwin, Faulkner, and Hecht (2006) look to the etymological roots of culture, through the French *culture,* derived from the Latin verb "*culturare*" (to cultivate). They note a "kinship among the words. *Cultus,* for example (from which we get "cult") refers to religious workshop, which might be seen as a way of bringing up ("cultivating") someone in a religious group" (6). Furthermore, in his 1983 work, *Keywords: A Vocabulary of Culture and Society,* Raymond Williams drew connections between culture, the arts, and education through referring to the genealogy of *Civilization* in the German *Kultur* (agricultural cultivation). Thus, culture for him was used in three categories, as "(i) the independent and abstract noun which describes a general process of intellectual, spiritual and aesthetic development, . . . (ii) the independent noun, whether used generally or specifically, which indicates a particular way of life, whether of a people, a period, a group, or humanity in general, . . . (iii) the independent and abstract noun which describes the works and practices of intellectual and especially artistic activity" (90).

In this way, culture can be seen to play a key role in forming our understandings of musical, educational, and religious practices. Yet, representations of culture as part of teaching and learning music are only the starting point of understanding, if such perfect clarity is at all achievable. As Baldwin, Faulkner, and Hecht (2006) caution, "any attempt to describe a 'culture' serves at best as a fuzzy snapshot. . . . First, it leaves out what is not within the frame of the camera's lens (obscuring the complexity, 'essentializing' a culture). Second, it reduces to a still picture what actually is a dynamic, ever-changing entity (it 'reifies' the cultural description of a group)" (17). In this sense, what is referred to as *culture* may be understood as a process wherein "phenomena [religious beliefs, communal rituals or shared traditions] are produced through systems of meaning, through structures of power, and through the institutions in which these are deployed" (Donald and Rattansi 1992, 4). This understanding of culture as something we *do* is also reflected in conceptualizations of music as social action (for example, Elliott and Silverman 2015; Small 1997). Thus, when we refer to culture, or cultural differences, as products of identity work, or expressions of belonging, we may simultaneously neglect the ideological conflicts of interest that continually (re)produce and shape our understandings of what these are in the first place. The notion of culture as the ongoing site of ideological contestation and a mechanism of control in each of the domains of music, education, and religion raises questions of how we might address accumulative blind spots and epistemic ignorance when attending to phenomena at the intersection of all three.

While the chapters in this volume aptly illustrate the complexity and challenge of pinning down exactly what we mean by culture—be it musical, educational, or religious—one future challenge that we share is to reflect on the power structures that define and confine culture. If, as Miettinen's (chap. 16) and Boyce Tillman's (chap. 15) chapters argue, we all live and act in the "in between," rather than doing away with the concepts of identification or cultural affiliation altogether, perhaps we can find meaning in the processes that produce them. In considering the political dimensions by which individuals claim or assign similarities or differences in relation to others, and the interpretations and roles we play in these processes as researchers, we ought to consider which outcomes are legitimized and made possible and which are not. Through whose value systems do we view the world (see also Boyce-Tillman 2014)? Whose voices are heard when we engage in intercultural encounters and negotiations? Who is it that we are writing about when we consider music "as a part of social and *cultural* experience" (Jorgensen, chap. 1)? Who are we advocating for, when we say that music offers possibilities to learn "about cultures and difference through performance . . . as social action" (Westerlund, Kallio, and Partti, chap. 3), or as a means to engage "youth culture" (Fletcher and Barrett, chap. 4)? As Marie McCarthy (2015) has argued, we need to move beyond representation in our efforts for inclusion. If we seek opportunities for "radical inclusion" (Boyce-Tillman, chap. 15), we need to consider not only the deficits in opportunities for participation but also deficits in the capacity to listen, understand, and engage with diverse voices, musics, spiritualties, cosmologies, pedagogies, and onto-epistemologies. These imperatives hold just as true when working within academic culture and research as when engaging in musical, educational, and religious practices.

Living and Learning in Relation

As the chapters of this book traverse the terrain of socioreligious, musical, and cultural differences, a central theme that arises is that of social change. Yet, as Yob notes in her chapter (17), change remains an elusive concept. In exploring what forms social change might take hold at the intersection of music, education, and religion, I follow a metaphor used by Marie McCarthy (2013), who describes the process of music making and learning as "a landscape of relational consciousness" (6), in conceptualizing of social change as relational, contextual, and always uncertain.

Boyce-Tillman's chapter (15) notes that in encountering musical difference, students may challenge their own value systems "and they move along on their own spiritual journey—to explore the 'betweens' within it." This notion of betweens is important and offers an additional consideration about encounters with differences that often focus on dichotomies of self and Other, sacred and secular. In her chapter (17), Yob describes a number of entities that have been conceptualized as distinct and in opposition to one another, such as town and gown, or community and university, and church and state. The social change that she envisions is located in betweens, in relational processes of "working *with* others" in ways that acknowledge difference. Elizabeth Ellsworth (2005) characterizes the unpredictability of learning as a relational, transitional space: "Learning never takes place in the absence of bodies, emotions, place, time, sound, image, self-experience, history. It always detours through memory, forgetting, desire, fear, pleasure, surprise, rewriting. And because learning takes place in relation, its detours take us up to and sometimes across the boundaries of habit, recognition, and the socially constructed identities within ourselves" (55).

Relationality is thus more than the drawing of connections between the self and Others in that it also involves the multiple relationships that one has with oneself, as well as those that one forges with "second worlds" of the "sacred sphere" (Spychiger, chap. 9). In this sense, forging new paths in relation requires an acceptance of uncertainty and "unfinishedness" (Freire 2014), as illustrated by the process of relational recognition and learning that Badarne and Ehrlich (chap. 18) have embarked upon.

Positioning music, education, and religion as relational *doings,* each may be seen as "a double-edged sword... [affecting] human beings for good or ill" (Kim, chap. 12). Acknowledging the betweenness arising from living-in-relation, a number of chapters also highlight the importance and complexity of navigating the middle paths forged toward socially just policies and practices. For instance, Westerlund, Kallio, and Partti (chap. 3) argue against assumptions of secular neutrality or consensus in favor of attending to the ethical, political, and agential dimensions of musical performance. Kertz-Welzel (chap. 11) and Badarne and Ehrlich (chap. 18) both emphasize the importance of a reflexive, dialectal approach, although in very different contexts. Yob (chap. 17) envisions social change as twofold, as "social justice (creating equity and fairness) or empowerment (building self-efficacy, self-esteem, and personal value)." These chapters all remind us that the notion of social justice itself is not impartial and can guide educators and scholars not only toward inclusion and positive social change but also toward exclusion and oppression. Jorgensen (chap. 1) offers the example of a young girl in Australia who "may learn to play the didgeridoo in a publicly supported school, even though she is denied it in her traditional culture." In this seemingly simple vignette, Jorgensen illustrates how social justice can be employed in line with the values of gender equality for the individual while simultaneously appealing to oppressive, colonial conceptions of "traditional culture" (which includes musical and cosmological beliefs and practices) as primitive and irrational. Such experiences open up new spaces to discuss the ideologies and values underpinning discourses of human rights, decolonization, and equality. Social justice, and practicing *respect,* is clearly a more complex endeavor than doing unto others "as you would have them do to you" (Lk 6:31, NIV).

Invitations and Imaginings

As the first edited volume attending to the intersection of music, education, and religion in recent decades, *Music, Education, and Religion: Intersections and Entanglements* embraces a wide range of perspectives in attending to the ways in which these three areas fuse, overlap, connect, or conflict in various contexts. Yet the questions arising within and between these chapters are far from resolved. Reaching beyond conceptions of music, education, and religion as distinct, fixed entities, this book invites the reader to consider the identities, cultures, values, and experiences of teachers, students, musicians, believers, and atheists alike as complex, dynamic, and always in (re)formation. Furthermore, it also serves as an invitation to reflect on our own ideological underpinnings and the voices, contexts, or beliefs not included within these pages. In critically attending to the questions of "who am I, why am I and what should I do as well as the questions of ultimate meaning, nature and purpose of life" (Ubani 2013, 43), this book offers new opportunities to also ask "who should I be, how can I be, and what is possible to do?" in looking to the future and engaging our own existential imaginations.

Acknowledgments

This chapter has been written as part of the Global Visions through Mobilizing Networks project funded by the Academy of Finland (project number 286162).

ALEXIS ANJA KALLIO is a music education researcher at the Sibelius Academy, University of the Arts–Helsinki, working as part of the Global Visions through Mobilizing Networks: Co-developing Intercultural Music Teacher Education in Finland, Israel, and Nepal project. She is coeditor of the *Nordic Yearbook of Music Education Research*.

References

Baldwin, John R., Sandra L. Faulkner, and Michael L. Hecht. 2006. "A Moving Target: The Illusive Definition of Culture." In *Redefining Culture: Perspectives across the Disciplines*, edited by John R. Baldwin, Sandra L. Faulkner, Michael L. Hecht, and Sheryl L. Lindsley, 3–26. Mahwah, NJ: Lawrence Erlbaum.
Bauman, Zygmunt. 2000. *Liquid Modernity*. Cambridge, UK: Polity.
Boyce-Tillman, June. 2014. *Unconventional Wisdom*. Oxon, UK: Routledge.
Donald, James, and Ali Rattansi. 1992. "Introduction." In *"Race," Culture and Difference*, edited by James Donald and Ali Rattansi, 1–10. London: Sage.
Elliott, David J., and Marissa Silverman. 2015. *Music Matters: A Philosophy of Music Education*. 2nd ed. Oxford: Oxford University Press.
Ellsworth, Elizabeth. 2005. *Places of Learning: Media, Architecture, Pedagogy*. New York: Routledge.
Flanagan, Keith. 2016. "Preface." In *Religion, Identity and Change: Perspectives on Global Transformations*, edited by Simon Coleman and Peter Collins, viii–xii. Oxon, UK: Routledge.
Freire, Paulo. 2014. *Pedagogy of the Oppressed*. 30th anniversary ed. Translated by M. Bergman Ramos. New York: Bloomsbury.
Giddens, Anthony. 1991. *Modernity and Self-Identity: Self and Society in the Late Modern Age*. Stanford, CA: Stanford University Press.
Habermas, Jürgen. 2010. *An Awareness of What's Missing: Faith and Reason in a Post-secular Age*. Cambridge, UK: Polity.
Kroeber, Alfred L., and Clyde Kluckhohn. 1952. *Culture: A Critical Review of Concepts and Definitions*. Cambridge, MA: Harvard University, Peabody Museum of American Archeology and Ethnology.

McCarthy, Marie. 2013. "Children's Spirituality and Music Learning: Exploring Deeper Resonances with Arts Based Research." *International Journal of Education and the Arts* 14, no. 4. http://www.ijea.org/v14n4/.

———. 2015. "Understanding Social Justice from the Perspective of Music Education History." In *The Oxford Handbook of Social Justice in Music Education*, edited by Cathy Bennedict, Patrick Schmidt, Gary Spruce, and Paul Woodford, 29–46. Oxford: Oxford University Press.

Moberg, Marcus, Kennet Granholm, and Peter Nynäs. 2012. "Trajectories of Post-secular Complexity: An Introduction." In *Post-Secular Society*, edited by Peter Nynäs, Mika Lassander, and Terhi Utriainen, 1–26. New Brunswick, NJ: Transaction.

Orsi, Robert A. 2005. *Between Heaven and Earth: The Religious Worlds People Make and the Scholars Who Study Them*. Princeton, NJ: Princeton University Press.

Robbins, Thomas, and Dick Anthony. 2017. *New Patterns of Religious Pluralism in America*. 2nd ed. Oxon, UK: Routledge.

Sium, Aman, Desai Chandi, and Eric Ritskes. 2012. "Towards the 'Tangible Unknown': Decolonization and the Indigenous Future." *Decolonization: Indigeneity, Education and Society* 1, no. 1: i–xiii.

Small, Christopher. 1997. *Musicking: The Meanings of Performing and Listening*. Middletown, CT: Wesleyan University Press.

Taylor, Charles. 2007. *A Secular Age*. Cambridge, MA: Belknap.

Taylor, Edward W., and Melissa J. Snyder. 2012. "A Critical Review of Research on Transformative Learning Theory, 2006–2010." In *The Handbook of Transformative Learning: Theory, Research, and Practice*, edited by Edward W. Taylor and Patricia Cranton, 37–55. San Francisco: Jossey-Bass.

Ubani, Martin. 2013. "Existentially Sensitive Education." In *The Routledge International Handbook of Education, Religion and Values*, edited by James Arthur and Terence Lovat, 42–54. Oxon, UK: Routledge.

Williams, Raymond. 1983. *Keywords: A Vocabulary of Culture and Society*. New York: Oxford University Press.

INDEX

Aarseth, Øystein, 208–11
additive hypothesis, 36–37
adolescents: Catholic teen case study, 4–5, 71–85, 274; use of music, 71–72
Adorno, Theodor W., 171, 173, 176, 177–78
aesthetics of sacred spaces, 145
aesthetic stage, 134–36
agency: and black metal, 211; and categories, 63; and community building, 56; and identity, 55, 62–64; and performance, 55–65; and sacred spaces, 153; scholarly focus on, 2; and social change, 9; teacher's, 42
Ahmadinejad, Mahmoud, 199
Akkerman, Sanne F., 239, 242, 243, 244, 245
altars, Thai, 91, 92–93
Anglican Church: and justice, 252–53; outreach programs, 250–59; radical inclusion in music education, 224–35, 274, 276, 277
anthems, 44
Anttonen, Veikko, 157–58
Apollonianism, 132
apologetics of music, 8, 183–93, 278
Apologia musices (Case), 8, 183, 185, 188–92
apostolicity, 229
apprentice/master relationship, 164–67
architecture and sacred spaces, 107, 145, 149
Aristotle, 45, 130, 136–40, 187, 189, 190
art: and aesthetics of sacred space, 145; arts as the otherworld, 6–7, 144, 149; educators' lack of understanding, 129–30
assumptive frames of reference, 18
Astin, Alexander, 162
Astin, Helen W., 162
atheism: as non-Finnish, 121n10; public opinion on, 39; rates of, 60; and Serbian children's choirs, 107; and spirituality, 232; in Western media, 159
atmosphere, 144, 145
Australia: Catholic education in, 72–73; Catholic teen identity case study, 4–5, 71–85, 274; restrictions on Aboriginal women in music, 23, 278

Bakhtin, Mikhail, 230
Bakker, Arthur, 239, 242, 243, 244, 245
Baldwin, John R., 276
ballet, 251, 257
Barnes, Joseph, 186

Bauman, Zygmunt, 239, 241, 242, 274, 275
believing-belonging paradigm, 5, 99–109, 273
Bell, Joshua, 254
Bernhard, Thomas, 129–30
beyondness, 149
Bildung: and community service programs, 251; and music education, 176, 177–78, 179; and spirituality, 117–20, 131; and *Suvivirsi*, 117–20; as term, 117
biological function circle, 142–43
Black Circle, 209–10
black metal, 8–9, 208–18
Bologna Accord, 251
both/and choice, 139
boundary crossing theory, 239, 242–43
boundary workers, Israel music teachers as, 9, 238–47, 274
Brenner, Brenda, 250–58
Buddhism: overview of Thai, 89–91; and Thai musical heritage in US, 5–6, 87, 88, 93–96; and violence, 38; Zen Buddhism, 33
Burzum (band), 210
Butler, Judith, 55, 58, 60, 62–64

Cannon, Dale, 158, 163, 167
carnivalesque, 230, 235n29
Case, John, 183, 188–92
Cassirer, Ernst, 149
categories: and agency, 63; and identity, 58, 59, 62–63, 64
Catholic Church: abuse scandals, 40; Catholic teen case study, 4–5, 71–85, 274; education in Australia, 72–73; and violence, 38
catholicity, 229
Cederlund, Uffe, 209
character development in Aristotle, 136–38
children's choirs in Serbia, 5, 104–8
choice: in Aristotle, 137, 139; in Kierkegaard, 6, 135, 136, 139; by students, 258, 270; by teachers, 138–39; and virtue, 137; and wisdom, 232–33
Christianity: deity in, 32; duty and service in, 252, 253; harms from, 38, 39–40; influence on popular music, 18; and Israeli education, 263, 264; Kierkegaard on, 134, 135–36; post-Christianity, 253; proselytizing, 253–54; and sacred spaces, 144, 145, 147; and Satanism, 211, 213–14; Serbia and believing-belonging

Christianity (*cont.*)
    paradigm, 5, 99–109, 273; *Suvivirsi* debate in Finland, 5, 60–61, 63, 111–13, 118–20; in Thailand, 89. *See also* Anglican Church; Catholic Church; Puritans
church burnings, 208, 210
classrooms. *See* learning environment
cognitive development, 150–51
cognitive emotions, 16
commonplace books, 187
community: and agency, 56; in Catholic teen case study, 81–82; and Foundation Music, 225, 227–28, 232–33, 250–59; and identity, 55–59, 64, 107–8, 275–76; music as community activity, 81–82; music making by, 2, 227–28, 256–57, 277; and need for belonging, 101; and performance, 56; and service programs, 9–10, 249–59, 277, 278; and Third Reich, 176, 177
concrete-operational stage, 150–51
congregational identity, 101
Coogan, Christa, 251–58
Coop Himmelb(l)au, 154n13
cosmopolitanism: and black metal, 8, 211–13, 215, 217; musical cosmopolitanism, 24
Count Grishnackh. *See* Vikernes, Kristian
country music, 18
creatures, sacred space, 146–47
culture: cultural identity, 273, 275–76; cultural memory, 102; improvisation in women's, 228; interconnection with music, 17–18, 20; and power structures, 276–77; and religious music, 46; as term, 20, 276; Thai musical heritage programs, 5–6, 87–96, 273. *See also* multiculturalism
curricula: Australian Catholic schools, 76; engaging religion through, 25, 26; Finnish, 55, 56, 59, 65, 114–15; Israeli, 263; and Kitsch, 175; queering, 224, 232, 233; as restricted, 15, 22, 59; Serbian, 102–3; Thai culture, 94, 96

Dalai Lama, 162
dance: in community service programs, 251–58; ecstatic, 266; as evil, 174, 175, 184; Thai, 87, 90, 91, 94, 95
Davie, Grace, 100, 101, 102
Dawkins, Richard, 159
Deathlike Silence Productions, 209, 210
death metal, 208–9. *See also* black metal
death of God movement, 253
De Botton, Alain, 101, 232
deep learning, 228
Dennett, Daniel, 159

detachment, 49
devil: in black metal, 208–18; dialectics of, 7, 171–79, 274
devil's advocate, 178–79, 218n10
Dewey, John, 20, 26, 42, 149, 231–32
dexterity, 200–204
dialectics and the devil, 7, 171–79, 274
didgeridoo, 23, 278
Die Wahlverwandtschaften (Goethe), 31–32
Dionysianism, 132–33
discrimination and religion, 39–40
disenchantment, 6, 133–34, 159–60
diversity. *See* multiculturalism
Doctor Faustus (Mann), 7, 171, 172–73, 177
drumming: in community service programs, 251; in Islam, 198, 266–67, 269
Durkheim, Émile, 2, 71, 115
duty, 134, 135, 136, 252, 253

ecological-semiotic function circle, 142–44, *143*
ecology, learning, 152
edification, 43
education: affinities with religion and music, 4, 35–36; Australian Catholic education, 72–73; Christian foundation of US, 230–31; defining, 33–34; in Finland, 55, 56, 59, 65, 114–15; focus on productivity, 41–42; goods from, 4, 35, 36–37, 45–46, 49–50; harms from, 4, 41–43, 45–46, 49–50, 278; and heritage, 88; indoctrination by, 5, 43, 118–20, 171, 175, 177, 274; Islam and coeducation, 58; liberal education, 42–43, 230–31; online education, 164; and sacred spaces, 145, 151–54, 168; and understanding of art, 129–30. *See also Bildung*; learning environment; music education; religious education
either/or choice, 6, 139
Ellsworth, Elizabeth, 277–78
embodiment, 8, 201–3
emotional cognitions, 16
emotions: and community engagement, 255–56; and Kitsch, 174–76, 179; and music, 16, 36, 73, 81–82, 102, 105, 107, 133, 139, 173, 193n15; and performance, 58, 166; and sacred spaces, 149, 167
empowerment: of Arab-Israeli girls, 268–69; and community service programs, 258–59; and political action, 27; of teachers, 25–26
enchanted reality, 160
enhancement thesis, 35–36
entertainment, 193n15
Entombed (band), 209
ethical stage, 134–36, 139

ethics: apologetics of music, 183, 184, 188, 189, 190–92; ethical melodies, 138; and goods, 35, 225; of performance, 61, 65; and role of education, 42, 83, 228, 231; and secularism, 55, 57, 59, 61–62, 64, 112, 116, 117, 120, 132, 253; and teachers, 165–66, 238, 246, 252. *See also* morality
ethnic identity and religion, 6, 95–96
Euronymous. *See* Aarseth, Øystein
European Central Bank, 154n13
European Convention of Human Rights, 118–19
European Court of Human Rights, 112
ExtrA, 143
ExtrO, 143

faith, leap of, 135–36
faith stage of life, 135–36
Faulkner, Sandra L., 276
Faust (Goethe), 7, 171, 172–73, 177
Feld, Steven, 28n5
feminist theology, 253
Finland: curriculum, 55, 56, 59, 65, 114–15; national identity, 116–17, 121n10; pagan music conflict, 60, 62–63; repertoire in music education, 5, 111–22, 274; *Suvivirsi* debate, 5, 60–61, 63, 111–13, 118–20
flow theory, 256
folk music: and death metal, 214, 217; Finnish, 60, 115; Thai, 80, 91
formal-operational stage, 150–51
formation of persons, 231–32
Foucault, Michel, 19, 43, 226
Foundation Music, 224–35, 250–59, 274
frames, 7, 18, 88–89, 161
frames of reference, assumptive, 18
Freire, Paolo, 43
function circle, 142–44, *143*
fundamentalism, 3, 19, 274

gender. *See* women
generalization, 26
Germany: service learning programs in, 251–58; during Third Reich, 172–73, 176–78, 177
Gillespie, Michael Allen, 161–62
glorification theology, 134
gnomes, 155n14
Goethe, Johann Wolfgang von, 7, 31–32, 171, 172–73, 177
Good Morning Iran, 196. *See also* television broadcast rules
goods: additive hypothesis, 36–37; of community programs, 10, 225–26; of music,

religion and education, 4, 35–37, 45–46, 49–50, 278
gospel music, 18
group identity, 80–81
guru-disciple relationship, 7, 164–67, 168
Gwinne, Matthew, 185–86

Habermas, Jürgen, 168, 275
hadith, 8, 197
hailing, 60
harms of music, religion and education, 4, 37–46, 49–50, 253–54, 274, 278
Harris, Sam, 159
heaven, *143*, 144, 162
heavy metal, 208. *See also* black metal
Hecht, Michael L., 276
Hegel, Georg W. F., 117
Helvete (record store), 209
heritage: as term, 88; Thai musical, 5–6, 87–96, 273
Higher Education Community Engagement Movement, 249
Hinduism: guru in, 165; Hindu identity in US, 95; supreme being in, 33; in Thai culture, 89, 91–92; and violence, 38
hip-hop music, 45
Hitchens, Christopher, 159
Hitler, Adolf, 172–73, 177
Hitler Youth, 179n3
Hmong music, 17
Holmes, Arthur F., 231
holy term, 154n1, 155n15
hooks, bell, 43, 167
hospitality, 24
humanities: marginalization of, 15, 16; music education as, 3, 15–28, 275
hybrid and hybridity, 147, 151, 245, 246

identification, 241
identity: and agency, 55, 62–64; and categories, 58, 59, 62–63, 64; in Catholic teen case study, 4–5, 71–85, 274; and community, 55–59, 64, 107–8, 275–76; congregational, 101; cultural, 273, 275–76; ethnic, 6, 95–96; and formation of persons, 231–32; and Foundation Music program, 226; group, 80–81; liquid, 241; musicians, 165; and the Other, 275–76, 277–78; and performativity, 55–59, 64; and popular music, 71–72, 133; religious, 101; and religious music, 58–59, 73, 77–84, 100–101; secularism's effect on, 59–64; and social cohesion, 107–8; sub-identities, 241; teachers, 9, 238–47, 269–70, 274; Thai musical heritage

Index 283

identity (*cont.*)
 in US, 6, 94, 95. *See also* national identity and nationalism
Immaculata Catholic College case study, 4–5, 71–85, 274
immanent frame, 7, 161
improvisation: in community programs, 251, 257, 259; in Iranian classical music, 201–3, 204; in jazz, 44, 203; in Southeast Asian music, 91; in Space for Peace event, 230; in women's culture, 228
Indiana University, 250–58
indoctrination: defining, 118; education's potential for, 5, 43, 118–20, 171, 175, 177, 274; and Kitsch, 175; *vs.* religious engagement, 24
ineffability of mystical experiences, 132
In Laudem Musices Oratio (Gwinne), 185–86
insight from mystical experiences, 132
interpenetration, 116–17, 118, 120
interrogation techniques and music, 45
intersectionality, 238, 239, 241, 246
IntrA, 143
IntrO, 143
Iran: music regulation in, 8, 196–205, 273–74; nationalism of, 198, 199
Islam: and coeducation, 58; dialogue between Jewish and Arab teachers, 10, 262–71, 278; fundamentalism, 3; music in, 8, 147, 197–98, 263, 265–68; music regulation in Iran, 8, 196–205, 273–74; Muslim students in Australian Catholic schools, 76, 84; and Satanism, 213; in Thailand, 89; and violence, 38–40
Israel: dialogue between Jewish and Arab teachers, 10, 262–71, 278; music teachers as boundary workers, 9, 238–47, 274; religious segregation in, 9, 10, 262–63, 264, 269, 271

James, William, 132
jazz, 18, 44, 174, 203
Joas, Hans, 148
Judaism: dialogue between Jewish and Arab teachers, 10, 262–71, 278; fundamentalism, 3; music in, 263, 265–66; ultra-Orthodox, 9, 238–46, 263, 265, 268–69, 274; and violence, 38, 39
justice: and community service programs, 252, 253–54, 258, 259; and education, 35; and Foundation Music program, 226, 227, 229; and gender equality, 278; and music education, 4, 9, 18, 23, 192, 278; and religion, 161, 190, 252–53, 274; in *Suvivirsi* debate, 64, 113, 118

Kaluli people, 28n5
Kant, Immanuel, 132
Karlsen, Sidsel, 57, 63
Khamenei, Ali, 38, 200
Khatami, Mohammad, 199
Khomeini, Ruhollah, 198, 199, 200
Kierkegaard, Søren, 6, 130, 134–36, 138–39
Kitsch, 7, 147, 171, 174–76, 179
Kokopelli, 146–47
Koran. *See* Qur'an

Lang, Alfred, 7, 142, 143, 148
Langer, Susanne, 149, 255–56
language. *See* translations
Latour, Bruno, 147, 151, 153
leap of faith, 135–36
learning: deep learning, 228; service learning, 9–10, 249–59; and social change, 277
learning ecology, 152
learning environment: online learning, 164; sacred spaces for, 152–53; as third space, 244–45, 246
Levinsky College, 263, 264–65
liberal education, 42–43, 230–31
liminal zones, 9, 244
Lindholm, Jennifer A., 162
Liquid Modernity, 239, 241, 275
Loki, 217n11
Luciferian principle, 215
Luther, Martin, 46
Lutheran Church: and Finnish identity, 116, 121n10; music in, 111, 114, 115. See also *Suvivirsi* debate

Magdalene Laundries, 40
magical thinking, 150, 151
Mann, Thomas, 7, 171, 172–73, 177
master/apprentice relationship, 164–67
maturity and modernization, 151
Mayhem (band), 208, 210
McCarthy, Marie, 277
McGill, Kathleen, 228
Melville, Andrew, 187
memory, cultural, 102
mentors, 165–67
Merbecke, John, 186
military use of music, 44
Miller, Lisa, 162
Milton, John, 173
misogyny, 39–40, 45
modernization: Liquid Modernity, 239, 241, 275; and maturity, 151; and secularization, 159–60, 161–62

284 *Index*

morality: apologetics of music, 8, 183–93; and music education, 174, 175, 184, 186, 187; polemics of music, 183, 184–85, 189, 190, 191; and teacher status in Israel, 269–70. *See also* ethics

multiculturalism: in Catholic teen case study, 72, 75–76; and cultural identity, 275–76; and exclusion of religious music, 22; in Finland, 113; and performance, 4, 55–65, 274, 278; radical inclusion in music education, 224–35, 274, 276, 277; in repertoire, 57; scholarly focus on, 2; as social ideal, 56

music: affinities with education and religion, 4, 17–18, 35–36; affinities within forms of, 34–35; apologetics of, 8, 183–93, 278; defining, 20–21, 34; devil in, 173–74; and engagement of self, 256; as form of worship, 103, 184, 185, 191; functions of, 136–38; goods from, 4, 35–37, 45–46, 49–50; harms from, 4, 43–46, 49–50, 274, 278; identity and popular, 71–72, 133; interconnection with culture, 17–18, 30; musical experiences compared to religious experiences, 6, 7, 47–49, 102, 129–39, 147, 231–32; polemics of, 183, 184–85, 189, 190, 191; regulation in Iran, 8, 196–205, 273–74; role in sacred spaces, 145, 146, 147; scholarly focus on music making, 1–2; as specialized, 17; use by adolescents, 71–72. *See also* musical instruments; music education; musicians; popular music; religious music

musical instruments: in outreach programs, 251; prohibitions on, 8, 147, 196, 200, 204; in sacred spaces, 147

music education: apologetics of, 8, 183–93; Australian teen case study, 4–5, 71–85, 274; and black metal, 8, 211, 215–17; of choristers in England, 184, 186–87; and cosmopolitanism, 217; defining, 20–22; and devil, 7, 171–79, 274; in Finland, 5, 111–22, 274; in Germany, 176–78; as a humanity, 3, 15–28, 275; in Iranian classical music, 200–202, 203–4; Israeli segregation in, 10, 262–63, 264; Kitsch in, 7, 171, 174–76; and layers of meaning, 6, 129–30, 138–39, 274; and learning ecology, 152; limits of, 19–20; and morality, 174, 175, 184, 186, 187; and national identity, 4; opportunities for women in, 18; and performance, 4, 55–65, 274, 278; queering of, 224–35; radical inclusion in, 224–35, 274, 276, 277; and ritual, 60, 61, 63, 91–93; as sacred practice, 7, 157–68, 274; sacred practices in, 7, 163–67; and sacred spaces, 152–54, 168; scholarship overview, 1–3; in Serbia, 104–8; as social ritual, 60, 61, 63; and specialization, 191; as technical, 15; of Thai musical heritage, 5–6, 87–96, 273; transformative role of, 158, 171–79. *See also* learning environment; teachers

musicians: black metal, 213–14; choristers' education, 184, 186–87; identity, 165; Iranian broadcast rules, 8, 196, 200, 204; morality and status of, 184, 185, 187, 190, 192

national identity and nationalism: Finnish, 116–17, 121n10; Irani, 198, 199; and music education, 4; Serbian, 102–3, 105; Thai, 90
National Socialism, 176–78
Necrobutcher. *See* Stubberud, Jørn
Newman, John Henry, 231
Nielsen, Frede V., 129, 138, 139
Nietzsche, Friedrich, 2, 132–33
nonreligious term, 65n2
Norway. *See* black metal
numinous, 48, 132, 144
Nut (goddess), 144

occulture, 211
Ohlin, Per, 210
online education, 164
Orpheus, 146
Orsi, Robert A., 274–75
Orthodoxy. *See* Serbian Orthodox Church; ultra-Orthodox Judaism
Ostāds, 201–4
Other, the: avoidance of, 57; and identity, 275–76, 277–78; and multicultural repertoire, 57
otherworld: and learning environment, 153; sacred sphere as connector to, 6–7, 142–45, 158, 178; in secular societies, 6–7, 144, 148–49; as term, 154n2. *See also* sacred spaces
Otto, Rudolf, 48, 71, 132

Pan, 146
Pargament, Kenneth, 162–63
Pärt, Arvo, 18
peer-support, teacher, 243–44
Pelle Dead. *See* Ohlin, Per
perfomativity of performance, 55–65, 274, 278
performance: and agency, 55–65; in black metal, 214–15; and connection, 166; dexterity in, 200–204; and diversity in education, 4, 55–65, 274, 278; Iranian broadcast rules for, 8, 196, 200, 204; perfomativity of, 55–65, 274, 278; and rituals, 61, 91; and sacred spaces, 158

philistine, life of, 135
Piaget, Jean, 150–51
Plato, 136, 138, 190, 191
play, 216
pleasure in Aristotle, 136–38
polemics on music, 183, 184–85, 189, 190, 191
politics: debate over religious music in Finland, 5, 111–13; economy of education, 41; strategies for engaging religion, 25, 26–27
popular music: black metal, 8–9, 208–18; as evil, 174; and identity, 71–72, 133; influence of religious music on, 18; in Israeli music education, 240, 243, 267; jazz, 18, 44, 174, 203; and performance, 20; and social cohesion, 57
post-Christianity, 253
postsecularism, 3, 168, 274
Praise of Musicke, The, 8, 183, 185–88, 189, 190–92
praxialism, 56, 58, 256
preoperational stage, 150, 155n14
presentational symbols, 149, 255–56
privatization of education, 42
problem music, 174
productivity, focus on, 41–42
Prometheus, 217n11
prosperity theology, 134
psychological function circle, 143
public policy strategies for engaging religion, 25, 26–27
public spaces: performance as public, 56, 59; schools as, 59, 61, 63–64
Puritans, 133, 184–86, 188, 191
Putnam, Robert, 164
Puumalainen, Mikko, 112–13

queering music education, 224–35
Qur'an, 8, 197–98

racism, 39
radif, 201–2, 203
rationality: and disenchantment, 6, 130, 133–34, 159–60; faith as break with, 135–36; and secularization, 2, 159–61, 273
recognition and identity, 63
reflection: in Catholic teen case study, 76, 79–80, 82; as mode, 163; and religious music, 82–83; and sacred spaces, 149; by teachers, 129, 138, 239, 246, 254
religion: affinities with education and music, 4, 17–18, 35–36; affinities within forms of, 34–35; black metal as, 211–14, 215; defining, 33, 273; defining religious engagement, 23–24; and ethnic identity, 6, 95–96; goods from, 4, 35–37, 45–46, 49–50; harms from, 4, 37–41, 45–46, 49–50, 253–54, 274; modes of being religious, 163; official religions, 22, 89; religious as term, 65n2; religious education, 76, 102–4; religious engagement *vs.* indoctrination, 24; religious experiences compared to music experiences, 6, 7, 47–49, 102, 129–39, 147, 231–32; religious identity, 101; religious stage, 134–36; resurgences of, 3, 99, 273; and social cohesion, 115; *vs.* spirituality, 16–17, 47, 162–63; and teaching music as a humanity, 3, 15–28, 275. *See also* Anglican Church; Buddhism; Catholic Church; Lutheran Church; Puritans; religious music
religious education: in Catholic teen case study, 76; in Serbia, 102–4
religious music: in Catholic school case study, 4–5, 71–85, 274; in children's choirs, 5, 104–8; in classical repertoire, 18; critique of values in, 18–19; and culture, 46; exclusion of, 15, 22; in Finnish education, 114–15, 118–20; and group identity, 80–81; and identity, 58–59, 73, 77–84, 100–101; influence on popular music, 18; in Lutheran Church, 111; in Puritan church, 188; and reflection, 82–83; in Serbian education, 102–4; in Serbian Orthodoxy, 99, 102–4; as worship, 184, 185. See also *Suvivirsi* debate
religious stage, 134–36
repertoire: classical choral, 18; engaging religion through, 23–24, 25; in Finnish music education, 5, 111–22, 274; and identity, 57; in Israeli music education, 267; multiculturalism in, 57; perceptions of religiosity in, 60–61; in Serbian children's choirs, 104–5, 106–7
repetition: and agency, 62; in music education, 163; and Serbian children's choirs, 107
Rethinking Education (UNESCO), 249
ritual rationality, 133–34
rituals: music education as, 60, 61, 63; and performance, 61, 91; and sacred spaces, 147; and sacred time, 158; Thai music education, 90–93; *way khruu* rituals, 91, 92–93, 94
Rød Ungdom (Red Youth), 217n4
Rouhani, Hassan, 199
Rousseau, Jean-Jacques, 115
Russell, Bertrand, 42–43

Saarakkala, Vesa-Matti, 113
sacred spaces: architecture of, 107, 145, 149; and education, 145, 151–54, 168; and emotions,

149, 167; moment of silence as, 7, 157, 158, 166; sacred sphere, 6–7, 142–55, 158, 278; types of, 157
sacred sphere, 6–7, 142–55, 158, 278
sacred term, 157–58, 163, 168n2
Sacred term, 168n2
sacred time, 158
sacrifice and sacred spaces, 146
Sæther, Eva, 57
satanic music. *See* black metal
Satanism, 211, 213–14
Scheffler, Israel, 16, 19
Schleiermacher, Friedrich, 71
schools as public spaces, 59, 61, 63–64
searching areas, 153–54
A Secular Age (Taylor), 145, 147–48
secularism: as cognitive development, 150–51; as discriminatory, 59–60, 118–19; effect on identity, 59–64; and ethics, 55, 57, 59, 61–62, 64, 112, 116, 117, 120, 132, 253; and exclusion of religious music, 15, 22; as neutralizing, 59, 64; otherworld in, 6–7, 144, 148–49; overview of, 2–3; postsecularism, 3, 168, 274; rise of, 2–3, 159–62, 273–74; sacred spaces in, 142, 145–46, 147–50, 158; stages of, 160–61
segregation, Israeli, 9, 10, 262–63, 264, 269, 271
self-cultivation. See *Bildung*
self-engagement and music making, 256
Selvam, Sahaya G., 163
Serbia and believing-belonging paradigm, 5, 99–109, 273
Serbian Orthodox Church: religious education in Serbia, 102–4; Serbia and believing-belonging paradigm, 5, 99–109, 273
service programs, 9–10, 249–59, 277, 278
sexuality, sublimation of, 265–66
silence as moment of sacred space, 7, 157, 158, 166
situational thought and practice, 25–26
social change, 9–10, 249–61, 277, 278
social cohesion, 5, 9, 57, 107–8, 115
social contract, 115
social gospel movement, 253
social stratification, 44
Space for Peace event, 224, 226, 229–30
spirituality: as aesthetic experience, 47; atheist spirituality, 232; and *Bildung*, 117–20, 131; and community service programs, 252–56; expression in music, 24; in music education, 7, 47–48, 49, 158, 163–67; *vs.* religion, 16–17, 47, 162–63; spiritual experiences compared to music experiences, 6, 7, 129–39, 147, 231–32

stages on life's way, 130, 134–36
standardized testing, 42
Steel, Sean, 232
Stifoss-Hanssen, Hans, 163
Stubberud, Jørn, 210
Stubbes, Phillip, 185
students: as audience, 254; Catholic teen case study, 4–5, 71–85, 274; community building by, 225; guru-disciple relationship, 7, 164–67, 168; service learning, 9–10, 249–59; as spiritual seekers, 164
sublimation, 265–66
sublime, 48, 132, 133, 173, 216
Suvivirsi debate, 5, 60–61, 63, 111–13, 118–20
symbols: presentational, 149, 255–56; symbolic form, 149

Taylor, Charles: imminent frame, 7; on modernization, 131, 151; on rise of secularism, 159–61, 273–74; sacred spaces in secularism, 145–46, 147–48; stages of secularism, 160–61, 168
teachers: agency of, 42; choice by, 138–39; dialogue between Jewish and Arab, 10, 262–71, 278; empowerment of, 25–26; and ethics, 165–66, 238, 246, 252; guru-disciple relationship, 7, 164–67, 168; identity, 9, 238–47, 269–70, 274; pedagogical heroism, 175; peer-support, 243–44; reflection by, 129, 138, 239, 246, 254; status of, 265, 269–70; strategies for engaging religion, 25–27; stretching limits by, 10, 265, 266–68, 270–71; understanding layers of meaning, 6, 129–30, 138–39, 274; *way khruu* rituals, 91, 92–93, 94
Teasdale, Wayne, 162
television broadcast rules, 8, 196, 200, 204
testing, standardized, 42
Thailand: musical heritage, 5–6, 87–96, 273; overview of religion, 89–91
tham khwan rituals, 90
theater and polemics of music, 184, 189, 191
Theravada Buddhism, overview of, 89–91
Thet Mahachat (holiday), 90
Third Reich: in *Doctor Faustus* (Mann), 172–73, 177; music education in, 176–78
third spaces, 244–45, 246
time, sacred, 158
tonalities, 138
transcendence: of aesthetic experiences, 48; in music education, 163, 167, 168; and sacred spaces, 157, 158; and secularism, 161; as term, 33, 168n1
transfer effects, 175

Index 287

translations: mystical experiences as untranslatable, 132; and Serbian children's choirs, 106–7
tremendum et fascinans, 132
tricksters: Kokopelli, 146–47; Loki, 217n11; Luciferian principle, 215

Uexküll, Jakob von, 142–43
ultra-Orthodox Judaism: music teachers and, 9, 238–46, 274; and prohibition on women's voices, 240, 263, 268–69; role of women in, 240, 241, 265
UNESCO, 249
United States: Christian foundation of education, 230–31; exclusion of religious music in education, 15; service learning programs, 250–58; Thai music in, 87, 88, 90, 93–96
University of Music and Performing Arts Munich, 251–58
University of Winchester, 224–35, 250–59, 274
utilitarianism and music, 174, 175–76

Vikernes, Kristian, 210–11
violin service program, 251–58
Virsivisa, 122n18

virtue: as goal of education, 35; as goal of religion, 35; of music, 137, 138, 188, 190, 191–92; virtuous activity, 136–38

Watain (band), 213
way khruu rituals, 91, 92–93, 94
Weber, Max, 2, 6, 32, 133, 159, 160
Williams, Raymond, 276
wisdom: Aristotle on, 137; as decision making, 232–33; Foundation Music and, 231, 232–33; and role of education, 24, 26
women: in colonial singing schools, 23; dialogue between Jewish and Arab teachers, 10, 262–71, 278; feminist theology, 253; improvisation in women's culture, 228; Islam and coeducation, 58; Islamic women and music, 268; misogyny in hip-hop, 45; misogyny in religion, 39–40; opportunities in music education, 18; restrictions on, 23, 240, 263, 268–69, 278; in ultra-Orthodox Judaism, 238–46, 263, 265, 268–69

Zen Buddhism, 33
Zepf, Siegfried, 256
zones, liminal, 9, 244
zones of interpenetration, 116–17

www.ingramcontent.com/pod-product-compliance
Lightning Source LLC
Chambersburg PA
CBHW021348300426
44114CB00012B/1127